Religion in China To

Religion in China Today

The China Quarterly Special Issues
New Series, No. 3

Edited by

DANIEL L. OVERMYER

CAMBRIDGE
UNIVERSITY PRESS

CAMBRIDGE UNIVERSITY PRESS
Cambridge, New York, Melbourne, Madrid, Cape Town, Singapore, São Paulo

Cambridge University Press
The Edinburgh Building, Cambridge CB2 2RU, UK

Published in the United States of America by Cambridge University Press, New York

www.cambridge.org
Information on this title: www.cambridge.org/9780521538237

First published 2003

A catalogue record for this publication is available from the British Library

ISBN-13 978-0-521-53823-7 paperback
ISBN-10 0-521-53823-8 paperback

Transferred to digital printing 2006

Contents

Cover illustration Worship at Sanyuan gong Temple, Guangzhou,
1997. Photograph courtesy of Daniel L. Overmyer

Notes on Contributors

DANIEL H. BAYS is professor of history and director of the Asian studies programme at Calvin College, Grand Rapids, Michigan. He is professor emeritus at the University of Kansas. He is editor of *Christianity in China* (1996), and co-editor with Grant Wacker of *The Foreign Missionary Movement at Home* (2003).

RAOUL BIRNBAUM is professor of Buddhist studies at the University of California, Santa Cruz. His many publications focus on Buddhist practices and representations in China, from medieval times to the present.

NANCY N. CHEN is associate professor of anthropology at the University of California, Santa Cruz. A medical anthropologist, she is author of *Breathing Spaces: Qigong, Psychiatry, and Healing in China* (2003), and co-editor of *China Urban: Ethnographies of Contemporary Culture* (2001).

KENNETH DEAN is the Lee professor of Chinese culture in the department of East Asian studies, McGill University. He is the author of *First and Last Emperors: The Absolute State and the Body of the Despot* (with Brian Massumi), *Taoist Ritual and Popular Cults of Southeast China*, and *Lord of the Three in One: The Spread of a Cult in Southeast China*. He is currently editing several volumes of epigraphical materials on the history of religion in Fujian.

FAN LIZHU is professor of sociology at Fudan University, where she teaches sociology of religion, religion and Chinese society. Her most recent publication is *Religious Development in Contemporary China: A Case Study in Shenzhen*. Her current research focuses on temple festivals in northern China, and spiritual nourishment and religious development in China.

DRU C. GLADNEY is professor of Asian studies and anthropology at the University of Hawai'i at Manoa. He is author of *Muslim Chinese: Ethnic Nationalism in the People's Republic* (1996, second edition), *Ethnic Identity in China: The Making of a Muslim Minority Nationality* (1998), *Making Majorities: Constituting the Nation in Japan, China, Korea, Malaysia, Fiji, Turkey, and the U.S.* (editor, 1998), and *Dislocating China: Muslims, Minorities, and Other Sub-Altern Subjects* (in press). For online articles and research projects, see http://www.hawaii.edu/dru.

PAUL R. KATZ is an associate research fellow at the Institute of Modern History, Academia Sinica. He specializes in the study of local religious traditions in China and Taiwan. His most recent publications include *Demon Hordes and Burning Boats: The Cult of Marshal Wen in Late Imperial Chekiang* (1995), *The Cult of the Royal Lords in Taiwan* (in Chinese, 1997), and *Images of the Immortal. The Cult of Lü Dongbin at the Palace of Eternal Joy* (1999).

LAI CHI-TIM is associate professor of Daoism in the department of religion at the Chinese University of Hong Kong. He lectures on the history of Daoism, Daoist classics, Daoist ritual and Hong Kong Daoism. He received his PhD from the Divinity School, University of Chicago, in Daoism and the history of religion.

TIK-SANG LIU is assistant professor at the Hong Kong University of Science and Technology. His research interests focus on the coastal communities and local religious activities in the Zhu [Pearl] River estuary area of South China.

RICHARD MADSEN is professor of sociology at the University of California, San Diego. His most recent books include *China's Catholics: Tragedy and Hope in an Emerging Civil Society* (1998), and *Popular China: Unofficial Culture in a Globalizing Society*, co-edited with Perry Link and Paul Pickowicz (2002).

DANIEL L. OVERMYER is professor emeritus at the department of Asian studies and the Centre for Chinese Research, University of British Columbia. He researches the ideas, beliefs and values of ordinary people in China, and currently focuses on community rituals and beliefs of villages in Hebei province and on comparing such traditions in China with those in other parts of the world.

PITMAN B. POTTER is director of the Institute of Asian Research at the University of British Columbia. He is also professor of law and director of Chinese legal studies at UBC Law Faculty.

Religion in China Today: Introduction

Daniel L. Overmyer

In the last 20 years religious traditions in many parts of China have revived their activities and organizations and rebuilt their temples, mosques and churches, despite decades of strict regulation and repression by the government. This revival is an aspect of the greater social freedom that has accompanied the economic development and diversification of that period. The government is trying to maintain political control, and legal restrictions remain, but wherever local conditions permit, religious activities come bubbling to the surface, festivals for the gods are held, traditional funerals and burial rituals are restored, destroyed images and shrines are replaced, priests reappear to perform rituals, and congregations meet to worship. There is some outside help for these revived activities, from such sources as overseas Chinese lineages, temples for the same gods in Taiwan, Muslim and Buddhist organizations in the Near East and South-East Asia, and Christian missions, but the fundamental impetus is the faith and devotion of the Chinese people themselves. All of this involves both the partial restoration of older traditions and adaptation to the present economic and social situation. Religious beliefs and rituals are an important and growing reality in modern Chinese society, which cannot be fully understood without taking them into account. They are also an important political issue for the government, because according to orthodox Marxist theory religion is supposed to wither away as socialism is established, but this has not happened. On the contrary, religious traditions with completely non-Marxist ideologies are flourishing, which amounts to a challenge to the authority of the Party and state. A closely related issue is religious freedom, which is important in China's relations with many other countries, Christian, Muslim and Buddhist. It is our hope here to provide much-needed information about this vital aspect of contemporary Chinese life, culture and politics.

This special issue is co-sponsored by *The China Quarterly*, the Institute of Asian Research of the University of British Columbia, and the Fundação Oriente, an academic foundation in Portugal. Its eleven articles are all by scholars who are among the best in the world on their topics, from universities in Canada, the United States, China, Hong Kong and Taiwan, while one of the discussants/reviewers is Timothy Barrett of the University of London. The other reviewer is Diana Lary of the University of British Columbia. All of these authors have done fieldwork in China. The project began with discussion in 2001 among Pitman Potter, Diana Lary and Dan Overmyer of UBC, and Richard Louis Edmonds of the University of London, then the editor of *The China Quarterly*. We identified topics and scholars, and then solicited articles, the drafts of which were discussed at a conference in Arrábida, Portugal in the autumn of 2002, supported by the Fundação Oriente and its director, Mr João Amorim. We are grateful to the Fundação for this support, which was an important contribution to our project. There are many studies of contemporary Chinese politics and economics, but few of the current situation of Chinese religions, so the goal of this project is to provide the best available information about this topic for non-specialist readers.

The first of the following contributions, on Chinese government policies towards religion, is by Pitman Potter, a scholar of Chinese law and politics. For many hundreds of years the Chinese state in all its forms has assumed that it has the right and obligation to control every aspect of life, including religious beliefs and practices. The state has always been particularly concerned to control organized groups with their own allegiances, from family lineages and private academies to Buddhist monasteries and popular religious sects. Until the mid 20th century poor communications and weak local government administration hindered the application of this ideology of control, but in the People's Republic such administration has been much more effective, and policies toward religion more strict. According to the Chinese constitution, people have the freedom to believe or not believe in religion, but this refers to government-approved forms of five major traditions, Daoism, Buddhism, Islam, and Roman Catholic and Protestant Christianity. Independent groups associated with these traditions are proscribed, as are traditional Chinese popular religious sects, which were once widespread. But the most serious problem with this limited definition of approved religions is that it leaves out the beliefs and rituals of the great majority of the Chinese people as practised in families and local communities. This ancient and varied local tradition, institutionalized in the midst of ordinary social life, is based on the worship of ancestors and protective deities in domestic shrines and community temples. It has long provided community identity and cohesion, and support for traditional social values. However, in the People's Republic all of this has been labelled "feudal superstition" unworthy of recognition as religion, and hence subject to repression and destruction.

Pitman Potter discusses the recent history of government policies towards religion, and the changes that have taken place since the end of what is called the "Cultural Revolution," 1966–76, a period of particularly intense destruction of old social and cultural traditions. Though the state has continued its emphasis on social control, there has been a gradual liberalization of policies towards religion since about 1982, while in 1990 Jiang Zemin urged a "more tolerant management of religious organizations." Nevertheless, leaders of unauthorized Muslim, Roman Catholic and Protestant groups continue to be subject to arrest, as are Tibetan Buddhists who support the Dalai Lama and members of the outlawed *falun gong* movement discussed by Nancy Chen below. In some areas local ritual traditions and temples have been allowed to revive, but they still have no legal status or protection.

The term "religion" in this article means worship of symbols that are believed to represent extra-human power, either natural objects such as large rocks and trees, or personified deities. The goals of such worship range from seeking immediate practical aid like healing and safe childbirth to harmonizing oneself with cosmic forces. By this definition, the rituals and beliefs of Chinese local communities are as much religion as any other.[1] Since community traditions are the foundation and quantitative mainstream of Chinese religions, four of the contributions to this special issue are devoted to them as they appear in different areas of the country. The first of these is by Kenneth Dean, an anthropologist and historian of religions at McGill University in Montreal. His topic is local communal religion in contemporary South-east China, the area where such practices have most strongly revived in the last 20 years, in part because of the influence of Taiwan, just 90 miles from the coast of Fujian province. The opening pages of Dean's article provide a good definition of his topic, emphasizing communal rituals centred in temples dedicated to a variety of gods, annual festivals, individual offerings of incense, food and drink, and divination, all of which require complex local organization. He notes the destructive results of official policies and the "extraordinary acts of courage and devotion that enabled the survival and growth of local community religion in China today." Dean emphasizes that annual rituals mobilize the entire populations of rural villages, and can also connect the villages in a whole area through annual processions in honour of their gods. These temple networks can be the most immediate and effective form of local organization, "an unofficial level of local governance." Together with his Chinese colleagues Dean has surveyed the lineages, cults and ritual activities of over 600 villages in one area of Fujian. Though much has been revived, the effects of repression by both Republican and communist governments can still be seen in ruined temples and depleted rituals, with much variation among local areas. In the cities temples have been completely destroyed in most areas so that young people have no way of learning about traditional religious practices; hence, there can be sharp differences between urban and rural areas. However, even in rural areas symbols of modernity can be incorporated in tradition, so temple committees can provide for audio-visual records of festivals, and images of Mao Zedong and banners with official slogans can be carried in religious processions.

Fan Lizhu, a sociologist from Fudan University in Shanghai, deals with an example of local community religion in north China, the activities of a woman spirit-medium in a small village in Hebei province. This woman is believed to represent an ancient goddess, the Silkworm Mother, to whom people turn for healing illnesses not cured by Western or Chinese medicine, the cost of which they may not be able to afford. Several specific cases of such healing are discussed. This delightful little study takes us to the heart of Chinese village religion, with its emphasis on practical aid.

The survey of local community traditions is continued by Liu Tik-sang, an anthropologist from the Hong Kong University of Science and Tech-

1. The meaning of the term "cult" in this special issue is that of the Oxford English Dictionary, "Worship; reverential homage rendered to a divine being," that is, it is here intended as a neutral descriptive term without the pejorative meanings sometimes associated with it.

nology who is a specialist in the activities of ordinary people in Hong Kong and its surrounding Zhu (Pearl) River delta. His report emphasizes the mutually supportive relationship between rituals and the organization of local households, communities and lineages, all of them based on a traditional view of the close connections between humans, deities and extrahuman forces in the environment. He also discusses the ways in which people continue their worship in a new urban setting, and the importance of *fengshui*, the art of aligning buildings and graves in accord with cosmic forces believed to be present in the landscape. These and other popular practices are carried out in a completely matter-of-fact way by many thousands of people in the modern societies and economies of Hong Kong and Macau as expressions of their own identity and culture. As is the case with Taiwan, religious practices in these two areas have not been subject to severe repression, so are important manifestations of contemporary Chinese religious faith and practice.

The most vibrant religious scene in the Chinese-speaking world is in Taiwan, which now has a democratically elected government and complete religious freedom. Taiwan's modern society and economy are a standing refutation of the old idea that religion will fade away as modernity advances. On the contrary, new freedom and economic resources have led to an increase of religious activities of all kinds, including those of local temples, Buddhist monasteries and charitable organizations, and a variety of new religious groups. Long-suppressed religious sects now have magnificent new temples and publicly distribute their scriptures and tracts. Local religious traditions are understood as an integral part of Taiwanese identity, while politicians seek the support of gods and temples for their campaigns. All of this is discussed here by Paul R. Katz, a historian who has long taught and done research in Taiwan and is now at the Academia Sinica in Taipei. His focus is on the relationship of religion and the state, and on the role of religion in providing a Taiwan form of civil society, a social space between private life and the state. He also discusses the efforts by devotees of the goddess Mazu to visit older temples to her on the mainland, and to invite mainland worshippers to bring a famous image of the goddess to Taiwan. Many Taiwan scholars now study their own religious traditions, a Taiwan Association of Religious Studies has been established, and there are now eleven university departments of religious studies and a new graduate institute devoted to that topic. Though the repression of religious activities on Taiwan was never so severe as in the People's Republic, freedom of religion did not fully develop there until after the lifting of martial law in 1987, so here as in other areas Taiwan provides a good example for the People's Republic to follow.

The oldest religious traditions in China are those of local communities, the emperor and state, and Daoism, though Buddhism began to arrive from India and Central Asia in the first century CE at about the same time that the Daoist religious tradition started to develop. Rituals performed by the emperor and his officials died out in the early 20th century with the end of the Qing dynasty, though many of their forms, symbols and deities still influence local community traditions, where there is still an emperor of the gods. From its beginnings in the Han dynasty Daoism was distinguished by its own forms of organization, priests, rituals, beliefs and scripture texts, which the Daoists maintained were superior to the common traditions around them. Daoist gods are immortals or symbols of astral forces, not the deified human beings of community cults. Daoist priests, trained by masters or in monasteries, developed elaborate theologies and rituals devoted to these gods, so Daoism became a complete religious system in its own right. Nevertheless, since these priests were invited to participate in community rituals, they influenced local religion and in turn were influenced by it. Lai Chi Tim, a historian of religions at the Chinese University of Hong Kong, has contributed an article on the situation of Daoism from 1980 to the present, as it has emerged from the destruction of the Cultural Revolution. His emphasis is on the restoration of Daoist temples, liturgies and training for priests, as well as on the activities of priests outside the monasteries to perform rituals for local communities. Most of these activities are authorized by the government-established National Daoist Association, which has produced several sets of rules for them. Lai notes that some of the funds for this revival of Daoism have come from Hong Kong, Taiwan and Singapore, as well as from mainland devotees and from tourism at Daoist pilgrimage sites on sacred mountains. In 1989 the first ordinations of Daoist priests were held since 1947, with other ordination rituals held in the 1990s. With these ordinations Chinese Daoism is on the path to recovery.

Buddhism has been an integral part of Chinese religion and culture since the first century CE, and has long since developed such Chinese characteristics as a more world-affirming philosophy and a simple and direct method for attaining salvation by mindful recitation of the name of the Buddha Amitābha. Its ideas of karma and rebirth have influenced Chinese literature and popular mentality, and some of its Buddhas and bodhisattvas have been adopted as deities by local and popular sectarian traditions. Nevertheless, Chinese Buddhist intellectuals over the centuries have maintained the old classical philosophical teachings. The author of the contribution here on contemporary Chinese Buddhism is Raoul Birnbaum, a scholar of Buddhism at the University of California, Santa Cruz, who has more fieldwork experience with Chinese Buddhists than any other Western scholar now active. He begins his report with a discussion of important Buddhist leaders and reformers from the 19th century through the first half of the 20th, to clarify the integrity and self awareness of this tradition as it entered the time of the People's Republic. His focus is on monks and nuns, and lay devotees who have taken formal vows of allegiance.

For centuries many monasteries were supported by income from land donated to them by lay devotees, but after 1949 such land was confiscated, monasteries were destroyed or converted into schools, factories or residences, many monks and nuns were forced to return to lay life, and public assemblies of lay Buddhists ceased. A China Buddhist Association was formed at government direction to control the monastic activities that remained. However, beginning in the mid-1980s the situation began to improve, with financial support coming from lay donors and remuneration for rituals performed by monks, particularly for funerals. A key problem has been the lack of middle-aged leaders to instruct novices, but new academies are helping to fill this gap. Birnbaum concludes his essay with a discussion of the influence of Buddhist teachers outside the mainland and from Tibet. Though Tibetan Buddhism is different from that of Han Chinese, some Chinese Buddhists have gone to Tibet on pilgrimages and to study.

The Chinese government recognizes 56 different ethnic groups in the country, with the great majority being the Han people and the rest called "minority peoples." Though Han Chinese influence is everywhere, most of these groups have maintained at least some of their own cultural, language and religious traditions, but this topic is far too complex for a one-volume survey. Among the minorities are several who are Muslim, that is, whose religion is a form of Islam. There have been Muslims in China for about 1,400 years, living all over the country, but with a large concentration in Xinjiang province in the far west. There are over 20 million Muslims in China, more than in most Middle Eastern countries. The best informed Western scholar of contemporary Chinese Islam is Dru C. Gladney of the University of Hawaii, the author of our chapter on this topic. He is an anthropologist with extensive fieldwork experience in China and Central Asia. Gladney notes at the beginning of his report that "Muslims in China live in minority communities amid a sea of people, in their view, who are largely pork-eating, polytheist, secularist and kafir ('heathen')." His focus is on Muslim identity in China, and the wide variety of Muslim practices and ethnic groups. One of the largest of these groups is the Uyghur, with over seven million members, mostly living in the Uyghur Autonomous Region in Xinjiang. Gladney discusses in detail their history and divisions, including sometimes violent conflicts. Some Uyghur factions advocate independence from China, which is a matter of great concern to the government not only for political reasons but also because Xinjiang is an oil-producing area. Chinese Muslims are also important because of their contacts with Muslim nations in Central Asia and the Middle East. In the late 1990s over 6,000 Chinese pilgrims went on pilgrimages to Mecca, and some Chinese students are being educated in Islamic universities in Egypt and elsewhere. Gladney concludes by noting that the activities of some Chinese Muslims are part of the larger globalization that is affecting much of the country.

There have been Roman Catholic Christians in China since the 16th century, and they now total ten to 12 million, "more Catholics than in Ireland"! Most are active and devout, and many have risked "severe political harassment, even imprisonment, in order to practise their faith." These quotations are from the article here on Chinese Catholicism by Richard Madsen of the University of California at San Diego, a foremost scholar of this topic. Since the beginning of the People's Republic there has been a struggle between the Chinese government and the Vatican, because in 1949 Pope Pius XII "forbade Catholics, under pain of excommunication, to co-operate in any way with the new Chinese regime. For its part, the new regime was determined to bring the Catholic Church, as all other religions, under tight state control." To do this the government set up the Catholic Patriotic Association, and sought Catholic leaders who would consecrate bishops without Vatican approval. Most Catholics refused to co-operate with this, and "carried out their faith in secret, sometimes under threat of severe punishment." Some bishops and priests were imprisoned for long terms. The result was an underground church with six to eight million adherents. Madsen's focus is on the division of the Chinese church, which is still unresolved because of the issue of whom is to select and appoint bishops. All of this is exacerbated because the Vatican is now the only state in Western Europe that recognizes Taiwan. The author notes that since Chinese Catholics were cut off from the reforms of the Second Vatican Council in 1962–65 most of them remain quite conservative, especially in rural areas where the church is firmly embedded in the patterns of traditional village life. Persecution by the government continued in the 1990s, but this has not reduced the number of practising Catholics. In actual practice there is now some reconciliation between members of the official and unofficial church, but the great majority give their allegiance to the Vatican. The government cannot stop this, but neither can it bring itself to grant any autonomy to the church, so the stand-off remains.

There have been Protestant Christians in China since the early 19th century. In the People's Republic they have gone through the same cycle of repression and recovery as other religious traditions, but in this case the result has been rapid growth to a total estimated membership of 25 to 30 million, at least 20 times more than in 1949. Our authority on this topic is Daniel H. Bays, a historian at Calvin College, whose contribution here begins, "Protestant Christianity has been a prominent part of the general religious resurgence in China in the past two decades. Today, on any given Sunday, there are almost certainly more Protestants in church in China than in all of Europe." There are an officially recognized Three Self Patriotic Movement (self-government, self-support and self-propagation) and a China Christian Council, but the majority of Protestants are in unofficial "house churches." Though there is still Western missionary influence on the liturgy and theology of many congregations, some of the house churches are part of independent Chinese traditions founded in reaction to missionary control. While there are some large urban congregations, most Protestants live in rural areas where they are influenced by local social and religious traditions. Bays also notes "Cultural Christians," Chinese intellectuals attracted to some Christian teachings who are not themselves members of churches. They are particularly interested in the reputed role of such teachings in the development of modern capitalism. In my own view, Protestant Christianity is doing well in China in part because of its association with the West and because for a long time so much of the local religious competition was destroyed or discredited. Though Chinese Protestants are now in contact with churches and organizations outside China, they are fundamentally independent and self-sufficient, and have become part of Chinese religion and culture. From this foundation they are now prepared to make their own contribution to world Christianity.

The final contribution to this special issue of *The China Quarterly* is by Nancy N. Chen of the University of California, Santa Cruz, an anthropologist of modern Chinese popular culture. Her focus here is on contemporary movements to promote healing by refining and strengthening *qi*, the vital force of the body and spirit, which in traditional Chinese thought are not clearly distinguished. This activity is now called *qigong*, "*qi* practice." The ultimate source of such practice is Daoist meditative exercises going back to the fourth century BCE, but Chen's focus is on modern forms in the People's Republic which were widely practised until the 1990s, typically by groups of people in public parks. Many *qigong* masters appeared whose followers believed had special healing powers, which was an attraction in part because the cost of medical treatment had risen sharply. As the numbers of participants grew, the government became concerned to regulate *qigong* and to specify that it could be practised only according to scientific principles without mystical overtones. Following the wide interest in *qigong* healing, a man named Li Hongzhi began to lecture and to organize a movement called the *falun gong*, which combined forms of meditation and self-cultivation with Li's own views. Based on the testimony of its practitioners this movement spread rapidly. As early as 1994 the *falun gong* organized demonstrations to protest against denouncements of its claims to heal, and on 26 April 1999 over 10,000 of its members staged a silent vigil outside Zhongnanhai in Beijing, the official state compound where China's top leaders live. This demonstration took the government completely by surprise, and caused it great consternation because it represented an independent ability to mobilize thousands of people outside government control. Before long the *falun gong* was banned, and millions of its books and tracts were burned, accompanied by intense propaganda attacking the movement as an "evil cult." Li Hongzhi had fled to the United States in 1996, which led to an internationalizing of the *falun gong* and widespread communication via the internet. Though this movement has been largely suppressed in China, it continues to recruit and protest in many other parts of the world. The response of the Chinese government has been very severe, and there is concern that this will encourage a return to old repressive policies towards other traditions.

Concluding Comments

In such a brief survey there is of course much that is left out, such as the religious traditions of minority peoples, as noted above, local community religion in the central, south-western and other areas of China, and Christianity in Taiwan, Hong Kong and Macau. Fan Lizhu has also done research on religion in the modern city of Shenzhen that has revealed a variety of private practices by its largely new immigrant population. Her work provides a fresh start for a study of urban religion in contemporary China. For recent Chinese studies of local community traditions see the section on "New sources for the study of Chinese local religion" in Kenneth Dean's article, and two of my recent publications, "From 'feudal superstition' to 'popular beliefs': new directions in mainland Chinese studies of Chinese popular religion,"[2] and *Ethnography in China Today: A Critical Assessment of Methods and Results*.[3] For a survey of recent Western studies of Chinese religions in general, see my "Chinese religions: the state of the field."[4]

The religious situation of Tibet is not discussed here because as the organizer and editor of this special issue I am reluctant to contribute to the idea that Tibet is an integral part of China, a view not necessarily shared by other contributors to this volume. Confucianism is not addressed because its modern manifestation is more as an ethical philosophy than a religion. Confucian ethical principles permeated late traditional Chinese culture, and had much influence on the beliefs and values of religious traditions, particularly the veneration of ancestors that is a fundamental aspect of family, lineage and community religion. Wherever such values as filial reverence, respect for social superiors, justice, honesty and courtesy are promoted, there Confucian values are present. There are Confucian temples in Taiwan and elsewhere in the Chinese diaspora that are still active, with ancestral tablets of the master and his followers arranged in rows above the altars. I have visited some great old temples on the mainland which have images of these figures, though none that I have seen was still being used. In the past Confucius was also worshipped and meditated on in Confucian academies. In Daoism and community temples Confucius has long been treated as a god represented by images, and in Taiwan there are religious sects devoted to him. In the past students prayed to him for help in civil service examinations, and in Taiwan they still pray to deities who are believed to have special powers for this. On the whole, however, proper intellectuals have been supposed to venerate Confucius as a very special human being, but not as a god. In the 20th century there have been decades of fierce attacks on Confucius as a symbol of all that is decayed and backward, attacks that intensified in the People's Republic, but there is now an attempt in China to rediscover his ethical teachings, if only to fill the void left by the destruction of traditional social values. His hometown and burial place in Shandong province have been restored.[5] In Taiwan Confucius and his teachings have been promoted as a foundation of Chinese culture, in part as a response to the Cultural Revolution on the mainland.

2. *Cahiers d'Extrême-Asie*, No. 12 (2001), pp. 105–128.
3. Taipei: Yuan-liou Publishing Co., 2002.
4. Parts I and II, *Journal of Asian Studies*, Vol. 54, No. 1 (February 1995), pp. 124–160, and Vol. 54, No. 2 (May 1995), pp. 314–395. These articles are by ten co-authors.
5. For a summary of the revival after 1980 of discussions by Chinese scholars of Confucian thought and ethics, see ch. 15, "The new Confucian movement in mainland China," in Umberto Bresciani, *Reinventing Confucianism: The New Confucian Movement* (Taipei: Taipei Ricci Institute for Chinese Studies, 2001, Variétés Sinologiques New Series 90).

The impression one gets from reading this material is that despite government repression and restrictions, religions in China are doing better than might have been expected. All of them had difficulties in the decades before 1949 from social disorder, weak and corrupt government, civil wars and the Japanese invasion, so their situation was far from ideal when the People's Republic began, which makes their persistence today all the more remarkable. They are a tribute to the tenacity of the human spirit and religious faith. Nevertheless, the freedom of religion still has a long way to go in China, where the government still feels threatened by any significant social activity outside its control. In this area, old imperial Chinese and Leninist assumptions still rule, yet China will never become a fully modern and democratic country until these assumptions are abandoned. The example of Taiwan demonstrates that lively religious activities are not a danger to a fully modern society; indeed, they can strengthen social modernity by providing the people with a cultural arena of their own.

Belief in Control: Regulation of Religion in China*

Pitman B. Potter

ABSTRACT This article examines the regulation of religion in China, in the context of changing social expectations and resulting dilemmas of regime legitimacy. The post-Mao government has permitted limited freedom of religious belief, subject to legal and regulatory restrictions on religious behaviour. However, this distinction between belief and behaviour poses challenges for the regime's efforts to maintain political control while preserving an image of tolerance aimed at building legitimacy. By examining the regulation of religion in the context of patterns of compliance and resistance in religious conduct, the article attempts to explain how efforts to control religion raise challenges for regime legitimacy.

The relationship between religion and state power in China has long been contested. Dynastic relations with religious organizations and doctrine included attempts to capture legitimacy through sponsorship of ritual, while folk religions continued to thrive in local society despite ongoing attempts at official control.[1] In addition, religion was a significant source of resistance to imperial rule, often in the form of secret societies attempting to remain aloof from official control,[2] as well as through peasant uprisings inspired by religious devotion.[3] During the Maoist period, programmes of socialist transformation challenged the social bases for traditional Chinese folk religions, while policies of political monopoly attacked those limited examples of organized religion that could be identified and targeted.[4]

In post-Mao China, the regime adopted a somewhat more tolerant perspective on religion.[5] As a component of a new approach to building

* The research for this article was made possible by a strategic grant on Globalization and Social Cohesion in Asia from the Social Sciences and Humanities Research Council of Canada (SSHRC), for which I am grateful. I would like also to thank Meera Bawa, a graduate student and law student at UBC for her research assistance.
1. See generally Stephen Feuchtwang, "School-temple and city god," in Arthur P. Wolf (ed.), *Studies in Chinese Society* (Stanford: Stanford University Press, 1978), pp. 103–130; C.K. Yang, *Religion in Chinese Society* (Berkeley: University of California Press, 1961).
2. See e.g. David Ownby, *Brotherhoods and Secret Societies in mid-Qing China: The Formation of a Tradition* (Stanford: Stanford University Press, 1996).
3. See generally, Elizabeth J. Perry, *Challenging the Mandate of Heaven: Social Protest and State Power in China* (Armonk NY: M.E. Sharpe, 2001) and *Rebels and Revolutionaries in North China, 1845–1945* (Stanford: Stanford University Press, 1980); Susan Naquin, *Millenarian Rebellion in China: The Eight Trigrams Uprising of 1813* (New Haven: Yale University Press, 1976).
4. See generally, Rennselaer W. Lee III, "General aspects of Chinese communist religious policy, with Soviet comparisons," *The China Quarterly*, No. 19 (1964), pp. 161–173.
5. See generally Liu Peng, "Church and state relations in China: characteristics and trends," *Journal of Contemporary China*, Vol. 5, No. 11 (1996), pp. 69–79; Donald E. MacInnis, *Religion in China Today: Policy and Practice* (Maryknoll NY: Orbis, 1989); Chang

regime legitimacy,[6] the government accepted a trade-off of broader social and economic autonomy in exchange for continued political loyalty. Thus, beginning in the 1980s, a "zone of indifference"[7] into which the government chose not to intervene was cautiously expanded in areas of social and economic relations. While the government's concession of socio-economic autonomy was not enforceable through formal institutions or processes, it remained an important source of popular support that could not easily be repudiated except in response to perceived political disloyalty by the citizenry.

This tension between autonomy and loyalty is particularly evident in the area of religion. While China's expanding participation in the world economy has seen increased international criticism on human rights grounds of policies aimed at controlling religious practices,[8] the importance of the regulation of religion rests primarily on domestic factors of authority and legitimacy. Religion represents a fault line of sorts in the regime's effort to build legitimacy through social policy. As a rich array of religious belief systems re-emerges,[9] the regime faces continued challenges of maintaining sufficient authority to ensure political control while still presenting a broad image of tolerance. This article examines the regulation of religion in China in the context of these dimensions of legitimacy and political authority.

Regulation of Religion: Maintaining the Balance Between Autonomy and Loyalty

As with many features of social regulation in China, the regulation of religion proceeds essentially from the policy dictates of the Chinese Communist Party (CCP), which are then expressed and enforced in part through law and administrative regulation. Dissemination and enforcement of Party policies on religion is the responsibility of an intersecting network of Party and governmental organizations.[10] Prior to his retirement following the 16th National CCP Congress, Politburo Standing Committee member Li Ruihuan had particular responsibility for religious affairs, while Politburo member in charge of propaganda Ding Guangen

---

footnote continued

Chi-p'eng, "The CCP's policy toward religion," *Issues & Studies*, Vol. 19, No. 5 (September 1983), pp. 55–70.

6. See generally Pitman B. Potter, "Riding the tiger – legitimacy and legal culture in post-Mao China," *The China Quarterly*, No. 138 (1994), pp. 325–358.

7. Tang Tsou, *The Cultural Revolution and Post-Mao Reforms: A Historical Perspective* (Chicago: University of Chicago Press, 1986), p. 18.

8. See e.g. Human Rights Watch/Asia, *China: State Control of Religion* (1997), Human Rights Watch/Asia, *Continuing Religious Repression in China* (1993), US State Department Bureau of Democracy, Human Rights and Labor, "China country report on human rights practices, 2000" (23 February 2001).

9. See generally, Chan Kim-Kwong and Alan Hunter, "Religion and society in mainland China in the 1990s," *Issues & Studies*, Vol. 30, No. 8 (August 1994), pp. 52–68; Julia Ching, "Is there religious freedom in China?" *America*, Vol. 162, No. 22 (9 June 1990), pp. 566–570.

10. See generally, Human Rights Watch/Asia, *China: State Control of Religion* (1997), ch. 3; MacInnis, *Religion in China Today*, pp. 1–5.

also played an important role.[11] The Party's United Front Work Department is charged with detailed policy formulation and enforcement, subject to general Party policy directives.[12] The State Council's Religious Affairs Bureau has responsibility for regulatory initiatives and supervision aimed at implementing Party policy.[13] Public Security departments have taken broad responsibility to enforce regulations controlling religious activities, and have participated actively in suppression campaigns.

Party policy. Party policy on religion over the past 20 years has reflected a marked departure from the repressive policies of the Maoist period. The Third Plenum of the 11th CCP Central Committee in 1978 supported conclusions about the decline of class struggle.[14] This led in turn to gradual acceptance of broader diversity of social and economic practices, including a relaxation of Party policy on religion. The official summary of CCP policy on religion issued in 1982 as "Document 19" stated the basic policy as one of respect for and protection of the freedom of religious belief, pending such future time when religion itself will disappear.[15] While recognizing that religious belief was a private matter, and acknowledging that coercion to prevent religious belief would be counterproductive,[16] Party policy nevertheless privileged the freedom not

11. See "Li Ruihuan meets religious leaders," Beijing Xinhua Domestic Service 31 January 2000, in FBIS *Daily Report – China* (FBIS-CHI-2000–0201) 1 February 2000. In the official Xinhua report on the National Work Conference on Religion, 10–12 December 2001, Li Ruihuan was listed just after Li Peng and Zhu Rongji and ahead of Hu Jintao among the leaders attending. See "Quanguo zongjiao gongzuo huiyi zai jing juxing" ("National work conference on religion convenes in Beijing") *Renmin wang (People's Net)* (electronic service) (12 December 2001). Ding Guangen was listed first among the chairs of the Work Conference.
12. UFWD Director Wang Zhaoguo's public statements on united front work regarding religion have echoed the central tenets of Party policy on issues of Party and state guidance of religion and the need for religions to adapt to the needs of socialism. See e.g. "Wang Zhaoguo on PRC united front work," Beijing Xinhua Domestic Service, 8 January 2000, in FBIS-CHI-2000–0110, 11 January 2000.
13. See e.g. Ye Xiaowen, "China's current religious question: once again an inquiry into the five characteristics of religion" (22 March 1996), Appendix X in Human Rights Watch/Asia, *China: State Control of Religion* (1997), pp. 116–144.
14. See "Zhongguo gongchandang di shiyi jie zhongyang weiyuanhui di san ci quanti huiyi gongbao" ("Communiqué of the Third Plenum of the Eleventh CCP Central Committee"), *Hongqi (Red Flag)*, No. 1 (1979), pp. 14–21.
15. See "Guanyu woguo shehuizhuyi shiqi zongjiao wenti de jiben guandian he jiben zhengce" ("Basic viewpoints and policies on religious issues during our country's socialist period") (31 March 1982), in Xu Yucheng, *Zongjiao zhengce falü zhishi dawen (Responses to Questions about Knowledge of Law and Policy on Religion)* (Beijing: Chinese Academy of Social Sciences Press, 1997), pp. 287–305, at p. 292. An English translation appears as "Document 19," Appendix 2 in Mickey Spiegel, "Freedom of religion in China" (Washington, London and Brussels: Human Rights Watch/Asia, 1992), pp. 33–45. For discussion of circumstances surrounding the issue of Document 19, see Luo Guangwu, *Xin Zhongguo zongjiao gongzuo da shi yaojian (Outline of Major Events in Religious Work in the New China)* (Beijing: Chinese culture *(huawen)* press, 2001), pp. 298–304.
16. Herein perhaps lay a recognition of the limits of CCP policies that under Mao attempted to repress local religious practices and traditions. See generally, Edward Friedman, Paul G. Pickowicz and Mark Selden, *Chinese Village, Socialist State* (New Haven: Yale University Press, 1991), esp. pp. 234–35, 268–270. Also see Stephan Feuchtwang, "Religion as resistance," in Elizabeth J. Perry and Mark Selden (eds.), *Chinese Society: Change Conflict and Resistance* (London: Routledge, 2000), pp. 161–177.

to believe in religion. It also recognized only five religions, Buddhism, Daoism, Islam, Catholicism and Protestantism, in an effort to exclude folk religions, superstition and cults from the bounds of protection.[17] The Party was also committed to unremitting propaganda to support atheism, and to using its control over the educational system to marginalize religious belief.[18] Document 19 prohibited grants of "feudal privileges" to religious organizations and otherwise limited their capacity to recruit, proselytize and raise funds. Education of clergy and administration of religious organizations and buildings aimed to ensure that religious leaders remained loyal to principles of Party leadership, socialism, and national and ethnic unity. Document 19 also prohibited Party members from believing in or participating in religion.[19]

While the early 1980s signalled an important phase of liberalization in comparison to previous periods, the Party remained concerned primarily with enforcing social control, under the rubric of the dictatorship of the proletariat and the central role of Party leadership in the process of socialist modernization.[20] Significant social unrest in Tibet and Xinjiang in 1988–89,[21] coupled with the nation-wide crisis created by the 1989 democracy movement, posed particular challenges. In 1991, the CCP Central Committee/State Council's "Document No. 6" expressed the regime's policy response that attempted to co-opt religious adherents while also repressing challenges to Party power.[22] Document No. 6 emphasized increased regulatory control over all religious activities: "Implementing administration of religious affairs is aimed at bringing religious activities within the bounds of law, regulation, and policy, but not to interfere with normal religious activities or the internal affairs of religious organizations."[23] While the reference to non-interference seemed benign, the qualification that this extended only to "normal" activities suggested an overarching purpose to confine religion to the limits of law and policy.

Document No. 6 grew out of the State Council's National Work Conference on Religion on 5–9 December 1990, at which there was relatively frank discussion on the number of religious adherents in China and a recognition of the need for limited tolerance.[24] Following Li Peng's

---

17. *Ibid.* Also MacInnis, *Religion in China Today*, pp. 385–410. For parallels to religious policies under the Qing, see Ownby, *Brotherhoods and Secret Societies*; Naquin, *Millenarian Rebellion in China*.

18. See generally, MacInnis, *Religion in China Today*, pp. 411–19.

19. "Basic view points and policies," pp. 299–301.

20. See Preamble to the 1982 Constitution of the PRC (Beijing: Law Publishers, 1986).

21. On Tibet, see Melvyn Goldstein, "Tibet, China and the United States: reflections on the Tibet question," *Atlantic Council Occasional Paper* (April 1995), pp. 38–48. On Xinjiang, see Felix K. Chang, "China's Central Asian power and problems," *Orbis*, Vol. 41, No. 3 (Summer 1997), pp. 401–426.

22. "Guanyu jinyibu zuohao zongjiao gongzuo ruogan wenti de tongzhi" extracted in Luo Guangwu, pp. 434–37. English text appears as "Document 6: CCP Central Committee/State Council, circular on some problems concerning further improving work on religion" (5 February 1991), Appendix 1 in Spiegel, "Freedom of Religion in China," pp. 27–32.

23. See *Ibid.* pp. 435–36. Also see Chan Kim-Kwong and Alan Hunter, "New light on religious policy in the PRC," *Issues & Studies*, Vol. 31, No. 2 (February 1995), pp. 21–36

24. For discussion of the work conference, see Luo Guangwu, pp. 428–432.

exhortation to ensure strict enforcement of Party policy and state law on control of religion, Jiang Zemin took a more relaxed tack, calling for a united front approach that included tolerant management of religious organizations, policies on religion that were suited to broader pro-grammes of reform and opening up, and a recognition that religion "affects the masses of a billion people" (*shejidao qian baiwan qunzhong*) and that resolution of issues of religion would have significance for national stability, ethnic unity and the promotion of socialist culture. In anticipation of the issuance of Document No. 6, Jiang called the five leaders of national religious organizations to Zhongnanhai for a briefing, emphasizing the balance between limited tolerance of religious activities that conformed to Party policy, and repression of heterodoxy.[25]

Document No. 6 claimed to protect freedom of religious belief, while requiring believers to comply with imperatives of Party leadership, social stability and social interests. The document reiterated provisions of the 1982 Document No. 19, on the right not to believe in religion. Document No. 6 directed public security organs to take forceful measures to curb those who use religious activities to "engage in disruptive activities," "stir up trouble, endanger public safety, and weaken the unification of the country and national unity," or "collude with hostile forces outside the country to endanger China's security." Apart from their utility in justify-ing restrictions on religious activities in Tibet and Xinjiang and prohibi-tions against Christian practitioners from Taiwan,[26] these provisions also limited proselytization, recruitment, fund-raising and other activities in support of organized religion.[27]

Despite efforts at official control, a religious revival in China gathered significant momentum through the 1990s.[28] The Party's policy response recognized five basic characteristics of religion that had been identified and formalized by the CCP's United Front Work Department in the late 1950s and then reiterated in 1989.[29] These stressed the long-term charac-ter of religion and its mass base, national and international aspects, and complexity. The long-term character of religion militated in favour of patient persistence in Party policies of co-optation and control. The mass character served as a cautionary note that the Party could not easily

25. *Ibid.* pp. 432–34.
26. With increased (albeit indirect) travel between Taiwan and the mainland in the 1980s, the links between Taiwan relations and religious affairs became a matter of particular concern. See Religious Affairs Bureau and Taiwan Affairs Office, "Institutional secret, national edict on religion" (*guo zhongfa*), No. 128 (13 November 1989), in Chan and Hunter, "New light on religious policy in the PRC," pp. 21–36 at pp. 30–31.
27. Spiegel, "Freedom of religion in China," pp. 8–13.
28. See generally, Jaime Florcruz *et al.*, "Inside China's search for its soul," *Time*, Vol. 15, No. 14 (4 October 1999), pp. 68–72; Adam Brookes and Susan V. Lawrence, "Gods and demons," *Far Eastern Economic Review*, 13 May 1999, pp. 38–40; Arthur Waldron, "Religious revivals in Communist China," *Orbis*, Vol. 42, No. 2 (Spring 1998), pp. 323–332; Donald MacInnis, "From suppression to repression: religion in China today," *Current History*, Vol. 95 (September 1996), pp. 284–89; Matt Forney, "God's country," *Far Eastern Economic Review*, 6 June 1996, pp. 46–48.
29. Ye Xiaowen "China's current religious question: once again an inquiry into the five characteristics of religion" (22 March 1996), in Human Rights Watch/Asia, *China: State Control of Religion* (1997), pp. 116–144 at pp. 117–18.

ignore or control the some 100 million people believed to participate in religion. The links between religion and national and international questions called for attention to the interplay between ethnicity in such areas as Tibet and Xinjiang and the imported religions of Buddhism and Islam. The complexity of religion was seen to require careful analysis of the processes of popular belief as a prerequisite for effective policy.

In the face of these conditions, Party authorities on religion focused on strengthening administration of religious affairs according to law, and on actively guiding religions to enable them to adapt to socialist society.[30] While the educational function of Party policy represented a method of indirect control over clergy and believers,[31] administration according to law imposed criminal and administrative sanctions for religious activities used to "oppose the Party and the socialist system, undermine the unification of the country, social stability and national unity, or infringe on the legitimate interests of the state...."[32] Party policy was less tolerant of local sects seeking broader autonomy from the Party and the government,[33] while also urging vigilance against infiltration of China by hostile foreign elements under the guise of religion. The United States was portrayed as particularly interested in using religion to subvert China.[34]

The State Council's 1997 "White Paper on Freedom of Religious Belief in China" reiterated the point that "religion should be adapted to the society where it is prevalent" and the religions must "conduct their activities within the sphere prescribed by law and adapt to social and cultural progress."[35] Pursuant to these principles, the government remained committed to punishing those religions and religious believers who "are a serious danger to the normal life and productive activities of the people" or who "severely endanger the society and the public interest."[36] The coercive themes were reiterated at the United Front Work Department's national work conference in late December 1999 by Director Wang Zhaoguo: "We must comprehensively and correctly implement the Party's religious policy, strengthen administration of religious affairs according to law, and actively guide religions to adapt to socialist society."[37]

This theme was reinforced in RAB Director Ye Xiaowen's October

30. See Luo Shuze, "Some hot issues in our work on religion" (June 1996) in Human Rights Watch/Asia, *China: State Control of Religion* (1997), pp. 65–70
31. *Ibid.* pp. 68–70.
32. *Ibid.* p. 68. Also see Mickey Spiegel, "Control 'according to law': restrictions in religion," *China Rights Forum*, Spring 1998, pp. 22–27.
33. Luo Shuze, "Some hot issues in our work on religion," at pp. 66–67
34. *Ibid.* p. 65. This continues to be a focus of official policy statements on religion. See "US report on religious freedom seen as 'power politics'," Beijing Xinhua English Service, 11 December 1999, in FBIS-CHI-1999-1210, 13 December 1999; "PRC refutes charges on religious affairs," Beijing Xinhua English Service, 8 December 1999, in FBIS-CHI-1999-1208, 9 December 1999.
35. "Freedom of religious belief in China" (hereafter "1997 White Paper") in *White Papers of the Chinese Government, 1996–1999* (Beijing: Foreign Languages Press, 2000), pp. 227–257 at pp. 246–47.
36. *Ibid.* p. 247.
37. "Wang Zhaoguo on PRC united front work," Beijing Xinhua Domestic Service, 8 January 2000, in FBIS-CHI-2000-0110, 11 January 2000.

2000 essay on theory and policy.[38] Ye called for cadres to adhere to the "three sentences" (*san ju hua*) of Jiang Zemin extolling the need to enforce Party policies on religion, strengthen management of religion according to law, and actively lead the adaptation of religion and socialism.[39] Ye also reiterated four principles articulated during Jiang Zemin's July 1998 inspection tour of Xinjiang, namely the freedom to believe or not believe in religion, non-interference in religious activities, separation of politics from religion, and the interdependence between rights and obligations associated with religious activities. Ye cautioned cadres on the need for tolerance of approved religious activities in accordance with law, although he also urged punishment of violations. For Ye, the key to managing popular religious activity seemed to lie in educating the younger generations in historical materialism and atheism, rather than in coercion and repression of practitioners.

Despite the violent repression campaign against the *falun gong* in 2000–2001, Party policy continued to sound a theme of cautious accommodation with religion in general, under the theme of adaptation between religion and socialism. In his speech to the December 2001 National Work Conference on Religious Affairs, Jiang Zemin called once again for adaptation between religion and socialism.[40] The conference was intended originally to summarize the results of the campaign against the *falun gong* and to provide instructions for further action. However, by the time the meeting was held, policy consensus on repression of the *falun gong* had apparently progressed to the point where there was little left to discuss. As a result, the conference was used as an opportunity to summarize official policies. Jiang's speech instructed officials to adhere to policies on religious freedom, refrain from using administrative force to eliminate religion and accept that religion would be an integral part of Chinese society for a long time. These conciliatory elements were echoed in an influential article by Deputy Director of the State Council Office for Economic Restructuring Pan Yue, who is also an important official in the CCP's youth wing.[41] Pan suggested that the Party drop its long-standing prohibition of religious figures joining the Party and recognize that religion "has psychological, cultural and moral functions, as well as numerous uses, such as services and public welfare." Pan called for the Party to "abandon the policy of consistently suppressing and controlling religion and adopt [a policy] of unity and guidance and take advantage of the unifying power and appeal of religion to serve the CCP regime."

However, the December 2001 work conference also expressed the

38. Ye Xiaowen, "Dui zongjiao lilun he zhengce yaodian de fensi he guilei" ("Analysing and classifying the main points of religious theory and policy"), in Luo Guangwu, pp. 1–8.

39. These had been articulated in Ye's 14 March 1996 *Renmin ribao* editorial, which in turn harkened back to Jiang Zemin's 7 November 1993 speech to a national united front work conference. See Luo Guangwu, pp. 528–29, 465–68.

40. "Jiang Zemin, Zhu Rongji address religious work conference, other leaders take part," Beijing Xinhua Domestic Service, 12 December 2001 in FBIS-CHI-2001-1212, 19 December 2001.

41. "Report says CCP plans to allow religious figures to join Party," Hong Kong Sing Tao Jih Pao (internet version), in FBIS-CHI-2001-1224, 26 December 2001.

more conventional aspects of policies on control of religion. Jiang Zemin called for the Party and state to guide religion to conform to the needs of socialism, and to prevent religious adherents from interfering with the socialist system, the interests of the state and the requirements of social progress. Religious adherents were admonished to love the motherland, support the socialist system and the leadership of the Party, and obey the laws and policies of the state. The basic principles articulated in Document 19 of 1991 remain key to ensuring that religious activities would not thwart the goals of Party leadership and socialism. Zhu Rongji's remarks to the December 2001 meeting focused on the need for effective administration of the regulatory system for religion, particularly in rural and minority areas.[42] The theme of control was reiterated in *Tibet Daily*'s 13 December commentary on a Central Committee outline concerning implementing citizens' moral construction, which focused on "strengthening unity with the broad masses of people who do not believe in religion," supporting "normal and orderly religious activities" and strengthening Party leadership.[43] In addition, Politburo Politics and Law Chair Luo Gan's speech on tasks for 2002, given just prior to the work conference, stressed the need for suppression of disruptive religious activity.[44] Thus, despite recent suggestions about liberalization, the discourse of control remains strong.

Provision of Chinese law. The State Council's 1997 White Paper reiterated the distinction between religious belief which the state purports to protect, and "illegal and criminal activities being carried out under the banner of religion."[45] The distinction is made according to CCP policies, as expressed in the provisions of the Constitution and specific laws and regulations.

The Constitution of the PRC represents a formal articulation of Party policy. As Peng Zhen, then Vice-Chair of the Committee to Revise the Constitution, pointed out in 1980, "the Party leads the people in enacting the law and leads the people in observing the law" (*dang lingdao renmin zhiding falü, ye lingdao renmin zunshou falü*).[46] This edict remains a bulwark of the Party's approach to law making.[47] During the post-Mao

---

42. "Jiang Zemin, Zhu Rongji address religious work conference."
43. See "Xizang ribao commentator views implementation 'outline' on ethics building, Tibet's religious policy," *Xizang ribao* (*Tibet Daily*), 13 December 2001, in FBIS Doc. ID CPP20011217000175, 17 December 2001.
44. See "China's Luo Gan outlines tasks of political legal work in 2002," Beijing Xinhua Domestic Service, 4 December 2001, in FBIS-CHI-2001-1204, 7 December 2001.
45. "1997 White Paper," p. 247.
46. See e.g. Peng Zhen. "Guanyu difang ren-da changweihui de gongzuo" ("On the work of local people's congress standing committees") (18 April 1980). In *Peng Zhen wenxuan* (*Collected Works of Peng Zhen*) (Beijing: People's Press, 1991), pp. 383–391 at p. 389.
47. See e.g. Wu Fumin, "Zou yifa zhiguo lu" ("Walking the road of ruling the country by law"), in *Fazhi ribao* (*Legal System Daily*), 19 April 2000, pp. 1–2; Zhang Zhiming, *Cong minzhu xin lu dao yifa zhiguo* (*From the New Road of Democracy to Ruling the Country According to Law*) (Nanchang: Jiangxi Higher Education Press, 2000); Tian Jiyun (ed.), *Zhongguo gaige kaifang yu minzhu fazhi jianshe* (*China's Reform and Opening Up and Construction of Democracy and the Legal System*) (Beijing: China Democracy and Legal System Press, 2000), p. 412.

period, policies of limited tolerance for religion were reflected in the provisions of Article 36 of the 1982 Constitution:[48]

Citizens of the People's Republic of China enjoy freedom of religious belief.

No state organ, public organization or individual may compel citizens to believe in, or not to believe in, any religion: nor may they discriminate against citizens who believe in, or do not believe in any religion.

The state protects normal religious activities. No one may make use of religion to engage in activities that disrupt public order, impair the health of citizens or interfere with the educational system of the state.

Religious bodies and religious affairs are not subject to any foreign domination.

In explaining the meaning of Constitutional provisions on religious freedom, Peng Zhen noted that from a political perspective the common elements of patriotism and adherence to socialism bind those who believe in religion and those who do not.[49] This underscored the imperative of submission to party-state control as a condition for enjoyment of religious freedom. Protection of freedom of religion was qualified as well by provisions of the PRC Constitution Article 33 conditioning the exercise of citizens' rights on their performance of duties: "Every citizen enjoys the rights and at the same time must perform the duties prescribed by the Constitution and the law."[50] As explained by Peng Zhen, these duties included upholding the Four Basic Principles,[51] which impose a duty to uphold the socialist road, the dictatorship of the proletariat, leadership of the Party, and Marxism, Leninism, Mao Zedong Thought.[52] Thus, the freedom granted religious belief remained conditional not only on compliance with law and regulation, but more fundamentally on submission to the policies and edicts of the party-state.

The Constitution provides authority for specific legislation on the matter of religion. As yet, there is no comprehensive law on religion, although the principle of freedom of religious belief is articulated with qualifications in a number of specific laws.[53] Thus, the Law on Autonomy in Nationality Regions (1984, 2001) allows in Article 11 for freedom of religious belief, subject to qualifications against harm to social order, personal health and state education. The General Principles of Civil Law (1986) provides in Article 75 for protection of personal property includ-

48. PRC Constitution (1982) (Beijing: Publishing House of Law, 1986). The provisions of Article 36 were retained in the constitutional amendments of 1988, 1993 and 1999.

49. Peng Zhen, "Guanyu Zhonghua renmin gongheguo xianfa xiugai cao'an de shuoming" ("Explanation of the draft revisions to the Constitution of the PRC"), in Peng Zhen, *Lun xin shiqi de shehui minzhu yu fazhi jianshe* (*On Building Socialist Democracy and Legal System During the New Period*) (Beijing: Central Archives Press, 1989), pp. 100–115 at p. 109.

50. PRC Constitution (1982). This provision was retained in the 1988, 1993 and 1999 amendments.

51. Peng Zhen, "Guanyu Zhonghua renmin gongheguo xianfa xiugai cao'an de shuoming" ("Explanation of the draft revisions to the Constitution of the PRC"), in *Renmin ribao* (*People's Daily*), 6 December 1982.

52. Deng Xiaoping, "Jianchi si xiang jiben yuanze" ("Uphold the four basic principles"), in *Deng Xiaoping wenxuan: yijiuqiwu – yijiu ba'er* (*Collected Works of Deng Xiaoping: 1975–1982*) (Beijing: People's Press, 1983), pp. 144–170 at pp. 150–51.

53. "1997 White Paper," pp. 230, 232.

ing cultural items and in Article 77 for protection of property of religious organizations. The Law on Elections to National and Local People's Congresses (1986) provides in Article 3 for the right to stand for election regardless of religious belief, as does the Organization Law on the Village Committees (1987) in Article 9. The Education Law (1995) Article 9 prohibits discrimination in educational opportunity based on religion, although Article 8 provides that religion may not interfere with the state educational system. The Labour Law (1995) Article 12 prohibits discrimination in employment based on religion. The revised Criminal Law of the PRC (1997) provides in Article 251 for punishment of state personnel who unlawfully deprive citizens of their freedom of religious belief. As with the Constitutional provisions, these laws confine the scope of protection to the matter of religious belief, as qualified by requirements that religious practices not conflict with the state's political authority.

Authorized by the Constitution and informed by CCP policies, China's regulatory provisions on religion include measures of general application as well as edicts that apply to specific conduct or beliefs. Regulatory restrictions extend to places of worship, which must be formally registered and undergo annual inspections, and may not be used for activities that "harm national unity, the solidarity of ethnic groups, social stability or the physical health of citizens, or obstruct the educational system.[54] Religious education academies must implement CCP policy and submit to Party leadership, and their curricula, programmes and personnel are subject to approval by the Religious Affairs Bureau.[55] The officially approved curricula incorporate state policy into religious instruction.[56] Activities such as recruiting believers among primary and secondary school students, propagating religious ideology in school, establishing illegal (that is, not properly approved and registered) religious schools and enrolling young people, and travelling abroad to attend seminary are considered in violation of the provision that religion may not obstruct state education.[57]

---

54. "Guowuyuan guanyu zongjiao huodong changsuo guanli tiaoli" ("State Council regulations regarding the management of places of religious activities") (31 January 1994), in Xu Yucheng, *Respect to Questions*, pp. 308–310. English text of these measures, along with "Registration procedures for venues for religious activities" (1 May 1994); "Method for annual inspection of places of religious activity" (29 July 1996), appear in Human Rights Watch Asia, *China: State Control of Religion* (1997), pp. 106–108, 109–111, 112–14, respectively.

55. See e.g. Religious Affairs Bureau of the State Council, "Comments on enhancing the world of religious academies" (15 January 1988), in Chan and Hunter, "New light on religious policy in the PRC," at pp. 29–30.

56. See for example, "Excerpts from questions and answers on the patriotic education program in monasteries" (25 May 1997), in Human Rights Watch Asia, *China: State Control of Religion* (1997), pp. 100–103, where monastery students are required to master government policy attacking the Dalai Lama.

57. "Notice on the prevention of some places using religious activities to hinder school education" (26 November 1991), in Human Rights Watch/Asia, *Freedom of Religion in China* (1992), pp. 68–70. For further controls over students sent abroad for religious education, see Religious Affairs Bureau of the State Council, "Comments on the Protestant Church sending of students overseas" (21 May 1990), in Chan and Hunter, "New light on religious policy in the PRC," pp. 31–32.

Religious activities by foreigners are also subject to control. This derives in part from the conflicted history of China's relations with foreign missionaries, who are portrayed as instruments of imperialism. In addition, the government strives for control over religion by insulating religious practitioners and activities from their overseas counterparts.[58] Evangelical Christians from the United States and Korea have been cited as examples of foreign religious interests interfering with China's independence and autonomy in managing religious affairs, and building up anti-motherland, anti-government forces.[59] Religious broadcasts, internet information, and literature and materials brought into China from abroad are subject to special inspection and confiscation.[60] Foreigners are generally prohibited from proselytizing, recruiting candidates to go abroad for instruction, and bringing to China religious materials that endanger the public interest.[61]

The Religious Affairs Bureaus of China's provinces and major cities are empowered to issue local regulations on the control of religion.[62] These generally echo the tenets of central edicts.[63] The Regulations of the Shanghai Religious Affairs Bureau (1996), for example, mirror provisions of national regulations on the authority of the government to maintain lawful supervision over religious affairs, including registration and supervision of religious organizations, religious personnel, places of worship, and religious activities, education and property.[64]

Particular regulatory provisions are also aimed at specific religions. Mindful of the overlap between religious belief and ethnic tension, the

58. See generally, "Fourteen points from Christians in the People's Republic of China to Christians abroad" in MacInnis, *Religion in China Today*, pp. 61–70.

59. "Vigilance against infiltration by religious forces from abroad" (15 March 1991), in Human Rights Watch/Asia, *Freedom of Religion in China* (1992), pp. 52–54. Also see Human Rights Watch/Asia, *China: State Control of Religion* (1997), pp. 33–36.

60. See Religious Affairs Department of the State Council and the Ministry of Public Security, "Notification on stopping and dealing with those who use Christianity to conduct illegal activities" (18 October 1988); Religious Affairs Office, "Comments on handling religious publications that enter our borders" (16 June 1990), in Chan and Hunter, "New light on religious policy in the PRC," pp. 30 and 32, respectively. On internet controls, see "Computer information network and internet security, protection and management regulations" (30 December 1997) (author's copy).

61. "Guowuyuan guanyu Zhonghua renmin gongheguo jingnei waiguoren zongjiao huodong guanli guiding" ("State Council regulations on the management of religious activities of foreigners in the PRC") (31 January 1994), in Xu Yucheng, *Responses to Questions*, pp. 306–307. English text appears in Human Rights Watch/Asia, *China: State Control of Religion* (1997), pp. 104–105.

62. See generally, Richard Madsen and James Tong (eds.), "Local religious policy in China, 1980–1997," in *Chinese Law and Government*, Vol. 33, No. 3 May/June 2000, containing regulations from Guangdong, Fujian, Zhejiang, Shanghai, Shandong, Hebei, Henan, Qinghai, Xinjiang and Yunnan. Also see, "Regulations from the Shanghai Religious Affairs Bureau" (30 November 1995), in Human Rights Watch/Asia, *China: State Control of Religion* (1997), pp. 90–99; "Provisional regulations for the registration and management of places of religious activity in Fujian province," in Human Rights Watch/Asia, *Continuing Religious Repression in China* (1993), pp. 50–54

63. Richard Madsen, "Editor's introduction," in Richard Madsen and James Tong (eds.), "Local religious policy in China, 1980–1997," in *Chinese Law and Government*, Vol. 33, No. 3 (May/June 2000), pp. 5–11.

64. "Regulations from the Shanghai Religious Affairs Bureau" (30 November 1995), in Human Rights Watch/Asia, *China: State Control of Religion* (1997), pp. 90–99.

government regulates religious activities of minority nationalities in Tibet and Xinjiang closely to ensure repression of nationalist separatism.[65] Echoing Constitutional provisions and Party policy, the Law on Autonomy in Nationality Regions (1984) provides in Article 11 that "normal" religious activities are protected, but prohibits use of religion to "disrupt social order, the health of citizens, or interfere with the educational system of the state." In Tibet, regulation of religion aims at control of a religious revival in Buddhism and at political questions surrounding the authority of the Dalai Lama.[66] Reacting to an outbreak of anti-Chinese unrest in 1988–89, the government imposed martial law and stepped up efforts at securing political control.[67] Following the Dalai Lama's demurral to China's offer of negotiations, government regulation of religion in Tibet since 1994 has focused on a political agenda of attacking elements associated with the Dalai Lama.[68] Among the many measures taken in this campaign are control over education curricula to subordinate religion, refusal of negotiations with the Dalai Lama and the ban against display or possession of his photograph, the re-education and in some cases dismissal of monks over their loyalty to the Dalai Lama,[69] and the subversion of the Dalai Lama's selection of a new Panchen Lama.[70] Expulsion of nuns and the demolition of Buddhist institutes and monasteries reflect on ongoing commitment to ensuring control over religious education and instruction in Tibetan Buddhism.[71] The government's commitment to controlling those who challenge it was evident as well in efforts to persuade India to return the Karmapa Lama, whose flight from Lhasa shocked Beijing in early 2000.[72]

65. See T. Shakya, *The Dragon in the Land of Snows: A History of Modern Tibet Since 1947* (New York: Columbia University Press, 1999); International Rehabilitation Council for Torture Victims (ed.), *Torture in Tibet 1949–1999* (Copenhagen: IRCT, 1999); P. Wing, L. and J. Sims, "Human rights in Tibet: an emerging foreign policy issue," *Harvard Human Rights Journal*, Vol. 5 (1992), pp. 193–203. Also see Melvyn Goldstein and Matthew T. Kapstein (eds.), *Buddhism in Contemporary Tibet* (Berkeley: University of California Press, 1998). Cf. A. Rosett, "Legal structures for special treatment of minorities in the People's Republic of China," *Notre Dame Law Review*, Vol. 66, No. 5 (1991), pp. 1503–28.

66. See generally Goldstein and Kapstein, *Buddhism in Contemporary Tibet*; MacInnis, *Religion in China Today*, pp. 184–203.

67. See generally, Solomon M. Karmel, "Ethnic tension and the struggle for order: China's policies in Tibet," *Pacific Affairs*, Vol. 68, No. 4 (Winter 1995–96), pp. 485–508. Also see Amnesty International, *People's Republic of China: Repression in Tibet, 1987–1992* (1992).

68. See generally, Human Rights Watch/Asia, *China: State Control of Religion* (1997), pp. 43–50.

69. For an example, see "Education for ethnic minorities: diversity neglected in stress on manufactured unity," *China Rights Forum*, Summer 2001, pp. 12–15; "Excerpts from questions and answers on the patriotic education program in monasteries" (25 May 1997), in Human Rights Watch/Asia, *China: State Control of Religion* (1997), pp. 100–103.

70. Also see Hollis Liao, "The case of the two Panchen Lamas – a religious or political issue?" *Issues & Studies*, Vol. 31, No. 12 (December 1995), pp. 115–17; Jonathan Mirsky, "A Lamas' who's who," in *New York Review of Books*, 27 April 2000, p. 15.

71. Tibet Information Network, "Serthar teacher now in Chengdu: new information on expulsions of nuns at Buddhist institute" (8 November 2001); "China-Tibetan monk," Associated Press Wire Service (27 September 1991).

72. "PRC spokesman on asylum in India for Karmapa Lama," Agence France Presse HK, 11 January 2000, in FBIS-CHI-2000–0111, 12 January 2000.

Regulation of Islam in Xinjiang also appears to reflect conclusions about convergence between religion and nationalism.[73] Heavy emphasis is placed on prohibitions against using religion to oppose CCP leadership and the socialist system, or to engage in activities that split the motherland or destroy unity among nationalities.[74] Religious activities are not permitted to interfere with state administration, religious activities and personnel must remain within the localities where they are registered, and religious teaching and the distribution of religious materials is closely controlled. Education and training of religious personnel is permitted only by approved patriotic religious groups, while people in charge of scripture classes must support the leadership of the Party and the socialist system, and safeguard unity of all nationalities and unification of the motherland. Human rights reporting on Xinjiang provides many examples of harassment and repression of Islamic teachers, mosques, schools and practitioners who might contribute to secessionist sentiment.[75] Recently, Beijing has used the US-led war against terrorism to justify repression of Islamic activities in Xinjiang, through a concerted campaign of arrests and executions of alleged separatists.[76]

The Chinese regulatory framework gives special attention to Christianity. This is in part because of an historiography that links Christian missionary work with imperialism, and to fears of international subversion through religion.[77] The growth in popularity of Christianity during the post-Mao period has driven new efforts at control.[78] Catholic churches are primarily under the authority of the Chinese Catholic Patriotic Association and the Chinese Conference of Catholic Bishops, while Protestants are subject to the "Three Self" patriotic movement and the

73. See MacInnis, *Religion in China Today*, pp. 248–254. Also see Dru Gladney, *Muslim Chinese: Ethnic Nationalism in the People's Republic* (Cambridge MA: Harvard Council on East Asian Studies, 1991); He Yanji, "Adapting Islam to socialism in Xinjiang," in Luo Zhufeng (ed.), *Religion Under Socialism in China* (trans. MacInnis and Zheng) (Armonk NY: M.E. Sharpe, 1991), pp. 224–231.

74. "Provisional regulations on the administration of religious activities in the Xinjiang Uighur Autonomous Region" (1990), in Human Rights Watch/Asia, *Freedom of Religion in China* (1992), pp. 64–65.

75. See generally, Human Rights Watch/Asia, *China: State Control of Religion* (1997), pp. 39–42; Amnesty International, *People's Republic of China: Secret Violence, Human Rights Violations in Xinjiang* (1992).

76. See Information Office of PRC State Council, "East Turkistan terrorist forces cannot get away with impunity," Beijing Xinhua English Service, 21 January 2002, in FBIS-CHI-2002–01–21, 21 January 2002. Also see Willy Wo-Lap Lam, "Terrorism fight used to target China secessionists," CNN e-mail newsletter (23 October 2001); "China claims 'big victory' over separatists in Xinjiang," Agence France Presse (25 October 2001); Craig S. Smith, "China, in harsh crackdown, executes Muslim separatists," *New York Times*, 16 December 2001.

77. See e.g. Luo Shuze, "Some hot issues in our work on religion," pp. 65–66.

78. See e.g. discussion of the "Notice on preventing and clearing up the use of Christianity to carry out crimes and illegal activities" (Guanyu zhizhi liyong jidujiao jinxing weifa weifa huodong de tongzhi) issued October 1988 by Religious Affairs Bureau and Public Security Bureau, in Luo Guangwu, pp. 391–393. Also see Simon Elegant, "The great divide," *Far Eastern Economic Review*, 6 June 1996, p. 53; Betty L. Wong, "A paper tiger? An examination of the International Religious Freedom Act's impact on Christianity in China," *Hastings International and Comparative Law Review*, Vol. 24 (2001), p. 539.

China Christian Council.[79] With its longer history of missionary activity in China and more formalized hierarchy of clergy professing exclusive loyalty to the Vatican, the Catholic Church has posed particular problems for the CCP regime.[80] The government has devoted particular efforts to control over Catholic clergy and their activities. Those associated with the underground church who refuse to renounce the authority of the Vatican have regularly been singled out for criminal prosecution and repression.[81] Regulations issued in 1989 called for stepping up control over the Catholic Church, primarily through increased education and indoctrination of state-approved clergy, strengthening the organizational authority of the Catholic Patriotic Association, repression of "Catholic Underground Forces," and strengthening Party leadership.[82] Tensions with the Catholic Church have been compounded by the Vatican's diplomatic recognition of Taiwan, although normalization of relations with the mainland remains a possibility, driven by a combination of liberalization and political realism.[83]

The Protestant Church has reportedly received less attention, partly because of its autonomy from the Vatican.[84] However, the relative fluidity of Protestant organizational structures, particularly the role of lay clergy, has made it harder for the government to control, leading for calls to repress Protestant evangelical activities under the guise of controlling illegal "sects" (xiejiao).[85] The charter for the "Three Self" movement underscores its submission to Party leadership, support for the authority of the state and the socialist motherland, and obedience to the Consti-

79. See generally, MacInnis, *Religion in China Today*, pp. 263–67, 313–18; Human Rights Watch/Asia, *China: State Control of Religion* (1997), pp. 13–16. On the "Three-Self" movement during the Maoist period, see Wallace C. Merwin and Francis P. Jones, *Documents of the Three-Self Movement* (New York: National Council of the Churches of Christ in the USA, 1963).

80. See generally, Richard Madsen, *China's Catholics: Tragedy and Hope in an Emerging Civil Society* (Berkeley: University of California Press, 1998). Also see Freidman *et al.*, *Chinese Village, Socialist State*, p. 234.

81. See e.g. "What we learned from the trial of the case of the Zhu Hongsheng counterrevolutionary clique," in Human Rights Watch/Asia, *Continuing Religious Repression in China* (1993), pp. 41–47.

82. CCP United Front Work Department and State Council Religious Affairs Bureau, "Circular on stepping up control over the Catholic Church to meet the new situation" (24 February 1988), in Human Rights Watch/Asia, *Freedom of Religion in China* (1992), pp. 46–51.

83. See Melinda Liu and Katharine Hesse, "A blessing for China," *Newsweek*, 11 June 2001, pp. 27–31.

84. Hon S. Chan, "Christianity in post-Mao mainland China," *Issues & Studies*, Vol. 29, No. 3 (September 1993), pp. 106–132, at p. 124.

85. See John Pomfret, "China church chief said to protest in prison," *International Herald Tribune*, 7–8 December 2002, p. 2; Li Shixiong and Xiqiu (Bob) Fu, "Religion and national security in China: secret documents from China's security sector" (New York: Committee on Investigation of Persecution of Religious Freedom in China, 2002); Amnesty International, "Urgent action update: death penalty/fear of imminent execution/torture and ill-treatment," 5 February 2002, and "Urgent action update: death penalty/fear of imminent execution," 4 January 2002. For earlier documentation, see "A report on the development of Christian sects in China," Human Rights Watch/Asia, *Freedom of Religion in China* (1992), p. 76.

tution, laws, regulations and policies of the state.[86] The charter for the China Christian Council is less effusive in its support for Party leadership, but still expresses compliance with the party-state through a commitment to manage its churches according to China's constitutions, laws, regulations and policies.[87]

The attack on illegal sects also extends to the now-famous *falun gong* movement, which is not considered a religion and thus is not covered by the policies of limited tolerance articulated in Document 19 of 1982. Initially the government appeared to focus on the movement's challenge to state orthodoxy as the main grounds for suppression.[88] Shocked by the group's organized peaceful protest in front of Zhongnanhai in April 1999, the regime was alarmed further by the prospect of widespread *falun gong* membership among officials and Party members.[89] Although the government claimed in July that sufficient legal grounds already existed for banning *falun gong*,[90] in October 1999 special additional measures were enacted by the NPC Standing Committee outlawing heretical sects and activities.[91] The measures attacked activities that "under the guise of religion, *qigong* or other name disrupt social order or harm the people's lives, financial security and economic development." While examples of murder, rape and swindling were listed as among the criminal activities at which the measure was aimed, particular emphasis was given to harming enforcement of laws and regulations, causing public disturbance, and disrupting public order. Thus, the target was in essence non-compliance with established norms of political loyalty, as official interpretations focused particularly on sectarian activity that "destroyed normal social order and stability."[92] Reflecting the government's concern with the apparent international reach of *falun gong*, the law provided particularly heavy penalties for cases involving contacts among *falun gong* followers

86. "Constitution of the National Committee of the Three Self Patriotic Movement of the Protestant Churces of China" (2 January 1997), in Pik-wan Wong, Wing-ning Pang and James Tong (eds.), "The Three-Self churches and 'freedom' of religion in China, 1980–1997," *Chinese Law and Government*, Vol. 33, No. 6 (November/December 2000), pp. 37–39.

87. "Constitution of the China Christian Council" (1 January 1997), in *ibid*. pp. 39–42. For discussion of the link between compliance with the Chinese constitution and submission to Party leadership, see nn. 71,72 and accompanying text.

88. Elizabeth J. Perry, "Challenging the mandate of heaven: popular protest in modern China," in *Critical Asian Studies*, Vol. 33, No. 2 (2001), pp. 163–180.

89. See Ming Xia and Shiping Hua (guest eds.), "The battle between the Chinese government and the falun gong," *Chinese Law and Government*, Vol. 32, No. 5 (September/October 1999), especially documents 1–4 and 13, focusing on forbidding *falun gong* membership by Party members, non-Party members subject to the United Front Work Department, and state functionaries, and Communist Youth League members.

90. Document 11: "Laws exist for the banning of falun gong," in *ibid*. pp. 43–45.

91. "Quanguo renmin daibiao dahui changwu weiyuanhui guanyu qudi xiejiao zuzhi, fangfan he chengzhi xiejiao huodong de jueding" ("Decision of the NPC Standing Committee on outlawing heretical organizations and guarding against and punishing heretical activities") (30 October 1999), in State Council Legal System Office (ed.), *Zhonghua renmin gongheguo xin fagui huibian – 1999 no. 4 (Compilation of New Laws and Regulations of the PRC – 1999 no. 4)* (Beijing: Law Publishers, 1999), p. 148. Also see "NPC Standing Committee issues anti-cult law" and "More on China issues anti-cult law," Beijing Xinhua English Service, 30 October 1999, in FBIS-CHI-1999–1030, 20 November 1999.

92. "China passes law to 'smash' falungong, other cults," Agence France Presse HK, 30 October 1999, in FBIS-CHI-1999–1030, 20 November 1999.

in different provinces or abroad. The measures were used as well to attack other groups who allegedly threaten Communist Party rule.[93]

While the new measures were enforced vigorously in concert with an intense propaganda campaign,[94] the leadership remained concerned over its inability to eradicate the group.[95] More recently, the government has linked *falun gong* with Tibetan and Xinjiang separatists as threats to Communist Party leadership and the stability of China.[96] In addition, the campaign against *falun gong* has become internationalized because of the US residence of its leader Li Hongzhi, and is thus intertwined with the US and international concerns over China's human rights record.[97] Arrests of foreign citizen practitioners of *falun gong* has further complicated the international relations aspect of the issue,[98] and stern warnings from Beijing that *falun gong* activities would not be permitted in Hong Kong raised delicate questions about Hong Kong's autonomy.[99] Official fears that socio-economic impacts of China's accession to the WTO may bolster *falun gong*'s popularity reflect further the government's appreciation of the international dimensions of the movement.[100]

Ensuring Political Loyalty: Compliance and the Challenge of Legitimacy

The regulation of religion in China depends on compliance, not only to support enforcement but also as a basis for building political legitimacy. As changing socio-economic conditions limit the state's capacity to use force or political favouritism, compliance will depend increasingly on voluntary acceptance of regime norms legitimated through popular acceptance of the trade-off of autonomy for loyalty. Yet, to the extent that its enforcement of policies on control of religion appears to contradict the accepted balance between autonomy and loyalty, the regime may undermine its own legitimacy more broadly.

93. See Human Rights Watch, *HRW World Report 2000: China*, February 2000; Human Rights Watch, "China uses 'rule of law' to justify falun gong crackdown," 9 November 1999.
94. See e.g. instalments in "Shenru che pi 'Falun Gong' xiejiao benzhi" ("Basics of deepening the exposure and criticism of '*falun gong*' heresy"), *Fazhi ribao* (*Legal System Daily*), 3–7 February 2001.
95. "Experts say PRC's leadership 'increasingly alarmed' by falun gong's strength," Agence France Presse HK, 22 January 2001, in FBIS-CHI-2001–0122, 23 January 2001.
96. Human Rights Watch, "Dangerous meditation: China's campaign against falungong" (2002). Also see "Wei Jianxing, Luo Gan Address Conference on Public Security, Judicial Work," Beijing Xinhua Domestic Service, 2 December 2000, in FBIS-CHI-2000–1202, 13 December 2000.
97. See generally, Sarah Lubman, "A Chinese battle on US soil: persecuted group's campaign catches politicians in the middle," *San Jose Mercury News*, 23 December 2001, p. 1A.
98. John Pomfret, "China holds 40 foreign falun gong protesters: use of Westerners marks new tactic," *Washington Post*, 15 February 2002, p. A26.
99. See generally, " 'Roundup': falungong urged to abide by Hong Kong law," *Hong Kong China News Service* (Hong Kong Zhongguo tongxun she), 11 December 1999, in FBIS-CHI-1999–1211, 11 December 2001, and "Editorial views PRC comments against falungong activities in Hong Kong," *Hong Kong Mail*, 31 January 2001, in FBIS-CHI-2001–0131, 31 January 2001.
100. See "China's Luo Gan outlines tasks of political legal work in 2002," Beijing Xinhua Domestic Service, 4 December 2001, in FBIS-CHI-2001–1204, 7 December 2001.

Changing conditions of compliance. Accelerated efforts to build a market economy in China during the late 1990s have challenged the regime's ability to maintain a balance between socio-economic autonomy and political loyalty. While Party affiliation remains important, the day-to-day livelihood of members of society has come to depend less on political patronage and more on job skills, entrepreneurialism and material accumulation.[101] Although it has meted out harsh repression against public dissent, the Chinese state seems to mirror the classic "strong society/weak state" paradigm,[102] as it appears unable to prevent increased public cynicism and quiet resistance.[103] This dilemma extends to its efforts to control ever-expanding religious activity, which not only reveals the resilience of religious belief but also suggests limits to the state's capacity to control religious behaviour.

Made possible by the regime's grant of broader social autonomy, the increase in religious activity in China reveals patterns of compliance and resistance regarding norms of political loyalty. Patterns of compliance are evident in participation in religions that are formally registered with the Religious Affairs Bureau, such as strong public attendance at patriotic Christian churches,[104] Buddhist and Daoist temples,[105] and mosques.[106] Similarly, participation in family-centred folk religion expresses norms of compliance to the extent that open conflict with political authority is avoided. These models of compliance-based religious activities appear as a public norm for religious behaviour in China that is tolerated by the regime.

Patterns of resistance in religious behaviour are also evident, however. The audacity of *falun gong* practitioners in public displays of resistance has gained significant attention within China and internationally.[107] In Tibet, government crackdowns have politicized religious activities that are viewed locally as matters of national identity.[108] By its efforts to control or even suppress religious activities in Tibet, the government has set in motion forces of resistance that bring together the interrelated but

101. Merle Goldman and Roderick MacFarquhar, "Dynamic economy, declining party-state," in Goldman and MacFarquhar (eds.), *The Paradox of China's Post-Mao Reforms* (Cambridge, MA: Harvard University Press, 1999) pp. 3–29.

102. Joel Migdal, *Strong Societies and Weak States* (Princeton: Princeton University Press, 1988).

103. Elizabeth J. Perry and Mark Selden, "Introduction: reform and resistance in contemporary China," in Perry and Selden (eds.), *Chinese Society: Change, Conflict and Resistance* (London: Routledge, 2000), pp. 1–19.

104. "Chinese Christians flock to official, underground churches," Agence France Presse HK, 25 December 2000, in FBIS-CHI-2000–1225, 27 December 2000.

105. "PRC refutes charges on religious affairs," Beijing Xinhua English Service, 8 December 1999, in FBIS-CHI-1999–1208, 8 December 1999. Also see *China Daily*, 18 December 2002, p. 1.

106. *China Daily*, 12 December 2002, p. 1.

107. For discussion, see Richard Madsen, "Understanding falun gong," *Current History*, September 2000, pp. 243–47; Elizabeth J. Perry, "Challenging the mandate of heaven: popular protest in modern China," *Critical Asian Studies*, Vol. 33, No. 2 (2001), pp. 163–180.

108. See generally, Elliot Sperling, "Statement before US Senate Committee on Foreign Relations Subcommittee on East Asian and Pacific Affairs" (13 June 2000), Human Rights Watch.

quite distinct dynamics of national identity and nationalism. Resistance has included open demonstrations against Chinese, combined with underground efforts to promote independent education in Tibetan Buddhism and loyalty to the Dalai Lama, all of which present serious challenges to the Chinese government. In Xinjiang, Islam presents a fundamental challenge, due to the combination of religious resistance to political authority and ethnic resistance to Han-dominated imperialism.[109] While separatists have been emboldened by the Soviet defeat in Afghanistan and though Islamic revivalism is certainly in evidence,[110] most unrest in Xinjiang appears to be the result of Uyghur ethnic hostility to Chinese policies of Han migration and subordination of local language and culture, rather than the product of Islam per se.[111] And though tensions reportedly exist in Xinjiang between Sunni and Shi'ite (particularly Wahhabist) Muslims, these have not yet diminished resistance to Han dominance.

Unofficial Christian churches also reflect a dynamic of resistance. While Christianity offers perhaps a more salient example of foreign influence, it has become increasingly sinicized through the inclusion of features of folk religion and traditional cultural forms, thus making its expression of resistance all the more threatening to the regime.[112] The underground Catholic Church has been portrayed as particularly threatening to CCP policies of political control, although the Protestant house church movement is potentially a greater threat. The house churches are described by local and foreign observers as both larger and more deeply entrenched in Chinese society than the patriotic Christian churches associated with norms of compliance.[113] Moreover, the informal and decentralized processes for naming Church leaders defies the government's formalistic approach to control through registration and bureaucratic supervision. Periodic efforts to raid house church services and to imprison house church leaders have received little public attention, but are seen by many as an unwarranted intrusion in social affairs. Yet the house church movement continues to swell, such that the numbers of adherents is viewed as at least double the population in the patriotic registered Christian churches.

109. See generally, Dru Gladney, "Internal colonialism and China's Uyghur Muslim minority," *Regional Issues* (Leiden University Newsletter, 25 November 1988).
110. See Raphael Israeli, "A new wave of Muslim revivalism in mainland China," *Issues & Studies*, Vol. 33, No. 3 (March 1997), pp. 21–41.
111. See generally, Nicolas Becquelin, "Xinjiang in the nineties," *The China Journal*, No. 44 (July 2000), pp. 65–91, Felix Chang, "China's Central Asian power and problems: fresh perspectives on East Asia's future," *Orbis*, Vol. 41, No. 3 (Summer 1997), pp. 401–426; Sean L. Yom, "Uighur Muslims in Xinjiang," *Self Determination Conflict Profile* (2001); Colin Mackerras, "The minorities: achievements and problems in the economy, national integration and foreign relations," *China Review* 1998, pp. 281–311
112. Stephan Feuchtwang, "Religion as resistance," in Perry and Selden, *Chinese Society: Change, Conflict and Resistance*, pp. 161–177 at p. 167.
113. See e.g. "China shuts down, blows up churches, temples in religious crackdown," Agence France Presse HK, 12 December 2000, in FBIS-CHI-2000-1212, 14 December 2000; "Chinese Christians flock to official, underground churches," Agence France Presse HK, 25 December 2000, in FBIS-CHI-2000-1225, 27 December 2000.

The challenges to legitimacy. Changing conditions of compliance with government controls on religion pose problems for the regime's effort to build legitimacy for its regulatory efforts and for its political position generally. In light of the increasing numbers of religious believers in China, building legitimacy for government policies on religion will require compliance from believers themselves. Thus, the regime differentiates between religious practitioners engaged in compliance and resistance, through legal and regulatory provisions distinguishing "normal" from heretical religious practices. The regime's underlying imperative of stifling heterodoxy is evident in the fact that its targets tend to be sects within the recognized religions whose activities challenge Party and state authority.[114] At the December 2001 national work conference on religion, for example, senior leaders distinguished between "normal" religious activities and heretical conduct associated with sects.[115]

These efforts are consistent with the regime's historical practices of identifying and enforcing norms of social conformity by denigrating and attacking nonconformists. Regulation of religion in China is used not only to control religious practices but also to express the boundaries of tolerance and repression so as to isolate resistance and privilege communities loyal to the party-state. Thus, the government promises tolerance for the compliant and repression for the resistant.

Yet the effectiveness of these policies depends on a normative consensus around both the content of policy and law and the processes of enforcement.[116] As suggested by Lyman Miller in the context of the scientific community, when members of Chinese society owe their loyalty to norms more powerful than those articulated by the Chinese government, regime legitimacy becomes a critical problem.[117] Just as scientists, owe a higher loyalty to the norms of science, so too do religious believers owe a higher loyalty to their own religious norms that may force a choice between loyalty to the regime and faithfulness to belief. To the extent that policies on regulation of religion require a degree of subservience that is inconsistent with religious conviction, compliance will be elusive. And if enforcement of these policies can be achieved only through repression, the distinction between compliance and resistance may fade as religious believers find compliance unworkable and are driven even further underground.

A more fundamental dimension of legitimation concerns members of society at large, who view the religious question as emblematic of other elements of social policy where the grant of socio-economic autonomy is a key condition for continued political subservience. The regime's hand-

114. See e.g., Luo Shuze, "Some hot issues in our work on religion"; "Regulations from the Shanghai Religious Affairs Bureau," Articles 3–5.

115. "Jiang Zemin, Zhu Rongji address religious work conference."

116. See generally, Felix Scharpf, "Interdependence and democratic legitimation," in Susan J. Pharr and Robert D. Putnam (eds.), *Disaffected Democracies: What's Troubling the Trilateral Countries* (Princeton: Princeton University Press, 2000).

117. Lyman Miller, *Science and Dissent in Post-Mao China* (Seattle: University of Washington Press, 1996).

ling of religion serves notice to the general populace about the contours of the trade-off of autonomy and loyalty, and thus has implications for regime legitimacy more broadly. In this process the regime faces challenges of history, socio-economic change and bureaucracy. The challenge of history limits perceptions of and responses to current conditions, particularly concerning the relationship between religion and social stability.[118] The historical record suggests that dynastic weakness and instability tended to arise not from tolerance of pluralism and diversity, but rather from the government's inability to respond to socio-economic change. In the late Qing, for example, the court failed to respond effectively to the emergence of the private sector as a locus of power, and was thereby unable to protect its own political authority.[119] National unity during earlier dynasties was supported by transportation and logistics networks, currency policies, and market systems, rather than suppression of intellectual dissent.[120] Nevertheless, the historical myth that diversity in social relations and religious belief undermines the strength of the regime continues to inform Communist Party policy.

The link between religion and legitimacy is also evident in regime responses to socio-economic change, particularly economic dislocation brought on by the market reforms and the impact of globalization.[121] While the many informal networks and social safety nets already available in China will help cushion the shock, religion provides an important source of comfort for the dispossessed. This both reflects and contributes to the declining power of traditional ideological bases for regime legitimacy. As regime goals change from social well-being to market facilitation, regime legitimacy will depend increasingly on the delivery of public goods and services.[122] With economic reform, however, the Chinese state has become a vehicle for socio-economic inequality – facilitating economic opportunity for a few privileged individuals and groups, while deploying the mechanisms of repression to keep the rest of society in check.[123] In the face of its inability to protect public welfare, official repression of those outlets in religion to which increasing numbers of

---

118. W.J.F. Jenner, *The Tyranny of History: The Roots of China's Crisis* (London: Penguin, 1992), pp. 193–201.

119. See Susan Mann Jones and Philip A. Kuhn, "Dynastic decline and the roots of rebellion," in John K. Fairbank (ed.), *The Cambridge History of China: Volume 10 – Late Ch'ing 1800–1911 Part I* (Cambridge: Cambridge University Press, 1978), pp. 107–162.

120. See generally, Mark Elvin, *The Pattern of the Chinese Past: A Social and Economic Interpretation* (Stanford: Stanford University Press, 1973).

121. See e.g. Dorothy Solinger, "The cost of China's entry into WTO," *Asian Wall Street Journal*, 4 January 2002.

122. See generally, Nikolas Rose, "Governing liberty," in Richard V. Ericson and Nico Stehr (eds.), *Governing Modern Societies* (Toronto: University of Toronto Press, 2000), pp. 141–175.

123. See generally, Michael A. Santoro, *Profits and Principles: Global Capitalism and Human Rights in China* (Ithaca: Cornell University Press, 2000; Michael Dutton, *Streetlife China* (Cambridge: Cambridge University Press, 1998). The remarkable effort by Peking University's China Centre for Economic Research to support research and policy making in this area reflects recognition of the depth of the problem of economic inequality and the as-yet insufficient resources for resolving it.

people resort will be likely to contribute to the regime's legitimacy deficit.

Finally, the bureaucratic culture of the Chinese regulatory regime also poses problems for legitimacy. In the context of gradual social liberalization, which the regime has fostered, bureaucratic control of religion is seen by many as intruding on intensely personal matters.[124] The potential for popular alienation is compounded as the policy and regulatory frameworks by which the party-state defines and implements the parameters for accepted religious conduct remain relatively impervious to public scrutiny. The resilience of bureaucratic behaviour generally continues to entrench the habitual practices of state control mechanisms associated with Party policy on religion, undermining further their effectiveness in responding to changing social and spiritual needs. These needs include both religion as solace for socio-economic dislocation, and generalized expectations about social autonomy. So far, we search in vain for a parallel in China to what is described as the "European exception" where the church and state were driven by the challenge of heresy to transcend their institutional and ideological limitations and respond effectively to changing socio-economic conditions.[125] In the wake of bureaucratic stagnation in China, response to change remains problematic and legitimacy continues to decline.

Conclusion

The Chinese government's policies and practices on religion offer a useful example of the dilemmas of regulation of social relations generally. Through its policies supporting graduate liberalization of socio-economic relations, the party-state has created rising expectations about popular autonomy. While the regime faces the imperative of repressing aspects of socio-economic change that threaten its political authority, it must still present a general image of tolerance for increased autonomy among the populace at large. Maintaining this balance is particularly critical in the area of religion, which is both a highly personal and internalized system of norms for belief and behaviour, and a response to regime failures to provide well-being for its citizens. Regulation of religion reflects Party policies granting limited autonomy for accepted practices while attempting to repress activities that challenge political orthodoxy. Legitimacy remains a key ingredient, not only as a basis for effective government regulation of religion but also as a product of such regulation to the extent that it can acquire popular support for official preferences on the balance between autonomy and loyalty. The regime's ability to sustain legitimacy both for and through its regulation of religion remains uncertain however, as the utility and effectiveness of control remain contested.

124. Richard Madsen, *China's Catholics: Tragedy and Hope in an Emerging Civil Society* (Berkeley: University of California Press, 1998), p. 108
125. See Mihaly Vajda, "East-Central European perspectives," in John Keane (ed.), *Civil Society and the State* (London: Verso Press, 1988), pp. 333–360 at p. 346.

Local Communal Religion in Contemporary South-east China

Kenneth Dean

ABSTRACT   This article demonstrates that the local communal religion of the villages of China, sometimes referred to as "popular religion," has revived with great force in contemporary South-east China. In some areas, the networks of village temples have formed a second tier of local government, providing services, raising funds, and mobilizing entire communities to participate in collective rituals. The article is based on fieldwork in 600 villages of Putian, Fujian, but also discusses developments elsewhere in South-east China. The article concludes that local communal religious rituals are significant arenas for the negotiation of modernity in contemporary China.

Ritual events of Chinese local communal religion are performed in tens of thousands of villages in contemporary South-east China. Nevertheless, local Chinese religion resists definition. Definitions of religion derived from Western critical traditions (including Marxism in China) focus on four features: religious doctrine, institutional organization, a hierarchical priesthood and rites that express particular beliefs. These features are not particularly useful for understanding local communal religion, or "popular religion," in China, which involves participation in communal rituals centred in temples dedicated to a variety of gods from a vast pantheon, many of local origin. In addition to participating in communal rites on important annual ceremonies such as Chinese New Year and Lantern Festival, or on the birthdays of the gods, individuals can go to village temples any time to worship the local gods by bowing and praying, proclaiming vows, making offerings of food and drink, and burning incense and spirit money. These acts are usually followed by divination of the god's response by dropping divining blocks or consulting divinatory poetry. The actions are performed with great sincerity, reverence and solemnity. The fact that the temples of the gods have been rebuilt and that local communal rites are being actively performed across South-east China despite the devastation of the Cultural Revolution is a remarkable testimony to the faith, courage and commitment of millions of Chinese villagers.

Communal rites of collective worship of gods in local temples require complex local organization. Temple committees, often selected on the basis of rotation or divination, raise funds from every participating family, organize processions to each household in the community, arrange for and participate in performances of special Buddhist, Daoist or "Confucian" rites by ritual specialists from these traditions, and sponsor the performance of Chinese operas. These ritual specialists are also called upon on special occasions to perform rites of passage, propitiation and affliction, and various prophyaltic rites. Specialists in geomancy, exorcism, dream interpretation and prognostication contribute their skills to local communal religion. Spirit mediums play a particularly important role in temple festivals, and in other aspects of local religion, providing an important channel of communication to the gods and the ancestors. In many communities in South-east China some aspects of lineage ritual have also been revived. Moreover, ancestors and gods are often worshipped in individual homes as well, with offerings of food, drink and incense. Many of the rituals of local communal religion are intense, chaotic and stimulating events, filled with the smoke of incense and the sound of firecrackers, the simultaneous performance of opera, rituals and processions, and the participation of crowds.

Such ritual events are difficult to characterize in terms of doctrine, although most would agree that in general the rites are intended to beseech the gods for blessings. Instead of hierarchical institutional organizations there is a complex network of local temples dedicated to a rich pantheon of gods. Rather than a hierarchical priesthood one finds local leaders rotating into positions of responsibility for the organization of localized communal rituals. Daoist, Buddhist or "Confucian" ritual specialists are for the most part hired from outside the village to perform particular rites. Local spirit mediums are often possessed by the gods of the village temples, and display their acts of prowess and speak words of power during the rites. But their acts and utterances are too diverse and specific to local circumstances to take the form of a doctrine or a set of particular beliefs.

Thus Chinese official definitions of religion do not apply readily to "popular religion" as it is practised by hundreds of millions of people in South-east China. Nevertheless, these definitions have prevailed at the level of policy, and this impasse has led to disastrous results. For almost a century, Chinese governments have attacked aspects of Chinese local religion as "feudal superstition." During the Cultural Revolution, most of these practices were banned, and most temples were impounded or destroyed. Many ritual specialists, whether Daoist, Buddhist, or specialists in divination or geomancy, were imprisoned or attacked, along with countless local spirit mediums, temple caretakers and lay devotees.[1] It is impossible in the scope of this article to begin to document the pain and suffering experienced by so many individuals and communities during this period, or the extraordinary acts of courage and devotion that enabled the survival and growth of local communal religion in China today.

Chinese scholars of "popular religion" in China have tended to write almost exclusively about what they term "secret societies" and "sectarian" groups, which have often been linked in official sources with peasant rebellion.[2] These scholars have rarely discussed the temples dedi-

1. See Pitman Potter's article in this issue of *The China Quarterly*.
2. See Ma Xisha and Han Bingfang, *Zhongguo minjian zongjiaoshi* (*History of Chinese Popular Religion*) (Shanghai: Shanghai renmin chubanshe, 1992); but see also the massive new publication of ritual and theatrical texts, musical scores and first-hand accounts of rituals from the Chongqing region edited by Hu Tiancheng and Duan Ming, *Minjian jiyi yu yishixiju* (*Folk Sacrifice and Ceremony Drama*) (Guiyang: Guizhou minzu chubanshe, 1999).

cated to local gods that can be found in almost every village in South-east China. Little attention has been paid to the communal rituals that mobilize the entire population of rural villages. In fact, most so-called sectarian groups have been peaceful throughout their historical development, until forced into confrontation by official persecution.[3] Participation in these groups can best be understood as another level of voluntary involvement in a religious movement in addition to, or on top of, mandatory participation in communal village rituals. This is true despite the particular elements (special dress, diet or rites) used to differentiate the "sectarian" group from other religious groups in the community.

This article offers a preliminary survey of local religious practices in South-east China, an area of over 3,000 square miles with a population of several hundred million people. The *Language Atlas of China*[4] distinguishes approximately 51 dialects or sub-dialects in this region, which is made up of Zhejiang, Fujian, Guangdong, Jiangxi, Hunan and southern Anhui (Huizhou) provinces. The major dialect groups are Wu, Min, Keijia (Hakka) and Yue. Many of these dialect regions contain several distinct local cultures. Each local culture has its own historical dynamic, one expression of which can be seen in its own pantheon of hundreds of deities, many of local invention. Several minority groups, such as the She, Yao, Miao (Hmong) and Dan, add still more layers of cultural complexity to the region. The speakers of several sub-dialects of Hakka in the mountainous centre of South-east China are just the most prominent and one of the most recent of several waves of Han Chinese colonizers and immigrants who moved into the lands of the "hundred Bai Yue peoples" from Han times onwards.

There are still enormous holes in our knowledge of the local religious practices of this region. Maps of the distribution of the theatrical, musical and dance traditions of South-east China reveal complex patterns of trans-regional influences. Similar maps for the distribution of transregional cults dedicated to gods or ritual traditions do not yet exist. Worship of local gods can be compared with cults of the saints in medieval Europe or in parts of Catholic Europe today.[5] The term "cult" in this article is used in that sense, and carries no pejorative meaning. Many gods worshipped in village temples are deified local historical figures, although others are nature or astral gods. More than one god can be worshipped in a village temple and many villages have several temples, so the distribution of patterns of worship is difficult to document except on a very broad level. Thus, some gods are worshipped across China, such as Guanyin, Guandi and Tianhou (Mazu). Others are more

3. Daniel Overmyer, *Folk Buddhist Religion: Dissenting Sects in Late Traditional China* (Cambridge, MA: Harvard University Press, 1976). See also B.J. ter Haar *White Lotus Teachings in Chinese Religious History* (Leiden: Brill, 1996).

4. S. Wurm *et al.* (eds.), *Language Atlas of China* (Hong Kong: Longman Group Ltd., 1988).

5. Daniel Overmyer, "Convergence: Chinese gods and Christian saints," *Qingfeng* Vol. 40, No. 1 (March 1997), pp. 1–14.

specific to certain regions of South-east China, such as Guangze zun-wang, Sanping zushi, Dingguang fo and Xu Zhenjun. Some regional cults have historic ties of "incense division" between founding temples and branch temples. Others have looser networks, involving the circulation of god statues between temples. Still others involve patterns of convergence of processions from local temples to the founding temple or tomb of the god.

Ethnographic research into the temple festivals and communal rituals celebrated within these god cults has revealed the widespread distribution of Daoist ritual traditions in this area, including especially Zhengyi (Celestial Master Daoism) and variants of Lüshan Daoist ritual traditions. Various Buddhist ritual traditions (Pu'anjiao, Xianghua married monks and so on) are practised throughout this region, particularly for requiem services. Masters of ritual ceremony whose tradition may be linked to Confucian ritual texts for animal sacrifice provide liturgical guidance for sacrificial rites dedicated to local gods. Spirit mediums, male and female, are possessed by local gods or contact the souls of the dead. Many or all of these ritual specialists may take part in a temple festival. There are multiple liturgical frameworks at play in such rituals, further complicating the effort to specific their specific meaning. I have elsewhere suggested the concept of a syncretic field of Chinese religion to try to account for the multiplicity of frameworks and complexity of the interactions between villagers and ritual specialists in their ritual events.[6]

Most of the thousands of villages throughout the South-east Chinese region have one or more temples dedicated to community deities. A large number of these temples have been restored and village rituals have been celebrated in the past 20 years. The degree of activity of these temples and their village communities varies widely over the region. In the area where I have done fieldwork for over a decade, the Puxian region of coastal Fujian, a villager can attend 250 days of opera performed in temple festivals each year. A survey of lineages, cults and ritual activities in over 600 villages conducted in this region over the past six years reveals that, on average, the population of these villages is around 1,200 people, though some villages have more than 6,000 residents. There are 100 different surname groups, with the average village having 3.4 surnames, although some had 14 or more and 27 per cent were single-surname villages. The survey located 1,639 temples, an average of 2.7 per village, ranging from 18 in some villages down to just one in 36 per cent of villages. The 1,639 temples housed 6,960 god statues representing over 1,200 different deities. Each temple had an average of 4.3 gods, but some temples had as many as 31. The 600 villages are organized into 123 ritual alliances. Each village first holds its own procession of the gods in the

6. Kenneth Dean, *Lord of the Three in One: The Spread of a Cult in Southeast China* (Princeton: Princeton University Press, 1998). On Lüshan Daoism in Fujian, see Ye Mingsheng, "Fujian sheng Longyan shi Dongxiao zhen Lüshanjiao guangji tan keyiben" ("The ritual texts of the Guangji altar of the Lüshan sect in Dongxiao town, Longyan municipality, Fujian") in Wang Chiu-kuei (ed.), *Zhongguo chuantong keyiben huibian* (*Collection of Traditional Chinese Ritual Texts*) (Taipei: Hsin Wen feng Publishing Co., 1996).

first lunar month, usually accompanied by a Daoist ritual in the temple and performances of opera on the stages set across an open courtyard from the temple. Then each village joins in a larger procession to the other villages of the ritual alliance. Several ritual alliances join into still larger processions, usually based within irrigation systems. These latter processions can involve over 100 villages and last up to a week. The remarkably dense network of local temple alliances and clusters of nested hierarchies of temples in this area has taken on many local administrative tasks, forming an unofficial second tier of local governance. The gap in traditions caused by the Cultural Revolution has to some extent been sutured, due in part to the willingness of retired Party members to participate in temple committees. Taking a long view, this restoration of temple networks is a continuation of the transfer of duties from the centre to the localities that one can trace back to the mid Ming, if not before. This was a process of the slow development of a degree of local autonomy at the local level. A crucial point this article hopes to raise is that in many parts of South-east China, the ritual events of Chinese popular religion are not remnants of a rapidly vanishing traditional past but are instead arenas for the active negotiation of the forces of modernity.[7]

Virtually every village in South-east China has a temple or a shrine to the local tutelary divinity, the god of the earth. In addition to this and temples to local, regional or empire-wide deities, many villages or their nearby mountains have Buddhist monasteries or nunneries, and occasional Daoist belvederes. Lay Buddhist or "sectarian" religious groups have temples in many villages as well. Christian churches can be found in a smaller percentage of villages. Most non-urban areas have access to a scattering of Daoist and other ritual specialists working out of their homes, as well as a wide variety of local spirit mediums. Voluntary religious associations have developed in several regions, with their own ritual traditions. Ritual specialists of many kinds, but especially Daoist priests or ritual masters, are often invited to perform rites on the birthdays of the local gods, and on other important occasions of individual and family life. Most active temples, and many of the village temples of South-east China are very active, have temple committees which organize communal rituals, raise and dispense funds, and stage operas, marionettes, puppets or films in front of the temple. Thus the experiential field

7. For further information on current religious practices in the Putian area, see Kenneth Dean, "Lineage and territoriality," *Proceedings of the Third International Conference on Sinology* (Taipei: Academia Sinica, forthcoming, 2003); K. Dean, "China's second government: regional ritual systems of the Putian plains," in *Shehui, minzu yu wenhua zhanyan guoji yantaohui lunwenji* (*Collected papers from the International Conference on Social, Ethnic and Cultural Transformation*) (Taipei: Centre for Chinese Studies, 2001), pp. 77–109; K. Dean and Zheng Zhenman, "Group initiation and exorcistic dance in the Xinghua Region," *Min-su ch'u-i* (*Folklore and Theater*) Vol. 85 (1993), pp. 105–195. For historical background on this region see K. Dean, "The transformation of the *she* altar in the late Ming and Qing in the Xinghua region," *Cahiers d'Extrême-Asie*, Vol. 10 (1998), pp. 19–75, and Kenneth Dean and Zheng Zhenman (eds.), *Epigraphical Materials on the History of Religion in Fujian: The Xinghua Region* (Fuzhou: Fujian People's Publishing House, 1995), *The Quanzhou Region* (3 vols.) (2003).

of Chinese local religion is extraordinarily diverse and complex, as each community organizes itself through its temples and their rituals. Chinese local religion may be "diffused" as opposed to "institutional," as C.K. Yang[8] argued, but at the village level it is extremely organized.

Despite the extraordinary vitality and contemporaneousness of local religion in certain areas of China, it is nevertheless essential to realize the extent of the devastation and decline of many communal practices since the turn of the 20th century. In many parts of South-east China, lineage halls remain in ruins. Temples dedicated to local gods have been abandoned and the god statues have been destroyed, or stolen and sold. Communal rituals are performed, if at all, on a miniscule scale. This deterioration is the result of a combination of pressures, including political suppression of popular and ritual specialists of all kinds, and economic pressures. Many South-east Chinese villages are emptying as workers flood illegally into the rapidly expanding urban areas in the Zhu (Pearl) River delta and along the Fujian and Zhejiang coast. In order to comprehend these different regional patterns of religious revival and decline, it is necessary to examine both historical factors that provide a virtual reservoir of local cultural resources, and contemporary socio-economic forces and political pressures.

In very broad terms, the greatest change to local religious practice in South-east China since 1949 has been the decline in most areas of the lineage as a centre for socio-economic and especially ritual life. This feature of local life was particularly pronounced in pre-Revolutionary Guangdong and Fujian, as noted by Maurice Freedman. Although in some areas lineage halls have been rebuilt and lineage rituals resumed, lineages no longer have the landholdings and financial assets they commanded in the past. What has survived, and revived since 1979 with a remarkable tenacity, are the temples of the local gods and their rites, whether conducted by local spirit mediums or by Daoist, Buddhist or lay ritual specialists. However, the government has kept up the ban on the Pudu festivals for feeding the hungry ghosts of the seventh lunar month. This festival in many ways balanced and corresponded with the rites for the lunar new year. The latter have been revived but the former are now very rarely practised on a large scale. In many areas of South-east China, Overseas Chinese or Taiwanese connections play a key role in the reinvention of tradition. These temple festivals depend on fluid capitalization rather than entrenched class-based landholdings.

The revival of religious activities began and spread most rapidly in coastal Fujian, where connections with Overseas Chinese and Taiwanese compatriots provided economic support and political cover. In the early 1980s many temples were being rebuilt. By the mid-1980s local temple festivals had revived, complete with ceremonies led by Daoist priests. By the end of the decade there was a high tide of religious activities, as temple networks and regional ritual alliances were re-established through

---

8. C.K. Yang, *Religion in Chinese Society* (Berkeley: University of California Press, 1961).

the performance of collective processions and lengthy Daoist rituals at central temples. Regional opera troupes, puppet troupes and marionettists were performing more and more frequently. Daoist priests reassembled their collections of liturgical manuscripts by borrowing and copying from one another, but most lamented that much of the ritual tradition had been lost. Simplified rituals were performed, but increasingly there was a demand for the larger and more elaborate ones. This frenzy of activity settled down into a calmer steady state of ritual affairs by the mid-1990s. By the turn of the century, double-digit rates of economic growth led to massive urban "renewal," and most of the ancient sections of major cities like Quanzhou and Putian were torn down to make way for broader roads and apartment complexes. Nevertheless, even in these new high-rise developments, local temples to the earth god were being built alongside and in between rows of apartments.[9]

Certain key sites of local god cults remained under tight official control. A few were mummified into museums, with admission charges and no ritual activity allowed. Even these sites had a hard time containing the burning of incense and other signs of devotion. Many of the founding temples of local god cults in Fujian underwent an increasing de facto transfer of power to local devotees. This transfer was frequently facilitated by the involvement of retired Party officials in the temple committees. Some temples became so wealthy that they were able to establish scholarship funds, direct local infrastructure projects such as paving roads and laying down electricity, and dispense charity to beggars and impoverished families. They had become very significant cultural centres of village and town life. Officially sanctioned laorenhui (Old Folks Associations) were often based in them. They sponsored opera, cinema and rituals. Important collective decisions were reached within these cultural centres. Very careful accounts were kept of all donations, income and expenditures, and these were posted on a regular basis. The temples of the gods had returned to a central role in Chinese rural life. In the Fuzhou area, in some contrast to the Minnan and Puxian regions, major lineage halls were first re-established, and began playing an important role in local religion.

Other areas of South-east China lagged behind coastal Fujian. The Chaozhou region of Guangdong and the Wenzhou area of Zhejiang followed Fujian fairly closely in the process of rebuilding and reconsecrating temples, and reviving temple festivals and Daoist rites. The Zhu River delta saw a much more fragmented process of revival, often featuring the reconstruction of large temples that attracted individual worshippers in search of particularistic divine support. Inland provinces such as Jiangxi struggled with a strong legacy of conservative Maoism, because of the presence of revolutionary base areas and complex issues of provincial party politics. Poverty and out-migration seriously affected the process of religious revival. Moreover, there were periodic Party

---

9. See Kenneth Dean, *Taoist Ritual and Popular Cults of Southeast China* (Princeton: Princeton University Press, 1993).

campaigns to limit the scope of the revival of local religion. These led to the establishment of more and more regulations, including the 1994 requirement to register temples as "officially approved sites of religious activity." Regulations outlawing spirit-possession, exorcism, fortune telling, geomancy "and other feudal activities" were also posted in many temples. Other regulations were put in place to guarantee financial accountability, in a fascinating imitation of similar legal processes in Taiwan from the 1950s to the 1980s. Some local officials clamped down hard on the boom in temple construction. On 12 December 2000, Agence France reported on the destruction (sometimes with dynamite) of 1,200 temples and churches in the Wenzhou region. The claim was made that these temples had not registered properly, but the ferocity of the official response indicates a fundamental concern over the weakening legitimacy of the Party.[10]

The different rates of religious revival of the many local cultures of South-east China clearly reflect differences in local economic and political conditions. However, even more significant may be the different historical trajectories of these distinct local cultures. Each developed its own potentialities, based on the complexity of local social groups and their interactions, the depth and variety of localized ritual traditions, and the role of local managerial elites in negotiating space for growth from officialdom. Thus in order to understand aspects of the range of local religious activity in contemporary China, one must compare the historical development of different local cultures. But before considering this issue, another general feature of contemporary Chinese religious life must be addressed.

Urban and Rural Splits

Urban and rural splits in cultural activities and expectations are pronounced in contemporary China, and have become more so over the past 20 years. Neighbourhood temples played an essential role in Chinese cities and towns in the pre-Revolutionary period,[11] but have since been completely destroyed in most areas. Children growing up in cities have

10. For Guangdong see Helen Siu, "Recycling ritual," in P. Link, R. Madsen and P. Pickowiez (eds.), *Unofficial China: Popular Culture and Thought in the People's Republic* (Boulder: Westview, 1990), pp. 121–137; for the Hakka areas of Jiangxi, Minxi and Yuebei see John Lagerwey, "Introduction" to each volume of his *Traditional Hakka Society Series* (Hong Kong: International Hakka Studies Association and the Ecole Française d'Extrême-Orient, 1996–2002) 16 volumes to date, and his "A propos de la situation actuelle des pratiques religieuses traditionelles en Chine," in Catherine Clementin-Ohja (ed.), *Le renouveau religieuse en Asie* (Paris, EFEO, 1997), pp. 3–16. For Zhejiang see John Lagerwey and Lü Ch'ui-kuan, "Le taoïsme du district de Cangnan, Zhejiang," *Bulletin de l'École Française d'Extrême-Orient*, Vol. 79, No. 1 (1992), pp. 19–55; Paul Katz, "Recent developments in the study of Chinese ritual dramas: an assessment of Xu Hongtu's research on Zhejiang," in Daniel Overmyer, (ed.), *Ethnography in China Today: A Critical Assessment of Methods and Results.* (Taipei: Yuan-Liou Pub. Co., 2002), pp. 199–229; and Mayfair Yang, "Putting global capitalism in its place: economic hybridity, bataille, and ritual expenditure," *Current Anthropology*, Vol. 41, No. 4 (2000).

11. See Susan Naquin, *Peking: Temples and City Life, 1400–1900* (Berkeley: University of California Press, 2000). See also Kristofer Schipper, "Neighborhood cult associations in

little or no access to the communal ritual events of Chinese local religion which played a formative role in earlier times and which continue to have a major impact on rural life. Rural religious activity has flourished in many parts of China, particularly along the south-east coast, and throughout the south, including in south-western areas with large "minority" populations, as well as in Sichuan. While modernization models in the past often uncritically included de-traditionalization or secularization as inevitable correlates of "progress," such conceptions have been severely criticized. Nevertheless, urban intellectuals in contemporary China once again feel cut off from rural culture, and have little integrated access to such activities. Thus the modes of analysis discussed in this article may provide a starting point for a discussion of cultural transformations and the potential for dialogue or interaction between urban and rural spheres.

Having drawn a sharp distinction between urban and rural cultural experience, it is important to note that cultural influences flow in both directions. Cinemas, television, video, karaoke, radio, dancehalls, telecommunications, commodities, advertising imagery, tourism, investment and technology flow from the urban centres into the rural towns and hinterlands. A flow of "floating labour" returns to the urban centres, and makes its own impact on urban culture. There is no clear dividing line between "urban" and "rural," despite an apparent cultural polarization.

Comparing Regional Cultures

Within Chinese studies to date, the most sophisticated model of inter-regional comparison was developed by G.W. Skinner. Skinner divided China into nine macroregions on the basis of geographic and economic criteria, and applied central place theory, core-periphery spatial analysis and diffusion theory to the Chinese data. In his most recent presentation of his ongoing research, he employs a composite index made up of nine variables to map central place hierarchies and core–periphery relations over the Lingnan macroregion based on 1990 data.[12] Skinner's model modifies formal location theory by taking into account the general features of large-scale drainage basins. His analysis integrates a vertical model of a nested hierarchy with a horizontal model of multiple core–peripheral relations, and demonstrates how technological changes are diffused down the hierarchy and outwards from cores to peripheries within the regional system treated by the intersection of these models.

Skinner's models have had a pronounced effect on Chinese studies. However, Naquin and Yu point out that temples are often "on the peripheries of regions, but their cachement areas could be much

---

footnote continued

traditional China," in G.W. Skinner (ed.), *The City in Late Imperial China* (Stanford: Stanford University Press, 1977), pp. 651–676.

12. G. William Skinner, "The structure of Chinese history," *Journal of Asian Studies*, Vol. 44 (1985), pp. 271–292; "Differential development in Lingnan," in Thomas Lyons and Victor Nee (eds.), *The Economic Transformation of South China: Reform and Development in the Post-Mao Era* (Ithaca, NY: East Asia Program, Cornell University, 1994), pp. 17–54.

greater."[13] Sangren argues that sacred sites outside the parameters of the marketing system can have an important impact on peasant cultural horizons.[14] Such sites are often the target of organized pilgrimages. In China, cultural horizons could expand to take in the five sacred mountains, the major Buddhist sacred sites, and a host of centres of local god cults and renowned temples. Sangren also raises fundamental questions about the assumptions linking a Western rational choice model of economically determined spatiality to Chinese cultural space. He critiques Skinner's approach by arguing that religious and cultural spatial systems (territorial cults, nested hierarchies of temples, pilgrimage circuits beyond the standard marketing area) determine regional or local cultural conceptions, rather than marketing systems. Faure and Siu also question the applicability of Skinner's model to local cultural systems.[15]

How useful are Skinner's conceptual models to the comparative analysis of regional cultural histories and ritual systems? The nested hierarchy of temples I have found in certain areas surveyed in Putian would appear to follow a central place vertical model. The core–periphery horizontal model could be applied to the sectarian religious movements in the area surveyed such as the Sanyijiao (Three in One) religious movement, in that hundreds of temples relate back to a central point. Diffusion models from high, central points (cult centres) to peripheral temples could be used to analyse division of incense networks that form by branching off at successive levels. However, it is difficult to locate stable positions for any element of an actual regional ritual system. Any individual may be involved in several different circuits, many of which would reach outside the most generalizable regional ritual system. Each village contains several temples dedicated to a group of gods. Each temple or even each god worshipped in the temple may act as a catalyst enabling involvement in a local circuit within a narrow regionally defined nested hierarchy, while at the same time establishing a pilgrimage relation to a more remote cult centre. Other temples or ancestral halls will connect certain groups, households or individuals to other spatial modes of organization such as the migration pattern of a lineage, or the localized network of a sectarian movement. Random changes or movements from one level or circuit to another are common in these open cultural systems.

Thomas Lyons has also used regional systems data and GIS desktop mapping systems to illustrate aspects of the economic geography of Fujian province, in particular changes in GDP and the diffusion of new crops from the mid-1980s to 1993.[16] However, there is a telling exclusion of cultural features in Lyon's work. The sole index of culture in his

13. Susan Naquin and Yu Chun-fang (eds.), *Pilgrims and Sacred Sites in China* (Berkeley: University of California Press, 1992), p. 92.

14. P. Stevan Sangren, *History and Magical Power in a Chinese Community* (Stanford: Stanford University Press, 1987).

15. David Faure and Helen Siu (eds), *Down to Earth: The Territorial Bond in South China* (Stanford: Stanford University Press, 1995).

16. Thomas Lyons, *Economic Geography of Fujian: A Sourcebook* (Ithaca, NY: Cornell East Asia Series, Vol. 82, 1996).

sourcebook is the number of cinemas in a particular area. Clearly, the implicit standard is a Western modernized lifestyle. What Skinner and Lyons do not address is the unique, specific, experiential and performative nature of local culture. One could devise a model that would rate the level of cultural complexity in different areas according to the number of temples per village, gods per temple, ritual events per year, or the number of theatrical productions or ritual specialists. But one would not be able to claim that a south Chinese coastal village has *more* culture than a northern Chinese village on the basis of such statistical comparisons. A more useful approach would be to combine surveys of religious practice with cultural historical research that would examine the processes of formation of the reservoir of cultural resources within any particular region.

The mapping of cultural features and the multiple regional ritual systems into which they are swept up reveals a rhizomatic labyrinth of circuits and levels of cultural identification within which groups, households and individuals move. Through local cultural practices, abstract space is transformed into meaningful place. The tracing of trans-regional flows of migration patterns, ritual traditions, performing arts traditions of music, song and dance reveal that no regional cultural system is complete in itself (no culture is a closed whole). Maps, flowcharts and diagrams can be developed for different phases in the local history of specific regions. Examining these features over time allows for the development of a topology of power in regional ritual systems.

The degree of cohesiveness of the temples, their managing committees and their village communities depends on many factors. Perhaps most important, although difficult to clarify, is the degree of local autonomy each local culture has achieved over a long historical process that can be traced back in some of these regions to the late Song, and in others to the mid-Ming or later. By local autonomy I mean not a separation from the state, but a tacit downwards distribution of responsibility over local issues to a managerial elite based in temples, lineages, literary societies and money-lending associations. This process took place differently in each region of South-east China. For each local culture of South-east China (Ningbo, Hangzhou, central Zhejiang, Wenzhou, Huizhou in Anhui, Mindong, Houguan, Puxian, Minbei, Quanzhang Minnan, Chaozhou, Huizhou in Guangdong, Hakka western Fujian and Gannan in Jiangxi, northern Jiangxi, northern Guangdong, the Zhu River delta, western Hunan, and the list goes on), one would like to compare the impact in different periods of Buddhist monastic estates, lineage formations, temple networks, regional ritual alliances, trans-regional Daoist and Buddhist ritual traditions, state cults and ritual policies, in addition to socio-economic factors of land-tenure, market networks, interregional and international trade, and the growth of merchant capitalism.

Another crucial factor distinguishing these regions is the degree of complexity of historically formed horizontal religious and communal networks and the numbers of ritually marked vertical levels between the state and the village. Horizontal networks were formed between temples on the basis of division of incense from the founding temple of a cult, or the exchange of a god between temples and regions, or through regional ritual alliances marked by processions and shared rites. Difference in vertical links between regions of South-east China depends upon the degree of cohesiveness of each level from neighbourhood earth god shrine to village temples and upwards into a variety of nested hierarchies of temples, culminating in some instances at city-god temples, or their equivalents, marking a kind of hinge between popular and official cults, Confucian temples and shrines to local officials. In contrast to Skinner's models, which emphasize the vertical ties of market distribution and rational choices, the horizontal networks of Chinese popular religion provide a remarkably complex and wide range of alternative options, obligations and potentialities to their participants.

Prasenjit Duara based his influential notion of the cultural nexus of power upon a reading of Mantetsu documents on a group of villages in Northern China.[17] However, Duara does not provide a great deal of historical information on the process of formation of the cultural nexus of power he found embedded within and between temple networks, irrigation systems and local lineages. His study also implied that the cultural nexus of power suffered an irreparable rupture with the anti-religion campaigns and other modern reforms and abuses of the Republican era. Current developments challenge that assumption. A comparative analysis of potentially even more complex nexuses of power in South-east China may bring the issue of the historical development and the future potentiality of such networks into sharper focus.

New Sources for the Study of Chinese Local Religion

Although ethnographic research on minorities was supported by the state, especially in the South-western provinces, very little research on Han Chinese folklore, religion or culture was authorized from the Revolution until the early 1980s, when Departments of Anthropology were re-established in a few universities. But these departments often had a developmental anthropological focus, as figures such as Fei Xiaotong were drawn into policy debates on models of urban reform and developmental policies for townships and local marketing networks. Cultural anthropology has just begun to establish itself in China, with the large-scale translation of key theoretical texts.

Information on contemporary religious practice in China can now be obtained from several new sets of source materials on local religion that have recently been published. These include a series by the Central Art Institute on a province-by-province basis divided into ten different categories such as regional theatre, popular dance forms, folk music and sayings. Several of the relevant volumes for the South-eastern area

17. Prasenjit Duara, *Culture, Power, and the State: Rural North China: 1900–1942* (Stanford: Stanford University Press, 1988). The objectivity of the Mantetsu research has been the subject of considerable controversy.

include tantalizing information on Daoist ritual dance, masked ritual theatre and ritual music.[18] These materials have been presented from a purely artistic point of view, and are thus divorced from their ritual performance contexts. A second set of publications includes Tanaka Issei's volumes on Chinese regional theatre in relation to lineage forms and market networks, and in particular his study of Chinese shamanistic theatre, which examines a variety of masked ritual theatre.[19] This form of theatre attracted the attention of Chinese researchers in the drama field, and has a nation-wide organization of researchers, directors and opera troupes. This resulted in several conferences, a spate of publications, and "salvage performances" of forms of regional Nuoxi (masked exorcistic theatre) and Mulian plays.[20]

More direct ethnographic material on religious practices in South-east China are available in 20 of the 80-volume series on Chinese ritual, theatre and folklore edited by Wang Ch'iu-kuei.[21] These studies include collections of materials on the history of regional ritual drama and other rites, edited and annotated scripts, and fieldwork reports on the perform-ance of particular rituals or ritual dramas that were observed by the authors. For the most part written by specialists in theatre rather than anthropologists, these studies provide general introductions to the social contexts underlying the performances rather than detailed interpretations or analyses. Nevertheless, they often provide crucial documentation on the performance of rites and ritual dramas that would be otherwise unavailable. They include photographs of aspects of the rites, and provide facsimiles of the liturgical or theatrical manuscripts employed by the ritual specialists. Wang Ch'iu-kuei has also edited a series of detailed studies of single Daoist or Buddhist ritual specialists. These provide facsimiles of the ritual masters' entire working liturgical manuscript collections and contextualizes their work within their cultural environ-ment. The materials can be compared with similar collections of Daoist texts from Taiwan, and with earlier liturgical texts included in the Daoist Canon. In this way, scholars can gain a deeper understanding of develop-ments within Daoist liturgy in relation to popular cults across South China after the Ming dynasty.

18. Dong Zhenya (ed.), *Zhongguo minzu minjian wudao jicheng: Anhui juan* (*Com-pendium of Chinese Nationalities Popular Dance: Anhui Volume*) (2 vols.) (Beijing: Xinhua shuju, 1995); Li Jian (ed.), *Zhongguo minzu minjian wudao jicheng: Jiangxi juan* (*Compendium of Chinese Nationalities Popular Dance: Jiangxi Volume* (2 vols.) (Beijing: Xinhua shuju, 1992).
19. Tanaka Issei, *Chūgoku fukei engeki kenkyū* (*Research on Chinese Shamanistic Theatre*) (Tokyo: Tōkyō Daigaku Tōyō bunka kenkyūjo hōkoku, 1993).
20. Many of these sources are summarized in Wang Ch'iu-kuei (ed.), *Zhongguo nuoxi nuowenhua yanjiu tongxun* (*Research Newsletter on Chinese Exorcistic Drama and Chinese Exorcistic Culture*) (2 vols.) (Taipei: Shih Ho-cheng Folk Culture Foundation, 1992–93).
21. Wang Ch'iu-kuei (ed.), *Min-su ch'ü-i ts'ung-shu* (*Studies in Chinese Ritual, Theatre and Folklore*) (80 vols.) (Taipei: Shih Ho-cheng Folk Culture Foundation, 1993). Shorter field reports with up-to-date information on contemporary Chinese local religion are published in the journal *Min-su ch'ü-i* also published by the Shih Ho-cheng Folk Culture Foundation. For English-language reviews of many of the volumes in this and John Lagerwey's series, see Overmyer, *Ethnography in China Today*.

Another important set of ethnographic reports covering the Hakka regions of South-east China is John Lagerwey's *Traditional Hakka Society Series*. So far 19 volumes of essays documenting lineage society, temple festivals, ritual traditions, local cults, and local economic history of Western Fujian, North-west Guangdong and South-east Jiangxi have been published. These volumes are arranged on an area-by-area basis. They consist primarily of detailed essays written by elderly local intellectuals recalling the religious practices of the pre-Revolutionary period. In this sense they resemble the local literary and historical materials (*wenshi ziliao*) published by the Political Consultative Congresses of local governments, although the latter rarely touch on issues of religion or ritual. The *Traditional Hakka Society Series* therefore provides an invaluable baseline for a study of changes to practices in the present day. With new materials such as these becoming available, it becomes even more urgent to try to explain the divergent developments of the many different local cultures of South-east China, in order to expand current understanding of the future potential of Chinese local religion to survive and interact as a vital force within China's future.

Comparative Local Histories: Cultural Unification or Lines of Differentiation?

Recent studies of local cultural history in China seem to be haunted by the legacy of an earlier generation of Neo-Confucian studies. The basic premise of recent work in regional social and cultural history by Faure, Siu and Liu appears to be that South-east Chinese society evolved into an increasingly Confucian society, with the spread of Confucian ideals and Confucian institutions into families and lineages.[22] What is even more striking in this effort to document in local historical context the supposed Confucianization or gentrification of local society is that these Confucian ideals and ritual forms are believed to have largely replaced, overcome or superseded earlier forms of local culture. This is a developmental model of the evolution of Chinese culture, in which the end result is always the same, no matter which area is being discussed. The emperor always ends up in the village, the state in the family. The end result is the triumphant cultural unification of China. The only question remaining for historians is to determine when and where these processes took root. Faure and Liu suggest that integration with the state began in coastal Fujian in the Song dynasty through the enfeoffment of local gods by the court, while it was

22. Faure and Siu, *Down to Earth*; Ke Dawei (David Faure), "Guojia yu liyi: Song zhi Qing zhongye Zhujiang sanjiaozhou difang shehui de guojia rentong" ("State and rituals: the integration of local society into the Chinese state in the Pearl River Delta from Northern Song to mid-Qing"), *Zhongshan daxue xuebao (Journal of Sun Yatsen University: Social Science)*, Vol. 39, No. 5, General No. 161 (1999), pp. 65–72; Ke Dawei (David Faure) and Liu Zhiwei, "Zongzu yu difang shehui de guojiarentong: Ming Qing Huanan diqu fazhan de yishi xingtai jichu" ("Lineages and the integration of local society into the Chinese state: the ideological foundations of Southern Chinese regional development"), *Lishi yanjiu (Historical Research)*, No. 3 (2000), pp. 3–14; D. Faure, "The emperor in the village: representing the state in south China," in J. P. McDermott (ed.), *State and Court Ritual in China* (Cambridge: Cambridge University Press, 1999), pp. 267–298.

the adoption of Confucian lineage forms that enabled the integration of the local society of the Zhu River delta of Guangdong with the Chinese state in the mid-Ming. The means may have been different, but the end result was the same – cultural integration.

Many of these scholars perceive this model of cultural unification as a more enlightened alternative to an even darker vision of Chinese state–society relations. Karl Wittfogel's notorious hydraulic empire model of a totalitarian Chinese imperial state was fleshed out in the 1960s by his student Hsiao Kung-ch'uan in the latter's study of ideological control in 19th-century rural China.[23] Hsiao outlined a variety of state institutions all designed to exercise control over the hearts and minds of the rural populace. But he was too good an institutional historian to avoid noting the decline of many of these institutions, leaving his readers with an ugly picture of a corrupted state apparatus desirous only of extracting taxes and torturing troublemakers. Historians working with somewhat broader social scientific concepts in the 1970s and 1980s began to dispute Wittfogel and Hsiao's vision of a rapacious totalitarian state. They pointed out a variety of semi-autonomous sectors, and attempted to outline the powers specific to local scholarly and merchant elites. Some examined the positive contributions of activist officials who attempted to mobilize both state institutions and local social forces to combat natural disasters, or to offset class conflicts or other sources of social disorder. Those historians dealing with long-term changes in particular locales drew upon cultural anthropological theories of cultural assimilation to explain the spread of Confucian ideals and rites. They pointed to what they saw as a model of empowerment fore-grounding the agency of local elites in their creative efforts to adapt the ideals and institutions of the state to local contexts.

Although these accounts are compelling, and in particular help to explain the shifting of ethnic identities in the Zhu River delta, I would like to suggest a different model of cultural transformation, one which might be described as neo-evolutionistic, or even better, as a creative involution model. Rather than seeing Confucian ideals and institutions overcoming local shamanic ritual traditions, or homogenizing multiple ethnicities, or hierarchizing gender relations, one can instead trace a series of unintended consequences of institutional reforms and local mutations as they became tangled in an ever more complex network of local and regional cults, localized and higher order lineages, segmentary societies, and voluntary associations. With a concept of these events as ever-accumulating, increasingly complex additional dimensions of a virtual plane of non-contradiction (or adding to a reservoir of cultural potential) one can more readily explore processes of "dephasing," in which seeming remnants of prior phases in the cultural history of a particular local culture, such as temple festivals, Daoist rituals, spirit possession and collective processions, continue to release their own different forms of temporality and spatiality in an ongoing negotiation

23. Hsiao Kung-ch'uan, *Rural Control in Nineteenth Century China* (Seattle: University of Washington Press, 1960).

with the forces of modernity in contemporary South-east China. These local cultural systems have achieved a staggering complexity. The entire populations of hundreds of villages are mobilized in ritual events and processions, which draw upon their entire reservoir of cultural forms and practices through their specific forms of communal self-expression.

The "syncretic field of Chinese religion" is a concept I have elaborated to express the workings of the reservoir of cultural potential of local communal religion. This concept challenges both the form and content of earlier social-scientific/Confucianist models of a unified Chinese culture.[24] The syncretic field is a constantly self-differentiating field of potentiality stretched between polar attractors of Confucian *sheng* (hierarchical, ordering, centring power) and *ling* (immediate, localized, unpredicatable spiritual efficacy), marked by complex, hybrid forms of religious ritual and collective experimentation. The syncretic field has taken on very particular configurations and actualizations as it changes over time. Different phases will show distinct nodes of attraction (official temples and shrines, Neo-Confucian academies, Buddhist monasteries, ancestral hall rites, Daoist rituals, popular cults) in different relations to one another in different regions (official temples and shrines to officials, academies and shrines to literati, Buddhist ritual, ancestral rites, Daoist rituals, popular cults to a cross-section of community members). Any conceptualization of the current morphings of the syncretic field of Chinese popular religion would have to take into account CCP claims to enlightenment, rationality and reflexivity (counter-alienation) in relation to earlier polar attractors. The modern-state institutions and discourses (socialist as well as modernizing and capitalist) continue to generate great gaps and discontinuities in which local autonomous forms of collective desire and cultural experimentation, employing "pre-modern" modalities, continue to flourish.

In order to uncover instances of creative involution in the local history of Putian or any other local culture of South-east China, one can re-examine state institutions from a local perspective over time, to examine their local mutations and unintended consequences. When one traces the various lines of institutional change over time, one discovers the cracks that form as the lines give rise to blocks of becoming that move across state–society relations in unpredictable ways. In time Putian would become the most refined of all the districts in South-east China in its production of officials. It was also amongst the first regions to experiment with lineage forms of ancestral worship, a point noted with some concern by the leading Neo-Confucian scholar Zhu Xi (1130–1200), who sensed that developments in ancestral worship were rapidly getting out of control there. But rather than abandon past experience in a whole-scale conversion to Confucianism, the cultural resources of the Putian area continued to pile up new dimensions on the plane of

24. For further discussion of this concept, see Dean, *Lord of the Three in One*, and Edward L. Davis, *Society and the Supernatural in Song China* (Honolulu: University of Hawaii Press, 2002).

non-contradiction. Successive state institutional initiatives encountered an incomprehensibly complex ground of local and trans-regional ritual traditions, cult networks, voluntary associations, kin and pseudo-kinship groups, regional alliances, and flows of capital, ideas, images and practices from throughout the Asian trading network.

One could point to several "blocks of becoming" in the creative involution of the ritual systems of the Putian irrigated plains. These include the unintended consequences of the empire-wide establishment in the early Ming of official altars of the soil. These altars were gradually incorporated into local god temples, only to proliferate and mutate into a self-organizing, complex network of interlinking temples claiming local legitimacy. Current ritual networks and territories can be traced back to these local mutations. Another unintended effect of state institutional reform of the household registration and taxation systems known as the Single Whip Reforms in the mid to late Ming and early Qing was the gradual downloading of many forms of local self-governance on to local elites, working within local and higher order lineages, regional ritual alliances, cult networks, and a host of other networks. These took over responsibility for the upkeep of much of the local infrastructure (irrigation, local education, social order, charity, ritual observances) when local government funding ran dry. Such shifts are the origins of the current spheres of local autonomy under construction by many villages in South-east China.

There were many other instances of such blocks of becoming in Putian local history. The success of the Confucian lineage form in the early to mid-Ming would give way to a much more complicated range of lineage and pseudo-lineage forms closer to joint-stock corporations. The rise of the Three in One religious movement as a viable alternative as well as a reduplicative local ritual system beginning in the late Ming is another example of creative involution in the Xinghua area of Putian and Xianyou.

These blocks of becoming were transversal modes of social change because they worked through and transformed other institutional dimensions of individual villagers' lives as well, including potentially their identities in belonging to different orders or kinds of lineages, ritual territories and cult networks, but also their official household registration and taxation or corvée responsibilities, and their access to or understanding of the state, official schooling, the civil service examinations and official positions. Similar effects can be observed in China today, when villagers state their address in terms that mix the revived ritual topography with official spatial categories. Thus villagers in Putian, Fujian state their address in the following categories: *zhen* (current official township), *li* (Ming-dynasty ritually differentiated sub-canton), *qijing* (current village ritual-alliance territory), *cun* (current village name), *miao* (village temple), and finally the *jiaoluo* (village neighbourhood) in which they live. Each of these spaces is seen as belonging to or encompassing the others.

The pre-suppositions of social scientific models of elite control over village organizations in late imperial and contemporary times require some reconsideration. Communal self-organization is rooted in collective ritual processes that unfold within villages, temples and lineage halls. Collective rites express deep-seated communal values, rather than some outside imposed morality. In certain respects, leadership within the temple committees and lineage halls was more significant than the traditional marks of scholar-literati status. Scholar-literati could certainly be members, as could wealthy merchants. Individuals with official titles also were often included in the temple leadership, although usually when in retirement or on leave back in their home villages. However, membership in a temple committee is usually determined by rotation or by divination from within the group of all eligible villagers (usually male, but this too is changing), regardless of wealth or rank. Nevertheless, the powers associated with membership are substantial. Leadership at the local level means that whoever is capable of seizing on to, steering and articulating the flow of these shared values and the flow of the ritual event can attain a temporary leadership role. Thus membership in the local "elite" as defined by sociological criteria misses the remarkably fluid but nevertheless deeply flowing nature of the leadership of ritual events. These features of communal belonging, rotating leadership and collective decision-making continue to characterize Chinese local communal religion.

To conclude, I would argue that the interest of the newly available ethnographic material on local religious activity from South-east China lies in its diversity, rather than its similarity. Every region or local culture developed differently, attaining a degree of integration with the state (or having it imposed), while preserving their unique and singular qualities. On the other hand, no local culture developed in isolation from the state, or from trans-regional cultural flows, or trans-national flows of capital. The widespread evidence of the revival of local communal religion in many regions of China suggests that these cultural resources are again coming into play, enabling new responses to the forces of change.

Reflections on Ritual and Modernity in South-east China

I would like to raise a number of points about ritual and modernity in contemporary South-east China. I referred above to the temple networks of Putian as a second government – providing services to the locale but also collecting funds and mobilizing populations. This level of local governance and relative local autonomy has evolved slowly since the mid-Ming, and has shown an ability to respond to the retreat of the state from control over everyday life in contemporary China. The history of this gradual establishment of the institutions, techniques and practices of local autonomy is an important chapter in the socio-cultural development of China with many implications for the future.

First, the ritual events of Chinese local communal religion are embedded in historically complex processes of the construction of elaborate local systems of social organization and regional networks of temples.

Temple festivals and ritual alliances capture, deform and transduce lines of force traversing the spaces they create, whether these be forces of state, lineage or god cult territorialization, or capitalist, technological or cultural forces of deterritorialization. In other words, these singular ritual events and the changing spaces they produce and mobilize have been involved in a constantly changing confrontation with capital and different state and social formations for centuries.

The second point concerns the nature of everyday life in Putian. I suggest that ritual events in rural Fujian are intensifications of everyday relations, rather than moments figuring a mythological or cyclic temporality or plane of unification, which is how they are often conceived in the mode of the romantic peasant, or in terms of tradition versus modernity. Moreover, the ritual events of rural South-east China have not yet become commodified events. They are instead moments for the confrontation of the ever-new in the always the same. This includes the fascinating process of the self-reflective incorporation of new audio-visual and electronic technologies that increasingly permeate everyday life into ritual events, and the self-conscious appropriation of everyday political symbols within ritual. Images of Mao Zedong and the other fathers of the communist revolution are carried at the head of religious processions, while banners proclaim official slogans. Video documentation of religious festivals is paid for by temple committees and CD ROMs containing the latest innovations in ritual performance are exchanged between temples.

It is worth emphasizing the imperceptible intensification of everyday social relationality into ritual events. As mentioned above, ritual events in some particularly active and complex areas of South-east China can take place 250 days out of the year, all within an easy walk. Participation in these events is nearly total, with the exception of certain Christian families. The mobilization of the entire community to greater or lesser degrees on an everyday basis is one of the most significant features of these events.

It is difficult to locate precise frames or thresholds around ritual activity in current South-east China. In the everyday of Fujian rural ritual, time is twisted into a Möebius strip linking zones of indiscernability; at a certain level of intensity the everyday merges into the ritual event. Within ritual events multiple temporalities are brought to bear, including the reversal of forward-flowing time in Daoist meditation, the accessing within Daoist rites of the time of the prior heavens to replenish the latter heavens of actualized time, and the acceleration of cosmic cycles of time in the revelation and recitation of scripture. Space too is stretched. The body of the priest and the bodies of many participants are like multiple Möebius strips linking internal bodily spaces to planes of space, some actual spaces such as the intercorporeal spaces of the crowd, or the charged space of the temple, the courtyard or the procession, some drawn from the virtual and the imaginary such as multiple planes of inscription of cosmic forces. These planes of inscription of infinite semiotics are perhaps best illustrated in the indecipherable talisman, a figural morphing of cosmic forces of a-signifying semiotics that has a direct impact on space, time and the body.

The third point is that these ritual events are moments of formation of fluid emergent community, of community as an ontological sense of collective experimentation, but that they also re-inscribe hierarchical, patriarchal and sometimes outright oppressive stratifications. The ritual event is the totality of the experience for all involved; there is no outer term of reference like society, and even the notion of community is open. Each ritual is a gamble requiring negotiation with local government and Party officials and complex mobilization of community desires and resources. Many ritual events are still restricted or prohibited, and organizers are always in some sense under threat. Every communal ritual performance is therefore both a potential disaster, and at the same time a step in the construction of a temporary autonomous zone. The successful completion of a communal ritual is cause for celebration at many levels.

The fourth point is that the ritual events of Chinese communal religion have been interpreted by some scholars as moments of collective sacrifice of excess in response to the impact of capitalism. This would entail interpreting them as key elements in a sacrificial general economy that strives to obviate or challenge or forestall capitalist relations. However, it is clear that the economies of scale of these events are quite specific, and after all, it is capitalism itself in Bataille's analysis that is engaged in an all-consuming self-sacrifice of excess. Moreover, if I am correct to argue that these ritual events can be seen as a form of creative involutionary feedback of local cultural forms upon local–state and local capitalist relations, then it is important to see this as an evolving pattern of response and mutation, including to the forces and flows of capitalism. There are also issues of spatial scale at play. Local geographic features frame most ritual networks. An ecology of local power holds ritual networks back from direct confrontation with the state. Instead, the networks expand and become more complex within effective, appropriate levels and niches in the continually evolving, agonistic relation with state power.

Finally, I would like comment on the refusal of the participants in ritual events to engage in a dialogue with the discourses of modernization, such as debates on civil society or public spheres. Neither can these vital ritual events be confined within a discourse of "salvage ethnography" that would attempt to enshrine "Chinese tradition" as the obverse of modernity – a form of bad historicism.[25] This is not to say that they are lacking in discourses; on the contrary, proclamations, posters, banners, messages from the gods, extreme forms of calligraphy and Daoist talismans are visible everywhere, and the very ritual dances and processions inscribe intricate patterns of choreography into the heart of the community. The ritual discourse emphasizes deeply felt communal values and understandings of the efficacy of the gods. Beyond the semantic level,

25. Kenneth Dean, "Popular religion or civil society: disruptive communities and alternative conceptions," in T. Brook and B. Frolic (eds.), *Civil Society in China* (Boulder, CO: Westview Press, 1997), pp. 172–195.

there is an infinite semiotics at play in these events that can be seen in the inscription of every possible surface and the evocation of many impossible surfaces (supernatural planes mobilized by incantation, mudras and talismans). There is a different notion of language underlying ritual events. The ritual event is communal self-expression, not an act of inter-subjective communication.

What the ritual events of the Fujian countryside are engaged in could be seen as the "dephasing" of ritual practices that re-emerge from the syncretic field (the plane of non-contradiction, the virtual reservoir of cultural forms of local knowledge) and release alternative temporalities and spatialities in a ceaseless negotiation with the forces of modernity. These concrete ritual practices developed over time, but they have accumulated within the reservoir of local cultural memory and can be brought to bear upon contemporary social configurations. Here "tradition" is not opposed to "modernity." Instead, seemingly "pre-modern" communal practices like spirit possession and Daoist ritual are brought to the surface of the positive unconscious of the local community in ways felt viscerally throughout a collectivity. A person who has grown up in South-east China over the past 30 years will have performed many different roles in ritual events, carrying lanterns, marching in procession, carrying the sedan chair of the gods, perhaps becoming possessed by the gods. Such people can expect to continue to expand their experience in relationship to the evolving community through these ritual events in the future as they take on roles in the temple committee, in fund-raising, or by developing more specialized forms of ritual expertise. Although individual experience expands in the communal self-expression of ritual events, neither of these terms is pre-determined or stable. The ritual events of South-east China mould temporary autonomous zones which are spaces of emergent community, which can only exist in movement and transformation.

The Cult of the Silkworm Mother as a Core of Local Community Religion in a North China Village: Field Study in Zhiwuying, Boading, Hebei

Fan Lizhu

ABSTRACT This article deals with an example of local community religion in north China, the activities of a woman spirit-medium in a small village in Hebei province. This woman is believed to represent an ancient goddess, the Silkworm Mother (*Cangu nainai*), to whom people turn for healing illnesses not cured by Western or Chinese medicine. This study shows that local popular religion is very much alive in contemporary China.

In the year 2000, a research team of Daniel Overmyer from the University of British Columbia, Hou Jie from Nankai University and I launched a project for the study of temple festivals in rural north China. Its aim was to try to make sense of north Chinese rural communities by looking at the various symbolic practices by which the peasants traditionally and contemporarily express their value systems and seek to preserve and improve their lives.

Local religious practices and beliefs carried out by ordinary people in their daily life have long been the quantitative mainstream of the history of Chinese religions, and a fundamental support for traditional society, culture and moral values. Unfortunately, this significant part of Chinese culture has been ignored for a long time by academic studies. In the 20th century, Chinese popular religious practices and beliefs were criticized by scholars and destroyed by wars and political movement. Despite the best efforts of a half-century of communist propaganda against religion and the violent destruction of temples and statues during the Cultural Revolution (1966–76), devotion to local deities continues to thrive in China. Temples are being rebuilt; the sale of incense sticks and paper money is once again big business; and mediums who represent these gods are to be found everywhere. Popular religion is alive and well-developed in the rural areas of mainland China. Our research aimed to find out what makes popular religious practices revive, and what is the pattern of local people's religious practices?

According to a survey by Daniel Overmyer, in the last ten years Chinese scholars have produced a substantial number of studies of the religious traditions of ordinary people, and excellent fieldwork investigations have been carried out in some areas by Chinese scholars in collaboration with European, Canadian and US colleagues, and published in Hong Kong or Taiwan. However, the studies published in China have so far involved little fieldwork, except among minority peoples, and collaborative fieldwork has been done primarily in the south-eastern provinces of Fujian and Guangdong. With a few important exceptions such fieldwork has not been carried out in north China, the traditional centre of Chinese culture and government administration. Some of the northern villages we studied are in counties studied in the 1930s, particularly those in Ding county, concerning which substantial volumes were published by Sidney Gamble and Li Jinghan.[1] In the Ding xian (Ting Hsien) experimental district in western Hebei there was an average of seven temples per village in 1882, and this number was only slightly lower when a militantly secularizing magistrate arrived in 1914; thereafter the number declined sharply.[2] Six of Sidney Gamble's "sample villages" in Hebei, surveyed in the early 1930s, had a total of 38 temples, with 15 in one village alone. Gamble had "no reports" on temples in another five sample villages, suggesting that his investigators reported only the larger temples.[3] More recent studies of village life in north China have focused primarily on political, social and economic factors, without much attention to religious traditions. Important exceptions are studies of northern pilgrimages and death rituals by Susan Naquin, and of local religion in Shanxi province by David Johnson. Richard Madsen has recently published a book on Chinese Catholics that also includes material on north China communities.[4] R. David Arkush published in 1995 a book on north Chinese folk materials and popular mentality. Luo Hongguan studied the temple rituals in a village from northern Shanxi province in 1998.

This project on temple festivals in north China involved fieldwork in Baoding, Langfang, Handan, Xingtai and Shijiazhuang in Hebei province. In 2000, we went to a small village, named Zhiwuying, located in Xushui county in the Baoding area. There I unexpectedly met a local spirit-medium, an old lady, Mrs Wu, Silkworm Mother (*Cangu nainai*). According to local belief, Mrs Wu is believed to be an incarnation of the Silkworm Mother goddess. The devotees of this popular form of religiousness seek a personal and direct access to a divine power that can heal their various ills. Lay leaders figure prominently in popular religion, as opposed to the professional leaders of institutional religion. At times these lay leaders become mediums or shamans who mediate the efficacious power of the gods to ordinary folk.

Many different local communities, operating largely on their own, have produced Chinese gods. It is well known that some of the gods worshipped by ordinary people in traditional Chinese society and its continuations are deified spirits of local humans believed to have the power to respond to prayers and petitions. This power is manifested in healing,

1. D. Overmyer, "From 'feudal superstition' to 'popular beliefs'; new directions in mainland Chinese studies of Chinese popular religion," *Cahiers d'Extrême-Asie*, No. 12 (2001).

2. Sidney D. Gamble, *Ting Hsien: A North China Rural Community* (Stanford: Stanford University Press, 1968), reprint of the 1954 ed., pp. 405–407.

3. Sidney D. Gamble, *North China Villages: Social, Political, and Economic Activities Before 1933* (Berkeley: University of California Press, 1963), p. 119.

4. Richard Madsen, *China's Catholics: Tragedy and Hope in an Emerging Civil Society* (Berkeley: University of California Press, 1999).

protection and support, and in advice and moral teachings among villagers. The gods are believed to have independent power in their own right. Their beneficent and moral dimensions are widely developed in local society. These gods are believed to dwell in temples, represented by images and by human beings. Because they are powerful in popular culture, they are widely accepted and believed in by ordinary people. Meanwhile, their power not only exists in temples and images, but is also transferred to their representatives (mediums). Mediums are recognized as temporary manifestations of gods with divine power to help people solve difficulties and answer questions.

This study is based on fieldwork in Zhiwuying village in the Baoding area of Hebei province. It is in Dawangdian township in Xushui county, 100 miles south of Beijing. In this small village, the religious situation is different from the religious practices of south-east China. There are no big temples and ancestral shrines. There is no one big lineage that plays an important role in the village's business, but many small lineages. In the south, according to the fieldwork reports of John Lagerwey, temple festivals are the most important and complex manifestations of community religion; preparations for them can involve hiring an opera or puppet troupe, arranging for rituals to be conducted by Daoist priests or Buddhist monks, erecting sheds for operas and offerings, preparing food and many other activities. It is important to note that religious activities are organized by lay people from influential families, not priests, since lineage tradition is very powerful in southern communities.[5]

In the summer of 2000, we were told that there was a new Guanyin temple in Zhiwuying village. It was a small temple built among houses in the village, but it was locked and a village resident told us that an old lady living just behind the temple kept the key. We went to see her to ask for the key. She was sitting on the *kang* (clay bed) and appeared to be blind, but she recognized that we were not her neighbours, and even asked whether there was a foreigner with us since Professor Overmyer was with us. At first she refused to give the key to the head of the township who was with us as she seemed to feel that he was not a good worshipper. Finally, I talked with her in a gentle and peaceful way, and she gave the key to me. I found there was a small and shabby altar in her room with some offerings, incense and candles. On the top of this small altar there was a dirty red curtain. I lifted the curtain, to find that there was a paper picture with a female god and several smaller figures with Chinese characters saying "all the gods are here" (*quan shen luozuo*). In a brief talk with the old lady, Mrs Wu, I learned that this room is the local worship and healing centre of the Silkworm Mother goddess. So I decided to come back to learn more about the cult of the goddess. In 2000 and 2001, I returned twice and stayed in the village. I was able to stay in

---

5. See Fang Xuejia (ed.), *Meizhou Heyuan diqu de cunluo wenhua* (*Village Religion and Culture in Northeastern Guangdong*) (Hong Kong: Traditional Hakka Society Series, Vol. 5, 1997).

Mrs Wu's home watching her communicate with the people seeking help and healing those in need. I interviewed believers from the village and outside it, and also unbelievers from the village. I even visited believers' homes to see the sacred place where they communicated with and worshipped the Silkworm Mother.

This report discusses how Mrs Wu found herself "called" to serve as the medium of the ancient god-figure known as the Silkworm Mother, and how this popular belief has developed in the past 20 years in Zhiwuying village and influenced other villages. The cult of the Silkworm Mother has deep historical roots and was but one of the many religious devotions that were violently suppressed during the Cultural Revolution. Today this worship is once again thriving.

This report shows that local popular religion is very much alive in contemporary China, as well as the specific role of mediums in this style of religiousness. It also indicates how communities and individuals turn to these religious practices in their search for meaning and their moral concerns. Their beliefs have the power to push the development of popular religion in folk society, to help in the fight for survival and dealing with relationships with others in daily life. The basic features of Chinese local popular religion seem to be indestructible. The cult of the Silkworm Mother is a visible expression of people's interests, and public worship in it represented the periodic mustering of the community for the demonstration of common beliefs and common interests.

To move from the meagre and formulaic descriptions of religious and calendarical festival provided by local chronicles (*difangzhi*) to accounts based on fieldwork, filled with vivid details about elaborate rituals and colourful customs that are not even mentioned in printed sources, is to move into a new world. However, it is important to realize that the informants here are providing descriptions that reveal what a local popular religion is really like.

The Cult of the Silkworm Mother and Religious Tradition in Zhiwuying Village

The function of community integration is especially apparent in cults of sufficient general importance to stimulate the religious interest of the entire community. Leading among such cults are those dedicated to deities of elements of nature, which have always dominated the consciousness of the peasant population.[6] The cult of the Silkworm Mother is an old tradition among ordinary people in the Baoding area. As a female deity, the Silkworm Mother's status in the Baoding area is similar to that of the Goddess of Taishan in Shandong.

According to numerous historical documents, worship of the Silkworm Mother was very popular in local society, and spread out among different

6. C.K. Yang, *Religion in Chinese Society* (Berkeley, University of California Press, 1967), pp. 60–70.

areas, such as Hebei, Jiangsu, Sichuan and Zhejiang.[7] Silk production was a traditional industry in China, and women were the major producers. In common with other folk gods and goddess, tales of the silkworm mother are found in different areas, with different versions and stories, but the practices and rituals were quite similar. The original responsibility of the Silkworm Mother was to protect the silk industry. She dwelled in temples, and also in households. Worship of the Silkworm Mother became broader because she was believed to have more and more sacred power to protect people and meet their many needs, beyond silk production, so that even though the silk industry declined in some areas, the cult of the Silkworm Mother did not fade away. People may not be very clear about the tales and myths related to the Silkworm Mother, but this kind of folk belief is deeply rooted in popular culture. This is what is happening in Zhiwuying village.

From my interviews with villagers, I learned that there are different stories about the Silkworm Mother's identity. In Chinese religious tradition, the spirits of humans could be deified because of their good deeds, courage and strength in life. The Silkworm Mother had just the above characteristics. For local believers, she was not a fictitious figure but a real human being who had lived in this area many years ago. It is said that the Silkworm Mother was born ten thousand years ago in Balizhuang, Rongcheng, a village near Zhiwuying. Her family was named Yang. People believed that the Silkworm Mother helped to solve various difficulties and problems. She had the ability to possess shamans, perform cures, send sons and work miracles, which made her more accessible and appealing than other gods. Above all, the Silkworm Mother is a local god; she is identified as a neighbour by villagers.

So, people not only celebrated her birthday at a temple festival on the 20th of the first lunar month, but another special day is also celebrated according to the local tradition. The ninth day of the ninth month is the time for married women to return to visit their parents. Since the Silkworm Mother was a young girl from Balizhuang, Rongcheng, many believers in that area make a pilgrimage trip to the temple located there, as well as to the main Silkworm Mother temple on West Mountain 50 kilometres away.

The cult of the Silkworm Mother is part of local religious activities in Zhiwuying village. Historically, there were more than ten temples in this village, including Tudi (Earth God) Temple, Sanyue Temple and Laoye Temple. They were destroyed several times, in the Sino-Japanese War, the Land Reform Movement and the Cultural Revolution. In recent years, some temples have been rebuilt by villagers. Most donations came from fund-rising for the Silkworm Mother, showing that she still has a very strong influence among villagers.

The cult of the Silkworm Mother is an old tradition in this area; however it ceased during the Cultural Revolution but was revived in the

---

7. Li Qiao, *Zhongguo hangye shen chongbai* (*Trade God Worship In China*) (Overseas Chinese Press, 1990).

late 1970s. How did this happen? It was because of a woman named Mrs Wu, who is believed to be the incarnation of the Silkworm Mother with divine power to help people.

The Story of the Incarnation of the Silkworm Mother, Mrs Wu

Villagers' beliefs and customs are based on the needs of pre-modern agricultural village life. Chinese gods are numerous and specialized; in the household, for example, there are deities of the gate, door, kitchen stove, marital bed, well and latrine, as well as ancestral tablets and images of more powerful gods on the household altar. People believe that the divine power of deities not only exists in temples and shrines, but also can be attached to human beings. Mediums commonly claimed to be possessed by deities with divine power, so, sometimes the mediums were thought of as the deity itself. This happened in Zhiwuying village. Mrs Wu, now an old woman, claimed that she was possessed by the Silkworm Mother 20 years ago after long suffering from serious pain in her legs. Now, villagers call her the Silkworm Mother.

She was an ordinary woman, no different from her female neighbours, and has two sons and three daughters. Her husband died when she was 50 and she had no intention of being a medium at that time. She says that she did not practise any religion: "I was too poor to believe in god." However, she knew about the cult of the Silkworm Mother from her childhood. She also knew something of the history of the Silkworm Mother, but like many other villagers, she was not much concerned about it. She took it for granted. In her view, the Silkworm Mother was born ten thousand years ago.

In 1977, when Mrs Wu was sixty, she had serious pain in her legs. She could not move or even dress herself and medicines did not heal her. After suffering for two months, one night she had strange dream. There were a lot of people with costumes and weapons, but she was not afraid. One man said: "We have looked for you for many years, now finally we have got you." They pulled her outside. The next day, she continued to experience this strange dream. It seemed that she did not fall into a sound sleep, because she saw mountains and rivers very clearly where she had never been before. There were several gods talking to her, including the Queen Mother of West, the Silkworm Mother and the Horse King. She was asked to report her life history. She told them her own history from when she was ten years old, including about her family members. She answered many questions, such as the name of her relatives, whether they did bad things, and so on. She said that it was amazing that she even knew her great grandfather's name, which she had not known before. The Silkworm Mother told her that she had been noticed for many years, and exhorted her to do good deeds and manage the affairs of her family. In the end, she was asked to hang up a picture of all the gods (*quan shen*). She did not understand, so she did not take it seriously. Unfortunately, she suffered the pain in her legs at that night, so she promised that she would hang up the picture of all the gods if the pain left.

The next morning, she bought a big sheet of red paper. She took it to her parents' family and asked her brother to write "all the gods are here." Her brother was very angry when he learned the story from her. He said: "Everyone has dreams, don't take it seriously. I don't have pen. I don't have ink. You are already too old, don't think about becoming a medium. It is very troublesome." She became angry too, "OK. I won't ask you any more." Unexpectedly, she said loudly to her brother just as if she were announcing a big decision to the world: "I am the Silkworm Mother, I am coming here to heal people who have disease. Nobody can stop me. If he wants to stop me, he will be blamed." Her brother was extremely surprised, then he wrote for her on the red paper, "all the gods are here."

However, Mrs Wu had never had medical training so she dared not treat people. She doubted whether she was able to cure illness. This lack of confidence lasted for quite a long time. At that time, nobody knew she was the incarnation of the Silkworm Mother. One day, when she was at a clinic for her leg pain, the doctor said to her, "you don't have to continue your treatment, you arc recovered already." Then, he took her out and said to her secretly, "you are a god now, you are a god now." He did not say what god she was. Later, this doctor sent one of his relatives to Mrs Wu to receive treatment for pain in her arms, which acupuncture did not help. Mrs Wu did not know how to treat it, until, suddenly, she felt power coming into her arms, so she massaged the patient. Fortunately, this patient got better. Mrs Wu was very surprised with herself: "How do I have such power? Why do my hands know how to treat patients?" Since then, for more than 20 years, she has had a reputation among the devotees of the Silkworm Mother in the village. People called her the Silkworm Mother.

Because of her popularity, Mrs Wu or the Silkworm Mother is recognized not only by people living in Zhiwuying village, but also those from nearby villages and some from remote places. Mrs Wu has been a very important figure for stimulating the cult of the Silkworm Mother in Zhiwuying and other villages near by. Both her physical treatment and her spiritual assistance to ordinary people from her motherly personality mean that the Silkworm Mother is becoming an important regional deity worshipped by individuals and organized groups in this area.

The Interaction Between the Silkworm Mother and Believers

Most people come to Mrs Wu with physical problems; some of them have psychological problems, manifested physically. Before they see her they have already tried medical treatment from both Western and Chinese doctors. She says: "People come to me with strange illnesses. They don't know those are not really strange illnesses, but from ghosts, ancestors or supernatural beings (*shi gui, shi zuxian, xianjia nongde*). So hospitals have nothing to do with this kind of patient."

In Chinese tradition, there are two types of illness. One is physical problems that can be treated by a medical doctor. The other is getting in trouble with the nether world for which one needs the help of gods. Normally, when people are sick, they go to see a doctor. After the failure of a doctor's treatment, they will go to mediums. Villagers in Zhiwuying know that Mrs Wu is an ordinary woman, nothing special, so why do they believe in her sacred power to cure disease? Because they believe that Mrs Wu is now a representative of The Silkworm Mother: "The cult of the Silkworm Mother is inherited from our ancestors, which is same with the cult of the Taishan Immortal Mother and the Taishan Old Ancestor." As with other popular gods, the Silkworm Mother has legitimacy from local culture. So, Mrs Wu is playing the role of a semi-human being and deity in village life. As she says: "The Silkworm Mother saves China, helps peasants and guards the country, so she is a god with sacred power. With sacred power, I can heal any disease. Otherwise I am not divine. I won't come with sacred power without the help of Silkworm Mother. There is only one god lasting thousands and thousands of years, thousands and ten of thousands of years, which is the Silkworm Mother."

Mrs Wu does not touch her patients but checks the causes of disease by "asking about the case history" (*wen'an*) and "solving the case" (*po'an*). Usually, she sits on the bed and closes her eyes in meditation style. She asks patients or their relatives to tell her the situation. She states that the treatment depends on whether the Ancestor God (*laozushen*; it does not refer to any particular god, similar to Old Heaven *laotian*) is willing to help. If the Ancestor God helps, the patients will recover soon; otherwise they will be in serious trouble. Usually, she tells the patients or their relatives how to worship the Silkworm Mother at home, by burning incense, asking for medicines, making vows and so on. People follow her suggestion and commands, because they believe that the Silkworm Mother gives them guidance with the aid of Mrs Wu. For example, they may believe that medicine comes from the Silkworm Mother. If they prepare a bowl of water and put it on the table in the direction of the Silkworm Mother and then ask the Silkworm Mother to give them the medicines they need, they believe the medicines for healing their disease will be put into their bowl of water. Then, they drink it.

Case studies: case 1: Mrs Li is about 50 years old. Two years ago, she had a strange problem with her back. Medicines from the hospital did not help. She almost gave up hope. Then she went to see a medium, an old lady in her village, but her pain was still not reduced. She then went to see Mrs Wu. Mrs Wu's explanation of her suffering was that she did not worship the real Buddha, but a false one. The old lady Mrs Li had gone to see was a horse-monkey demon (*mahoujing*). This surprised Mrs Li. Both the old lady and Mrs Wu were neighbours, why was one demon and one a god? However, it did not take Mrs Li much time to convert to worship the cult of the Silkworm Mother by going to see Mrs Wu. But she did not recover immediately. After several days she went to Mrs Wu again, and said: "Silkworm Mother, I followed your directions to pray every night. Why has the disease not stopped?" Mrs Wu was quiet for a moment, and sang with the music of Hebei opera. She told Mrs Li that there must be some unclean stuff close to the altar of the Silkworm Mother which were making the Silkworm Mother unwilling to help. Mrs Li ran home and found that there was a knife, steelyard hook and steelyard, used by her husband for selling pork. She suddenly realized why she suffered from bad illness: "My Heaven (God), the Silkworm Mother really knows everything." For her, the cult of the Silkworm Mother and Mrs Wu became the same thing. After a certain period of worshipping the Silkworm Mother, she recovered. Now she is the one of the most active devotees of the Cult of the Silkworm Mother; she goes to visit Mrs Wu almost every day.

During her treatment, Mrs Li followed the Mrs Wu's directions. She prayed to the Silkworm Mother every night to ask for medicines. She put a piece of white paper in front of the altar where she was burning incense. She prayed, "Silkworm Mother, save me and help me." Finally, some white powder appeared on the paper, which she believed to be medicine provided by the Silkworm Mother. Sometimes, she put out a bowl with water to ask for medicine. She believed that the medicine came into the water after her prayers. So she drank it twice a day.

Case 2: Mrs Wang, over 30 years old, is from Xiaoxicun, a nearby village. She had a bad headache. After the failure of hospital treatment, she went to see Mrs Wu. Mrs Wu did not ask the cause of disease, but about her relationship with her parents-in-law. She said to Mrs Wang: "You don't have any physical problem. You are not filial, and you treat your parents-in-law badly. So the Silkworm Mother is punishing you." She demonstrated her point by burning a candle in front of the picture of Silkworm Mother. First, the candle light was very even, but when Mrs Wu repeated that Mrs Wang was not filial, the candle flared up. Mrs Wu told Mrs Wang the fire showed the Silkworm Mother testing her. It was a big surprise for Mrs Wang. She believed that God knew about her behaviour. She accepted this explanation of her pain and corrected her attitude and behaviour towards her parents-in-law. Soon, when Mrs Wang came to visit Mrs Wu again, she looked healthy and in a good mood.

Case 3: One day, when I observed Mrs Wu at her home, a sister and brother of a Zhang family came. They said loudly "Silkworm Mother, please tell us how our mother can recover as soon as possible." Their mother was in a hospital after surgery. They did not tell Mrs Wu her exact sickness, but asked for her help. Mrs Wu did not ask them any questions, but she sang Heibei opera music. From her singing, people knew that she was trying to search for the causes of disease. After keeping quiet for a while, she said "Tell me the truth. Did you move the stones and bricks from temples or graves when you built your house? Did you kill any snakes?" The brother answered: "We did get some stones and bricks from a river bed. I did not think we stole bricks from temples or graves." Mrs Wu continued singing. "A flood burst the Dragon King temple, where the stones and bricks were from. Once you tell the truth, the Silkworm Mother can help you to investigate your mother's sickness. If you don't tell the truth, it is impossible to know the cause of disease." The brother said: "We probably got some bricks from temples. I remember that my elder brother threw a snake from his house, but I am not sure whether the snake was dead or not." Mrs Wu asked, "where did your brother throw the snake?" The brother answered, "he threw it into a ditch."

After a while, Mrs Wu sang: "If you want your mother get better, you must worship the Silkworm Mother." The sister said: "Yes, yes, we will. Tell us how to worship and how to burn the incense." Mrs Wu said: "You must promise to worship the Silkworm Mother after she recovers, don't forget to go to West Mountain to worship the Silkworm Mother. You pray toward the West where the Silkworm Mother is in your yard. Now your mother is in the hospital, you fix the time at 9 pm every evening. Prepare a bowl of water for your mother, when you pray at home. After praying, serve your mother the water, this water has the sacred power of the Silkworm Mother. Leave 20 *yuan* to buy candles and incense for the Silkworm Mother. Because it is not enough that your own family prays I will pray for you too in order to get more power." The sister and brother left feeling very satisfied.

The above cases show that Mrs Wu is a folk medium, playing a very important role in village society, mostly because the cult of the Silkworm Mother is still influential among ordinary people. For ordinary folk what counts is the goddess's efficacious power manifested in aid and healing. What really counts is community support of the cult.

According to medical anthropological studies every medical treatment system has its own structure of the causes of disease. The reason for the existence of folk medical treatments in modern society is that these treatments pay attention to the illness and the relevant social elements of illness. Physical problems are not the only causes of disease, which can also be caused by the relationship of the patient with others and immoral behaviour.[8] Mediums, like local doctors, are familiar with people's problems and beliefs, so they can explain the causes of disease which are supported by their patients' belief in the existence of sacred power. Normally, people go to see both folk doctors and medical doctors for both Western and Chinese treatment.

Mrs Wu has been a folk doctor healing people for more than 20 years, and has a very good reputation. Of course, people treat her not as an old country lady but as the Silkworm Mother. We can say that the cult of the Silkworm Mother goes beyond folk medicine. The cult of the Silkworm Mother, represented by Mrs Wu, is supported by popular culture and ordinary people. It demonstrates the kind of order and logic which has been accepted by the people for many years, including moral concern, balance between nature and human beings, and worship of ancestor gods. Mrs Wu's treatment is never simple medical service in the village,

8. See Zhang Xun, *Disease and Culture* (Daoxiang Press, 1994).

because she is a symbol of popular religion. Chinese gods are expressions of the concern of ordinary people to have personal and direct access to divine power in their own local areas. Vows to gods are contracts between them and their devotees for which no clerical intermediaries are necessary.

The Influence of the Cult of the Silkworm Mother

In China, popular religious activities with lay leaders have been active in local society, characterized by their own forms of organizations, activities, ritual and belief. Symbols of local divine power who were also once human are believed to sympathize with and respond to their worshippers; they are present in their shrines, represented by images, and also by mediums. To the ordinary people, a deep understanding of religious doctrines and myths is not really necessary. What is most important to them is whether the gods they are praying to are *ling*, have efficacious divine power; are they able to respond effectively to prayers and petitions? These divine symbols take on special roles beyond that of community patron, including the healing of specific diseases, help with childbirth, and the support of occupations and professions.

Twenty years ago Mrs Wu was an ordinary woman without special ability; she even once suffered family abuse from her husband. But after a period of difficult experience, she believed she was possessed by a deity, and now represents the Silkworm Mother. From this perspective, Mrs Wu is not treated as a simple country woman, but as a divine medium. This divine power is not available to other people in the community. So, for more than 20 years, Mrs Wu has been the only one with this particular function. When I asked her whether she had disciples and whether she intended to teach others her skill, she replied: "No. It is impossible for common people to learn it. One needs the help of gods." Even her daughter and daughter-in-law cannot obtain this power.

Mrs Wu has power from people's belief in the cult of the Silkworm Mother, and has established her reputation in the local area for healing specific diseases and solving people's frustrating problems. She told me: "At first, I did not want to do this, because I didn't want to have a bad name among neighbours. If I could not help them, people would be angry. It would be terrible." The Silkworm Mother's reputation is the same as Mrs Wu's. As more and more people get help from Mrs Wu, they believe that the cult of The Silkworm Mother is *ling*. So efficacious divine power makes the cult of the Silkworm Mother become more and more influential. People now come to see Mrs Wu from distant places, such as Beijing Shijiangzhuang and other cities. Those people testify that they have benefited from worshipping the Silkworm Mother and spread the good news about Mrs Wu, which has made the cult of the Silkworm Mother more and more popular. On the ninth day of the ninth lunar month in 2001, about 150 people gathered in Mrs Wu's house to make a pilgrimage to the Silkworm Mother Temple located on West Mountain 200 miles away.

At present there are no religious associations in Zhiwuying village, but this does not mean that people do not take part in religious activities and rituals. The cult of the Silkworm Mother in Zhiwuying village demonstrates that there are demands in local society for religious belief and rituals. Villagers pool their resources in order to contribute to rebuilding temples. I have heard that several temples have been built or rebuilt with the power of the Silkworm Mother in recent years. In Zhiwuying village, there is also a brand new Guanyin temple. A new Silkworm Mother temple has been built in Yang village near the place where the Silkworm Mother was born; in addition the Silkworm Mother temple on West Mountain has been rebuilt, and other religious sites are being constructed. Temple festivals also take place for the cult of the Silkworm Mother. These are lively affairs lasting several days that include offerings in temples, and the performance of operas or puppet-plays, with many villagers worshipping.

Now the question is, to whom do these religious establishments belong and who controls their assets? Where does the money come from to construct and maintain the buildings, purchase the images and ritual paraphernalia, pay for the incense and candles, and support the resident clerics, if any? From my interview information, most donations for rebuilding temples have come from the devotees of the cult of the Silkworm Mother. In some cases, Mrs Wu plays the key role in organizing people to take part in the temple festivals.

Mrs Wu does not ask people to give her extra money. She asks for a very limited amount for the costs of candle and incense. Ten years ago, only 0.20 *yuan* per visit was requested; now, it is 2.00 *yuan* per visit. However, she asks the patients to promise not only to offer the Silkworm Mother daily worship, but also to donate money to temple building in the Silkworm Mother's name. If people try to leave her extra money, she always refuses to accept it. She says: "Don't give me money, you should appreciate the Silkworm Mother, she helps you. So whenever or wherever, the Silkworm Mother builds a temple, you can make your contribution." In Chinese tradition, there is no merit greater than that of establishing a temple. So most people are willing to contribute money or labour in order to accumulate merit.

These religious activities and practices spread from Zhiwuying village to other villages in the Boading area. What is the attitude of village cadres towards the cult of the Silkworm Mother and the rebuilding of temples, organized by Mrs Wu? In interviews residents indicate that there is no controversy between Mrs Wu and village cadres. The power of village administration is weaker since peasants have more freedom to choose their life styles and mode of production. The leaders of Zhiwuying did not stop the development of the cult of the Silkworm Mother, most importantly because Mrs Wu as the representative of the Silkworm Mother is an old lady. She is thought to be superstitious (*shenshen guigui*), but it is not big deal. Village leaders did not interrupt temple rebuilding. Mrs Wu says, "we did not ask money from the village, so they have no reason to stop us." However, she is not satisfied with village leaders' inactive attitude towards temple rebuilding. She has some more ambitious plans, which can't be completed without strong support from village cadres. It reminds of me the cult of the patriarch Han in Beiqi village in Ding county which is supported by village leaders, who helped with getting a religious association licence and money to rebuild the temples and run temple festivals.

I would like to suggest that there are different local models in China for religious development between south and north. The development of popular religion depends on the situation. It may have a medium as the core of a popular cult in the village with weak village leaders; or it may be organized by strong village leaders or powerful lineages. However, no matter which model exists, popular religious development definitely has support from ordinary people.

Conclusion

This report is from the first stage of fieldwork. We are still carrying out studies on popular beliefs in rural areas in north China. I would like to conclude by making the following points.

First, although we have many reasons to believe that villagers are intensely conservative, especially where ritual and religion are concerned, I still doubt that contemporary Chinese popular religion is merely a revival of tradition. Popular religion is also an expression of the social conditions of modern life. Social dislocation generates new spiritual questions; greater economic comfort evokes new questions of meaning. The traditional Chinese/Confucian world view was severely challenged early in the 20th century, first by modernization efforts that opened China to Western political and scientific models, and later by Marxism. Most social theory would predict that, under these pressures of modernization, the persuasiveness of a traditional world view necessarily diminishes, even to the point of bankruptcy. Yet research among peasants in Zhiwuying village demonstrates that the traditional world view of Chinese religiousness, associated with fate, *fengshui*, Chinese medicine and so on, appears far from bankrupt.

Secondly, scholars have used the term of "folk Buddhism" to show that Buddhist ideas and symbols are almost totally subsumed by the concerns of village religion. Nevertheless, "folk Buddhism" is getting more diffused in the Zhiwuying village. People are not much concerned about the origins of the gods they worship. They seemed take them for granted. So the discourse of Mrs Wu and her followers is of mixed popular religious beliefs. When they talked about a sectarian Eternal Mother (*wu sheng lao mu*) they did not know her origins. Another example is that Mrs Wu's followers recited the "Book of Buddha," though in fact that paragraph is from a popular sectarian scripture.

Finally, popular religious belief as social capital functions not only to provide possible means to heal people's disease, but also to frame people's moral concerns. Since people still worship and fear ancestors, ghosts and spirits, they have a sense that human efforts cannot succeed without divine approval and support. With the help of folk belief, people are confident that through divination and rituals these superhuman powers can be known and dealt with; they believe that they can discover whether or not a problem is being caused by an angry ancestor, and why; when a sacrifice should be performed, and with what offerings. It is possible to draw a richly detailed picture of village symbolic life and religious practices from ethnographic reports from fieldwork.

A Nameless but Active Religion: An Anthropologist's View of Local Religion in Hong Kong and Macau*

Tik-sang Liu

ABSTRACT Tik-sang Liu examines local religious practices in Hong Kong and Macau. He states that these constitute the foundation of local social organizations; they are the means with which local society is organized, local people are mobilized, communal activities are co-ordinated and people are prepared for their various stages in life.

In Hong Kong and Macau, people regularly organize temple festivals to celebrate the birthdays of their patron deities. People also regularly visit temples seeking the deities' blessings. A temple visit may be to ask for assistance when believers are facing difficulties or when they have health problems. Often people visit various patron deities, returning frequently until the problems are resolved. In order to communicate with the supernatural beings, people perform their own private rituals in temples, at ritual sites or in front of their own domestic altars. Interestingly, however, there is no agreed-upon name for these religious activities; some would even argue that they have no religious beliefs. Many people refer to their religious practices as "worshipping deities" (*baishen*) or "superstition" (*mixin*). Although people are aware of the negative implication of the word "superstition," they claim that it is the only known term to describe their religious practices. Some name their religious activities Buddhism or Daoism, as similar elements can be found in formal Buddhist or Daoist rituals. Professional Daoist priests or Buddhist monks and nuns are always hired to perform life cycle and communal rituals. To ordinary people, there is no clear boundary between Buddhism, Daoism and local religious practices.

In Hong Kong, there is no specific government office for religious affairs. In the government's view, Buddhism and Daoism are defined as "traditional Chinese religions." The deities in Chinese temples are considered either Buddhist or Daoist, while traditional festivals are defined as

* I would like to thank Kenneth Dean, Paul R. Katz and Daniel L. Overmyer for helpful comments on this article. I am particularly grateful to James L. Watson and Rubie S. Watson for their teaching and unfailing support. Fieldwork in Hong Kong's New Territories in 1990–91 was supported by a grant from the Joint Committee on Chinese Studies of the American Council of Learned Society and the Social Science Research Council. Further research in Macau and Hong Kong's New Territories in 2001 was made possible by a Direct Allocation Grant from the Hong Kong University of Science and Technology.

the practices of Chinese custom. Local religion is not an administrative category for the government.[1]

As for Hong Kong's local religion, there is no Hong Kong-wide organization or scripture accepted by all practitioners. However, local religion is very important to many Hong Kong people, is expressed in many different forms and plays an integral part in the practitioners' daily lives. People carry out ancestral worship at home, in ancestral halls or at the graves of their ancestors. People worship different deities, and participate in deity birthday festivals, communal Jiao festivals and Hungry Ghost festivals. Hong Kong residents try to locate their settlements, houses and ancestral graves according to the principles of geomancy, or *fengshui*.[2]

It is common to see local and individual variations in the celebration of the same festival as local religious activities are organized by local leaders with participants coming from diverse social backgrounds. The forms of religious expression are determined by local traditions, leadership and the availability of financial resources. Although lacking a unifying institution, local religion makes good use of elements coming from other religions and socio-cultural institutions. Hong Kong local religion is a flexible and highly adaptable cultural institution.

Religion is any human behaviour that relates humans to the supernatural world. Religion includes not only the ritual practices and organization, but also gives people a way to understand their world and the universe. People organize themselves as they organize religious activities; religion also explains for people the implications of their past, present and future. Anthropologists are interested in people's religious behaviour and thoughts.[3]

Many studies show that Chinese local religion operates in a passive mode. Based on his studies in Taiwan, Wolf argues that local religion is a reflection of people's conception of their social reality. The Chinese pantheon of deities is a mirror image of the imperial bureaucratic relations, while the ancestors and ghosts are a projection of the Chinese patrilineal kinship system.[4]

Anthropological studies of Hong Kong local religion show that local religious activities play an active role in ordinary people's social and daily life. Ward's study of Cantonese opera performances as part of temple festivals reveals that the content of the opera reflects people's view of the cosmos, and that the performance of the opera itself is also

1. Hong Kong Government, *Hong Kong 2001* (Hong Kong: Information Services Department, Hong Kong Special Administrative Region Government, 2002), pp. 393–98.

2. See Maurice Freedman, "Chinese geomancy: some observations in Hong Kong," in William Skinner (selected and introduced), *The Study of Chinese Society: Essays by Maurice Freedman* (Stanford: Stanford University Press, 1979), pp. 189–211.

3. See Clifford Geertz, "Religion as a cultural system, in his *The Interpretation of Cultures* (New York: Basic Books, 1973), pp. 87–125; Andrew B. Kipnis, "The flourishing of religion in post-Mao China and the anthropological category of religion," *Australian Journal of Anthropology*, Vol. 12, No. 1 (2001), pp. 32–46.

4. Arthur P. Wolf, "Gods, ghosts, and ancestors," in Arthur P. Wolf (ed.), *Religion and Ritual in Chinese Society* (Stanford: Stanford University Press, 1974), pp. 131–182.

an organized institution. The opera troupe operates according to strict religious tenets; it is an offering to the deity and a ritual to expel evil spirits[5] as well as a marker to reinforce (sub)ethnic identity.[6] Potter's study of a group séance held by three shamans in Ping Shan demonstrates that shamanism functions as a means of local social control. The women involved, both dead and alive, none of whom had any formal status in local politics, attempted, with the aid of malevolent ghosts, to influence the rich and successful men in the community.[7] After conducting a study in Ha Tsuen, Rubie Watson argues that grave rites performed by the Tang in Hong Kong's New Territories are ways of staging political and status conflicts, an opportunity for the Tang to claim their new political status.[8] James Watson illustrates that people in the New Territories have success-fully altered the functions of one of their local religious activities, the Jiao festival, from a parade defining territory to a ritual presentation express-ing their wealth and status. Furthermore, social and political order are of a real concern to the local dominant powers and to the state. The powerful lineages demand that the subordinate villagers participate in religious activities as a show of loyalty, whereas the state officials are concerned with orthopraxy, the correct forms of religious activities. When religious activities are arranged in the proper way, religious belief is not a problematic issue for the local powers and for the state.[9]

A Religion With No Political Boundary

Hong Kong is an immigrant society with a large section of its population coming from South China, especially from the neighbouring Zhu (Pearl) River Delta area. Most of these immigrants arrived after 1949, at the time of the Great Leap Forward, or the Cultural Revolution. Hong Kong shares local religious activities and cultural traditions with neighbouring communities in the South China region, although there are always local variations. Many temples and ancestral halls in China have

5. Barbara E. Ward, "Not merely players: drama, art and ritual in traditional China," *Man*, Vol. 14, No. 1 (1979), pp. 18–39.

6. Barbara E. Ward, "Regional operas and their audiences: evidence from Hong Kong," in David Johnson, Andrew J. Nathan and Evelyn S. Rawski (eds.), *Popular Culture in Late Imperial China* (Berkeley: University of California Press, 1985), pp. 161–187; Chi-cheung Choi's study of the annual Jiao festival in Cheung Chau demonstrates that the festival consistently reinforces the social boundaries among various (sub)ethnic groups on the island. "Reinforcing ethnicity: the Jiao Festival in Cheung Chau," in David Faure and Helen Siu (eds.), *Down to Earth: The Territorial Bond in South China* (Stanford: Stanford University Press, 1995), pp. 104–122.

7. Jack M. Potter, "Cantonese shamanism," in Wolf, *Religion and Ritual in Chinese Society*, pp. 207–232.

8. Rubie S. Watson, "Remembering the dead: graves and politics in southeastern China," in James Watson and Evelyn Rawski (eds.), *Death Ritual in Late Imperial and Modern China* (Berkeley: University of California Press, 1988), pp. 203–227.

9. James L. Watson, "Fighting with operas: processionals, politics, and the spectre of violence in rural Hong Kong," in David Parkin, Lionel Caplan and Humphrey Fisher (eds.), *The Politics of Cultural Performance: Essays in Honour of Abner Cohen* (London: Berghahn Books, 1996), pp. 145–159; see also his "The structure of Chinese funerary rites: elementary forms, ritual sequence, and the primacy of performance," in Watson and Rawski, *Death Ritual in Late Imperial and Modern China*, pp. 3–19.

been demolished over the last few decades; local religious activities have been attacked and banned, and in general have suffered from strong political suppression. Fortunately, local religious activities were allowed in Hong Kong and Macau,[10] as they pose no threat to the ruling colonial governments. There are religious exchanges between Hong Kong and Macau; for example, Hong Kong opera troupes are often hired to perform in temple festivals in Macau. My research on the western coast of Hong Kong[11] shows that there are constant exchanges between these two places, especially among fisherfolk who make their living at the mouth of the Zhu River estuary. The fisherfolk participate in temple festivals and religious events in both places, as a result of their mobility from their fishing activities.

The fisherfolk in Hong Kong's Tai O and in Macau worship Immortal Zhu (*Zhudaxian*) who was a deity from Pinghai, a fishing port 80 kilometres east of Hong Kong, along the South China coast. Those in Macau celebrate the deity's birthday in the first lunar month,[12] while in Hong Kong they celebrate the festival two months later. Both festivals follow the form of a Jiao festival, which pacifies the wandering ghosts near and in the water. Some of the fisherfolk continued participating in the festival in Macau even after they settled in Hong Kong, but others switched to the festival in Tai O.[13]

Hong Kong and Macau were hubs of local religious activities when "feudalistic and superstitious practices" were being eliminated on the mainland.[14] It is a mistake, however, to think that the two colonies have preserved the original religious activities, as these have been modified according to the colonial context.[15] It is fascinating to observe how these

10. For the historical development of temples in Macau, see Jonathan Porter, *Macau: The Imaginary City: Culture and Society, 1557 to the Present* (Boulder: Westview Press, 1996), pp. 161–186; Keith G. Stevens conducted a comprehensive study of 450 temples in Hong Kong and Macau. Although he divides all the temples into the categories of Buddhist, Confucian, Daoist and folk religion, temples in the two colonies share no major geographical distinctions. "Chinese monasteries, temples, shrines and altars in Hong Kong and Macau," *Journal of the Hong Kong Branch of the Royal Asiatic Society*, Vol. 20 (1980), pp. 1–33d.

11. See Tik-sang Liu, "Becoming marginal: a fluid community and shamanism in the Pearl River Delta of South China," PhD dissertation, UMI, Ann Arbor 1995; Liao Disheng (Tik-sang Liu) and Zhang Zhaohe (Siu-woo Cheung), *Da'ao: cong yugang dao dongfang Weinisi (Tai O: From a Fishing Village to "Oriental Venice")* (Hong Kong: Joint Publishing (HK) Co. Ltd., forthcoming).

12. Maritime Museum, *Da Jiu Festival of Macao's Fishing Community and the Cult of Chu Tai Sin* (Macau: Maritime Museum, Maritime Administration of the Macao Special Administrative Region, 2001).

13. Chen Yande, "Cong Aomen minsu kan dangdi jumin de Mazu chongbai" ("The folklore of local Mazu cult in Macau"), in Xu Xiaowang and Chen Yande (eds.), *Aomen Mazu wenhua yanjiu (The Study of Mazu Culture in Macau)* (Macau: Aomen jijinhui, 1998), p. 130; Liao and Zhang, *Tai O*.

14. See Anita Chan, Richard Madsen and Jonathan Unger, *Chen Village: The Recent History of a Peasant Community in Mao's China* (Berkeley: University of California Press, 1984), pp. 87–90.

15. See Liao Disheng (Tik-sang Liu), "You lianxiang miaoyu dao difang wenhua: Xianggang Xinjie Tianhou dan de difang zhengzhi yiyi" ("From an alliance temple to a local cultural symbol: the local political meaning of Tian Hou Cult in Hong Kong's New Territories"), in Lin Meirong, Zhang Xun and Cai Xianghui (eds.), *Mazu xinyang di fazhan*

local religious elements have been reintroduced to the mainland since China's gradual opening in the early 1980s.[16]

The Supernatural World and Supernatural Powers

Practitioners of local religion in Hong Kong and Macau believe that there are many different deities residing in the supernatural world, all under the leadership of a supreme deity, the Jade Emperor. Guandi (God of War), Beidi (God of the North), Tian Hou (Empress of Heaven), and Hongsheng (God of the South Sea) are common gods of the middle rank, while Earth Gods are on the lowest level. As Wolf suggests, the deities make up a hierarchical pantheon, which is a reflection of the practitioners' view of the official imperial structure: under the rule of an emperor, there are high-ranking officers as well as numerous local officials.[17] The outer and inner design of a typical temple resembles a government office, *yamen*, from the imperial time. This same government office appears in Cantonese operas as well as in television series and films about ancient stories. When worshippers of local religion seek a deity's blessing or assistance, they act in the same way people in the past were believed to do when they sought help from local government officials. Worshippers kneel, offer incense, food and paper products to the deity, much as they would have shown respect and offered gifts to officials in the government in the past.

Believers in local religion also think that all animals and natural landscapes have their individual spirits who can chose to help people with their supernatural powers. Despite their position at the bottom of the pantheon of gods and spirits, earth spirits can cause trouble for human beings if not taken care of and shown respect. In Hong Kong and Macau, people may worship old trees, rocks with special shapes and Earth Gods represented by rocks.

People also do their best to work with the supernatural power embedded in the natural landscape by following the system of *fengshui*,[18] in which "air" (*qi*) and "dragon vein" (*longmai*) are very important. In *fengshui*, one determines the location and direction of the "dragon vein" or "air" in the natural landscape and can then capture the supernatural force in the natural environment by manipulating the positions and directions of houses, settlements and ancestral graves.

---

footnote continued

yu bianqian (*The Development and Changes of Mazu Cult*) (Taiwan: Taiwan Association for Religious Studies, forthcoming).

16. Liao Disheng (Liu Tik-sang), "Chuanjian xin miaoyu: shenmei de suzao yu xinzhong de canyu" ("The construction of a new temple: a shaman's initiation and the devotees' participation"), in Centre for Chinese Studies (ed.), *Simiao yu minjian wenhua yantaohui lunwenji* (*Proceedings of Conference on Temples and Popular Culture*) (Taiwan: Council for Cultural Planning and Development of the Executive Yuen, 1995), pp. 693–94; Tik-sang Liu, *Becoming Marginal*, pp. 180–192.

17. Wolf, "Gods, ghosts, and ancestors," p. 145.

18. See also Jack M. Potter, "Wind, water, bones, and souls: the religious world of the Cantonese peasant," *Journal of Oriental Studies*, Vol. 8 (1970), pp. 139–153.

Localized Deities

Although people believe that the Jade Emperor occupies the highest position in the pantheon, he does not have the greatest power in solving people's problems. If a deity does not answer a devotee's requests, the devotee does not then go on to seek help from the Jade Emperor. In the eyes of the worshippers, different deities have different areas of expertise. Worshippers seek the god who will help them most in the area of difficulty; a minor Earth God might be the best choice.

Gods who share the same name may have different characteristics depending on the community. People accord local or ethnic distinctions to deities,[19] perhaps turning a popular regional deity into a local patron god and using the patron deity's temple festival to unite community members and to define the community boundaries.[20]

In the literary tradition, the Tian Hou worshipped in Hong Kong and the Mazu worshipped in Taiwan and Fujian are the same deity. The Taiwan Mazu temples trace their genealogical roots to the ancestral temple in Fujian's Meizhou.[21] In Hong Kong, however, the local communities are not concerned as to whether the deity they call Tian Hou has any relationship with the Mazu temple in Fujian or with Taiwan. Hong Kong worshippers do not trace the genealogical origin of their Tian Hou as do people in Taiwan. Tian Hou is considered to be a localized deity in Hong Kong, Macau and Guangdong. The common origin myth of a Tian Hou temple is that a deity image was found washed up on the beach, and a small shrine was built to house it. The small shrine was then rebuilt into a bigger one, and finally the deity became the community's patron god. People give their own Tian Hou a localized name, using the name of the place of the community as a prefix to the deity's name. Neighbouring Tian Hou goddesses are treated as sisters of their own deity and this sibling relationship justifies the worship of other Tian Hou deities in nearby communities. In this way, local religion becomes a reflection of the local social and political situation and the relationship among temple deities shows the relationship of neighbouring communities.[22]

The pantheon of local religion is an "open" system. New deities are introduced and others are ignored, forgotten and finally disappear from people's view. Also, the meaning and the role of a deity can be changed when society is undergoing transformation. Tian Hou became the most important deity along the South China coast when she was promoted by

19. John T. Myers, "Traditional Chinese religious practices in an urban-industrial setting: the example of Kwun Tong," in Ambrose Y.C. King and Rance P.L. Lee (eds.), *Social Life and Development in Hong Kong* (Hong Kong: Chinese University Press, 1981), pp. 284–86.
20. Watson, "Fighting with operas," pp. 150–51.
21. Steven P. Sangren, "Power and transcendence in the Ma Tsu pilgrimages of Taiwan," *American Ethnologist*, Vol. 20, No. 3 (1993), pp. 564–582.
22. Liao Disheng (Tik-sang Liu), "Difang rentong de suzao: Xianggang Tianhou chongbai de wenhua quanshi" ("The construction of local identity: the cultural interpretation of Tian Hou Cult in Hong Kong"), in Chi-tim Lai (ed.), *Daojiao yu minjian zongjiao (Daoism and Popular Religion)* (Hong Kong: Xuefeng wenhua shiye, 1999), pp. 118–134.

the imperial state.[23] Local societies do have a say in choosing their deities, though. They pick their own patron deities and neglect others. The fishing communities in Tai O and Tuen Mun are closely related through kinship and business ties, but they worship different patron deities.[24] The fisherfolk in Tuen Mun worship Tian Hou, while the Tai O fisherfolk worship Yanghouwang (General Yang). After salt producers and merchants took control of the Tian Hou temple in Tai O in the early Qing period, the fisherfolk shifted their attention to Yanghouwang, whose temple was located at the outskirts of the local town, and adopted him as their patron deity.[25]

During the last few decades, new deities have been introduced in urban areas. Wong Tai Sin[26] (Immortal Huang), a Daoist deity, was introduced in Hong Kong by some immigrants who were his devotees in Guangzhou, the capital of Guangdong province.[27] A small shrine for Wong Tai Sin was established in 1921 in a squatter area where the immigrants lived. He has grown in popularity with the growth of the immigrant population. The area around the temple has been developed into large government housing projects, and the first project,[28] completed in 1958, was named after the deity. In the early 1980s, Wong Tai Sin also became the name of an administrative district as well as the name of a station for Hong Kong's first subway, which brings in devotees from every corner of urban society.

The development of a new settlement and the introduction of the electric railway system helped change another little-known deity, Chegong (General Che), into a popular one. Chegong was originally a patron deity of a cluster of villages in Shatin. Shatin is now a town of about 628,000 residents,[29] and the railway brings in devotees from all over Hong Kong.[30] Recently, it has become a convention that the local leaders and government officials conduct a public divination to ask for fortune for Hong Kong people in the temple festival during the Lunar Chinese New Year.

23. James L. Watson, "Standardizing the gods: the promotion of T'ien Hou ('Empress of Heaven') along the South China coast, 960–1960," in Johnson, Nathan and Rawski, *Popular Culture in Late Imperial China*, pp. 292–324.

24. Eugene N. Anderson, *The Floating World of Castle Peak Bay* (Washington, DC: American Anthropological Association, 1970), pp. 160–61.

25. Liao and Zhang, *Tai O*.

26. The local form of romanization, Wong Tai Sin, is adopted in this article since it is an official place name in Hong Kong. The Mandarin form is Huangdaxian.

27. Graeme Lang and Lars Ragvald, "Upward mobility of a refugee god: Hong Kong's Huang Daxian," *Stockholm Journal of East Asian Studies*, No. 1 (1988), pp. 54–87; Graeme Lang and Lars Ragvald, *The Rise of a Refugee God: Hong Kong's Wong Tai Sin* (Hong Kong: Oxford University Press, 1993).

28. Currently, around 380,000 people reside in the government housing projects in the Wong Tai Sin district. See Home Affairs Department of the Government of the Hong Kong Special Administrative Region, "Wong Tai Sin: district highlights," in http://www.districtcouncils.gov.hk/wts/english/welcome.htm, 15 December 2002.

29. See Home Affairs Department of the Government of the Hong Kong Special Administrative Region, "Special features of Sha Tin," in http://www.districtcouncils.gov.hk/st/english/welcome.htm, 15 December 2002.

30. See also Graeme Lang, "Sacred power in the metropolis: shrines and temples in Hong Kong," in Grant Evans and Maria Tam (eds.), *Hong Kong: The Anthropology of a Chinese Metropolis* (Richmond: Curzon Press, 1997), p. 252.

There are Yanghouwang, Wong Tai Sin and Chegong temples in other parts of Hong Kong, but they are not as popular as the three temples mentioned above.

Religious Elements in a Household

In addition to temples, there are altars for ancestors and patron deities in individual households. As different as temple festivals in various communities may be from one another, most household altars are quite similar. The tablets for ancestors, Master of the Site (*dizhu*), Heaven God (*dangtian*), Kitchen God (*zaojun*) and Door God (*menguan*) are commonly found in families practising local religion. Guanyin (Goddess of Mercy), Guandi (God of War), and Luzu (Immortal Lü) are the most popular deity images people set up at home in order to invite fortune. Incense sticks are offered daily to the ancestors and deities, and more elaborate offerings are presented during major Chinese festivals and family members' life cycle rituals. In these domestic rituals, known as "worshipping deities" (*baishen*), the ancestors are the first to be worshipped, then the patron deities in the house, and last, the Master of the Site and the Door God. The order in which the gods are worshipped shows their hierarchical relationship in the household.

A household's religious set-up is made up of deities from the lower rank of the hierarchical pantheon, with the Door God and the Master of the Site being the very lowest rank.[31] This hierarchical pantheon links the household, from the bottom up, to the community and the state. In Wolf's reflection model, this is the people's ideal for the state's bureaucratic structure.[32]

Temple Festivals and Religious Organizations

In Hong Kong and Macau, temple festivals are organized to celebrate the deities' birthdays.[33] A temple festival is normally held for three or four days, with the deities' birthday falling in the middle of the celebration. Cantonese opera is the major activity and constitutes an offering to the deity. The opera is performed twice a day with a different four-hour play in the afternoon and evening. A large temporary stage is built in front of the temple, allowing the deity, on the altar inside the temple on the central axis, a good view. If the temporary stage has to be built away from the temple, a small travelling deity image must be carried to it. When this deity image is carried to the temporary stage, the procession is usually turned into a parade that ritually purifies "the deity's territory."

---

31. When people move away from their houses, many do not carry with them the deity images worshipped in their former houses. They rather leave those of lower rank gods in Earth God shrines or along the sides of a temple in the neighbourhood. People would acquire a new set of deity images for their new homes. This practice suggests that the deities belong to a special territory, where they are left by their worshippers.
32. Wolf, "Gods, ghosts, and ancestors."
33. See Chen Yande, "The folklore of local Mazu cult in Macau," pp. 136–140.

A temporary shrine is set up at the opposite side of the stage for the travelling deity image, and the community members may worship the deity when they attend the opera performance.

Before the 1970s, the "flower-cannon catching" activity (*qianghuapao*) was a popular activity on the day of the deity's birthday. "Flower-cannons" (*huapao*), made of colourful paper decorations, each carrying a small deity image which was empowered with the deity's blessing, were distributed to devotees.[34] Participants won a flower-cannon by catching a short, numbered stick shot out of a mini rocket. Whoever got a stick could keep the flower-cannon represented for a year, returning it the next year for someone else. To increase their chances, people formed flower-cannon associations (*huapaohui*). Violent fights among rival groups at popular temple festivals were frequently reported.[35] Subsequently, the police attempted to quell the violence by pushing organizers to distribute the flower-cannons by lottery.

Flower-cannon associations, large or small, are the popular form of participation in local religious events. People form associations based on religion, locality, ethnicity, gender or occupation. Most of the flower-cannon associations stop operating after the temple festival and resume their activities at the next year's festival. Social networks built on their membership, however, are maintained throughout the year. When the colonial governments restricted the formation of local social organizations and limited local political participation, flower-cannon associations became one of the popular ways people organized themselves at the local level.

Jiao Festival

A Jiao festival is a large-scale communal ritual staged in order to pacify wandering ghosts, to purify the community's territory and to reach a cosmic renewal. There is no common set time for a Jiao festival. On Cheung Chau, an island in Hong Kong, it is held once a year, but in some places, it is arranged in either a 30- or 60-year interval.[36] Most of the Jiao festivals are organized once every seven or ten years. The main Jiao ritual is usually held in the winter; a divination is conducted at the patron deity's temple at the beginning of the Chinese New Year in order to pick the ritual representatives among male community members for the forthcoming festival. A fortune-teller is hired to arrange the schedule of the Jiao activities believed to be beneficial to all participants. The fortune-

34. See also Liao Disheng (Tik-sang Liu), *Xianggang Tianhou chongbai* (*The Cult of Tian Hou in Hong Kong*) (Hong Kong: Joint Publishing (HK) Co. Ltd., 2000), pp. 79–95; Graham E. Johnson, "From rural committee to spirit medium cult: voluntary associations in the development of a Chinese town," *Contributions to Asian Studies*, Vol. 1, No. 1 (1971), pp. 141–42.

35. Watson, "Fighting with operas," pp. 153–54; Liao Disheng, "From an alliance temple to a local cultural symbol."

36. Cai Zhixiang (Chi-cheung Choi), *Da jiao: Xianggang de jieri he diyu shehui* (*Da Jiao: Festival and Local Societies in Hong Kong*) (Hong Kong: Joint Publishing (HK) Co. Ltd., 2000), pp. 10–11.

teller bases these calculations on the birth date and birth time of all the ritual representatives. Two smaller rituals to inform heaven of the Jiao festival are arranged in the middle of the year. For the major Jiao event, a huge temporary stage is constructed for the Daoist rituals and the Cantonese opera. Professional Daoist priests are hired to perform rituals – lasting several days – to pacify the wandering ghosts in the community. Everyone in the community eats only vegetarian foods during this period. After the Daoist ritual, a Cantonese opera is performed, also several days long, to celebrate the beginning of a new cosmic cycle.[37] To mark this new start, people in the community begin to eat meat once more.

A Jiao festival is a communal event, and all the temple deities as well as the local Earth Gods are invited to participate. Daoist priests lead the ritual representatives in carrying the travelling images of the temple deities to the ritual site, while villagers send the paper tablets of the neighbourhood Earth Gods. These invited deities have the responsibility of monitoring the rituals and also partake in the fun of watching the Cantonese opera.

In many Jiao festivals, a "walking the sub-district" (xingxiang)[38] ritual is arranged. The Daoist priests, ritual representatives and participating villagers walk over the community's territory.[39] Community leaders go with the ritual troupe to visit their alliance villages. The Jiao festival is a large-scale religious and social activity. It requires the social and financial support of local organizations; it is an event expressing the unity of the community.

Ancestral Halls and Deity Halls in Traditional Communities

The powerful dominant lineages in Hong Kong's rural area have a long settlement history. They occupy fertile land that had been used as rice paddies for hundreds of years until the early 1970s. These lineages operate under the principle of patrilineal descent so that the male members are united under the symbol of their apical ancestor, who is worshipped in the ancestral hall.[40] The lineage members register their names in the genealogy, thus justifying their right to claims on all lineage resources. The lineage's inalienable assets, usually in the form of land, are leased out to generate rental income. This supports regular ancestral worship activities as well as the maintenance of the ancestral hall. Until the early 1980s, a local security force (xunding) was organized by the

---

37. The arrangement of the opera performance in a Jiao festival is same as the ones in temple festivals. See also Ward, "Regional operas and their audiences."
38. In Cantonese, the name of the ritual has another homonymous meaning of "walking the incense."
39. See Watson, "Fighting with operas," pp. 150–51.
40. See Maurice Freedman, "Ancestor worship: two facets of the Chinese case," in Skinner, The Study of Chinese Society, pp. 296–312.

lineage to protect its community. The area patrolled by this security force included the ritual and political territory.[41]

The ancestors of a lineage are represented in the form of tablets kept on a huge altar at the centre of the ancestral hall. In this hall, lineage members conduct ancestral worship, and meet to discuss issues of the lineage community. The big ancestral halls have a large courtyard for collective rituals and meetings, and a kitchen to prepare food for hundreds of people who attend the collective activities.[42] The size and appearance of an ancestral hall shows the wealth and status of the lineage.

Lineage members call their first ancestor the "foundation-building ancestor" (*kaijizu*) or "carrying-pole-releasing ancestor" (*luodanzu*). He is recognized as the creator of the lineage, the one who bequeathed to his descendants the land where the lineage members now live. In the supernatural domain, the ancestors have the responsibility of protecting their descendants, and to help their descendants with the geomancy power transmitted through their graves.[43]

Under the patrilineal descent principle, only men can become members of their lineage and eventually become ancestors. The ancestors are the icons uniting all lineage members. The male members' life cycle rituals are conducted in the ancestral hall before the ancestors. During the first lunar month of the lunar year, the "lantern lighting" rituals (*diandeng*) are arranged at the ancestral hall for families of newborn babies. At a wedding, the new couple and the groom's father must go to the ancestral hall to worship the ancestors. Although death rituals are not conducted in the ancestral hall,[44] the souls of the dead are believed to join the other ancestors' souls in the collective tablet in the ancestral hall.[45]

Birth and marriage rituals are very important for newborn sons and married-in wives in order to confirm their inclusion in the lineage.[46] The ancestors are not only a religious symbol, but also a symbol of political unity: an extremely important symbol of local politics, religion and economy.

For several centuries, the fertile plains in Hong Kong's New Territories have been occupied by big lineages. Latecomers could only settle along the coast and in mountainous areas not suitable for paddy rice culti-

41. Hugh D. R. Baker, *A Chinese Lineage Village: Sheung Shui* (Stanford: Stanford University Press, 1968), pp. 79–83; Rubie S. Watson, *Inequality among Brothers: Class and Kinship in South China* (Cambridge: Cambridge University Press, 1985), pp. 94–97.

42. James L. Watson, "From the common pot: feasting with equals in Chinese society," *Anthropos*, No. 82 (1982), pp. 389–401.

43. See Watson, "Remembering the dead," p. 207.

44. James L. Watson, "Of flesh and bones: the management of death pollution in Cantonese society," in Maurice Bloch and Jonathan Parry (eds.), *Death and the Regeneration of Life* (London: Cambridge University Press, 1982), pp. 155–186.

45. See Watson, "Remembering the dead," p. 208.

46. A daughter does not have the right to inherit her father or the lineage's property, but her parents would prepare her a dowry for her wedding. After a woman marries, she has the right to be buried in her husband's lineage's territory and has a position in her son's ancestral altar when she dies. For the discussion of women's status in a lineage in Hong Kong's New Territories see Rubie S. Watson, "The named and the nameless: gender and kinship in the Hong Kong region, 1900–1940," *American Ethnologist*, Vol. 13, No. 4 (1986), pp. 619–631.

vation.[47] Working hard to survive with limited local resources and political power, these latecomers were not able to develop into dominant lineages. Some managed to form small single-lineage villages,[48] with their own ancestral halls and lineage worship activities. Some of the surname groups formed multi-surname villages: villages consisting of several surname groups.[49] The surname groups have their own small ancestral halls, but share a common temple, known as the deity hall (*shenting*), which is the centre for the village's religious activities. Some of the ritual activities which are normally performed in the ancestral halls have been moved and are now conducted in the common temple. The temple has become the centre of community activities for the different surname groups in a single village.

Alliance Temples

In imperial times, state power rarely reached China's southern edge. Local societies in Hong Kong's New Territories had to take care of their own security matters and resolve their own conflicts. Local politics were controlled by the big lineages, whose members firmly controlled local resources and defended their territories. Small villages had to depend on these powerful lineages for protection. To maintain their power, the large lineages solicited the support of their satellite villages by forming a regional alliance, *yue* (in Cantonese, *yuek*).[50] In areas where there was no powerful dominant lineage, villages joined together in a similar way in order to protect themselves against aggressive neighbours. These regional alliances united the lineages and villages within a particular territory sharing a common irrigation system, as Brim argues.[51]

Rather than choosing one lineage's ancestor to unite people with different surnames, people who formed a regional alliance would choose a patron deity as a symbol of their unity. The deity's temple became the place where *yue* members met for religious activities and political discussions.[52] *Yue* became the local political units involved in discussing disputes over land and water rights, something which sometimes resulted in local battles.[53] Those killed in the battles were worshipped in the

47. See Nicole Constable, *Christian Souls and Chinese Spirits: A Hakka Community in Hong Kong* (Berkeley: University of California Press, 1994), pp. 40–42; Tik-sang Liu, *Becoming Marginal*, pp. 12–20.
48. James L. Watson, "Hereditary tenancy and corporate landlordism in traditional China: a case study," *Modern Asian Studies*, Vol. 11, No. 2 (1977), pp. 161–182.
49. Judith Stauch, "Community and kinship in southeastern China: the view from the multilineage village of Hong Kong," *Journal of Asian Studies*, Vol. 43, No. 1 (1983), pp. 21–50.
50. David Faure, *The Structure of Chinese Rural Society: Lineage and Village in the Eastern New Territories, Hong Kong* (New York: Oxford University Press, 1986), pp. 100–127.
51. John Brim, "Village alliance temples in Hong Kong," in Wolf, *Religion and Ritual in Chinese Society*, pp. 93–103; see also Patrick Hase, "The alliance of ten: settlement and politics in the Sha Tau Kok area," in Faure and Siu, *Down to Earth*, pp. 123–160.
52. Brim, "Village alliance temples in Hong Kong."
53. See Watson, "Fighting with operas," pp. 148–49; Liao Disheng, "From an alliance temple to a local cultural symbol."

alliance temples. The heroes' altars are kept in a side chamber called Hero Hall. These kinds of altars are found in the Guanyin temple in Pat Heung, the Tian Hou temple in Shap Pat Heung, the Tian Hou temple in Lam Tsuen and the Tian Hou temple in Tsuen Wan.

Annual festivals at the alliance temples are events where the people of the member villages within the *yue* territory meet and express *yue* unity as well as define territorial borders. Jiao festivals take place regularly in order to pacify wandering ghosts, to renew community and the universe, and to thank the deities for protecting the community.[54] The alliance temple deity is the chief deity in the Jiao festivals. Participation of the member villages as well as the parade taking place during the Jiao festival are important acts in defining the community and the territorial boundaries.

Religious Activities in the Urban Setting

There are many old temples in the urban area, but this community's involvement in temple activities is not as great as that of the rural community. Many people would say that this is because the rapidly changing urban area and the highly mobile population makes it difficult to maintain a neighbourhood and a community identity. Another reason is probably the Hong Kong government's control of major temples in the urban area, discussed below. Urban people do continue to participate in religious activities, however.

During the last few decades, the size of Hong Kong's population has been affected by the social and political situation in China. Immigrants from China formed a large part of Hong Kong's population, especially during the 1950s and 1960s when there was political turmoil in China. Most of these immigrants first lived as squatters and then gradually moved to better and more secure areas when they had enough money to do so. It is very difficult for local religious activities to be established in a highly congested urban environment where there is such a shortage of space. In some early squatter settlements and government housing projects, newcomers established local altars or shrines housed in very simple structures. These have become hubs for local religious activities, as temple festivals were an opportunity for new immigrants to nurture their local identity. In the 1970s, for example, many shrines were established in many immigrant communities in Kwun Tong, Sau Mau Ping, Ngau Tau Kok, Chai Wan, Lok Fu and Tsuen Wan.[55] However, these local communities have to struggle with government officials in order to maintain the permanent shrines in their areas, and successful cases are very limited. Many of these temples are facing removal as the original communities have been resettled and the government is beginning to develop the land on which they once lived.

54. Chi-cheung Choi, "Reinforcing ethnicity"; Faure, *The Structure of Chinese Rural Society*, pp. 80–86.

55. Myers, "Traditional Chinese religious practices in an urban-industrial setting," pp. 275–288.

Like people in the country, people in urban settings feel that they must attend to wandering ghosts in the supernatural realm. In traditional communities, this is done by staging Jiao festivals. In the urban setting, people organize the Yulan, or Hungry Ghost, festival in the seventh lunar month. Many of these festivals are initiated and organized by the Chaozhou immigrants, but local residents and shopkeepers also support the events.[56] Many of the festivals take place in government housing projects where the immigrants live.

For a Yulan festival, a temporary stage is constructed in an open space, usually a basketball court or football field. To express their (sub)ethnic identity, Chaozhou Daoist priests are hired to perform the ritual for the ghosts, and a Chaozhou opera performance is arranged.[57] Recently, there has been a shortage of Chaozhou Daoist priests and opera troupes in Hong Kong, so organizers have taken to hiring priests and opera troupes from their home villages in Chaozhou.

The relationship between immigrants and their home villages is important when looking at local religious activities in the urban context. Although there are not many communal religious activities in the urban area, some immigrants participate in communal religious events in their home communities. The immigrants have their relatives, friends, lineage organizations, ancestral hall and ancestral graves in their home villages. When they conduct their rituals or ancestral worship at home, the rituals are not only just an urban event, but are directly tied to their native places.

Other Popular Beliefs

Many different schools of thought have grown up to explain the impact of the natural landscape on human settlements, and the methods of discovering the sacred force. The basic assumption is that the geomantic power can benefit all living things, but that the destruction of the natural landscape will generate "killing air" (*shaqi*)[58] that people must avoid.[59] Geomantic power is like a hidden treasure waiting for people to discover. In an anthropological sense, geomancy is magic; the acquisition of geomantic force has nothing to do with the morality of the discoverer. Anyone can hire a good *fengshui* master to identify the location of the force. One captures the beneficial power and avoids the harmful forces by manipulating the setting and direction of a building or the decorations

56. See Hang-shi Chiu, "Yaumatei and the Yu Lan festival," in P.H. Hase (ed), *In the Heart of the Metropolis: Yaumatei and its People* (Hong Kong: Joint Publishing (HK) Co. Ltd., 1999), pp. 150–59.

57. See Chen Shouren (Sau-yan Chan), *Shengongxi zai Xianggang: Yueju, Chaoju ji Fulaoju* (*Sacred Operas in Hong Kong: Guangdong, Chaozhou, and Fulao Operas*) (Hong Kong: Joint Publication (HK) Co. Ltd., 1996), pp. 29–32; Myers, "Traditional Chinese religious practices in an urban-industrial setting," p. 286.

58. The killing air could also be generated by a corpse when the flesh decomposed. Watson, "Of flesh and bones," pp. 158–59.

59. James Hayes, *The Rural Communities of Hong Kong: Studies and Themes* (Hong Kong: Oxford University Press, 1983), pp. 153–55.

inside a building. If an ancestor is buried in an ideal *fengshui* location, the ancestor's bones can transmit beneficial power to his descendants.[60]

In the country, the geomantic set-up of ancestral halls and ancestral graves is believed to affect the prosperity of the lineage, while the geomancy of a temple influences its supporting community. Although urbanites do not unite around ancestral halls, ancestral graves or temples, geomancy is still very popular. This belief that there are always beneficial and harmful forces affecting every aspect of people's daily life causes people to manipulate the interior design and decoration of their apartments in order to capture the geomancy force and expel evil forces.[61] Geomantic validations are often available when a new housing project is for sale.

Geomancy is a form of belief constituting the foundation of the local religion in South China. Interestingly, in an anthropological sense, the religious significance of *fengshui* has been turned into a language explaining human inequality and conflict. In the New Territories, *fengshui* explains the economic differences among branches of families who trace their descent from a common ancestor. The supernatural explanation of wealth eliminates possible conflicts between the rich and the poor.[62]

Fengshui is also a weapon used by local people to confront government or land developers when they destroy the natural landscape for construction projects.[63] It has become a resource used to halt the development or to negotiate for compensation. When the government compensates a community for a development project in which the natural landscape is destroyed, it is often set aside for a ritual to regain balance in the natural environment.[64]

In the city, the real estate business is very involved in *fengshui*. When a new housing project is ready to go on the market, developers release information showing that the building has good *fengshui*, much better than other buildings for sale. Like people in rural areas, urbanites also use *fengshui* to express and manipulate human conflicts. Once in a while, there is news of fighting among neighbours over *fengshui* conflicts.

Fengshui even became an issue on the state level during Hong Kong's return to China in 1997. There was a *fengshui* conflict between the Governor's House and the Bank of China building, a 70-storey skyscraper designed by the famous architect I.M. Pei. The triangular shape of the building was seen to be like a knife, with the sharp edge aimed at

60. See Watson, "Remembering the dead."
61. See also Charles F. Emmons, "Hong Kong's *feng shui*: popular magic in a modern urban setting," *Journal of Popular Culture*, Vol. 26, No. 1 (1992), pp. 39–49.
62. Watson, "Remembering the dead," pp. 214–15.
63. See also Hayes, *The Rural Communities of Hong Kong*, pp. 146–152; Sidney C. H. Cheung, "Land use and *fung-shui*: negotiation in the New Territories, Hong Kong," *Cultural Survival Quarterly*, Vol. 25, No. 2 (2001), pp. 70–71.
64. James Hayes, "Local reactions to the disturbance of 'fung shui' on Tsing Yi Island, Hong Kong, September 1977–March 1978," *Journal of the Hong Kong Branch of the Royal Asiatic Society*, Vol. 19 (1979), pp. 213–16.

the Governor's House, causing difficulties for the British side in the conflictual negotiations over Hong Kong's future.[65] The story goes that the British wisely planted a willow tree in the Governor's House garden between the two buildings. The branches of the willow tree were supposed to repel the evil effect of the bank building, solving the problem.

The Bank of China Building in Macau was completed in 1991, but it was built facing the Ferreira do Amaral Equestrian Monument, a five-ton bronze statue of "one of the most outstanding governors of Macau." In 1992, this monument was shipped back to Portugal to symbolize the decolonization process. It was popularly believed that the monument had really been removed because it was creating a harmful geomantic force against the Bank of China building.[66]

Beliefs about language also play a strong part in people's daily lives. During major festivals and life cycle rituals, people always want to hear auspicious remarks, which are believed to affect their fortune. If a remark has a negative implication, this could adversely affect one's future. In present-day Hong Kong, manipulating the meaning of numbers is also popular. The homonyms of some numbers are believed to bring the users good or bad luck. People want to have auspicious numbers for their home addresses, for the floor of the building they live in, for their licence plates and for their telephone numbers. The number "three" sounds like the word for "alive," and the number "eight" sounds like "prosperity," while the number "four" is avoided as it sounds like "death." Even if one does not completely believe the importance of obtaining some numbers and avoiding others, having good numbers shows a person's status, as it often takes substantial funds to get them.

Links to the Other World

Deities, ancestors and ghosts live in an invisible supernatural world which coexists with the natural world, allowing spirits to be closely involved in human matters. Once a human being leaves the natural world, people believe he or she enters the supernatural world as either a spirit or a ghost. All supernatural beings have the ability to affect human matters in the natural world.

The belief is that after death, people who have committed many faults during their lives are sent to hell to be tried. The dead people's children and relatives must hire specialists to conduct rituals in order to reduce the sufferings of the deceased in hell. Rituals are considered "virtue and merits" (*gongde*), and can counteract wrongdoing.[67] Spirits who do not get any of this attention become dangerous and can disturb people in the

65. Christina Miu-bing Cheng, "Resurgent Chinese power in postmodern disguise: the new Bank of China buildings in Hong Kong and Macau," in Evans and Tam, *Hong Kong: The Anthropology of a Chinese Metropolis*, pp. 102–123.

66. *Ibid.*

67. For the discussion of the Buddhist's concept of *gongde*, see Holmes Welch, *The Practice of Chinese Buddhism, 1900–1950* (Cambridge, MA: Harvard University Press, 1967), pp. 377–382.

natural world. Responsible descendants should worship their ancestors and provide them with sufficient paper and food offerings to deter them from turning into wild ghosts.[68] When the deceased has accumulated enough virtue and merits from living a good life and having been tended properly by descendants, he or she will go back to the natural world and be born a human being once more. The two worlds are linked by ghosts and by reborn human beings. Buddhist rituals are often arranged for dead people, as the Buddhist belief in rebirth fits the people's expectations.[69]

When people are in need of something, they seek help from the spirits, expressing their needs to the deities through simple rituals. Some people believe that a better result will be attained if the ritual is conducted by a specialist. Professional Daoist priests, known as *nanwu* (*nam mo* in Cantonese) are hired for the most important festivals or major life cycle rituals. These Daoist priests maintain their religious traditions by transferring their knowledge of rituals and of ritual techniques to apprentices, as well as making available standardized handbooks on rituals. Using standardized rituals, the Daoist priests deliver the clients' messages and ritual offerings to the supernatural world. The priests claim that they have to follow their traditions in order to conduct the rituals, but the local people who are their clients also demand they incorporate local practices, which have been passed down from their ancestors. It is common to see the "great" (the Daoist) and the "little" (the local) traditions presented in local religious rituals. Each ritual expresses the identity of the local community as well as the relationship between the local society and the state. In these rituals, the path of communication is a one-way street: the ritual specialists cannot read what the spirits may want to say to the people asking for their help.

In order to hear what the spirits have to say, some clients seek help from professional shamans, known locally as "rice-asking women" (*wenmipo*). The shamans go into a trance, and it is believed that they are possessed by spirits who can then communicate directly with those in the natural world.[70] In this way, clients can understand the needs of the spirits and take care of them, thus resolving their own problems which they believe have been caused by unhappy spirits.

Sacred Time

In local religion, time is regarded as a supernatural element to which attention must be paid. The popular almanac, *tongsheng*, is used to help pick the most auspicious timing for ritual activities. This almanac pro-

68. To express care for their ancestors, people not only offer traditional paper items, but also paper products in shape of items existing in the ordinary daily life, such as cellular phones, watches, sports shoes, houses, airplanes, cars, yachts or even domestic helpers. See Janet Lee Scott, "Traditional values and modern meanings in the paper offering industry of Hong Kong," in Evans and Tam, *Hong Kong: The Anthropology of a Chinese Metropolis*, pp. 223–241.

69. For the discussion of the Buddhist's concept of rebirth, see Welch, *The Practice of Chinese Buddhism*, pp. 179–181.

70. See Liao Disheng, "The construction of a new temple"; Potter, "Cantonese shamanism."

vides guidance based on the lunar calendar about the best and worst times of every day and every hour to perform various activities. The timing of a ritual, however, is not determined simply by the almanac; specialists are also hired. Based on the birth dates and times of the participants in the ritual or festival, an ideal timing is calculated in order to avoid evil impact and have the most auspicious results. For example, the rites included in a wedding are determined by the couple's birth dates and times. These rituals are believed to affect the life of the couple after the wedding, and are therefore very important and must be carefully timed. For a Jiao festival, the entire schedule of events is determined by calculations using the birth dates and times of all the participants in the ritual. Thus, the life cycles of individuals are linked to the major communal rituals.

People usually arrange communal temple festivals during the deities' birthdays. In order to achieve the best result, people often pick a particular time of day to begin the festival. For the Tian Hou festival at Yuen Long Shap Pat Heung, the organizers worship the deity on the eve of the festival, at midnight. They believe that this is the beginning of the festival. Most communities celebrate the festival at midday on the 23rd day of the third lunar month.

A Tradition of Opposition to Local Religion

The Chinese Confucian elite has a long tradition of disregarding local religions; "gods" and "ghosts" are considered inappropriate topics for discussion. Starting with the May Fourth movement, local religion in China was considerably beaten down. Considered "feudal superstition" and blamed for China's poverty and backwardness, local religious practices were criticized for not being scientific as they relied on divination to solve problems. Local religions were said to nurture people's selfish and utilitarian attitudes which were now obstacles to the industrialization and modernization of China.[71]

The educated elite in Hong Kong inherited some of this anti-local religious tradition and tend to ignore the existence of local religion. The school curriculum, for example, pushes the anti-local religion tradition, aided and abetted by the prevalence of Christian organizations in Hong Kong's school system. A large number of Hong Kong schools are run by volunteer associations with the government subsidizing their operational costs; many of these organizations are Protestant and Roman Catholic, and because of their own agendas, they are not eager to promote local religion.[72]

---

71. See also Myron L. Cohen, "Being Chinese: the peripheralization of traditional identity," *Daedalus*, Vol. 120, No. 2 (1991), pp. 127–29; Shuk-wah Poon, "Refashioning popular religion: common people and the state in Republican Guangzhou, 1911–1937," PhD dissertation, Hong Kong University of Science and Technology, 2001, pp. 80–113.

72. In 2001, the Protestant organizations operated 609 schools and kindergartens, while the Roman Catholic organizations operated 327 schools and kindergartens in Hong Kong. Hong Kong Government, *Hong Kong 2001*, pp. 393–98.

Co-optation and Suppression

There was no formal political participation at the local level in Hong Kong until 1982, when the District Board system was introduced allowing a general election of local political leaders. In the New Territories, there has been a Rural Committee system since the 1950s. Villagers elect representatives on to the Rural Committees which make suggestions to the government on local issues. In the colonial establishment, the District Board councillors or village representatives did not have much political influence on government decisions, the office being instead a symbol of social status. Local religious activities are also events where local leaders can show off their organizational and political skills.

The temple and Jiao festivals are communal events requiring the co-ordination and participation of community members. Each festival attracts tens of thousands of people. These events give local leaders the opportunity to exercise their leadership and management skills. Government officials fully understand the situation and are willing to participate in the ceremonies in order to endorse the local leaders' positions. There is always a presentation in religious events where government officials, guests and chief donors are publicly presented with gifts.

The presence of the government officials sends a clear signal of their power in the local community, and they are also endorsing the local leaders' positions. Most local leaders do not have a formal position in the local political structure, however, as they are co-opted into government politics by the officials' presence in local events.

Community members organize themselves into religious organizations in order to participate in temple festivals and in flower-cannon activities. The police require all religious organizations to apply for permission in order to organize a lion or dragon dance troupe to appear at a festival. Lighting firecrackers had always been popular celebratory activity, but after the riots of 1968 the government banned the use of fireworks on any occasion, although villagers do not really observe the regulation when they conduct major rituals. The government further suppressed any violence that might erupt during flower-cannon activities by encouraging their distribution by lottery.

Resources for the Heritage and Tourism Industry

Temple festivals and the like have recently become tourist draws in Hong Kong and Macau. A 20-metre marble Mazu (Tian Hou) statue,[73] a duplicate of the one in Mazu's homeland in China, was built on Macau's Coloane Island in 1998. In 2001, the Macau government organized a Mazu festival to promote tourism. This ritual, officiated by the Chief Executive of Macau, took place on the hill where the Mazu statue stands. A troupe of performers was brought in from Fujian to perform the

---

73. The official record of the height of the statue is 19.99 metres. It was reported to be the tallest Mazu statue in the world. *Wenhui bao* (*Wenhui Daily*), 29 October 1998.

"official" Mazu rite, and pilgrims from Taiwan's *Dajia Zhenlangong*[74] also participated by shipping their ritual possession decorations and the travelling Mazu deity to the festival.

The Hong Kong government does not play an active role in promoting local religious activities. Similar to Macau, however, tourism has been one of the reasons the government is interested in regulating religious activities. The most successful case in this respect is the conversion into touristic and sporting events of local dragon boat races held during the Duanwu festival. Local dragon boats race to have the honour of representing their communities in the International Dragon Boat Race, the winners of which will represent Hong Kong in other countries. Organizers successfully eliminated the religious element of this event, which was originally about pacifying wandering ghosts in the water.[75]

In recent years, many religious buildings have been declared to be part of Hong Kong's heritage. Many temples and ancestral halls, identified as historical buildings, have been renovated or preserved. The Hong Kong government provides funding and guidance in the renovation projects.[76] The function of these religious buildings changes, however, after renovation, as the religious centre is turned into a museum and is open to the public. The religious buildings in Ping Shan and Lung Yeuk Tau are featured under two "Heritage Trails,"[77] tours for the benefit of tourists, and these formerly religious buildings have become a cultural resource for the Hong Kong tourist industry.[78]

Conclusion

In the case of Hong Kong and Macau, local religion does not exist passively, but actively organizes local society. It is impossible to separate local religious activities from people's daily lives. Religious practices constitute the foundations of local social organizations; they are the means with which local society is organized, local people are mobilized, communal activities are co-ordinated and people are prepared for their various stages in life.

People organize religious activities for ancestors, gods and ghosts. Ancestral worship gives people a way to organize themselves according to the patrilineal descent principle. An apical ancestor binds his offspring's family to form a lineage, the most popular form of social

74. The same organization organizes the famous annual Mazu pilgrimage in Taiwan. For details see Meiying Huang, *Taiwan Mazu de xianghuo yu yishi* (*The Incense and Rituals of Taiwan Mazu*) (Taiwan: Zili wanbaoshe wenhua chubanbu, 1994).

75. See Yoshiro Shiratori (ed.), *The Dragon Boat Festival in Hong Kong* (Tokyo: Ethnohistorical Research Project, Sophia University, 1985).

76. In the last two years, the renovation of a temple and of an ancestral hall each won an award from UNESCO for local involvement in the preservation of local heritage.

77. See also Sidney C. H. Cheung, "The meanings of a heritage trail in Hong Kong," *Annals of Tourism Research*, Vol. 26, No. 3 (1999), pp. 570–588.

78. See Rubie S. Watson and James L. Watson, "From hall of worship to tourist center: an ancestral hall in Hong Kong's New Territories," *Cultural Survival Quarterly*, Vol. 21, No. 1 (1997), pp. 33–35.

organization in South China. All the lineage members are linked through the worship of their common ancestor, and their common assets are maintained under the name of the ancestor.

In an area where more than one surname group resides, a patron deity can act as a symbol to tie the different groups together. Once a state-approved deity is picked for worship, the local society has a legitimate reason to organize itself into social groups and gather together for festivals at a temple. The deity's birthday celebration is an event which mobilizes people, forms local social organizations and expresses unity. People also mobilize to pacify wandering ghosts, who are dangerous spirits that need to be dealt with. To do this, people organize Jiao festivals in the New Territories and Yulan festivals in the urban areas.

Gods, ghosts and ancestors are religious and philosophical concepts that are sanctioned by the state and by the educated elite. To maintain state authority over religious unity, the meaning of these concepts are tightly controlled and defined solely by state-approved philosophers and religions. However, they may not have any local meaning. There has always been a tendency for local societies to co-opt the concepts and make them part of their own cultures. In this localization process, geomancy plays a very important role. It explains how the local environment empowers deities, ancestors and even ghosts. It gives reasons for why one particular temple deity is more powerful than another, and how an ancestral grave can benefit the lineage members. Geomancy can also work in the opposite way, interacting with dangerous ghosts to harm local residents. Local people who believe in geomancy link the natural world to the supernatural world and connect the supernatural power of animatism with animated spirits.

The magical nature of geomancy gives it a "scientific" outlook, which gives it justification in the modern world. The assumption that it is scientific allows people to reject the attack of local religion as being superstition. Geomancy has been incorporated into the design of modern architecture, playing a part in explaining harmony as well as conflict between members of the hegemonic states in two colonies.

In the process of rapid urbanization, the size of supporting communities of communal religious activities is shrinking. Some local societies are having difficulty in raising funds for frequent religious celebrations. A few of them received support from their emigrant members who came home seeking their native place identity. The expressive aspects of local religion are promoted, but always in the name of tourism or cultural preservation. The religious and social significance of temples and ancestral halls are overshadowed by emphasis on their importance to the region's cultural heritage. Religious buildings are being treated as museums, while religious rituals are regarded as traditional performances.

Interestingly, these recently recognized elements of Hong Kong's cultural heritage have become the "authentic models" for South China's local societies to replicate. On the other hand, genealogical links are being established between temples in the mainland on one side and temples in Hong Kong and Macau on the other. In the near future, local religion will become a significant cultural linkage binding the three places within the "one country two systems."

Religion and the State in Post-war Taiwan

Paul R. Katz

ABSTRACT This article explores the development of local religious traditions in post-war Taiwan, particularly since the ending of martial law in 1987. It focuses on the factors underlying the ongoing popularity of temple cults to local deities such as Mazu (originally the goddess of the sea, now worshipped as an all-powerful protective deity) and the Royal Lords (*Wangye*; plague deities now invoked to counter all manner of calamities). Special attention is devoted to the complex relationship between local community-based religious traditions and the state, including the loosening of restrictions on festivals, the use of temples as sites for political rallies during local elections, and the recent controversy over attempts to stage direct pilgrimages to mainland China. Other issues include debates over the "indigenization" of religious traditions in Taiwan and the growth of academic organizations devoted to the study of Taiwanese religion.

This article explores the development of religion in post-war Taiwan, particularly since the ending of martial law in 1987. In contrast with China, where religion is only now gradually emerging from the shadow of long-term oppression by a totalitarian regime,[1] in Taiwan religion is thriving and even expanding. Freedom of religion has always been guaranteed under the constitution of the Republic of China, article 13 of which clearly states, "the people shall have freedom of religious beliefs." However, now that Taiwan has developed into a democracy, people can practise the religious tradition of their choice without fear of state suppression. Members of any religious faith are free to congregate and introduce their belief systems to others, while previously outlawed sectarian religions such as the Unity Sect (*yiguan dao*) now operate openly and continue to expand. Taiwan's democratic environment has also furthered the growth of large-scale groups of lay Buddhists and the sangha, such as the Compassionate Relief Merit Society (*ciji gongde hui*).

Another striking facet of religion in Taiwan is that economic growth and technological development have not resulted in the decline of religious practice; on the contrary, many educated men and women who surf the web on a daily basis apparently feel no qualms about practising religion (in fact, most large religious organizations and temples now have their own websites). Religion continues to play an integral role in individual, family and community life, and temple cults in particular have retained their importance as sites for daily worship, community service and massive festivals. Popular deities such as Mazu (originally the goddess of the sea, now worshipped as an all-powerful protective deity) and the Royal Lords (*Wangye*; originally plague deities but now invoked

---

1. See the articles by Daniel Bays, Raoul Birnbaum, Nancy Chen, Kenneth Dean, Fan Li-chu, Richard Madsen and Pitman Potter in this issue.

to counter all manner of calamities) are still worshipped for their ability to provide health and prosperity, while temples themselves continue to contribute to the formation of local identity.

Government statistics about temples, albeit unreliable in their categorizing all temples as either Buddhist or Daoist, as well as their failure to count unregistered temples and household shrines (*shentan*),[2] can give some sense of the ongoing growth of temple cults. For example, according to the *Revised Edition of the Taiwan Provincial Gazetteer* (*Chongxiu Taiwan sheng tongzhi*), the number of "Buddhist" and "Daoist" temples in Taiwan had nearly doubled in the space of 50 years, from 3,661 in 1930 to 5,531 in 1981.[3] According to statistics compiled by the Ministry of the Interior, by 2001 Taiwan was home to a total of 9,707 "Buddhist" and "Daoist" temples that had registered with the state. These temples currently operate a total of 20 hospitals and clinics (as opposed to 35 hospitals and clinics run by Catholic organizations, and 26 hospitals and clinics run by Protestant organizations), as well as 180 schools ranging from kindergarten to university (186 Catholic; 158 Protestant).[4]

In recent years, some scholars have begun to consider the degree to which political and socio-economic changes have influenced the development of religious traditions. For example, David Jordan cites four major transformations in post-war Taiwan that have affected its religious development: increasing wealth, changes in government policy, more widespread education and increasing geographic mobility. Jordan shows that greater wealth has led to the construction of ever more ornate temples, but that in urban areas exorbitant real estate prices may be inhibiting the building of new temples. In terms of government policy, he notes a trend from suppression and control to tolerance combined with gentler attempts to "reform" practices deemed to be wasteful or otherwise undesirable (see below). Jordan also claims that education may be prompting a greater degree of religious "standardization," and that greater geographic mobility has reduced traditional ideas of regionalism and may even be contributing to the formation of a pan-Taiwanese identity.[5]

Scholars like Robert Weller and Meir Shahar have also studied the ways in which religious traditions have the potential to resist state attempts at imposing cultural hegemony. Their research has centred on cults associated with the unruly dead, or eccentric deities like Jigong, a 12th-century monk renowned for his spiritual powers despite a distinct penchant for eating meat and drinking wine. Such cults became extremely popular during the Everybody's Happy (*dajia le*) lottery craze of the

2. See for example Sung Kuang-yü, *Gaoxiong shi gequ simiao shentan minglu* (*A List of Temples and Altars in Kaohsiung's Districts*) (Kaohsiung: Kaohsiung City Documents Commission, 1993).

3. See *Chongxiu Taiwan sheng tongzhi, juan 3, zhumin zhi, zongjiao pian* (*Revised Edition of the Taiwan Provincial Gazetter, Volume 3, Treatise on Inhabitants, Chapter on Religion*) (Nantou: Taiwan sheng wenxian weiyuan hui, 1992), pp. 975–1065.

4. For more details, see the Ministry of the Interior's website: www.moi.gov.tw/.

5. David K. Jordan, "Changes in postwar Taiwan and their impact on the popular practice of religion," in Stevan A. Harrell and Huang Chün-chieh (eds.), *Cultural Change in Postwar Taiwan* (Boulder, CO: Westview Press, 1994), p. 138.

1980s. Weller's fascinating case study of the cult of the 18 Lords (Shiba wang gong) in post-war Taiwan describes how the spirits of 17 men and their loyal canine companion ended up receiving offerings of cigarettes and other items from people wishing to make a quick profit, including prostitutes and members of Taiwan's criminal underworld. Efforts by the state and even the temple committee itself to mould popular opinion proved largely fruitless, which reflects the ability of local society to fulfil its own spiritual and ritual needs while proving largely impervious to attempts at state control.[6] The recent inauguration of the Lotto lottery in January 2002 has prompted a new wave of worship of Taiwan's unruly gods, although the current fervour has been somewhat tempered by the fact that more and more Taiwanese are choosing to rely on computer programs to try to predict winning numbers.[7]

Perhaps the greatest amount of research has been done on sectarian religions, lay Buddhist movements and so-called "new religions" (xin-xing zongjiao), all of which are credited for stressing "religious neo-traditionalism" while also focusing on the needs of the individual. However, the majority of this research has treated the histories of such religions, biographies of their leaders or textual analyses of their scriptures, especially so-called "morality books" (shanshu).[8] Only a few scholars, notably Philip Clart, David Jordan, Daniel Overmyer and Gary Seaman, have paid much attention to the sociological aspects of sectarian religions in Taiwan.[9] In recent years scholars like Chiang Ts'an-t'eng, Charles B. Jones, André Laliberté and Robert P. Weller have begun to study how

6. See Meir Shahar, *Crazy Ji. Chinese Religion and Popular Literature* (Cambridge, MA: Harvard University Press, 1998); Robert P. Weller, "Identity and social change in Taiwanese religion," in Murray A. Rubinstein (ed.), *Taiwan. A New History* (Armonk: M.E. Sharpe, 1999), pp. 352–56.

7. Those interested in the current links between local religion and Lotto in Taiwan should visit the following website (http://tw.yahoo.com/) and input the key word *shenming pai.*

8. See for example Joseph Bosco, "Yiguan dao: 'heterodoxy' and popular religion in Taiwan," in Murray A. Rubinstein (ed.), *The Other Taiwan, 1945 to the Present* (Armonk, NY: M.E. Sharpe, 1994), pp. 423–444; Cheng Chih-ming, *Taiwan xinxing zongjiao xianxiang: chuantong xinyang pian (The New Religions Phenomenon in Taiwan: Traditional Beliefs)* (Ta-lin: Nan-hua Business College, 1999); Soo Khin Wah. "A study of the Yiguan dao (Unity Sect) and its development in peninsular Malaysia," PhD thesis, University of British Columbia, 1997; Sung Kuang-yü, *Tiandao chuandeng – Yiguan dao yu xiandai shehui (The Celestial Way and the Transmission of the Lamp – The Unity Sect and Modern Society)* (Taipei: San-yang Publishing Company, 1996); Wang Chien-ch'uan and Li Shih-wei, *Taiwan de zongjiao yu wenhua (Religion and Culture in Taiwan)* (Lu-chou: Po-yang wen-hua, 1999); Wang Chien-ch'uan and Li Shih-wei, *Taiwan de minjian zongjiao yu xinyang (Popular Religion and Beliefs in Taiwan)* (Lu-chou: Po-yang wen-hua, 2000); Wang Chih-yü, *Taiwan de Enzhugong xinyang (The Cult of the Lords of Benevolence in Taiwan)* (Taipei: Wen-chin Publishing Company, 1997).

9. See Philip A. Clart, "The ritual context of morality books: a case study of a Taiwanese spirit-writing cult," PhD thesis, University of British Columbia, 1996; Philip A. Clart, "The phoenix and the mother: the interaction of spirit writing cults and popular sects in Taiwan," *Journal of Chinese Religions*, No. 25 (1997), pp. 1–32; David K. Jordan and Daniel L. Overmyer, *The Flying Phoenix: Aspects of Chinese Sectarianism in Taiwan* (Princeton: Princeton University Press, 1986); Gary Seaman, *Temple Organization in a Chinese Village*, in Lou Tzu-K'uang (ed.), *Asian Folklore and Social Life Monographs*, Volume 101 (Taipei: The Orient Cultural Service, 1978).

Buddhism has interacted with the state.[10] Their research has centred on the Unity Sect, as well as the Compassionate Relief Merit Society, and the data they have collected convincingly demonstrate the importance of religious activity in modern Taiwan.

The contributions of the scholars cited above have been many and varied, but many have tended to overlook the importance of local religious traditions, especially community temple cults, in contributing to the relationship between state and society in post-war Taiwan. For example, in his recent book *Alternate Civilities*, Robert P. Weller demonstrates how certain religious organizations and institutions have contributed to Taiwan's democratization and socio-economic development. Weller's research rightly emphasizes the importance of supposedly new religious phenomena such as sectarian religions and lay Buddhist movements. For example, he convincingly argues that the Compassionate Relief Merit Society is perhaps the largest civil organization in Taiwan, and serves as an intermediate institution between the private world and the state. He also points out that sectarian organizations like the Unity Sect are voluntary associations that transcend traditional ties of community and kinship, and that both sectarian religions and lay Buddhist organizations fit criteria for civil society in being voluntary and popular nation-wide. In these respects, Weller argues, they differ from temple cults, which are often ascriptive and popular on the local and regional levels.[11]

Weller's data and arguments are highly convincing, but also raise some important questions. For example, he may overstate the novelty of sectarian religions and lay Buddhist associations. Such organizations flourished throughout Chinese history, particularly during periods of dynastic transition or rapid socio-economic growth.[12] What appears new

10. See Chiang Ts'an-t'eng, *Taiwan Fojiao bainianshi zhi yanjiu, 1895–1945* (*The History of Buddhism in Taiwan during the Past Hundred Years, 1895–1945*) (Taipei: SMC Publishing Company, 1996); Chiang Ts'an-t'eng, *Dangdai Taiwan Fojiao* (*Buddhism in Contemporary Taiwan*) (Taipei: SMC Publishing Company, 1997); Charles B. Jones, *Buddhism in Taiwan: Religion and the State, 1660–1990* (Honolulu: University of Hawai'i Press, 1999); André Laliberté, "Mainstream Buddhist organizations and the Kuo Min Tang, 1947–1996," in Philip A. Clart and Charles B. Jones, (eds.), *Religion in Postwar Taiwan* (Honolulu: University of Hawai'i Press, forthcoming)

11. See Robert P. Weller, *Alternate Civilities: Democracy and Culture in China and Taiwan* (Boulder, CO: Westview Press, 1999), pp. 14–16, 83–84, 87–88, 93, 99–101, 357–58. Weller tends to overlook the importance of Presbyterianism. See Murray A. Rubinstein, "Mission of faith, burden of witness: the Presbyterian Church in the evolution of modern Taiwan, 1865–1989," *American Asian Review*, Vol. 9, No. 2 (1991), pp. 70–108; Murray A. Rubinstein, "Christianity and democratization in modern Taiwan," in Clart and Jones, *Religion in Postwar Taiwan*.

12. See for example Kenneth Dean, *Lord of the Three in One: The Spread of a Cult in Southeast China* (Princeton: Princeton University Press, 1998); Susan Naquin, "The transmission of White Lotus sectarianism in late imperial China," in David Johnson *et al.* (eds.), *Popular Culture in Late Imperial China* (Berkeley: University of California Press, 1985), pp. 255–291; Daniel Overmyer, "Values in Chinese sectarian literature: Ming and Ch'ing *pao-chüan*," in *ibid.* pp. 219–254; Daniel Overmyer, *Precious Volumes: An Introduction to Chinese Sectarian Scriptures from the Sixteenth and Seventeenth Centuries* (Cambridge, MA: Harvard University Press, 1999); Barend ter Haar, *The White Lotus Teachings in Chinese Religious History* (Leiden: E. J. Brill, 1992).

in the post-war era is that women can now participate in public activities with enhanced legitimacy, and that in Taiwan such organizations now operate on the national level. Perhaps most importantly, however, Weller overlooks the ways in which temple cults have begun to influence Taiwanese culture and politics.[13] This article argues that the importance of temple cults has not only persisted but even increased in modern Taiwan, because temples are no longer strictly local but now play a role on the national stage as well. This issue is examined in two ways: tracing changes in state policy towards local religious traditions, and documenting ways in which religious beliefs and practices have affected the state. Therefore, while this article begins by describing state policies towards religion and the changing role of the Council on Cultural Affairs (Wen-hua jianshe weiyuanhui or Wenjian hui for short; hereafter abbreviated as CCA) in attempting to assert state control over temples and festivals, it then proceeds to discuss attempts by candidates to utilize local religion to shape the outcome of elections, and the recent controversy over attempts by certain Mazu temples to undertake direct pilgrimage to the goddess's natal home in Meizhou (Fujian). Other related issues include the roles temples still play in resolving legal disputes, debates over the indigenization of religion in Taiwan and the growth of academic organizations devoted to the study of Taiwanese religion.

Government Policy

One of the main problems confronting Taiwan's post-war rulers has been how to maintain some measure of state control over local religious traditions in the face of increasing democratization and cosmopolitanism. Such concerns are grounded in the Chinese state's traditionally ambivalent attitude towards its localities. In his article above about state regulation of religion in China, Pitman B. Potter observes that in China, the relationship between religion and state power has long been contested. Dynastic relations with religious organizations included attempts to capture legitimacy through ritual, while local religious traditions continued to thrive outside official control. As scholars like Hsiao Kung-ch'üan have documented, the Chinese imperial state endeavoured to control local society and culture through a combination of coercive and persuasive policies.[14] In the realm of religion, for example, the state attempted to sponsor or symbolically support local cults that matched its "orthodox" or "Confucian" agenda in an attempt to "standardize" local religion and

13. The fact that Weller downplays the importance of temple cults as forces on the national level may be because he often relies on the work of scholars whose work has focused on the late imperial or early republican eras, when temple cults rarely attained importance at the national level. See for example Prasenjit Duara, *Culture, Power, and the State: Rural North China, 1900–1942* (Stanford: Stanford University Press, 1988); James Watson, "Standardizing the gods: the promotion of Tien Hou ('Empress of Heaven') along the South China Coast, 960–1960," in *Popular Culture in Late Imperial China*, pp. 292–324.

14. Hsiao Kung-ch'üan, *Rural China: Imperial Control in the Nineteenth Century* (Seattle & London: University of Washington Press, 1960).

"superscribe" the state's political agenda on to local society.[15] At the same time, however, the state frequently attempted to suppress sectarian religions and so-called "secret societies," particularly groups that openly espoused millenarian ideologies with the potential to resist or overthrow the established order.[16] The success or failure of the Chinese state's cultural policies varied depending on the state's strength in a particular region at a particular time, but its agenda tended to remain relatively fixed over time.

State attempts to control local culture became somewhat more complex during the late 19th and early 20th centuries, as a result of the impact of Western technology and culture. During the May Fourth Movement in 1919, some intellectuals called for the widespread adoption of Western culture, arguing that traditional Chinese culture was preventing China's successful modernization.[17] Such views were highly prevalent during the Republican era, but were by no means universal or unchallenged. For example, other intellectuals continued to advocate the study of Chinese history and traditional culture despite being influenced by Western ideas, while a group of folklorists began detailed research on China's popular culture.[18] For its part, the Nationalist (Kuomintang or KMT) state attempted to find a middle ground between these two positions, while also promoting policies such as the New Life Movement (*Xin shenghuo yundong*) of 1934, which attempted to use traditional "Confucian" values and Sun Yat-sen's "Three Principles of the People" (*San min zhuyi*) to maintain social stability and unify popular support for the KMT.[19]

The history of cultural policies in Taiwan overlaps somewhat with that of China, but also features some important differences. As John Shepherd has shown, the Qing dynasty also attempted to implement various cultural policies after it assumed control over Taiwan. These policies, like those in the rest of Qing China, centred on the areas of education and religion, and had the common goal of maintaining social control and asserting cultural hegemony.[20] However, things began to change when the Japanese took over Taiwan following the Sino-Japanese War. During the colonial era (1895–1945), the colonial government was largely tolerant of Taiwan's indigenous culture, with the exception of those groups that resisted

15. Daniel Overmyer, "Attitudes toward popular religion in the ritual texts of the Chinese state: *The Collected Statutes of the Great Ming*," *Cahiers d'Extrême-Asie*, No. 5 (1989–1990), pp. 191–221. See also Duara, *Culture, Power, and the State*; Watson, "Standardizing the gods."

16. See especially ter Haar, *The White Lotus Teachings*; ter Haar, *Ritual and Mythology of the Chinese Triads: Creating an Identity* (Leiden: E.J. Brill, 1998).

17. See Chow Tse-tsung, *The May Fourth Movement: Intellectual Revolution in Modern China* (Cambridge, MA: Harvard University Press, 1960); Vera Schwarcz, *The Chinese Enlightenment: Intellectuals and the Legacy of the May Fourth Movement of 1919* (Berkeley: University of California Press, 1986).

18. See Hung Chang-tai, *Going to the People: Chinese Intellectuals and Folk Literature, 1918–1937* (Cambridge, MA: Council on East Asian Studies, 1985).

19. For an overview, see Jonathan D. Spence, *The Search for Modern China* (New York: Norton, 1990), pp. 361–434.

20. See John R. Shepherd, *Statecraft and Political Economy on the Taiwan Frontier, 1600–1800* (Stanford: Stanford University Press 1993), pp. 208–214.

its authority, particularly sectarian organizations. By the 1930s and 1940s, though, the advent of Japanese military campaigns in East Asia caused the colonial government to promote the Kōminka Movement (1938–45) in Taiwan (and Korea as well), when the authorities attempted the "Japanization" of their colonial subjects. During these years, the authorities displayed a much more repressive attitude towards Taiwanese culture and religion, destroying a number of temples and their statues and persecuting some local religious specialists.[21]

After the Nationalist government assumed control over Taiwan following the end of the Second World War, it was acutely aware of the impact of Japanese culture on the Taiwanese people during the colonial era, and attempted to implement changes that would promote a form of state-approved Chinese culture and enhance the KMT's legitimacy. However, before these policies could be implemented mismanagement combined with economic depression and various misunderstandings sparked the February 28 Uprising.[22] In the years following these tragic events, KMT cultural policy appears to have evolved according to a three-stage pattern described by Edwin Winckler.[23] During the first stage (1945–60), KMT policies tended to focus on negative control, especially in the realms of language and education. The second stage (1960–75) marked a period of gradual transition. The KMT began to spend more money on the natural sciences, the social sciences and the humanities (particularly at Academia Sinica), but also had to confront a significant brain drain as members of the elite who went abroad often failed to return. At the same time, however, it continued its policy of cultural restraint, especially in terms of suppressing the media.[24] The third stage (1975–90) saw the KMT faced by a series of crises on both the domestic and international fronts. In terms of cultural policies, it responded to these problems by investing more heavily in science and technology, as well as placing greater emphasis on and providing increased funding for cultural programmes.

Murray Rubinstein has made the important observation that during the first two stages the Nationalist government actively attempted to discourage pan-Taiwanese cults, a policy that only began to change during the 1980s and has now been almost completely abandoned.[25] For example, as

21. See Chou Wan-yao, "The Kōminka Movement in Taiwan and Korea: comparisons and interpretations," in Peter Duus, Ramon H. Myers and Mark R. Peattie (eds.), The Japanese Wartime Empire, 1931–1945 (Princeton: Princeton University Press, 1996), pp. 40–68; Ts'ai Chin-t'ang, Nihon teikoku shūgi ka Taiwan no shūkyō seisaku (Religious Policies during the Period of Japanese Rule over Taiwan) (Tokyo: Dohsei Publishing Company, 1994).

22. See Lai Tsehan, Ramon H. Myers and Wei Wou, A Tragic Beginning: The Taiwan Uprising of February 28, 1947 (Stanford: Stanford University Press, 1991). See also Steven E. Phillips, "Between assimilation and independence: the Taiwanese elite under Nationalist Chinese rule, 1945–1950," PhD thesis, Georgetown University, 1998.

23. See Edwin A. Winckler, "Cultural policy in postwar Taiwan," in Harrell and Huang, Cultural Change in Postwar Taiwan, pp. 28–35.

24. See especially Ming-Yeh T. and Gary D. Rawnsley, Critical Security, Democratization, and Television in Taiwan (London: Ashgate Publishing Company, 2000).

25. See Murray A. Rubinstein, "Statement formation and institutional conflict in the Mazu Cult: temples, temple-created media, and temple rivalry in contemporary Taiwan," in Chou Tsung-hsien (ed.), The International Academic Conference on the History of Taiwan: Society, Economics, and Colonization (Taipei: Kuo-shih kuan, 1995), pp. 189–224.

early as 1968 the Ministry of the Interior promoted a series of guidelines in an attempt to regulate local religion by "improving frugality in folk sacrifices" (*gaishan minjian jidian jieyue banfa*).[26] Emily Martin Ahern's study of festivals in the northern Taiwanese town of San-hsia clearly shows that such policies did have an impact on local religion during the 1970s, despite local resentment and attempts at passive resistance.[27] However, as David Jordan points out, in the long run the reduction in the scale of festivals and feasting may be less attributable to government policy than the transition from an agricultural to an urbanized society.[28] During this period, many intellectuals sided with the state, and did not hesitate to label local religious traditions as "superstition" (*mixin*) in their writings.[29]

As Taiwan's Nationalist government began to shift the emphasis of its cultural policies from mere negative control to promotion of its own agenda combined with regulation of cultural elements it found unsavoury, two government agencies were formed to be responsible for supervising the island's local culture.[30] The larger and more important of these was the Committee for the Revival of Chinese Culture (Zhonghua wenhua fuxing weiyuan hui or Wenfu hui for short; hereafter abbreviated as CRCC), which was established in August 1967 as a response to the Cultural Revolution in China (1966–76). This agency was mainly responsible for promoting the KMT's vision of Chinese culture (referred to as Zhongyuan wenhua or Zhonghua wenhua), which combined traditional Confucian values such as loyalty to the state and filial piety with doctrines created by party leaders like Sun Yat-sen and Chiang Kai-shek. The CRCC enacted a number of programmes to inculcate these ideas, including: "What citizens should know about daily life [activities]" (*Guomin shenghuo xuzhi*),[31] which focused on patriotic values and proper

---

26. For more on these and other government regulations, see Chiu Hei-yuan, "Zhonghua minguo youguan zongjiao 'faling' ji faling caoan huibian" ("Compendium of laws and draft bills concerning religion in the Republic of China"), *Field Materials, Institute of Ethnology, Academic Sinica*, No. 2 (1990), pp. 113–139; Chiu Hei-yuan, "Changing relationships between state and Church in Taiwan," paper presented at international conference entitled Taiwan: State and Society in Transition, University of Illinois at Urbana-Champaign, 21–23 September 1997. See also *Taiwan sheng jingwu dang'an huibian – Minsu zongjiao pian* (*Taiwan Police Administration Archives – Folk Religion*) (Taipei: National History Office, 1996).

27. See Emily Martin Ahern, "The Thai Ti Kong Festival," in Emily Martin Ahern and Hill Gates (eds.), *The Anthropology of Taiwanese Society* (Stanford: Stanford University Press, 1981), pp. 416–425. See also Hill Gates Rosenow, "Prosperity settlement: the politics of Paipai in Taipei, Taiwan," PhD thesis, University of Michigan.

28. Jordan, "Changes in Postwar Taiwan," pp. 148–150.

29. See for example Juan Ch'ang-jui, "Ruhe duanzheng minjian zongjiao xinyang" ("How to reform popular religion and beliefs"), in Li Yih-yuan and Chuang Ying-chang (eds.), *Minjian zongjiao yishi zhi jiantao yantaohui lunwenji* (*Proceedings of the Conference on Evaluating the Rituals of Popular Religion*) (Nankang: Institute of Ethnology, Academia Sinica, 1985), pp. 130–144.

30. For more on these two agencies, see Shih Chih-hui, " 'Zhonghua wenhua fuxing yundong' yanjiu" ("Research on the Movement to Revive Chinese Culture"), MA thesis, National Taiwan Normal University, 1995.

31. This movement was modified in the mid-1980s, and renamed "What modern citizens should know about daily life [activities]" (Xiandai guomin shenghuo xuzhi).

behaviour; and "Models for citizens' rites and ceremonies" (*Guomin liyi fanli*), which attempted to shape religious practice by stressing the importance of good manners and simple (that is, not lavish or expensive) rituals (see above). The CRCC drew up handbooks to promote these movements, and their contents were widely publicized through the mass media, as well as at schools and government offices. Throughout most of its existence, the CRCC stood for the KMT's ideal of a pan-Chinese culture, and tended to oppose the growth of indigenous Taiwanese culture, including temple cults. By the late 1980s, ongoing democratization and the rise of opposition parties such as the Democratic Progressive Party (DPP) had begun to affect the degree to which the CRCC could enact the programmes it desired. In the summer of 1990, stiff opposition in the Legislative Yuan resulted in the elimination of the CRCC's budget, thus marking the formal end of this agency. The KMT preserved a portion of the CRCC in the spring of 1991 by creating a non-government organization known as the General Committee of the Movement to Revive Chinese Culture (Zhonghua wenhua fuxing yun-dong zonghui).[32]

The second government agency responsible for cultural policies was the Bureau of Culture (Wenhua ju), which was created by the Ministry of Education in November 1967 and existed until May 1973. This agency assisted the CRCC in promoting the KMT vision of Chinese culture, although its efforts tended to concentrate more on the realm of education. For example, the Bureau helped the CRCC set up 96 branch offices in various colleges and universities, and sponsored over 300 lectures at these schools during its brief seven-year existence. In addition, it also engaged in various publication projects, and sponsored a number of local and international conferences on Chinese culture.

The current agency in charge of cultural policy, the Council on Cultural Affairs (CCA), was formed during the third stage of KMT cultural policy, at a time when Taiwan was gradually becoming a more cosmopolitan society and taking its first steps towards democracy. The establishment of the CCA, which was known as the Cultural Council for Planning and Development (CCPD) until 1995, can be traced back to an administrative report to the Legislative Yuan delivered on 23 September 1977 by the late president Chiang Ching-kuo, who was serving as premier at the time. This report, and a subsequent report to the Legislative Yuan in February 1978, stressed the importance of preserving and developing Taiwan's culture. In order to implement these ideas successfully, the Executive Yuan announced "Proposals for strengthening cultural and recreational activities" in February 1979 and began to plan for establishing an agency to carry out these proposals, the CCPD. The Executive Yuan officially established the CCPD on 11 November 1981. It was listed

32. For an introduction to the General Committee of the Movement to Revive Chinese Culture, please see www.ncatw.org.tw/Info.php.

as a first-level agency (the functional equivalent of a ministry), and placed under the direct control of the Executive Yuan.[33]

At the time of its founding, the CCPD was placed in charge of ten tasks, including the research and drafting of important policies for cultural development, the promotion and protection of cultural assets, and the establishment of local cultural centres (*wenhua zhongxin*).[34] These goals have changed somewhat. According to the "Guiding principles and objectives" (*shizheng linian yu mubiao*) section of the CCA's website, its current goals include: rectifying Taiwan's "fast-food culture" mentality, unifying cultural administrative authority, encouraging corporate sponsorship, investment or patronage of arts groups and activities, and integrating culture and technology.[35]

One of the most striking features of the CCA's self-proclaimed goals is their failure to mention one of the key nodes of traditional Taiwanese culture, namely temples. This contrasts with the early years of its existence, when the CCPD seemed to be working to replace temples and other traditional public spaces as a focus for promoting and even controlling Taiwanese culture. Such an attitude can be seen in the following statement presented by Shen Hsüeh-yung, the third chairperson of the CCPD, in a report to the Central Standing Committee of the KMT on 21 October 1993:

Let us look at our history in retrospect. How did our society evolve? How did the traditional villages, towns and communities consolidate their common identity through various folk art and cultural activities before the cultural centres and the government's cultural administrative systems came on to the scene? What bonded them to a system of mutual ethical beliefs, rituals and rules of order? A unique and united society was created ... under the auspices of temples and through various cultural and artistic temple activities ... In the face of dramatic social transitions, the traditional social structure in Taiwan, bonded by a common religious belief, has broken down irreversibly. Is there an alternative system ... to take over the social function performed by community temples in the past? ... We have always hoped that the municipal and county community activity centres and cultural centres would be able to shoulder the responsibility of social construction ... I believe that through planned campaigns these [state-sponsored activities] will penetrate levels of communities more deeply ... The political connotation of this strategy is apparent. If government authorities do not give priority to the absorption of the private sector's

33. This discussion of the CCPD/CCA is based on Paul R. Katz, "Cultural policies in late twentieth century Taiwan: a case study of the Council on Cultural Planning and Development," paper presented at the conference Taiwan: State and Society in Transition. For more on the history of the CCPD/CCA, as well as its current activities, see www.cca.gov.tw.

34. See Chen Chi-lu, "Xingzheng yuan Wenhua jianshe weiyuanhui gongzuo baogao" ("Report on work undertaken by the CCPD of the Executive Yuan"), *Yijiubasi nian Beimei huaren xueshu yantaohui taolun beijing cankao ziliao* (*Reference Materials on the Background of the North American Chinese Conference of 1984*), pp. 1–22.

35. For more on the CCA's current goals, see www.cca.gov.tw.

social resources, then the ruling party is handing this valuable asset over to its opponent.[36]

This remarkable statement is particularly notable because it reflects the government's increasing appreciation of the constructive roles temples have played (and in fact still do play) in Taiwanese society. This represents a significant change in traditional Chinese policy, which in the past tended to focus on reforming local cults, reducing the size of festivals and otherwise combating "superstition" (see above). In recent years, the government has attempted to reform some festivals by helping to sponsor them while also attempting to regulate their contents (for example, the Floating Lanterns' Festival in Keelung and the Boat Festival of Tung-kang (East Haven), albeit with rather mixed results.[37] Whether the CCA and its cultural centres (many of which are now run by the bureaus of culture of county governments) can actually replace temples as key public spaces is far from certain, but the very fact that the government is paying attention to this problem indicates a major transformation in state attitudes towards Taiwan's local religious traditions. At the same time, more and more temples in Taiwan are beginning to compete with the CCA by sponsoring their own cultural activities, from chess tournaments to classes in traditional music, literature and calligraphy to large-scale re-enactments of Koxinga's landing at Luerhmen. Some temples have even been co-operating with the CCPD/CCA in planning and carrying out some cultural projects.[38] If one enters the Chinese term for temple (*simiao*) into the search engine for the CCA's website, it will provide a total of 133 entries consisting of reports or articles published in the mass media that detail this agency's links with temples from the 1990s to the present day. These data indicate that officials at the CCPD/CCA have begun to show more restraint in attempting to reform local religious traditions, and have begun to appreciate the importance of temples as public spaces that contribute to the formation or strengthening of Taiwanese culture.

The data presented above clearly show that the state has had to give ground in its efforts to control community temple cults in post-war Taiwan. However, since Taiwan began to democratize during the 1980s, temple cults have been more than passive observers of government policy; they have played an important role in furthering local interests and asserting local identity. The sections below discuss the following examples of this phenomenon: the roles temples play in local elections, the ways in which elites who manage some renowned Mazu temples have

36. See Shen Hsüeh-yung, "Special topical report to the Central Standing Committee of the Kuomintang," 21 October 1993. See also "Report to the Education Committee of the Legislative Yuan, Second Session, Second Triennial," 8 December 1993.

37. See Chuang Ying-chang and Huang Mei-ying, "Guanguang yu minsu zongjiao de jiehe – yici guanban yingshen saihui zhi jiantao" ("The combination of tourism and folk religion – an evaluation of one state-sponsored festival"), in Li and Chuang, *Proceedings of the Conference on Evaluating the Rituals of Popular Religion*, pp. 56–68.

38. See Virginia Sheng, "Sacred bases for secular service," *Free China Review*, Vol. 45, No. 10 (1995), pp. 26–33.

attempted to influence Taiwan's cross-straits policy, and the importance of judicial rituals performed at temples.

Local Religion and the Electoral Process

One striking example of the diverse forms of interaction between local religious traditions and the state may be found in the presidential election of 2000, during which candidates such as Chen Shui-bian, Hsü Hsin-liang, Lien Chan and James Soong (Sung Ch'u-yü) attempted to attract grass-roots support and work with local elites by actively campaigning at temples to popular local deities such as Mazu. According to an article published in the 14–18 March 2000 issue of the weekly magazine *The Journalist* (*Hsin hsin-wen* (*Xin xinwen*)), representatives of the Lien campaign actively publicized supposedly miraculous events that occurred at temples, including the spontaneous flaring up of incense burners, while Lien himself professed to be optimistic about his chances after one of his supporters drew an auspicious poem (*qianshi*) in the course of a divination ritual. Other KMT legislators claimed that Jigong had declared his intention to support Lien. Not to be outdone, supporters of Soong, especially Yen Ch'ing-piao, the chairman of one of the island's most popular Mazu temples (the Zhenlan Gong of Ta-chia in Taichung county; see below), held divination rituals of their own to demonstrate that the goddess was solidly behind Sung. As for the eventual winner, Chen Shui-bian, he attempted to shore up his strongest base of support in southern Taiwan by claiming that the region's Royal Lords supported his cause. In addition, his party (the Democratic Progressive Party or DPP) set up a special sub-committee to organize rallies held at temples, as well as publicize supposedly miraculous occurrences linked to the Chen campaign and those of candidates for the Legislative Yuan. One example involved predictions of Chen's victory by the Golden Mother of the Jasper Pool (Yaochi jinmu) during spirit-writing rituals.

Local Religion and Cross-Straits Links

While Taiwan's political establishment has attempted to take advantage of local temples to win elections, some aspiring local politicians have attempted to turn the tables by using temple cults to advance their own interests against those of the state. One recent example of the intense and also complex links between religion, politics and identity in contemporary Taiwan involves the attempt by the Zhenlan Gong to undertake a direct pilgrimage to Mazu's ancestral temple in Meizhou.[39] When Taiwan and China established informal contacts back in 1987, people from Taiwan who rushed across the Taiwan Straits included war veterans who had accompanied Chiang Kai-shek from China to Taiwan after the fall of

---

39. For a lengthier account of the events summarized above, see the introduction to Paul R. Katz and Murray Rubinstein (eds.), *Religion, Culture, and the Creation of Taiwanese Identities* (New York: St. Martin's Press, forthcoming).

the Republic of China in 1949, as well as businessmen and industrialists seeking a chance to make a profit. However, one of the largest and most visible groups of travellers was pilgrims from Taiwan seeking their religious roots in China. One of the first pilgrimages to China was undertaken by the Zhenlan Gong, which took advantage of the occasion to assert its legitimacy and authority as one of Taiwan's leading Mazu temples. Between 1987 and 2000, numerous temples organized pilgrimages to China, but because of restrictions on cross-strait contacts were always forced to take indirect routes through third countries such as Hong Kong. More recently, Chinese worshippers and officials also brought a statue of Mazu from Meizhou to Taiwan (via Hong Kong) for a pilgrimage of their own in 1998, a move which caused great controversy among Taiwanese Mazu temples concerning which of them were willing to welcome this "Chinese Mazu".

During the winter of 2000, however, some of Taiwan's Mazu temples laid plans to challenge the status quo. The leadership of the Zhenlan Gong, which included the former Speaker of the Taichung County Council Yen Ch'ing-piao, initiated an effort to organize a direct pilgrimage from Ta-chia to Meizhou. It was around this time that Yen attempted to establish himself as local elite, religious leader and political kingmaker, by declaring his support for the presidential candidacy of James Soong. The issue of direct pilgrimage to China became more pressing during the spring and early summer, with Yen Ch'ing-piao and KMT members of the Legislative Yuan and National Assembly from central Taiwan gathering at the Zhenlan Gong on 4 June to throw divination blocks in order to determine a date for the pilgrimage. The ritual proceeded smoothly, with the goddess setting 16 July as the departure date. From this point, a political tug-of-war ensued between Chen Shui-bian's new government (which tends to oppose reunification with China) and members of the opposition, including elected representatives of the KMT, the New Party and Soong's newly formed People First Party (PFP). At the same time, Chinese officials, particularly local officials from Fujian who anticipated a windfall yet were also well aware of the symbolic importance of Taiwanese pilgrims travelling directly to China, made every effort to express their willingness to allow a direct pilgrimage, albeit with some strings attached (for example, only vessels from China or Hong Kong could be used to transport pilgrims). Caught in the middle were members of the government's Mainland Affairs Council, who pointed out that regulations governing direct links between Taiwan and China had not been passed, and that there was no way to guarantee the safety or rights of pilgrims who participated in this event. As for Chen Shui-bian, he attempted to persuade the Taiwanese people that going on direct pilgrimage to China would only serve China's propaganda efforts. Finally, the Zhenlan Gong relented, and chose to take the usual indirect route through Hong Kong. On the surface, this represented a victory for the DPP, but representatives of local temples who also enjoy nation-wide influence continue to pressure the new government to change its policies.

The situation has changed since the opening of the "Small three links" (*xiao san tong*) in January 2001, which allowed direct shipping links between Chin-men (Quemoy) and Matsu, and Xiamen and Mawei in Fujian province. On 2 October 2002 a large group of Taiwanese pilgrims made a direct voyage to China from Kaohsiung via Chin-men. The 426-member delegation, jointly organized by ten temples dedicated to Mazu, was the largest pilgrimage group to visit China since the opening of direct Chin-men–Xiamen shipping services. More such activities are highly likely to occur in the future.

Local Religion and the Judicial System[40]

Another fascinating example of how some temples work to bridge the gap between state and society involves the performance of judicial rituals, especially oaths and indictments made in the presence of gods of the underworld. The rite of making an oath before a god has long played an important role in local election campaigns, and in some cases candidates accused of lying or vote-buying would behead live chickens in temples dedicated to the gods of the underworld as a way of demonstrating their innocence.[41] Chicken beheadings are not performed often in Taiwan today, mainly due to pressure from local animal rights groups, opposition on the part of temples where such rites used to be staged and a general sense of disgust at their bloody nature. However, chicken-beheading rituals occasionally function as a metaphor in local political campaigns. For example, when James Soong was accused of wrongdoing during his presidential campaign, a local political cartoon depicted him performing a chicken-beheading ritual in order to emphasize his innocence.[42] Oaths unaccompanied by chicken beheadings are still performed today as a form of dispute resolution, and political figures will not hesitate to make oaths in popular local temples. In one example, when Yen Ch'ing-piao was accused of extortion and attempted murder, he made an oath in the Zhenlan Gong proclaiming his innocence.[43]

Indictment rituals, which date back at least a millennium, continue to be popular in Taiwan today, perhaps in part due to ongoing dissatisfaction with the legal system. For example, at sites like the Dizang Abbey (Dizang An), a popular temple in the city of Hsin-chuang in Taipei county, jointly dedicated to the Bodhisattva Dizang (Dizang wang pusa) and a controller of unruly ghosts known as the "Lord of the Hordes" (Dazhong ye), over 3,000 people a year continue to file indictments against individuals they feel have wronged them. Perhaps the most renowned indictment was filed at this temple by the television actress Pai

40. For more on the significance of judicial rituals, see Paul R. Katz "Divine justice: chicken-beheading rituals in Japanese occupation Taiwan and their historical antecedents," in Wang Ch'iu-kuei, Chuang Ying-chang and Chen Chung-min (eds.), *Proceedings of the International Conference on Society, Ethnicity, and Cultural Performance* (Taipei: Centre for Chinese Studies, 2001), pp. 111–160.

41. See Li Yih-yuan, "Zhan jitou" ("Chicken-beheading rituals"), in *Shitu, shenhua, yu qita* (*Master-Pupil, Myth, and Other Things*) (Taipei: Cheng-chung, 1983).

42. See the 18 December 1999 issue of *Ziyou shibao* (*The Liberty Times*), p. 15.

43. See the 30 April 2001 issue of *Zhongguo shibao* (*The China Times*), p. 6.

Ping-ping, following the kidnap and brutal murder of her teenage daughter Pai Hsiao-yen by three local gangsters. Members of the temple committee followed the case with intense interest, and crossed out photographs of each man on a wanted poster circulated by the police as each one was captured or killed. Local police and prosecutors have also been known to burn incense and/or file indictments at the temple in order to help solve difficult criminal cases. For example, when an investigation into a major bank robbery dragged on for months without a breakthrough, the Chief of the Police Administration made offerings at the Abbey, following which the robber was apprehended. In another case, a suspected arsonist refused to confess until prosecutors brought him to the Abbey and filed an indictment with the Lord of the Hordes.

Academic Research on Local Religion

Like the state, Taiwanese intellectuals have begun to change their traditionally conservative attitudes towards local religious traditions, and the vast majority now present religion in a positive light in their writings. The past decades have witnessed the publication of a substantial body of research about the importance of religion in post-war Taiwan. The *Bibliography of Taiwanese Folk Religion*, edited by Lin Mei-rong, remains the most comprehensive collection of bibliographic data available to date, although Laurence G. Thompson's *Chinese Religions: Publications in Western Languages* provides better coverage of Western research.[44] In addition, Chang Hsün, Chiang Ts'an-t'eng and Randall Nadeau have completed thorough state of the field reports with detailed bibliographic data.[45] David Jordan and Yü Guang-hong have published well-written analyses of religious growth in post-war Taiwan, while *Religion in Postwar Taiwan*, edited by Philip A. Clart and Charles B. Jones, contains numerous essays on this subject.[46]

Social scientists, especially a group led by Chiu Hei-yuan of the Institute of Sociology, Academia Sinica, have completed substantial

44. See Lin Mei-rong (ed.), *Taiwan minjian xinyang yanjiu shumu (zengding ban)* (*A Bibliography of Taiwanese Folk Religion (Revised and Enlarged Edition)*) (Nankang: Institute of Ethnology, Academia Sinica, 1997). The Association of Asian Studies has published three volumes of Thompson's bibliography: the first up to 1980, the second from 1981 and 1990, and the third (also edited by Gary Seaman) from 1991 to 1995. Philip A. Clart has continuously updated the bibliography, and the fruits of his efforts may be found at http://web.missouri.edu/ ~ religpc/bibliography CPR.html.

45. See Chang Hsün, "Guangfu hou Taiwan renleixue Hanren zongjiao yanjiu zhi huigu" ("A review of anthropological studies of Han Chinese religion in Taiwan"), *Bulletin of the Institute of Ethnology, Academia Sinica*, No. 81 (1996), pp. 163–215; Chiang Ts'an-t'eng and Chang Hsün (eds.), *Taiwan bentu zongjiao yanjiu daolun* (*Reader in Contemporary Religious Studies in Taiwan*) (Taipei: SMC Publishing Inc., 2001); Randall Nadeau and Chang Hsün, "Gods, ghosts, and ancestors: religious studies and the question of 'Taiwanese Identity',' in Clart and Jones, *Religion in Postwar Taiwan*.

46. See Jordan, "Changes in postwar Taiwan and their impact on the popular practice of religion"; Yü Guang-hong, "Taiwan diqu minjian zongjiao de fazhan" ("The development of popular religion in Taiwan"), *Bulletin of the Institute of Ethnology, Academia Sinica*, No. 53 (1983), pp. 67–105; Clart and Jones, *Religion in Modern Taiwan*.

research on Taiwan's religious traditions.[47] The results of their most recent project, based on questionnaires administered to 2,333 individuals, provide valuable data on religious beliefs and practices in Taiwan today. For example, the data indicate that sūtra-recitation, breath control and meditation are common among members of both sectarian and lay Buddhist movements. Other important topics include the impact of urbanization and rural–urban migration on religious beliefs, as well as forms of charitable giving to temples and religious movements.[48] There appear to be some methodological problems, however: categories like "Daoism" (*Daojiao*) and "folk beliefs" (*minjian xinyang*) are not rigorously defined, and while 1,851 questionnaires were administered at random, 482 were distributed to the leadership of small-scale religious movements to administer to their own believers. Nevertheless, these data go a long way towards quantifying the changes observed by many other historians and ethnographers.

One key step forward is the formation of the Taiwan Association of Religious Studies (Taiwan zongjiao xuehui; hereafter abbreviated as TARS). TARS was founded on 18 April 1999 when 37 professors and researchers from academic institutions throughout Taiwan gathered for an inaugural ceremony at the Institute of Ethnology, Academia Sinica. During the past two years, membership has increased to well over 400, including faculty, students, independent scholars, religious practitioners and religious organizations. Long before TARS came into existence, many scholars in Taiwan from fields like history and anthropology had been doing research on religion. However, at that time religious studies had not been established as an independent discipline. Taiwan's first Department of Religious Studies was founded in 1992 at Catholic Fu-jen University, and in the next few years ten other universities followed suit. More recently, National Chengchi University established an Institute of Religion in 1999, which has an MA programme in religious studies.[49] As a result, Taiwanese scholars became increasingly aware of the need for establishing a professional association for individuals interested in studying religion. TARS was created as a response to this awareness. It also attempts to reflect the multi-disciplinary nature of religious studies in Taiwan by being a broadly inclusive organization. Moreover, its membership is not restricted to academics; members of religious organizations are also welcome to join.

At present, TARS holds lectures and seminars on a monthly basis, and has begun to publish the *Taiwan Journal for Religious Studies*. It continues its efforts to bring together individuals from different back-

47. See Chiu Hei-yuan, "Taiwan diqu minzhong de zongjiao xinyang yu zongjiao taidu" ("Popular religious beliefs and attitudes in the Taiwan region"), in Yang Kuo-shu and Chiu Hei-yuan (eds.), *Bianqian zhong de Taiwan shehui (Taiwan Society in Transition)* (Nankang: Institute of Ethnology, Academia Sinica, 1988), pp. 239–276.
48. See the essays presented in *Zongjiao yu shehui bianqian (Religion and Social Change)*, Conference Proceedings, Academia Sinica, Institute of Sociology, 23–24 February 2001, especially pp. 17–18, 63, 87, 114, 196.
49. The Institute's website is located at www.religion.nccu.edu.tw.

grounds who are pursuing work in religious studies. Its lectures and seminars, as well as publications like the newsletter and the new journal, facilitate the circulation and exchange of data and ideas among scholars and members of the religious community in Taiwan. However, TARS does not intend to be simply an organization for Taiwanese; it also includes members from other nations, including China, Japan, Europe, Canada and the United States.[50]

Taiwanese scholars also frequently refer to local religion as part of the ongoing debate over cultural identity. Like other debates about identity the world over, this discourse has centred less on discernible and objective distinctions between two groups of people (in this case mainland Chinese and Taiwanese) than on perceived differences often inextricable from the realm of sentiments and beliefs. Some papers presented at academic conferences over the past few years have been notable in their attempts to define Taiwanese religion as a cultural phenomenon unique to Taiwan. These papers also view religion in Taiwan as being based on a sense of identity that largely excludes China as a source of cultural tradition. Whether this new sense of identity has gained widespread acceptance among the people of Taiwan, or has only been embraced by some of the island's intellectuals and politicians, remains to be determined. Nevertheless, the impact of such arguments on academic discourse has been considerable, with an increasing number of scholars attempting to find ways in which southern Chinese religious traditions have adapted to Taiwan's unique historical conditions. At the same time, however, such arguments appear to have had little impact on the general public, and local religion does not appear to be deepening divisions between the island's different ethnic and sub-ethnic groups.[51]

Conclusion

The evidence presented above shows that the relationship between state and society in post-war Taiwan is entering a new phase, in part a result of the island's political development and economic growth, but also in part a result of the increasing influence of local religious traditions at the national level. As noted at the beginning of this article, local community-based religious traditions in traditional China tended to survive in local societies beyond the scope of state control. In Taiwan today, however, local religious traditions are not merely autonomous but

50. Those interested in learning more about TARS can visit its website at http://140 109 24 171/taoist/.
51. For more on identity debates in Taiwan, see Thomas B. Gold, "Civil society and Taiwan's quest for identity," in Harrell and Huang, *Cultural Change in Postwar Taiwan*, pp. 50–53, 59, and Alan M. Wachman, *Taiwan: National Identity and Democratization* (Armonk: M.E. Sharpe, 1994). For more on how identity debates have influenced the study of Taiwanese religion, see Paul R. Katz, "Morality books and Taiwanese identity – the texts of the palace of guidance," *Journal of Chinese Religions*, No. 27 (1999), pp. 69–92; Katz and Rubinstein, *Religion, Culture, and the Creation of Taiwanese Identities*; Nadeau and Chang, "Gods, ghosts, and ancestors"; P. Steven Sangren, "Anthropology and identity politics in Taiwan: the relevance of local religion," *Fairbank Center Working Papers*, No. 15, 1996.

actively involved in attempting to mould state policy to meet community needs. Not only are cults and festivals flourishing, they are also intricately connected to Taiwan's political, social and even judicial realms.

The fact that this has occurred should not come as a surprise to those who have studied religion and society during the late imperial and modern eras. Temple cults have long constituted one of the most important public spaces or arenas in late imperial Chinese or Taiwanese society, and have been key arenas where elites and representatives of the state vied to assert or reinforce their dominance over local society. Evidence in the form of temple inscriptions (*miaobei*) and placards (*bian'e*) reveals that for centuries officials have not hesitated to support prominent local temples, particularly those to deities who had been included in the state cult. Thus, both representatives of the state and local elites had vested interests in supporting local religious traditions. Although their goals may have differed (officials tended to be more interested in control, while elites endeavoured to enhance their power and legitimacy), both recognized that temples were important public spaces where state and society could interact.[52] In Taiwan today, democratization has further enhanced the importance of local power, and prompted representatives of the state to be more proactive in terms of tapping into local resources, particularly key public spaces such as temples. A similar process may be beginning in China. Kenneth Dean's article in this issue indicates that local society is reasserting its autonomy in South-east China, while temple networks are once again functioning as a second government in the sense of providing services and mobilizing the population. The extent to which the growth of local religious traditions may have a long-term impact on the relationship between state and society in China, Taiwan and Hong Kong remains to be seen, but the outpouring of new ethnographic work on China, as well as the continuing efforts of scholars researching Taiwan and Hong Kong, should give us a more comprehensive perspective on this issue in the future.[53]

52. See Paul R. Katz, "Temple cults and the creation of Hsin-chuang Local Society," in T'ang Hsi-yung (ed.), *Papers from the Seventh Conference on Chinese Maritime History* (Nankang: Sun Yat-sen Institute of Social Sciences, 1999), pp. 735–798. See also Ch'en Shih-jung, "Qingdai Taoyuan de kaifa yu difang shehui jiangou" ("The settlement of Taoyuan and the construction of local society during the Qing"), MA thesis, National Central University, 1999.

53. See Daniel L. Overmyer with Chao Shin-yi (eds.), *Ethnography in China Today: A Critical Assessment of Methods and Results*, (Taipei: Yuan-liou Publishing Co. Ltd., 2002).

Daoism in China Today, 1980–2002*

Lai Chi-Tim

ABSTRACT Drawing on Daoist Association sources, fieldwork and interviews, this article analyses some major aspects of Daoism in China today. It first presents the revival of destroyed Daoist temples, the return of liturgical activities in Daoist temples and the establishment of training classes for young Daoists. It also discusses the restoration of ordinations of Daoists at the Quanzhen monastery Baiyun guan and the Halls of Zhengyi Tianshi at Longhu shan. Based upon the National Daoist Association's statistics from 1996, there were about 20,000 "Daoist priests who live at home," called *sanju daoshi*, who perform Daoist ritual outside monasteries in local communities across China. Despite the state's policy of controlling *sanju daoshi*, the revival of Daoist ritual tradition in village temples in China today reveals that Daoism is still very much alive in Chinese communities.

Daoism has remained a central part of the daily life of the Chinese people. Although the category of "Daoism" has different contents for different scholars, such as the aspects relating to philosophical mysticism, mythology, immortals, nourishing life, meditation and liturgies, Daoism can be seen as a religious and liturgical institution profoundly rooted in the "social body of the local communities."[1] From Ming times on, Daoism comprised two main schools: that of the Zhengyi Heavenly Masters, passed on hereditarily since the Han dynasty in the second century AD, and that of the school of Total Perfection (Quanzhen). The former fostered local communities and temple organizations and provided them with their liturgical framework and ritual specialists,[2] while the latter was based, on the Buddhist model, in monastic communities.

This article draws on three main sources of reference material that are helpful in understanding the recent situation and development of Daoism in China after years of suppression under the rule of the People's Republic.[3] The first is my own observation during the past three years while carrying out research into Daoism in China. I have visited Daoist

* This article is based on a research project entitled "History of Heavenly Master Daoism in the Six Dynasties Period." The project was generously funded by the Research Grants Council of the Universities Grants Committee (ref. CUHK4019/99H). I would like to thank Franciscus Verellen, Daniel Overmyer, Timothy Barrett, Kenneth Dean and Paul Katz for their comments and suggestions.
    1. Kristofer Schipper, *The Taoist Body*, trans. by Karen C. Duval (Berkeley: University of California Press, 1993), p. 4. On the discussion of the definitions of "Daoism" in the Chinese and Western studies of Daoism, see Russel Kirkland, Timothy Barrett and Livia Kohn, "Introduction," in Livia Kohn (ed.), *Daoism Handbook* (Brill: Leiden, 2000), pp. xi–xviii.
    2. Kristofer Schipper, "Taoism: the story of the way," in Stephen Little (ed.), *Taoism and the Arts of China* (Chicago: The Art Institution of Chicago in association with University of California Press, 2000), p. 52.
    3. On the suppression of Daoist priests during the period of Cultural Revolution, see Li Yangzheng, *Dangdai Zhongguo daojiao* (Beijing: Zhongguo shehui kexue chubanshe, 1993), pp. 15–16, 231.

temples in Beijing, Chengdu, Xinjin (Sichuan), Heming shan (Dayi, Sichuan), Longhu shan, Maoshan, Suzhou, Nanjing, Shanghai, Luofu shan (Huizhou) and Guangzhou. Because I am now engaged in a research project on Daoist ritual traditions on the southern coast of Guangdong province, I have also had the opportunity to observe Daoist rituals in that region's villages and talk to the "Daoists living at home" (*huoju daoshi*) who perform these rituals.

My second source of reference material is the two most representative journals of Daoism in China, *Zhongguo daojiao* and *Shanghai daojiao*. Since 1987, the *Zhongguo daojiao* has been a nation-wide, bimonthly publication of the National Daoist Association of China.[4] The *Shanghai daojiao* is a regional publication of the Shanghai Daoist Association.[5] These journals provide valuable information on three main topics: news of Daoist Associations, especially their religious activities, meetings and policy documents, at both national and provincial levels; repairs to and openings of Daoist temples; and the religious life and conditions of the Daoist priests who reside in temples.

The third source of reference material is academic reports on Daoism in China today; for example, recent publications by Li Yangzheng, Jan Yün-hua, Thomas H. Hahn, Kenneth Dean, Hachiya Kunio, John Lagerwey, Liu Jingfeng and Daniel Overmyer.[6]

This article covers the period from 1980 to the present day and focuses on three main aspects: the religious activities of Daoist temples and the conditions of administration of these temples under the Daoist Associations, at the national or provincial level; the restoration of ordination

---

4. Before the publication of *Zhongguo daojiao*, the National Daoist Association published a journal, *Daoxie huikan*, but this publication was only for inside information and could not be subscribed to by others.

5. There are three other regional journals of Daoism published in China today: *Sanqin Daojiao*, *Fujian daojiao* and *Maoshao daojiao*.

6. See Li Yangzheng, *Dangdai Zhongguo daojiao*; Li Yangzheng, *Dangdai daojiao* (Beijing: Dongfang chubanshe, 2000); Jan Yün-hua, "The religious situation and the studies of Buddhism and Taoism in China: an incomplete and imbalanced picture," *Journal of Chinese Religions*, Vol. 12 (1985), pp. 37–64; Thomas H. Hahn, "New developments concerning Buddhist and Taoist monasteries," in Julian F. Pas (ed.), *The Turning of the Tide: Religion in China Today* (Hong Kong: Royal Asiatic Society, Hong Kong Branch, in association with Oxford University Press, 1989), pp. 79–101 and "On doing fieldwork in Daoist studies in the People's Republic – conditions and results," *Cahiers d'Extrême-Asie*, Vol. 2 (1986), pp. 211–17; Kenneth Dean, "Field notes on two Taoist *jiao* observed in Zhangzhou in December 1985," *Cahiers d'Extrême-Asie*, Vol. 2 (1986), pp. 191–209, "Funerals in Fujian," *Cahiers d'Extrême-Asie*, Vol. 4 (1988), pp. 19–78, "Revival of religious practices in Fujian: a case study," in Pas, *The Turning of the Tide*, pp. 51–77, *Taoist Ritual and Popular Cults of South-east China* (Princeton: Princeton University Press, 1995), "Taoism in contemporary China," ch. 24, in D. Lopez (ed.), *Chinese Religion in Practice* (Princeton: Princeton University Press, 1996), pp. 306–326, and *Lord of the Three in One: The Spread of a Cult in Southeast China* (Princeton: Princeton University Press, 1998); Hachiya Kunio, *Chugoku no Dokyo: sono katsudo to dokan no genjo* (Tokyo: Tokyo daigaku toyo bunka kenkyojo, 1995); John Lagerwey, "Fujian sheng Jianyan diqu de daojiao," *Misu quyi*, No. 84 (1993), pp. 43–82; Liu Jingfeng, *Gannan zongjiao shehui yu daojiao wenhua yanjiu* (Hong Kong: International Hakka Studies Association, Ecole Française D'Extrême Orient, Overseas Chinese Archives, 2000); Daniel L. Overmyer (ed.), *Ethnography in China Today: A Critical Assessment of Methods and Results* (Taipei: Yuan-Liou Publishing Co. Ltd., 2002).

ceremonies for Quanzhen *daoshi* and Zhengyi *daoshi*; and popular Daoism and professional ritual specialists, commonly known as *huoju daoshi*, especially their ritual services and ceremonies outside Daoist temples. Because of the lack of a common definition of "Daoist believers" (*daojiao xintu*) and accurate data on the Daoist population of the laity in China, I do not deal with lay believers of Daoism, but focus on the institutional and clerical aspects of Daoism in China since the 1980s.

Daoist Associations, Daoist Temples and Daoists

Like most other national religious organizations in China following the Cultural Revolution, the National Daoist Association, originally founded in 1957, was re-established and held its third National Congress in 1980.[7] Following its re-establishment, the first task of the National Daoist Association was to restore the Daoist temples that had been destroyed by the Red Guards or occupied by non-religious organizations during the Ten Years' Chaos.[8]

Thomas Hahn's fieldwork report on Daoism in China between 1980 and 1986 has already pointed out that this initial phase of "Daoist recovery" was characterized by the revival of destroyed Daoist temples and the return of old Daoist priests nation-wide. Despite a suspicious "wait-and-see attitude" maintained by certain Western observers and scholars towards the changing religious policy in China after the years of destructive annihilation, Daoist temples, like other religious centres, have been rebuilt one by one and opened to the public since 1980.[9] In 1982, 21 of the best-known Daoist temples in 17 provinces or on famous mountains were the first temples to be re-opened, and received government approval when they were classified as nationally protected religious centres. Although some restored Daoist temples, such as Longhu shan in Jiangxi and Maoshan in Jiangsu, are of the Zhengyi order, most belong to the public monasteries (*shifang conglin*) of Quanzhen Daoism.[10] Since then, the speed of restoration and reconstruction of Daoist temples has

---

7. On the founding history of the National Daoist Association before 1980, see Li Yangzheng, *Dangdai daojiao*, pp. 38–70. In 1998, the National Daoist Association held its sixth national Congress. The Congress then elected the present members of executive committee of the National Doaist Association. Ming Zhiting is presently the chairman, and there are nine vice-chairmen, who are Zhang Jiyu, Ren Farong, Liu Huaiyuan, Wang Guangde, Huang Xinyang, Huang Zhi'an, Ding Changyun, Tang Chengqing, Lai Baorong and Yuan Bingdong.

8. *Daoxie huikan*, No. 13 (1984), pp. 1–8.

9. Julian F. Pas, "Introduction: Chinese religion in transition," in Pas, *The Turning of the Tide*, p. 1.

10. The 21 restored Daoist temples are Bixiaci in Taishan, Taiqing gong in Laoshan (Liaoning), Mao shan daoyuan in Jiangsu, Baopu daoyuan in Hangzhou, Longhu shan tianshifu in Jiangxi, Wudangshan zixiaogong in Hubei, Wudangshan taiyue taihe gong, Changchun guan in Wuhan, Chongxu guan in Huizhou, Tianshidong in Qingcheng shan (Sichuan), Zushidian in Qingcheng shan, Qingyang gong in Chengdu, Louguan tai in Zongnan shan (Sha'anxi), Baxian gong in Xi'an, Yuquan daoyuan in Huashan, Jiutian gong in Huashan, Zhenyue gong in Huashan, Wuliang guan in Qianshan (Liaoning), Taiqing gong in Shenyang, Zhongyue miao in Songshan (Henan), and Baiyun guan in Beijing.

accelerated. During the 1990s, restoration of Daoist temples expanded from those located in metropolitan cities to those in more rural, county areas. According to the "official" numbers and statistics disclosed by the National Daoist Association, about 400 Daoist temples were opened in 1992, 1,200 in 1995 and 1,600 in 1998.[11] Li Yangzhen, the associate director of the National Daoist College, claims a total of 1,722 Daoist temples established up until 1996.[12] In the case of Jiangsu province, it is reported that in 1993 there were only five Daoist temples, but this had increased to 42 in 1999.[13] It is not known whether there are instances in which main temples have established branch temples, or whether there are economic ties or dependence between temples.

Because of the lack of comparable data, it is not possible to obtain an accurate estimate for the number of Daoist priests that belong to the Quanzhen or Zhengyi orders. However, Li Yangzhen's account suggests that the number of resident Daoist priests rose to 7,135 in 1996, of whom 4,139 were Quanzhen monks, 2,311 Quanzhen nuns and 685 Zhengyi priests.[14] Furthermore, based on the geographical distribution of the Quanzhen and Zhengyi priests who were ordained in Qingcheng shan and Longhu shan in 1995, it is known that those who were ordained as Quanzhen monks and nuns came mainly from the Baixian gong (Xi'an), Louguan tai (Sha'anxi), Changchun guan (Wuhan), Wudangshan (Hubei), Qingcheng shan and Taiqing gong (Liaoning). In comparison, the Zhengyi ordained priests were from Daoist temples or Daoist Association in 12 provinces and one city, such as Jiangsu, Shanghai, Hunan, Hubei, Anhui, Zhejiang, Guangdong, Jiangxi, Yunnan, Fujian and Henan.[15]

Because of the state's administrative need for effective management and control of Daoist temples and their members, the establishment of local organizational authorities, such as Daoist Associations, continues. It is known that, by 1999, 133 regional Daoist Associations had already been established at a nation-wide level.[16] All Daoist Associations are under the administration of the Religious Affairs Bureau (*zongjiao shi-wuju*) at the district level.[17] Regional Daoist Associations are responsible for the management of temples, providing liturgical and scriptural training for their resident members, negotiating with the government over the repair of temples, and recruiting young members into Daoist temples.

It is evident that the tasks and concerns of Daoist Associations, at both the national and district level, have gradually changed during the years since the revival of Daoism in the 1980s. As mentioned above, the first phase of Daoist revival in the early 1980s was characterized by the restoration and repair of destroyed temples, as well as the recruitment of

---

11. *Zhongguo daojiao*, No. 3 (1992), p.10; No.5 (1999), p. 4.
12. Li Yangzheng, *Dangdai daojiao*, p.185.
13. *Zhongguo daojiao*, No. 1 (2001), p.9.
14. Li Yangzheng, *Dangdai daojiao*, p.185.
15. *Zhongguo daojiao*, No. 4 (1994), p.15; No. 1 (1996), pp.11–12.
16. *Zhongguo daojiao*, No. 5 (1999), p.4.
17. Li Yangzheng, *Daojiao shi lüejiang* (Beijing: Zhongguo daojiao xueyuan, 1997), p. 537.

young members into temples. The National Daoist Association, which was established with the aim of training young members, started a half-yearly programme called the "Higher educational class for Daoists" (*daojiao zhishi zhuanxiuban*) in 1982, which continued in 1984, 1986, 1987 and 1988.[18] The 1988 class was arranged especially for Daoist nuns, and 62 recommended students were admitted. It is reported that many graduates, especially from the first and second classes, have already achieved high positions in Daoist temples or Associations.[19] Meanwhile, many provincial and local Daoist Associations, for instance in Shanghai, Wuhan, Chengdu, Maoshan, Suzhou, Sha'anxi and Zhejiang, all started their own training classes for young Daoist priests in the late 1980s.[20]

In comparison with the condition of Daoism in China in the early 1980s, it seems that the problems regarding the legitimacy of Daoist temples, or of accusations being made against religious ceremonies being performed in temples, have not been heard since the 1990s. Instead of a problem of survival, the Daoist Associations (at all levels) have shifted their attention to focus more on the rules and orders relating to the internal affairs of Daoist temples and their staff members. They are now more concerned with ensuring effective means of managing and administrating the so-called "corrected" temple activities, the religious life of resident members, and, most importantly, the "Daoists living at home," who perform ritual services and ceremonies outside temples.

In the past ten years, the National Daoist Association has sought to enforce four influential policy documents in connection with issues concerning temple management, rules for the ordination of Quanzhen and Zhengyi priests, and a definition of the "corrected" religious activities of "Daoists living at home." The four paper documents are: "Methods for administering Daoist temples" (*Guanyu daojiao gongguan guanli banfa*) in 1992; "Tentative methods related to the administration of the Zhengyi priests who live at home" (*Guanyu daojiao sanju zhengyipai daoshi guanli shixing banfa*) in 1992; "Rules about the transmission of precepts for the Quanzhen order" (*Guanyu quanzhenpai chuanjie de guiding*) in 1994; and "Rules related to conferring registers of ordination for the Zhengyi priests" (*Guanyu zhengyi pai daoshi shoulu guiding*) in 1994.[21]

As it is no longer a question of prophecy, we shall try to explain the phenomenon of the rapid growth of restored Daoist temples in present-day China. The spiritual and religious needs of many Daoist believers are of course important, but the following three aspects play an equally important role. First, because of the lack of comparable evidence, it may

18. *Zhongguo daojiao*, No. 1 (1987), pp. 53–54, No. 3 (1987), pp.63–64; Li Yangzheng, *Dangdai Zhongguo daojiao*, pp.100–102. In 1990, a National Daoist College was established in the Baiyun guan at Beijing. There were two different classes, the "higher" and "advanced" programmes of Daoist education. See *Zhongguo daojiao*, No. 3 (1990), p.3.

19. *Zhongguo daojiao*, No. 1 (1987). For example, the present abbot of Baiyun guan, Huang Xinyang and the vice-president of National Daoist Association, Zhang Jiyu were graduates in the 1985 class.

20. Li Yangzheng, *Dangdai Zhongguo daojiao*, pp.107–112.

21. *Zhongguo daojiao*, No.4 (1992), pp.6–7; No.4 (1994), p.14; No.5 (1999), p.4; Li Yangzheng, *Dangdai Zhongguo daojiao*, pp.316–322.

be difficult to imagine that anti-religious attitudes towards Daoism have been completely withdrawn in China. Because Daoist Associations at all levels are constitutionally governed by the Religious Affairs Offices, it is hard not to imagine the government authority's consistent influence on these religious establishments.[22] Whatever the relationship between the government authority and religious bodies in China, it is a fact that basic religious activities in Daoist temples have been considerably revived and continuously expanded. Without doubt, the number of temples and priests has grown rapidly in the last decade.

Secondly, it is clear that, since the 1980s, money for repairing and reconstructing Daoist temples in China has been continuously raised by, and has always depended upon, Chinese Daoist institutions based in Hong Kong, Taiwan and Singapore. Guangdong and Fujian are two particular cases where money from foreign sources has been invested in Daoist temples.[23] Indeed, cadres and officials from the provinces or cities realize that such financial sources, used for rebuilding Daoist temples, can be one of the most effective means of attracting further money to invest in public works and establishments at the district level, such as schools, universities, hospitals, tourism, improvement of village education and so on.

Thirdly, the revival of Daoist temples has undoubtedly benefited from the boom in economic growth in China during the past two decades, which has resulted in the growth of personal income and the rapid development of private companies. It is not surprising to discover a close link between the recovery of Daoist temples and the nation-wide expansion of the tourist industry. In the summer of 1999, when I visited the Yuanfu Wanninggong temple at Maoshan, Nanjing, which was restored and opened to the public in 1988,[24] I was told that, "in 1997, a total of 650,000 pilgrims and tourists visited the Maoshan, and as a result, the total income from tourism amounted to 10 million [RMB]. Since the 1990s, the Maoshan Daoist temple's yearly income has increased by 500 thousand [RMB] every year, and it had made a profit of 6.5 million [RMB] up until 1999."[25] In 1996, supported by such a large income from tourism, the Yuanfu Wanninggong decided to build the largest bronze statute of Laozi in the world at Maoshan. In co-operation with a city-based company, the Yuanfu Wanninggong invested a total of 30 million RMB in its construction. There was an official public celebration in November 1998, when the giant Laozi bronze statue, 33 metres high, was opened to the public.[26]

22. Li Yangzheng, *Dangdai Zhongguo daojiao*, p.77.
23. Thomas H. Hahn, "New developments concerning Buddhist and Taoist monasteries," pp.81–83.
24. *Zhongguo daojiao*, No.3 (1989), p. 23.
25. Maoshan daojiao wenhua yanjiushi (ed.), *Maoshan daoyuan*, p.20. According the newsletter published by the Daoist Temple of Maoshan, *Maoshan daoyuan*, No. 9 (2000), the Maoshan temple has earned 6.6 million RMB in the first eight months of 2000.
26. *Maoshan daoyuan*, No. 1 (2001), p.3.

Ordinations of Quanzhen and Zhengyi Daoists

The revival of Daoism in present-day China advanced to a new phase with the renewal of its ordination practice, held by the Quanzhen order at the Baiyun guan, in 1989. This was the first Daoist ordination ceremony since the takeover of the communist government in China. In 1995, the Quanzhen and Zhengyi orders of Daoism held ordination ceremonies in the Qingcheng shan and Longhu shan respectively. The key to Daoism's survival crisis in China is clearly the succession of a new generation of young priests, which led the National Daoist Association to consider seriously the renewal of ordination, which had not taken place since the 1940s.[27]

With regard to the history of Quanzhen ordination ceremonies, Yoshioka Yoshitoyo found that 31 ordinations were held at the Baiyun guan between 1808 and 1927.[28] Until the period of the Republic of China, the Quanzhen sect had no bureaucratic institution for ordination, although it had to take place in a public *shifang* monastery.[29] From the Ming dynasty onwards, the Daoist priests of the Zhengyi order received their ordination within a loose Heavenly Master's family system, whose head was the Tianshi himself.[30] Until the early Qing, the Heavenly Master was entrusted to hold a nation-wide ordination at the Longhu shan, or to visit the various provinces to hold ordination platforms.[31] In the fifth month of Qianlong 4 (1739), the Heavenly Master's role as the nominal head of a nation-wide ordination system was banned.[32] Whereas the state tended to keep abreast of the Heavenly Master's nominal authority within the administration of Zhengyi Daoism, it is known that the Heavenly Master was still confirmed as guardian of orthodoxy within Daoism. He continued to issue registers to individuals who went to the Longhu shan for ordination, or selected other Daoists of the Heavenly Master's office (*Zhenren fu*) in his name and gave local Daoists licences (*zhizhao*)

27. *Zhongguo daojiao*, No. 4 (1994), pp.14–15. According to Li Yangzheng, *Dangdai daojiao*, p.123, the last ordination of Quanzhen order held before the takeover of communist government was in the Erxian An, Chengdu, in 1947.

28. Yoshioka Yoshitoyo, "Taoist monastic life," in Holmes Welch and Anna Seidel (eds.), *Facets of Taoism* (New Haven: Yale University Press, 1979), p.236.

29. Vincent Goossaert, "The Quanzhen clergy, 1700–1950," in John Lagerwey (ed.), *Religion and Chinese Society: The Transformation of a Field* (Hong Kong: Ecole Française d'Extrême-Orient and Chinese University of Hong Kong, 2003), pp.10,18. Goosaaert's study shows that Beijing's Baiyun guan and Shenyang's Taiqing gong were the two major Quanzhen ordination centres of North-eastern China. There were 1,740 Daoists ordained at the Taiqing gong between 1823 and 1929 in 8 ordinations and 5,460 at the Baiyun guan between 1807 and 1927 in 31 ordinations.

30. On the ordination in the Zhengyi tradition, see Kristofer Schipper, "Taoist ordination ranks in the Tunhuang manuscripts," in Gert Naudorf, Karl-Heinz Pohl and Hans-Herrman Schmidt (eds.), *Religion und Philosophie in Ostasien (Festschrift für Hans Steininger)* (Königshausen: Neumann, 1985), pp.127–148.

31. Vincent Goossaert, "Counting the monks: the 1736–1739 census of the Chinese clergy," *Late Imperial China*, Vol. 21 (2000), pp. 53–55.

32. Hosoya Yoshio, "Kenryû chô no Seiikyô" ("The Zhengyi order under the Qianlong reign"), in Akizuki Kan'ei (ed.), *Dôkyô to shûkyô bunka (Daoism and Religious Culture)* (Tokyo: Hirakawa, 1987), pp.577–78. Goossaert, "Counting the monks," p.54.

bearing his seal.[33] According to Li Yangzhen, the last ordination ceremony for the Zhengyi *daoshi* at the Longhu shan was held in 1946.[34]

With the takeover of the communist government, the Daoists were prohibited from performing any ordinations. With the renewal of the ceremony at the Baiyun guang in 1989, the period of the Quanzhen ordination procedure (*chuanjie*) was shortened to 20 days from the traditional 100 days.[35] There were 75 ordinands, 30 (40 per cent) of whom were women, and all of whom had already lived within a proper monastery for more than three years.[36] The oldest was aged 75 and the youngest was 21. At the end of the ceremony, the ordinands received the so-called Great Precepts of the Threefold Altar (*santan dajie*): the Initial Precepts of Perfection (*chuzhen jie*), the Intermediate Precepts (*zhongji jie*), and the Great Precepts of the Celestial Immortals (*tianxian dajie*).[37] In November 1995, a second Quanzhen ordination was held at the Changdao guan, also named the Tianshi dong, at the Qingcheng shan. Master Fu Yuantian was the abbot (*fangzhang*) of the Qingcheng shan, and thus took the presiding position of the Ordination Master (*chuanjie lüshi*).[38] Some 400 Quanzhen monks and nuns underwent the 1995 ordination.

The re-establishment of the Zhengyi ordination ceremony seems to have been more complicated. Restoration of the Zhengyi transferral of Register (*shoulu*) was first discussed in 1989, and a final agreement was reached in 1994, following the introduction of the "Tentative methods for administering the Zhengyi priests who live at home" for two years.[39]

Although the Quanzhen order of Daoism, which was established during the 12th century, attempted to follow the Buddhist ideal of a celibate and monastic life, the majority of the Zhengyi *daoshi* lived a married *daoshi* life at home, wearing ritual vestments for the performing of ritual, a practice which continues today.[40] These married *daoshi* were called the

33. *Ibid.* p.54. One copy of such a licence issued in 1704 has recently been found in the possession of a Daoist family from Hunan. It quotes that the early Qing imperial administration still entrusted the Heavenly Master with maintaining orthodoxy within Daoism by conferring on local Daoists the quality of a practitioner of pure Daoist liturgy. See Liu Jingfeng, *Gannan zongjiao shehui yu daojiao wenhua yanjiu*, p.263.

34. *Zhongguo daojiao*, No. 2 (1990), p.4. See also Li Yangzheng, *Dangdai daojiao*, p.124.

35. During the early 19th century, the duration of Quanzhen ordination had been shortened to 52 days at the Baiyun guan. See Goossaert, "The Quanzhen Clergy, 1700–1950," p. 21, n.63.

36. *Zhongguo daojiao*, No. 3 (1989), p.5.

37. Li Yangzheng, *Dangdai daojiao*, pp. 121–23. Cf. Yoshioka Yoshitoyo, "Taoist monastic life," pp. 235–36; Goossaert, "The Quanzhen Clergy, 1700–1950," p.21; Monica Esposito, "Longmen Taoism in Qing China: doctrinal ideal and local reality," *Journal of Chinese Religions*, Vol. 29 (2001), pp. 193–95.

38. *Zhongguo daojiao*, No. 1 (1996), pp. 7–11; Li Yangzheng, *Dangdai daojiao*, p.123. There were ten senior monks to be selected with different titles of ordination offices for the function of assisting the presiding master. They are Xie Zongxin, Wu Lichong, Cao Xiangzhen, Jiang Zhilin, Han Renquan, Tian Chengqi, Zhou Zhiqing, Huang Zhi'an, Wu Yuanzhen and Huang Xinyang.

39. *Shanghai daojiao*, No. 2 (1994), pp. 54–55.

40. Schipper, *The Taoist Body*, p.54 claims that: "On the basis of historical and contemporary observations, we can state that Taoism never was a monastic religion, for celibacy, is, in fact, inconsistent with its fundamental conception of the body. From the early

huoju daoshi, nowadays known in China as the *sanju daoshi*. However, under the Ming, Qing and the Republican periods, "*Daoshi* living at home" were always questioned and given a choice between a normal religious life, in which they would reside in a temple, or a return to lay status.[41] The state has always wanted the Daoists to conform to the Buddhist ideal of celibacy and a monastic life. Theoretically, it was illegal to perform ritual services and ceremonies outside Daoist temples. After the takeover by the communist government, all *huoju daoshi* were banned. Almost all of the ritual manuscripts that these Daoists possessed were taken from them and burnt or lost during the Cultural Revolution.[42] Nevertheless, since the beginning of the 1980s, traditional Zhengyi rituals, including the *Jiao* offering rituals and *Zhai* funeral rituals, have been extensively revived in China, especially in the villages of southern China.[43]

Despite the enormous resurgence of Zhengyi rituals in local society, the question of the married *sanju daoshi*'s "official" status, and how to manage them effectively, has perplexed the National Daoist Association since the 1990s. Above all, since these Daoist ritual specialists have always performed services and ceremonies in the context of the cults of various gods in local temples, they may not be so easily distinguished from temple shamans, whose religious activities are still criticized as superstitious. Therefore, it should be understood that the National Daoist Association's restoration of the ordination of the Zhengyi order in 1995 was not an easy accomplishment in the light of Daoism's modern history in China. However, the Zhengyi ordination actually took place under the guidance of the 1992 "Tentative methods for administrating the Zhengyi priests who live at home."[44] The rule is aimed at determining and classifying who are the "correct" and "recognized" *sanju daoshi* of the Zhengyi order.[45] Basically, a Zhengyi *sanju daoshi* is qualified and recognized only if he has successfully obtained a "Daoist certificate belonging to the Zhengyi sect" (*Zhengyipai daoshizheng*), which is uniformly issued by the National Daoist Association.[46] Theoretically, it is illegal for the *sanju daoshi* to perform liturgical services and ceremonies

---

footnote continued

times of the independent local communities of the Heavenly Masters' government, the *tao-shih*, men and women, were married people."

41. Goossaert, "Counting the monks," p.46.

42. Dean, "Field notes on two Taoist *jiao* observed in Zhangzhou in December 1985," p.195.

43. Cf. Kenneth Dean, "Revival of religious practices in Fujian: a case study," in Pas, *The Turning of the Tide*, pp.51–77; "Taoism in Southern Fujian: field notes, fall, 1985," in Tsao Pen-yeh and Daniel Law (eds.), *Studies of Taoist Rituals and Music of Today* (Hong Kong: The Society for Ethnomusicological research in Hong Kong, 1989), pp. 74–87; and *Taoist Ritual and Popular Cults of South-east China*.

44. On 24 August 1998, the National Daoist Association reviewed the 1992 rule and renamed it as the "Provisional methods for administering the Zhengyi Priests who live at home." Cf. *Zhongguo daojiao*, No. 3 (2002), p.6.

45. About the details of the "Tentative methods related to the administration of the Zhengyi priests who live at home" (*Guanyu daojiao sanju daoshi guanli shixing banfa*), see Li Yangzheng, *Dangdai Zhongguo daojiao*, pp.321–22.

46. *Zhongguo daojiao*, No. 4 (1992), pp.6–7.

outside a Daoist temple or officially endorsed religious centre, without advance approval from the regional Daoist Association.[47]

The first modern Zhengyi ordination ceremony took place at the highest doctrinal altar (*zongtan*) of the Halls of Tianshi fu, at Longhu shan on 5 December 1995, and lasted for three days.[48] Instead of conceiving it as a revival of the Heavenly Master family system, this ordination of "conferring registers" (*shoulu*) was not organized by the Halls of Tianshi fu, but by the National Daoist Association. With no ecclesiastical connection with the hereditary Heavenly Master, the ordination was presided over by three primary masters of the Zhengyi order, He Canran as the "Master who initiates and transmits" (*chuandu shi*), Chen Liansheng as the "Master who examines" (*jiandu shi*) and Zhou Niankao as the "Master who guarantees" (*baoju shi*). In fact, after the 63rd Heavenly Master, Zhang Enpu (1904–69), fled to Taiwan in 1949, the hereditary office of Heavenly Master Zhang was no longer recognized and has not been restored in China.

Around 200 ordinands, traditionally called the "students of registers" (*lusheng*) took part in this ordination ceremony.[49] Their ages ranged from 20 to over 80. At the end of the ordination, the ordained Zhengyi *daoshi* received a "registration certificate" (*zhidie*) (not "register of scriptures" *jinglu*) and a volume of "collected essays on the scriptures and instructions [given] for the ordination of Zhengyi sect of Daoism" (*daojiao zhengyipai shoulu chuandu jingjiaoji*).[50] Despite the lack of data on their religious background, it is certain that some of them must have belonged to the kind of *sanju daoshi* who must obtain the official "Daoist certificate, stating that they belong to the Zhengyi order." The officials of the National Daoist Association hoped that the apparently disordered situation of *sanju daoshi* could be further improved and structured by restoring ordination, and could thus achieve a more effective system of managing them.[51]

Regarding the purpose of this article, the restoration of the ordination system in the mid-1990s is evidence of Daoism's improved situation in China. The problem of succession in Daoism has been properly addressed. Whether Daoist ordinations will continue and to what extent they

47. *Ibid.* p.7.

48. Before the 1995 Zhengyi ordination ceremony held at Longhu shan, the Halls of Tianshi, on 3–9 October 1991, had held an ordination ceremony for 36 Zhengyi daoshi who came from Taiwan, Singapore and Malaysia. Cf. *Shanghai daojiao*, No. 4 (1991), p.28; *Zhongguo daojiao*, No.1 (1992), pp.5–6.

49. *Zhongguo daojiao*, No. 1 (1996), pp.11–12; *Shanghai daojiao*, No. 1 (1996), pp.7–11; Li Yangzheng, *Dangdai daojiao*, pp. 125–26.

50. *Zhongguo daojiao*, No. 4 (2001), p.12; Li Yangzheng, *Dangdai daojiao*, p.126. In the past, after ordination, the Zhengyi Daoist priest would receive the so-called "register of scriptures" (*jinglu*), disciplinary rules (*jie*), and scriptures from the Heavenly Master. The register was a list of names of the spirit generals contained in the sacred scriptures and thus gave the Daoist masters command over the specific graded number of spirit generals. Cf. Schipper, *The Daoist Body*, p.60 and "Taoist ordination ranks in the Tunhuang manuscripts," pp.128, 140; Franciscus Verellen, "The twenty-four dioceses and Zhang Daoling: spatio-liturgical organization in early Heavenly Master Taoism," in Phyllis Granoff and Koichi Shinohara (eds.), *Pilgrims and Place: Localizing Sanctity in Asian Religions* (Vancouver: University of British Columbia Press, 2003), pp. 15–67.

51. *Shanghai daojiao*, No. 2 (1994), pp.54–55.

will become normalized in the future is not known at this moment. Nevertheless, as a leading Zhengyi master, Chen Liansheng, pointed out in his speech on the issue of "the significance of the conferral of registers to Zhengyi Daoists" (*Guanyu zhengyipai daoshi shoulu de yiyi*), the Zhengyi ritual tradition may not yet have been properly legitimized because of some "inappropriate" policies that are maintained by local government officials.[52] According to Chen Liansheng, the restoration of the Zhengyi ordination tradition plays an important role in ensuring the healthy, protected and ordered development of this long established Daoist tradition.[53]

Sanju daoshi, Local Cults and Temple Festivals

Unknown to most outside observers of Chinese religions, traditional Daoist rituals, local cults and popular culture have revived and increased their activities in China today, especially in rural villages.[54] Although we have access to a number of reports on the resurgence of Daoism in local society, we still know surprisingly little about the present situation of popular Daoism and, in particular, the figures and religious activities of *sanju daoshi* who live among the common people.[55] Despite their responsibility for governing Daoist activities, the Daoist Association has described the *sanju daoshi*'s ritual activities as being in a serious state of disorder and sometimes criticize them as being superstitious.[56]

Until the 1990s, district Daoist Associations did not have statistics for the number of *sanju daoshi*.[57] In the early 1990s, in order to control and handle them more easily and effectively, they started to investigate the real situation regarding *sanju daoshi*. The Daoist Association in the city of Wenzhou reported that there were 1,605 *sanju daoshi* of the Zhengyi sect in 1992.[58] The Daoist Association in Fujian province quoted a total of 4,000 Zhengyi *daoshi* in the cities of Quanzhou, Putian and Jinjiang.[59] The Daoist Association in Gansu province verified that, until 1993, there were about 1,200 Zhengyi *daoshi* registered with the association.[60] It was reported that there were 1,000 Zhengyi *daoshi* in Shanghai in 1990. In

52. *Shanghai daojiao*, No. 3 (1995), p.34.
53. *Shanghai daojiao*, No. 2 (1994), pp.4–5. On Chen's other essays related to the aim of the restoration of Zhengyi ordination, see Chen Liansheng, *Daofeng ji* (*Collected Essays of the Wind of the Dao*) (Shanghai: Shanghai shehui kexueyuan chubanshe, 1996).
54. Dean, *Taoist Ritual and Popular Cults of South-East China*, p.3.
55. The 80 volumes of the monograph series of "Studies in Chinese ritual, theatre and folklore" (*Minsu quyi congshu*, Taibei: Shih Hocheng Foundation, 1993-) edited by Wang Qiugui have contributed to a better understanding of popular Daoism in county level in the past decade. Other ethnographic reports covering the Hakka regions of South-east China (*Traditional Hakka Society Series*, Hong Kong: EFEO, 1997-) directed by John Lagerwey also cover local Daoist ritual in that region. See Daniel Overmyer, "Introduction," in Overmyer, *Ethnography in China Today*, pp.3–4.
56. *Zhongguo daojiao*, No. 3 (1992), p.25.
57. Hann, "New developments concerning Buddhist and Taoist monasteries," p.15.
58. *Zhongguo daojiao*, No. 3 (1992), p.25–26.
59. *Zhongguo daojiao*, No. 1 (1989), p.10.
60. *Zhongguo daojiao*, No. 3 (1994), p.7.

Jiangsu province, the number of registered *sanju daoshi* exceeded 4,000 in 2000.[61] I have also had access to all the materials published by the Daoist Associations and have found only one report that presents the total number of Zhengyi *daoshi* in China today. Li Yangzheng reports that, based on the National Daoist Association's statistics from 1996, there were about 20,000 *sanju daoshi* in local society.[62]

It is not difficult to find evidence of the Daoist Associations' enthusiasm for setting up district bureaucratic control of *sanju daoshi*, especially since the late 1990s. For example, in the city of Suzhou a special monitoring committee and administration office for *sanju daoshi* were set up in 1997. Under the committee's governance, similar management task forces were set up in districts, counties and villages. By law, the "corrected" *sanju daoshi* have to register with their local Daoist Association, and thus receive a "Daoist certificate belonging to the Zhengyi sect" which legally permits them to perform ritual services and ceremonies outside Daoist temples. Standardized ritual vestments, manuscripts and instruments are also provided, which the *sanju daoshi* are requested to use when they perform rituals.[63] Accordingly, the renewal of their Daoist certificate is based on an annual examination of their religious activities.[64]

Bureaucratic control of the "Daoists living at home" (*huoju daoshi*) has existed since the Ming period and probably continues to the present day.[65] In the Hongwu reign, the Ming state took steps towards setting up a clerical bureaucracy to supervise all Daoist priests at a national level, the *daolu si* in the Board of Rites and the *daohui si* in the counties.[66] According to Vincent Goossaert's study of *huoju daoshi* in the Qing period, the state's policy for controlling "Daoists living at home" was evident in its religious policy that granted a ministry's licence (*buzhao*) to a select number of non-Quanzhen Daoists through the secular authorities of the *daolu si* or the *daohui si*.[67] Apart from this official method of gaining recognition, it is known that some Daoists went to Longhu shan for the Heavenly Master's ordination and returned home afterwards. Whereas there are two different ways, secular and religious, of identifying Zhengyi *daoshi*, it is still not clear how far they can help to identify the so-called *huoju* type of Zhengyi *daoshi* in the Qing period.

In addition to the *huoju daoshi* of the Zhengyi tradition, there must

61. *Zhongguo daojiao*, No. 1 (2000), p.9.
62. Li Yangzheng, *Dongdai daojiao*, p.185.
63. *Zhongguo daojiao*, No. 3 (2002), pp.6–8.
64. *Zhongguo daojiao*, No. 5 (1999), pp.17–19.
65. On the traditional Chinese state's control of religious activities of the people, see Daniel L. Overmyer, "Attitudes toward popular religion in ritual texts of the Chinese state: the collected statutes of the Great Ming," *Cahiers d'Extrême-Asie*, No. 5 (1989–90), pp.191–221 and Anthony C. Yu, "On state and religion in China: a brief historical reflection," unpublished paper, 2002.
66. *Ming huidian*, Vol. 226, pp.4435–37. See also Ishida Kenji, "Mindai Dôkyô shijo no Zenshin to Seii" ("The Quanzhen and Zhengyi orders in Daoist history during the Ming dynasty"), in Sakai Tadao (ed.), *Taiwan no shûkyô to Chugoku bunka* (*Religion in Taiwan and Chinese Culture*) (Tokyo: Fukyosha, 1992), pp. 145–195.
67. Goossaert, "Counting the monks," pp.42–47.

have been a large number of "Daoists living at home" independent of either official registration or religious ordination by the Heavenly Master. More attention has been recently given to the widespread distribution of the mixture of Daoist ritual tradition and shamanistic cults across Chongqing, Guizhou, Fujian and southern China.[68] As representative variants of Zhengyi ritual specialists in local regions, vernacular Daoists of Lüshan traditions (*shigong*) in northern Fujian and of the Duangong rites around the Guo related altar in Guizhou are professional ritual specialists, who live among the common people and are often invited to perform rites on the birthdays of local gods, consecrations of village temples, healing, exorcism and so on.[69] These vernacular Daoist priests do not receive their ordination from the Heavenly Master, but are ordained locally by their masters, who pass them religious names (*fahao*) belonging to their own Daoist altars (*daotan*).[70]

Although Daoism is not defined in this article, its liturgical function and unification seem to be the key that causes all *huoju duoshi* to call themselves Daoists. Kristofer Schipper points out: "Rather than his way of life, then it is his liturgical function, his role as ritual specialist, that defines the position of the *tao-shih*," and that, "it is in towns and urban areas that one most frequently finds the families of *tao-shih*."[71] This is the Daoism of China's common people.[72] Although the state has always tried to control them, the "Daoists living at home" continued their liturgical life unhindered before the destruction of Daoist sanctuaries between the late Qing period and the Cultural Revolution.[73] Looking at Daoism in this way leads to a better understanding of the great significance of the enormous revival of Daoist ritual services and ceremonies in local society and temples in China today.

Without doubt, scholars' recent fieldwork and researches on Daoism in Fujian have demonstrated the huge revival of Daoist ritual tradition in local society.[74] In his meticulous account of Daoism in contemporary Fujian, Kenneth Dean arrives at the same conclusion as Schipper did in

---

68. See Dean, *Taoist Ritual and Popular Cults of South-east China*, pp.28, 42; John Lagerwey, "The altar of celebration ritual in Lushan county, Sichuan," and "Duangong ritual and ritual theatre in the Chongqing area: a survey of the work of Hu Tiancheng," in Daniel L. Overmyer (ed.), *Ethnography in China Today: A Critical Assessment of Methods and Results*, pp.75–108.

69. On the study of Nuo related *duandong* ritual tradition, see Hu Tiancheng, "Vernacular priest plays of Jielong in Sichuan," Vols. 1, 2, and 3 (*Minsu qui congshu*, Nos. 18, 34, and 35) published in 1993 and 1995. On the study of Lüshan ritual tradition, see Ye Mingsheng, "Fujiansheng Longyanshi Dongxiaozhen *Lüshanjiao guangjitan keyiben*" ("The ritual texts of the Guangji altar of the Lushan sect in Dongxiao town, Longyan municipality, Fujian"), in Wang Qiugui (ed.), *Zhongguo chuantong keyiben huibian* (*Collection of Traditional Chinese Ritual Texts*) (Taibei: Xinwenfeng Publishing Co., 1999).

70. Dean, *Taoist Ritual and Popular Cults of South-east China*, pp.53–58; Liu Jingfeng, *Gannan zongjiao shehui yu daojiao wenhua yanjiu*, pp.217–231.

71. Schipper, *The Taoist Body*, pp.56–57.

72. There are other kinds of "Daoism," which are called monastic, mystical and philosophical Daoism.

73. Schipper, *The Taoist Body*, pp.16–19.

74. On books and reports on the revival of Daoist ritual in local levels, see n.3.

his study of Daoism in the city of Tainan, Taiwan in the late 1960s.[75] The liturgical tradition of the "Masters of the Gods" has an indispensable relationship with the local cults of temple deities. Given the important role of Daoism in popular cults, Dean presents many examples which show that "Taoists must consecrate the temples. The festival of the gods must be blessed by Taoists. Purification ceremonies are conducted by Taoists. Processions are initiated and led by Taoists. Great Offerings are consecrated by Taoists."[76]

In my fieldwork in a village in Bao'an, close to the Futian airport of the city of Shenzhen (Guangdong), I travelled with a Daoist family named Chen, whose Daoist altar is called Guangsheng tang. Without receiving any ordination certificate by the Heavenly Master, there have been at least four generations of Daoist priests in the Chen family since the late Qing. At present, four brothers of the present generation have resumed their performance of Daoist rituals. They still remember the story of their father who, like other contemporary *huoju daohsi*, had been banned from performing Daoist rituals since the 1950s. In the Chen family's village, several other Daoist altars are openly active at the present time. In the course of my fieldwork, I observed the Chen Daoists performing rituals for the consecration (*kaiguang*) of a rebuilt ancestral hall, the birthday festival of Tianhou in a temple, and the *Zhai* ritual for the dead. The interaction between Daoist rituals and the local community's daily religious life has been a constant manifestation of popular Daoism in local society throughout its history until the present day. Daoists perform rituals that are a part of the local religion of common people.[77]

Conclusion

This presentation of the major aspects of Daoism in China today does not invite overly optimistic speculation that the age-old Daoism has already returned to modern China. Without doubt, Daoism is present today, as it was in former times. Nevertheless, the progressive destruction of Daoist sanctuaries, priests and ritual traditions over the past century has not yet been forgotten.[78] Modernization, anti-religious policies and government officials' misunderstanding of Daoism still present a great challenge to the survival of this indigenous religious tradition in China. As Schipper has pointed out, Daoism was never a purely monastic religion, nor did it depend on any definite form of temple existence, but is supported by a variety of religious rituals and festivals in the lives of local society. As some scholars of Chinese religion have shown, various

75. Dean, *Taoist Ritual and Popular Cults of South-east China*, pp. 15–17.
76. *Ibid.* p.13.
77. For recent fieldwork reports on the interaction of popular Daoism with local temple festivals during 1990s, see Liu Jingfeng, *Gannan zongjiao shehui yu daojiao wenhua yanjiu*, especially pp.177–347 and Overmyer, *Ethnography in China Today*.
78. On the destruction of Daoism in the past century, see Schipper, *The Taoist Body*, pp. 16–19, and Lai Chi-tim, "Minguo shiqi guangzhoushi nahm-mouh daoyuan delishih kuojiu" ("History of 'nahm-mouh Daoist halls' in early Republican Canton"), *Bulletin of the Institute of Modern History of Academia Sinica*, Vol. 37 (2002), pp. 1–40.

socio-economic policies, or the state's political exploitation of the local community in early modern China, had a destructive effect on temple cults and cult organization in local society.[79] In a similar way, the future of Daoism, with particular regard to the important role of Daoism in Chinese local culture, is equally dependent on the extent of openness and the balance of the controlling policies that the state adopts towards local Daoism and its related professional ritual specialists, "Daoists living at home."

---

79. Cf. Prasenjit Duara, *Culture, Power, and the State: Rural North China, 1900–1942* (Stanford: Stanford University Press, 1988) and Barend J. ter Haar, "Local society and the organization of cults in early modern China: a preliminary study," *Studies in Central and East Asian Religions*, Vol. 8 (1995), pp. 1–43.

Buddhist China at the Century's Turn

Raoul Birnbaum

ABSTRACT Based on fieldwork and studies of historical and contemporary materials, this article investigates several issues key to Buddhist life in the present-day PRC, focusing on Han Buddhists, especially the monastic tradition. It argues that many current practices take their shape from the innovations that transformed Chinese Buddhist life in the late Qing and Republican periods. While profound political, economic and social changes have occurred in the past few decades, some of the most pressing issues are extensions of questions raised at that time. The most significant question of the earlier period – what is the Buddhist monastic vocation, and what training and leadership are required to safeguard that ideal? – remains central to present-day activities and conceptions. To consider how to answer this question, or indeed how it is posed within present circumstances, three interconnected matters are investigated: current training methods, the economics of monasteries and the issue of leadership. In this context, Han–Tibetan interchange in the Buddhist field and the influence of overseas Chinese Buddhists on the mainland are also considered.

This article is not a "report" so much as an inquiry. Based on field experience and historical studies, I would like to raise some key issues regarding the state of Buddhist life in the People's Republic of China at the beginning of the 21st century.

A simple question strikes as the basis for this discussion: what is it, or who is it, that could constitute the subject of this article? An initial definition of the field of inquiry appears reasonably straightforward: a corporate body of individuals conventionally self-identified as Buddhist (the religious professionals – monks and nuns – and a lay community), their range of activities (including what might be thought of as "religious life"), and the sites of those activities (most especially monasteries, shrines, pilgrimage sites such as mountains, and *jushi lin*, or lay association halls).

The textured reality of these interconnected topics is complex, and points to difficulties at the heart of this inquiry. Some of these complications arise from an attempt to make meaningful statements about an extraordinary variety of individuals, who are found within a system that in its lived realities operates with acutely layered social practices. In addition, there are distinctive regional variations across Chinese territory, as well as striking differences among the various types of sites even within a single locality.

Another concern is where to set the bounds of affiliation, and thus how far one extends discussion. This is not a small point. In this article I define these limits in accordance with the practices of the formal tradition. "Monks and nuns" are understood to include both novices and their seniors, the fully ordained members of the clergy. They are easily recognized by such external characteristics as shaven heads and distinctive monastic attire. Fully ordained clergy possess ordination certificates (*jiedie*), which they may be asked to produce when they request temporary or permanent lodging at a monastery. The great majority may also be recognized by the *jieba*, "ordination scars" on their scalps ranging in number from three to 12, received following completion of the third and final stage of full ordination, the acceptance of bodhisattva vows to seek liberation in order to aid all beings.[1]

"Laypeople" within the Buddhist community are not so easily recognized. A Buddhist temple filled with worshippers who offer incense and bow before deity images is not necessarily filled with Buddhists. Such visitors may well respond to the atmosphere and the many images just as they would in any type of Chinese temple, with prayers and offerings made to powerful spirits in order to seek good fortune for themselves and others. Some may feel a special devotion to one of the figures of the Buddhist pantheon, especially the compassionate figure of Guanyin, whose popularity is widespread, but these worshippers are not necessarily "Buddhist." From the point of view of those within the system, lay Buddhists have made a conscious commitment to a Buddhist path and have affirmed that formal commitment by going through the Triple Refuge ceremony, sponsored by a monk or nun. Like the monks and nuns, they receive a "Dharma name" (*faming*) and thus enter the Buddhist "family." This is recorded on a certificate (*guiyi zheng*), with the individual's photograph attached, which serves as an essential identification document when a layperson (*jushi*) seeks admission to a temple without paying the gate fee charged to tourists and other outsiders, or seeks temporary monastic lodging while on pilgrimage.

To further complicate any account of contemporary Buddhist life in China, the situation on the ground has been changing rapidly within the past ten or 15 years. This undermines the usefulness of making certain types of generalizations or statements of "fact" (including the parroting of statistics, for which the methods of compilation are not clear). In setting forth discussion below, while I focus principally on some distinctive aspects of monastic life, I will attempt to address at least some of the complications noted above in relation to the basic points of inquiry. However due to space limitations there can be no pretence of covering the whole field. I will proceed with a highly selective approach in which I seek to pursue several lines of coherence with the aim of drawing attention to a few key issues. Within the wider social frame, it focuses especially on monks (that is, male monastics), because of the broader range of written sources and the nature of my own fieldwork carried out over the past few decades.

The present era, I will suggest, is not an entirely anomalous point of disjuncture, despite its strange feel. Although confronted by enormous changes in social, political and economic life that have occurred since the

---

1. The practice of branding the scalp with incense burns at ordinations, which appears to date back at least to the Yuan, has been discouraged at some sites over the past few years, but still continues as an optional procedure. For historical consideration of Chinese Buddhist practices of offering the body through fire, see James A. Benn, "Burning for the Buddha: a history of self-immolation in Chinese Buddhism," PhD dissertation, UCLA, 2001.

early 1950s, with some acute disruptions such as the Cultural Revolution and its sporadic aftershocks, for Buddhists many key practices and discourse issues of this present moment arise directly from the profound changes in Chinese Buddhist life that were established during the late Qing and Republic. But of course that is not the full story.

This article describes some principal currents of Buddhist life during that earlier period, and then examines aspects of the present against this backdrop in order to gain a sense of continuity and change. To some readers, these historical matters may appear peripheral, even a digression, but this background cannot be separated from the story that I seek to tell. There are two key points at the base of this approach. First, to understand a progression of events and key issues in the aftermath of a convulsive period of religious persecution, it is instructive and indeed essential to consider Buddhist developments following a previous devastating calamity in China some 100 years earlier. I certainly do not propose a reductive view in which "history repeats itself," but familiarity with essential points of the near past may cast some light on the processes of the present. Secondly, while indeed one may provide a descriptive report on present-day Buddhist life without reference to what has produced that constellation of phenomena, such a report – by its "factual" barrage and anecdotal flair – can produce the satisfying *effect* of an apparent knowledge without any actual coherence. Therefore I have chosen this historicized approach, which looks at how things are now in the context of how they were just before.

As a final point in defining the scope of discussion, the geographic and social territory of present-day China encompasses at least three distinctly different "ethnicized" Buddhist traditions. (Such ethnic labels are intrinsically problematic, but for the sake of this present discussion I follow the divisions established within contemporary PRC discourse.) These traditions include Tibetan forms (also adopted by Mongols and some Manchus), the so-called "Southern" or non-Mahayana traditions ordinarily associated with South-East Asians, practised by Dai peoples in the border region of southern Yunnan, and the dominant form widespread across Chinese territory that may be termed "Han" Buddhism and generally has been thought of as "Chinese Buddhism." This article focuses on the latter form, whose practitioners are united by such elements as a standardized daily liturgy, an additional set of commonly practised rituals, and scriptures and other texts composed in Chinese; a sharply defined and commonly worshipped pantheon; a fairly consistent code of rules and etiquette; and an awareness of place within its wide-ranging lineage histories.

On the Tenor of Buddhist Practice and Discourse in the late Qing/Republican Period

The widespread destruction of Buddhist monasteries during the Taiping civil war (1851–64), both deliberate and circumstantial, had a profound effect on the material setting and structures of Buddhist life in south China, which had long been the heartland of Chinese Buddhist activity and support. In the decades immediately following the war's bloody conclusion, considerable energy was applied to campaigns to reconstruct fallen monasteries and temples. Fundraising and construction dominated.

In the aftermath of that turmoil and rebuilding effort, a cohort of figures appeared whose work and activities produced one of the most remarkable periods of Chinese Buddhist history. These individuals came to maturity and authority at the end of the Qing and during the early Republic. While their family origins were scattered across a variety of regions, for the most part they settled in the south-east Buddhist heartland. Buddhists were not separated from the political, social and intellectual transformations in the air at this time, and from various angles these individuals collectively produced a creative restatement of Chinese Buddhist life. Their teachings and reforms remain pervasive, dominant elements in present-day activities and discourse, such that any attempt to make sense of current modes requires familiarity with the basic positions of this earlier period.[2]

In the late 19th century, there were several types of sites where monks or nuns lived. They ranged from the large "public monasteries" (*shifang conglin*) that were understood as corporate property of the Buddhist sangha, with populations of long-term residents that could number in the hundreds; to equally large "hereditary monasteries" (*zisun miao*) controlled by specific lineages; to smaller complexes of the hereditary type, including sites with as few as one to five monastics in residence; to temples controlled by a local community or a group of laymen, sometimes as a profit-making venture, in which religious professionals were in a sense employees. There also were simple dwellings for solitary practitioners or small groups of monastics engaged in intensive practice, at isolated places in the countryside, usually at mountain sites. (All these institutional types still exist today.) Economic support for these institutions was varied, ranging from the rents paid on large land-holdings and profits made from investment of surplus income, to substantial gifts from wealthy families, to proceeds from ritual activities carried out for lay sponsors (usually tied to funerary or memorial matters), to small plots

---

2. Materials in this section are drawn most especially from readings in a wide range of primary sources; space limitations do not permit extensive citation. For primary and secondary sources in Chinese on some of the principal figures of this period, especially biographies and autobiographies, see Raoul Birnbaum, "Master Hongyi looks back: a 'modern man' becomes a monk in twentieth-century China," in Steven Heine and Charles Prebish (eds.), *Buddhism and the Modern World* (New York: Oxford University Press, forthcoming 2003). In English, the most important study remains the remarkable two-volume work of Holmes Welch: *The Practice of Chinese Buddhism 1900–1950* (Cambridge, MA: Harvard University Press, 1967) and *The Buddhist Revival in China* (Cambridge, MA: Harvard University Press, 1968). My analysis sometimes differs significantly from that of Welch, but I remain ever indebted to him for these works. In Chinese, the principal history of Buddhist activities during this period is Shi Dongchu, *Zhongguo fojiao jindai shi*, 2 vols. (Taipei: Zhonghua fojiao wenhua guan, 1974); this work should be read with the understanding that Dongchu was a disciple of Taixu, a principal figure in this history.

farmed by clerics themselves at remote places. Very importantly, there was no centralized authority internal to the system that exerted any real control over its many aspects.

While some clerics never travelled far from their native place (constrained in part by linguistic ties), many others roamed widely, sampling life at institutions in a variety of regions. They wandered through a remarkable nation-wide circulatory system that accumulated individuals at distinctive nodal points. These wanderers circulated ideas, practices, tales and gossip – essential factors in the construction of a linked system, rather than an atomized set of highly localized institutions. This circulatory system still retains its essential shape and functions. The best-known centres for practice and learning were mainly (although not exclusively) situated in the south-eastern provinces of Zhejiang, Jiangsu and Fujian. These regions also had especially large populations of lay followers, who were encouraged and instructed by the presence of numerous capable clerics, and in turn famously gave them support. Northern clerics who wanted to advance in their training, and those who wanted a more secure economic footing, tended to flow towards the major centres of the south-east.

In the late 19th and early 20th centuries, leading members of this cohort of monks, which loosely spanned two generations, were fairly consistent in their sharp critique of Buddhist life and the need for reform and renewal. Internally, levels of monastic training and practice were criticized. Put bluntly, there was considerable concern at the number of unlearned "rice buckets" within the system, whose adherence to monastic precepts was variable. The vital question concerned monastic vocation: what are the aims of monastic life, and by what means – training, leadership – can those aims be supported, achieved and sustained? This question was urgently felt. Externally, economic and political security were growing ever more tenuous, and there were voracious attempts at national, provincial and local levels to take over monastery buildings for "more productive" use as secular schools. There was a sense that the internal and external problems were linked, and that a higher level of monastic training and discipline would result in greater respect and support from the outside, as well as an inherent ability to ward off looming threats.

Significantly, while many of these prominent teachers did not ignore the work of the famous masters of the Tang and the Song, they turned for inspiration most especially to brilliant figures of the late 16th and 17th centuries (such as Zibo Zhenke, Hanshan Deqing, Yunqi Zhuhong, Ouyi Zhixu and Jianyue Duti), all of whom worked to renovate or even resuscitate the Buddhist practice traditions of their time, sometimes under very difficult conditions. There was, I think, a circumstantial kinship. Today, many look to the late Qing–Republican teachers for authoritative guidance, just as those teachers turned to their predecessors. This is a crucial point: Chinese Buddhists work within a historical continuum that neither ended in the Tang or Song, nor came to some final, memory-free halt with the Cultural Revolution.

The responses of this cohort group to the particular challenges of the age may be set into two distinctive categories: an approach powerfully framed within traditional discourse that in some ways may be viewed as "fundamentalist," and a call for comprehensive reform that consciously embraced a certain vision of modernity. The same question of vocation remains a central issue today, and present-day positions draw directly from these earlier responses, sometimes citing the main proponents as their authoritative sources.

The first response, sometimes (although misleadingly) termed "conservative," consisted of various positions taken by monks thought of as "practitioners" (*xiuxing ren*), some of whom also were renowned as scholars within the tradition. They spoke from a basis of traditionally constituted training and personal realization, and thus commanded considerable respect within the lay and monastic community. The most prominent figures included the Pure Land master Yinguang (1861–1940), the Vinaya master Hongyi (1880–1942), Chan teachers such as Yekai (1852–1922), Jing'an (Bazhi Toutuo, 1851–1913), Yuanying (1878–1953), Laiguo (1881–1953) and Xuyun (1840–1959), and Tiantai master Dixian (1858–1932) and his disciple Tanxu (1875–1963). There were many others with regional rather than national reputations. Some of these men were abbots of high-prestige monasteries, while others preferred a less settled, more itinerant teaching life. I have listed these many names, and could have added quite a few more, to give a sense of the exceptional number that constituted this era's stellar array of monks of high reputation.

The fundamentalist approach was characterized by an attempt at reform through a return to basics, but the notion of basics differed somewhat amongst the various proponents. Many voiced explicit concerns over what practices could be effective in such difficult historical times. For some, an insistence on basics was set in discourse that suggested an unbudging resistance to any other approach. What they produced was a paring down to essentials, with boundaries clearly set.

The result was a narrowed range of practices, with particular emphasis on singular practices as the core of activity. The principal modes were this: for pure land practice, *yixin nianfo* ("single-minded concentration on the buddha"); for Chan practice, internal investigation through vigilant concentration on the key phrase *nianfo shi shei?* ("who is it who is mindful of the buddha?" that is, "who am I?"). If diligently carried out, these are powerfully effective practices that produce tremendous mental focus. They are not unique in the history of Chinese Buddhist practice, but the paring down to the singularity of practice as a core procedure within each cultivation tradition and the constricted range of practice options overall are particular characteristics of this era.

Some of these teachers were text-literal. They looked for fundamentals and held to them without distraction or deviation, sometimes to a point that others might consider intolerant. By this time the vast range of scriptural texts was narrowed down to a core group that received thorough study. These included the "three big sutras," certain small ones and a few additional works. The three big sutras were the *Huayan jing*, the *Lotus Sutra* and the *Lengyan jing*. In addition, some Chan practitioners studied texts such as the *Sutra of Complete Awakening*, the Sixth Patriarch's *Platform Sutra*, and the *Vimalakirti Sutra*; the *Treatise on the Awakening of Faith in the Great Vehicle* also was studied across lineage tradition lines. The small sutras were mainly those that focused on individual buddhas and bodhisattvas, and the vows they have made to aid all beings. Their popularity reflects the strongly devotional qualities of Chinese Buddhist life, a meeting point that united practitioners across the range of Buddhist China, from the least educated to the most sophisticated traditional adherents. The short texts include works on Amita Buddha, the Healing Buddha and Dizang Bodhisattva, as well as individual chapters separated from long works, such as the chapter on Guanyin from the *Lotus*, and the chapter on Puxian Bodhisattva's vows and practices from the *Huayan*. In addition, the *Diamond Sutra* circulated widely. These texts were objects of intensive study, but also, very importantly, many of them – especially the short texts – were chanted rapidly as a religious exercise. The ability to chant such texts is not necessarily related to any engagement with the complex of conceptual meanings contained within them.

While certainly these texts contain enough to provide a lifetime of fruitful study, comparison of the limited range of these works to the extraordinary variety contained within formal compendia available at that time, such as the *Dragon Treasury* (*Longzang*, the Buddhist canon produced during the Qianlong period), points to the prevailing characteristic of identifying a core and concentrating on it. This approach to texts is not new in Chinese Buddhist history, but it does form part of a constellation of factors that gives this era its particular texture.

A principal mode of textual study at this time, and thus of intellectual and spiritual development, was carried out by lecture series in monasteries, often presented by visiting masters invited for this purpose. In the case of long texts, it could take several months or longer to work through the material, sentence by sentence, paragraph by paragraph. While many prominent sutra lecturers had a range of texts within their grasp, often they were recognized for one text in particular (this is a well-established phenomenon in Chinese Buddhist history). Eminent monks such as the men listed above were invited to lecture all over the country, and clerics would gather at the lectures in order to study with such famous figures. Significantly, clerics could attend these lectures and pursue this type of higher learning throughout their lives.

I would like to return to this issue of training shortly, for in the contestation to define the nature of monastic life, to define the fundamental principles of monastic vocation – a contestation that is basic to this earlier period and continues to the present day – questions of monastic training were and continue to be central.

In contrast to this first response, the seemingly tireless monk Taixu (1889–1947) proposed a programme of comprehensive modernizing reform.[3] Taixu's talent and keen intelligence were recognized early in his career, when he studied and had close contact with some of the most eminent of the practitioners, such as Jing'an, Yuanying and Yinguang. However, his later views and actions caused some very painful ruptures in these relationships. These ruptures continue to demarcate some of the fault lines in Chinese Buddhist communities. Taixu was strongly driven by his understanding of modernity, which in part was conceived as Westernization. He hoped to induce a radical modernization of the Buddhist sangha, in which the numbers would be greatly reduced and the level of learning greatly increased. Taixu was concerned with creating a 20th-century Buddhism – which included notions of religion derived from Christian models, as well as notions of Buddhism derived from European academic assumptions. He devised numerous schemes as proposals for action, and out of these many proposals he established some enduring and highly influential institutions.

Taixu's work had support within some elements of Chinese Buddhist worlds, including reform-minded monks and some prominent lay critics of the monastic establishment. He also was strongly encouraged by relations with foreigners, especially Protestant missionaries in China, who cheered on his rhetoric of "anti-superstition," drastic clerical reform and social action. He gained considerable prestige in certain circles at home when he embarked on a nine-month tour of Europe and the United States in 1928–29. Very importantly, Taixu's close ties to government officials during the Republican period – which provided mutual benefit – helped establish a modern model for "political monks."

Taixu's provocative stance articulated a profound conceptual turn away from the underlying basis of the practitioners' position. Their Buddhism at core was a radical break from conventional society, a deep and uncompromising critique of the conventional values of worldly life. They sought to strengthen institutions and provide means of training through which clerics could achieve a classically understood Buddhist liberation. Their so-called conservative position is so radical that, properly grasped, it could be understood to threaten the stability of some constructed social and political orders. But it also is such a sharp break that those with secular power could view Buddhist institutions as no threat at all. In contrast to the step back from wordly engagement of the practitioners, Taixu sought to reconstruct the Buddhist clergy as an elite corps of men and women who would deeply engage with the world as it was encountered, and seek to change it.

Taixu wanted to get rid of the buddhas and bodhisattvas, and eliminate the funerary rites that were a principal source of income for some clerics and their monasteries. The buddhas and bodhisattvas in their guise as

3. For his collected writings, see *Taixu dashi quanshu*, 32 vols. (Taipei: Shandao si fojing liutongchu, 1998). In addition to Taixu's autobiography, *Taixu dashi zizhuan* (*ibid.* Vol. 29, pp. 163–311), his disciple Yinshun's *Taixu dashi nianpu* (Xinzhu: Zhangwen chubanshe, 1998) is a principal starting point for study of his life. See also Li Mingyu, *Taixu jiqi renjian fojiao* (Hangzhou: Jiangxi renmin chubanshe, 2000). An English language study also exists: Don A. Pittman, *Toward a Modern Chinese Buddhism: Taixu's Reforms* (Honolulu: University of Hawai'i, 2001).

celestial benefactors are illusions, as is the Western Paradise of Amita Buddha, to which so many Chinese Buddhist devotees seek rebirth. He proposed that superstition-free Buddhists turn this place right here into a pure land, by bright mental training and compassionate activity. The training would be achieved in *foxue yuan*, Buddhist studies academies, with a carefully constructed curriculum that emphasized advanced studies in Yogacara and Madhyamika treatises, highly philosophical traditions whose study had been neglected for some centuries in China but were especially appreciated by European academics at that time. Compassionate activity most particularly would take the form of charitable action, as was seen in the work of Christian missionaries in China.

The first few decades of the 20th century marked the beginning of the era of *foxue yuan*. The institution of monastic academies for training novices and newly ordained monks, while encouraged by those seeking a better educated and more closely disciplined sangha, was hastened at this time by repeated attempts at local and national levels to convert monasteries or sections of them into secular schools. Even when support for a Buddhist studies academy was not whole-hearted, it was understood as an effective pre-emptive move to preserve monastic property and independence. It also was conceived by some, such as Taixu, as a deliberate and positive move toward modernity. Taixu's conception of learning and his notion of such schools (shared with other educational reformers active in the sangha) was tied closely to the model of a Western-style university. He founded several academies for monks where courses included foreign languages, modern history and mathematics, as well as aspects of Buddhist studies. This conception of monastic education differed sharply from the earlier and still-prevailing mode, which focused on one subject at a time (a text or group of texts) for several months or sometimes for years, under a master and his close disciples. While most of Taixu's schools were short-lived, the Minnan foxue yuan, which he transformed in Fujian in 1927 when he became abbot of Xiamen's Nanputuo Monastery, has endured and indeed flourishes today as a large and well-run institution.

It is all too easy to produce a portrait of Taixu that is merely a caricature. He provides more than enough encouragement by his repeated creation of "world-wide" or national Buddhist associations of very modest membership in which he was a principal officer, or his various grand schemes for a tightly controlled clergy that would wear new vestments of his design (who put him in charge of the Buddhist sangha?). Still, the main thrust of his concerns shows a thoughtful, serious and original approach to a meaningful place for Buddhist monastic life in a modern world. With an emphasis on productive activity and a harsh critique of "superstition," it was an approach that in some ways met the needs of the coming political discourse.

In considering these influential figures, the question of eminence, or at least of high reputation, is central. How did these men gain their authority at that time? From a very traditional point of view, one could say that practice accomplishment is recognized by peers in the same way that professional musicians will recognize the most capable amonst them. But as in the musical world, only a few of those most capable rise to meet the public eye.

The circumstances by which Buddhist monks stepped up to that position in the late Qing and Republican period are not entirely clear. Still, one can see – through study of autobiographies and biographies written by close disciples – certain points in common. Almost all these men spent significant time in one of the high prestige monasteries of the south-east, sites known for strict and thorough training. Almost all of them studied texts under the most celebrated lecturers of their time. In these two circumstances, they also met their peers – other monks, old and young, willing to endure hardship in order to receive serious training. Although Buddhist self-cultivation as traditionally understood is a personal matter that is generated from within, social factors can be very important, including mutual support and a kind of friendly competition when members of a cohort group share the same difficult aim. Following their training within monasteries, almost all these men also engaged in extensive solitary retreat practices (to be discussed below). In addition, and very importantly for the construction of a public reputation, most of them were verbally adept and were excellent writers, and they had access to the means for dissemination of their writings (sometimes through influential lay disciples involved in publishing houses). Most of these men knew each other, so in addition to some shared vertical relationships (training under famous masters, studying at the same elite monasteries), they developed horizontal relationships amongst each other.

I would like to conclude this discussion with a few comments on long-term retreat, since almost all the eminent monks of the late Qing and Republican period were veterans of this highly demanding practice, including Taixu. There are two main forms: "sealed retreat" (*biguan*) and solitary mountain retreat. Said to have begun in the Yuan period, *biguan* came to the fore as a special practice bearing great prestige during the late Qing. Sealed retreat was a formal, contractual procedure for a set period usually ranging from three months to three years. It was carried out in a special hut or chamber within a monastic compound, or in a cave or small building far from inhabitation. In contrast, mountain retreat was free and open-ended. This less formal retreat at mountains or other isolated places has a long history in China, where indigenous practices tallied with elements of the forest-dwelling traditions valued by some Indian Buddhists.

An emphasis on retreat for concentrated and focused practice, as a route to accomplishment and also as part of the path to eminence and authority, is a particular and striking characteristic of this period. Thus, very importantly, some of the most esteemed practices within the system in this period were carried forth outside the routine, or indeed even outside the walls, of monasteries. Many of those who sought the highest attainment felt it necessary to leave the monastic environment, which supposedly was constructed and organized for that purpose. Free of the monastery, they were at liberty to engage in concentrated practice. This flow outwards is an implicit but emphatic criticism of monastery life, and an experience that fuelled the reformist discourse of the age.

The Present Situation: Some Key Issues in Monastic Life

There is a historical break between the world of those eminent monks – most of whom had passed away by the 1940s or early 1950s – and the present. It encompasses not only the creation of the People's Republic of China and the rise of a pervasive official unsympathy for the Buddhist enterprise, but also the profound difficulties of the Cultural Revolution, the effects of which lasted well beyond the conventional "ten years of chaos." The land reforms of 1950 and afterwards took a substantial economic base away from the large monasteries, as well as from some principal lay donors. Leading monks in some regions were publicly reviled as "landlords" (*dizhu*) and suffered grievously. Other fierce pressures severely diminished the size of the clergy, and numerous monasteries were destroyed or converted into factories, warehouses, schools or housing. In contrast to some successful strategizing in the preceding era, there no longer was a way to resist comprehensive territorial incursions. Lay activities also came to a halt, at least in public.[4]

It was not until well into the 1980s that the Buddhist enterprise began to rebound, although fitfully so, with considerable regional variation. This process continues, but not always in sympathetic circumstances. Winds blow one way, and then they change course to blow in some other direction. What appears stable and secure can suddenly take on another cast. Set against the backdrop of the 2,000-year expanse of Buddhist history in China, in which there have been some very troubled moments, this particular period of difficulty has not been brief.

In keeping with other comprehensive changes in Chinese society, there has been a significant change in the way that Buddhist monastic life is organized, controlled and regularized. Of the many organizations that Taixu and his cohorts formed, the China Buddhist Association (Zhongguo fojiao xiehui) (CBA) has remained as a pivot point between Buddhist monastics and responsible agencies and figures in the government. This national organization is internal to the Buddhist world and bears responsibility for such matters as setting policy, overseeing monastic life, disbursing certain funds, transmitting government directives downwards, and also representing Buddhist interests in an official and unified manner. In addition to its national office in Beijing, the CBA also has provincial and county branches, as well as branches in large cities with substantial Buddhist presence.[5] Thus, it is thoroughly integrated into a wide range of

---

4. The only extended scholarly account in English of the Buddhist situation during this period is Holmes Welch, *Buddhism under Mao* (Cambridge, MA: Harvard University Press, 1972), which looks at the first two decades of communist rule, including the initial years of the Cultural Revolution.

5. Some CBA functions are well expressed by the organization's monthly magazine, *Fayin*, currently edited by the prominent monk Jinghui, which provides a mix of official notices and clarifications of positions and policy, scholarly and semi-scholarly articles, and news or announcements of events around the country. Also, there are many regional Buddhist magazines, usually sponsored by branches of the CBA, such as: *Shanghai fojiao, Ningbo fojiao, Taizhou fojiao, Fujian fojiao.*

Buddhist matters and activities, from the broad national level to the most local concerns. It has a scrutinizing and regularizing function. The officers who fill its many positions by and large are monks and nuns, ordinarily including the heads or administrators of the most important monasteries. Also, there have been several laymen with key positions at the national level, notably the long-time president Zhao Puchu (d. 2000). The CBA provides a structure for clerics to have some voice in self-governance. By their positions and responsibilities such monks and nuns are pulled inexorably into a complex political world.

Despite certain sharp breaks from the past, there also are distinctive human continuities. Many of the most prominent monks who rose to responsibility and authority in the first stage of the rebuilding process were the direct disciples of the Republican era leaders. While the vast majority of this generation now have passed away or are elderly and retired, some of their direct disciples carry on and are conscious of their place within lineage traditions.

Rather like the period after the Taiping war, the most pressing immediate issues have been to rebuild material circumstances – monasteries and systems of economic support – and to reconstitute a clergy. Both processes now are well-established and continue apace. But at the same time, the intensity of the most significant question of the earlier period – what is the Buddhist monastic vocation, and what training and leadership are required to establish and safeguard that ideal? – is no less diminished, particularly after the significant growth of the clergy over the past dozen years or so.

The two positions staked out in the Republican period remain the dominant poles today, and the principal authors of those positions are cited often. The particular ways in which this question of vocation was framed in the first half of the 20th century arose in part from the pressures of modernity, under which some traditional forms of life were questioned. Those pressures certainly were intensified under communist rule, as the whole country was urged to transform its ways, with an emphasis on material productivity. While the position of reformers such as Taixu – who proposed a purging of "superstition," a paring down of personnel to a highly controlled core, a focus on involvement in the world through social service – met some of the discourse needs of the new society, that position was contested. The situation is no less critical in the face of the destabilizing effects of a new wave of prosperity and apparent social freedom that began to open out in the mid-1990s. And of course, while this is a question of absolutely basic importance, it continues to play out as a political question: *who* will define the answers?

Let me try to sketch out several interconnected matters that are fundamental to how the question is answered, especially how the question is framed or posed to youngsters within the system, as they constitute the future of that system. These include current training methods, the economics of monasteries and the issue of leadership.

There is a generation gap in the Order that was problematic in the 1980s and early 1990s. Its long-term effect still is not clear. In Chinese

Buddhist history, the great majority of monks ordinarily entered the Order by their late teens or early 20s (some became novices at a much earlier age). In the mid-1960s, when many clerics were compelled to return to lay life and monasteries were closed, up to the mid-1970s and even later, it was extraordinarily difficult to become a monk, especially for a young, bright, able-bodied person. At the early stages of attempts to reconstitute the clergy, a small core group of old men – who either had managed to hold on through the preceding decades, or returned to monasteries from their sojourns in lay life, often leaving families behind, or to the side – was responsible for an increasingly large group of new, young recruits. What was missing at many sites was a crucial middle generation of experienced hands who could give the young recruits practical guidance and serve as a link to the old, frail survivors. There was no substantial presence of men and women who in their daily activities could provide visible examples of what it meant to be accomplished clerics in the prime of life. This gap was especially difficult for novices, not yet ordained, who needed the most basic training and socializing into the traditions of the system.

One result was that some sites at that time could be unruly: the young led each other, sometimes with a lack of understanding of what it was that they did not know. Because in the 1960s and 1970s the minds of the populace were strongly directed towards concentration on other matters, there was a knowledge gap. Some novices came into the system with sparse basic knowledge and quite a few fantasies about Buddhist life. This at times compounded the problem. And also the physical strength of youngsters was desperately needed for the rebuilding effort, which elders could envisage but not enact themselves. Although novices traditionally have contributed physical labour to their home monastery as an initial stage of training, in this period new recruits at many sites worked to an exceptional degree and had little energy for study or conventional Buddhist practice.

Now at the beginning of the 21st century the situation has grown more stable, and Taixu's dream of a network of Buddhist studies academies for monks and nuns, with a fairly consistent curriculum that highlights intellectual training in Buddhist philosophy, has been fulfilled. Clerics still receive initial training from their tonsure master, and more advanced training in precepts at the time of full ordination, but the traditional practice of life-long text study by participation in extended lecture series presented by famous masters has been cut off. Instead, young monks and nuns may apply to attend a Buddhist studies academy. Those who meet the increasingly selective admissions criteria (which now include competitive written examinations on a variety of topics) may enrol for a course of study, often for three years' duration. Graduation from the best of these institutions is considered the equivalent of a university degree. While in the past some *foxue yuan* were instituted to forestall takeovers of monastic property for use as secular schools, ironically the result has been a kind of takeover from the inside, in which this mode of study now dominates.

In the past, any cleric could attend a sutra lecture series. The illiterate kitchen worker Huiming (1859–1930) attended lectures in the 1880s at Tiantong Monastery in Zhejiang that proved crucial to his development. Huiming later became a famous lecturer himself, and though he still looked like a simple peasant, he even went on to become a distinguished abbot of Hangzhou's famous Lingyin Monastery.[6] Paradoxically, with the broadening of monastic education, opportunities for some have become more limited, so that for example an intelligent fellow from the countryside with limited educational background, whose family could not afford tuition fees beyond elementary school, would be screened out by the competitive exams and could not advance his learning in this particular institutionalized mode.

Several additional points are worth special note. Following the modern university model, students take a large number of courses, including mandatory political study as well as specifically Buddhist matters. They survey many topics at once, take examinations, and move on term by term, in contrast to the old system that focused on mastery of one text at a time. Thus, a choice has been made (by whom? in what consultation?) for scope rather than depth. Given the amount of material to be covered, familiarity with the long sutras most often is limited to study of sections, rather than the full extent of the text (there are exceptions at some academies). Also, admission is limited to younger clerics, with cut-off ages usually at 28 or 30.

Thus, this system is set up to produce an elite of young clerics who are well-grounded in the parameters of their system. While those committed to life-long study have constructed a base from which to proceed, others may well feel that having received a degree and thus a kind of certification they have studied enough. Because the curricula are fairly consistent, this network of academies has a regularizing effect on the intellectual life of a generation of younger clerics. Again, the long-term effects of this method are not yet clear. (Significantly, the Buddhist studies academies provide scholarly clerics with positions as instructors, and thus they have a safe niche: approved sites in which to engage in activity that now is deemed socially productive, in contrast to the earlier harsh objections of the 1960s and 1970s.)

Monastic life has long been a means of up-classing in Chinese society. Young men with no particular prospects can enter the Order and receive food, shelter and clothing. One day, they are no one in particular, and the next, when they don monastic dress, they are entitled to respect from laypeople, who may bow before them and give them monetary gifts. Those with bright minds who wish to study may have access to opportunities that otherwise would have been out of the question (although now there are filters on that access). Those with power ambitions may rise to positions of considerable authority through avenues that otherwise would

6. A collection of Huiming's lectures was published in 1936 and has been reprinted many times. More recent editions usually include the biographical essay "Ji Huiming fashi" by his disciple Leguan (originally published separately in 1966); see *Huiming fashi kaishi lu* (Gaoxiong: Puzhao fotang, 1999), pp. 4–16.

have been closed to persons of their background. These surely are not the sole reasons for joining the Order and remaining, but they are relevant in thinking about the social textures of this way of life.

While *foxue yuan* now have been established all across the country, they vary greatly in size (from a score of students up to several hundred), quality and reputation. Some monastery heads consider graduates of the most prestigious of these institutions as the elite of the young generation, and these graduates may be eagerly recruited for permanent residence at the wealthiest and most famous monastic sites, where life is considerably more comfortable than in a small poor temple in the hinterland. The political training that is part of the curriculum also prepares some clerics for leadership roles in major monasteries and within the China Buddhist Association. Thus, certain types of tangible rewards may accrue to graduates beyond an informed grounding in their chosen way of life.

The various academies may differ in lineage flavour, so that for example at Yunmen shan's Dajue si, a Chan monastery whose elderly abbot Foyuan was Xuyun's attendant and close disciple, there is a Chan emphasis to studies, while at Lingyan shan si outside Suzhou, Yinguang's Pure Land teachings dominate. Some sites are especially known for good *daofeng*, their atmosphere of serious religious practice, such as the two just mentioned, while others may be less orderly, less serious or more attuned to other kinds of ambitions.

Training also is carried out in the day-to-day experience at monasteries. Some large monasteries have excellent reputations within the system as centres for dedicated religious practice, and they serve as gathering places for like-minded individuals. These sites are widely admired, even by those monks who have no desire to live in such rigorous environments. They include (but are not limited to) sites such as Gaomin Monastery outside Yangzhou, Yunju shan in Jiangxi, Yunmen shan in northern Guangdong, Lingyan shan outside Suzhou, Wolong Monastery in Xi'an. It is no accident that most of these monasteries were closely associated with masters such as Laiguo, Xuyun and Yinguang. The institutions explicitly continue the traditions of serious practice those teachers established there. This is a direct legacy from the Republican period.

However, the monastic economy has changed, and this has had an impact on monastic life. The vast landholdings formerly controlled by some large monasteries are gone, although some institutions do have smaller agricultural holdings, which monks and nuns may work themselves. Beyond the food produced on limited acreage by some institutions, as well as sale of surplus crops or speciality items such as tea, economic sustenance at present appears to flow from several principal sources: lay donors (including not only individuals from local communities but also Buddhist devotees abroad), performance of sponsored rituals (as a kind of work for hire), and various types of governmental agencies.

Donations to monasteries from lay devotees are not new in Chinese Buddhist history, nor is ritual for hire. Both cases produce a meeting ground between the lay and monastic population that appears simple, but can be vexed in the social complexities of the exchange. Many monasteries, especially in the south-east heartland, now depend on ritual activities for a substantial portion of their sustaining income. While the rites have as a basic principle the aim of benefiting all beings, their constant, repetitive, exhausting practice may be understood as a necessary act to sustain a certain economic standard.

In some regions the ability to perform rituals is a basic qualification for admission as a permanent resident to a monastery, and mastery of the principal solo chant roles in such popularly-performed rites as the highly theatrical *fang yankou* ("releasing the burning mouths") makes one a prime catch. The ritualists receive a portion of whatever is paid to the monastery, and they also may receive "red envelopes" directly from lay sponsors. The regions of China's principal economic boom are precisely the areas where historically there have been large numbers of lay Buddhists, and it is there that sponsored ritual activity is most intense (and most lucrative). In the right locale, a skilled ritualist with a commanding voice and steadfast energy can earn substantial amounts of money. It is exhausting work, though, and potentially has a corrosive effect on those who began monastic life with high ideals. A focus on ritual, which brings with it attendant financial rewards, is very different from a quiet life concentrated on meditation or mindfulness of the buddha, study of texts and teaching. Monasteries where such rituals are the main activity may be pervaded by the atmosphere produced by that focus.

Monks ordinarily receive a set monthly stipend from their monastery, which varies according to region, wealth of a particular institution and level of monastic position. In addition to supplements earned through ritual performance, they receive monetary offerings from lay disciples (if they have them), as well as general offerings made by laypeople to monks of the entire monastery, especially on important holidays in the Buddhist and traditional calendar. They may need money for travel, for purchase of personal items, including sometimes cellphones and computers; some are able to support impoverished family members back home. Due to economic factors and the reputation of several key monasteries, the flow of monks from the north and hinterlands into the south-east Buddhist heartland continues as it did earlier.

Imperial sponsorship of certain monasteries had a long tradition in China, so one could say that the present economic support (or intrusion) by governmental agencies has a context. This support is most pronounced at large and famous monasteries, at the now-thriving four principal Buddhist mountain pilgrimage centres, and at some newly created sites. As part of the process of renovation and renewal begun in the 1980s, various government agencies have sponsored building projects at monasteries. This has had the short-term effect of infusing local economies, but especially a long-term effect in creating local and regional tourist attractions, with all the collateral economic benefits that could be imagined.

This is especially pronounced at many traditional pilgrimage sites, which now have been developed by local authorities as tourist destinations (in which religion forms a mildly exotic backdrop), and so from a Buddhist point of view there is a complicated mix of purity and defilement, dedication and sensual abandonment, all jostling in the same space. Monastic autonomy or self-direction sometimes becomes difficult under these conditions, and such monasteries may regain their quiet air only in the evening when the main gates finally are closed. In some large monasteries located in or near urban areas, or at prime pilgrimage sites, inhabitants are subjected to daily scrutiny as if they were part of a "living history" exhibit. As internal tourism rapidly expands in China, this experience grows with it. Of course, the tourist experience also provides opportunities for outsiders to come into contact with the Buddhist monastic world. In addition to supporting existing sites, some localities have created their own Buddhist holy places, apparently as business ventures, by such means as the construction of massive bronze or copper images, approached through a funnel of tourist facilities to which a small temple has been appended.

The institutionalization of charitable activities has become a conspicuous element of the expression of monastic economy at certain large and wealthy sites. Although there are precedents in Chinese Buddhist history, this particular mode seems to spring directly from the modernizing reformers' emphatic call to transform our world into a pure land. One notably active site for charitable work is Nanputuo Monastery in Xiamen, a place that bears the strong imprint of its former abbot Taixu.[7] Typically, aid is given for disaster relief, to old people, those who are sick or weak, and to children in schools in poor communities. This aid is given from one institution (the monastery or its charitable organization) to another (hospital, school and so on), but it is personalized by a ceremonial bestowal at the site of need by the monastery's abbot and assistants, as recorded with photographs. This very public charitable aid emphasizes Buddhist kindness that is expressed in material means. It presents a conspicuous display of productive responsibility to the nation. Some abbots also are notably attentive to a variety of needs personally brought before them, and can make a big difference in a private and unheralded way.

Let us turn now to the very serious matter of leadership. The long list of eminent teachers of the Republican period is unimaginable in the current scene. Of the men who made it through the storms of the 1950s, 1960s and 1970s and then were able to step up to lead monasteries in these last two decades, a few – for example, such widely admired teachers as Foyuan, Benhuan and Delin – remain as vibrant links to the now-legendary figures of the Republican era. But at this point most of the venerable *Dade* (Great Virtuous Ones) have passed away or stepped aside. Even if some of these elders have served merely as dignified figureheads, their absence is palpable in the current scene.

7. Nanputuo's charitable organization, the Xiamen Nanputuo si cishan shiye jijin hui, became a member of the China Charity Federation in 1995. Comprehensive reports are included in its annual publication, *Cishan*. The principal convent in Xiamen, Shishi chanyuan, an institution with an active Buddhist studies academy for nuns and close links to Nanputuo and its famous Minnan foxue yuan, also founded a charitable organization in March 2000.

In some cases they have been replaced by men of a different sort, whose reputations have been forged not in the rigours of the meditation hall but by proving themselves as capable administrators with well-honed political skills. Generally these monks are graduates of the Buddhist studies academies. Such men also may hold positions in local, provincial or even national political bodies, and thus they may well have mastered the kind of thinking and rhetoric required to protect and advance Buddhist interests in the current environment. At the same time, undeniably it is their Buddhist affiliation that provided the route to achieving this political station. Their position as leaders of large monasteries, sometimes surrounded by core teams of monk-administrators that they have brought with them, certainly has an effect on the atmosphere of those institutions. This may produce another notion of monastic vocation.

At the same time that this new route to prominence has been forged, some among the generation now in their late 20s and early 30s are beginning to emerge as talented and authoritative leaders in a traditional sense, respected by their peers for their practice accomplishments. These are men and women who have a decade or more of experience, who diligently sought out excellent guidance, and then applied themselves to the work at hand with such dedication that the result is immediately apparent. It is relevant, I think, that by the timing of their birth, members of this age-group are less scarred by grievous political events than those of immediately preceding generations, and they have come to maturity after the initial rebuilding efforts have been established.

It is significant that when one asks such men and women about their heroes and models, they invoke the names and the specific methods of the practitioner-leaders of the immediate past: Xuyun, Hongyi, Yinguang, Laiguo and their direct disciples. To pursue training and practice without interruption or intrusion, some have moved from the heartland to remote areas (to small, quiet temples in outlying areas or even to such places as caves in Gansu), to traditional zones for solitary retreat practice such as the Zhongnan Mountains, or to small and scarcely-noticed temples of their own in an urban environment (*jingshe*, as small as one or two rooms in size). The move out from the big monasteries at key points in the lives of some serious practitioners of the late Qing and Republic is mirrored in these contemporary acts. It, too, can be seen as an implicit criticism of the pressures and trends of contemporary monastic life.

Tibet and Abroad

Shifting, unstable notions of "inside" and "outside" link two additional matters of considerable importance. The first is the issue of relations with ethnic Chinese Buddhists, especially Buddhist teachers, living outside the PRC. Secondly, there is the matter of Han and Tibetan interchange in the Buddhist field. I mentioned earlier that a list of eminent, widely known Buddhist teachers of present-day China could not compare in number to that of the Republican period. Attempts to fill this space have been made by figures from abroad, as well as by teachers from Tibetan culture areas.

Many monks left the mainland in 1949 for Taiwan and Hong Kong.

Some were already eminent, such as the elderly Tanxu, who fled from the north-east to settle in Hong Kong. Others were young and unknown. A number ventured outwards through Asia, most especially Fujian natives who found natural connections to long-established Chinese communities of Fujian émigrés in Malaysia, Singapore and the Philippines. A few eventually moved farther afield to join overseas Chinese communities in places such as the United States, Canada and Australia. Some among these émigrés have risen to considerable prominence in their new locales, with large numbers of lay followers, devoted corps of monastic disciples and extensive international real estate holdings in the form of grand monastic establishments with numerous subsidiary branches. In a few cases, their teachings have had some impact on the mainland, especially (but not exclusively) among laypersons.

Among the Taiwan-based teachers, Xingyun (b. 1927), strongly influenced by Taixu's "humanistic Buddhism," is founder of the enormously wealthy and politically influential Foguang shan movement in Taiwan, with branches world-wide. Several others also are well-known in the PRC, such as the Chan teacher Shengyan (b. 1930), as well as the nun Zhengyan (b. 1937) and her very active Ciji charitable organization. Commentaries on precepts by the Vinaya master Guanghua (1924–96) have been used widely to train novices for monastic ordination.

A very traditional scholar-practitioner in the Tiantai tradition (the contemporary lineage running through Dixian and Tanxu), Miaojing (b. 1930) is well-regarded in corresponding circles in China. A native of the north-east, he lived in Hong Kong for many years, moved to California in the early 1970s, and recently established a monastic complex in the mountains of northern New Mexico.

The Chan teacher Xuanhua (1918–95) left his position under Xuyun at Nanhua Monastery to emigrate to Hong Kong in 1949, and later moved to the United States in 1962. He established a network of monasteries in North America and Asia, most importantly the City of Ten Thousand Buddhas in northern California, a trilingual (Chinese, Vietnamese, English) Buddhist community for lay and monastic practitioners. Many of his sutra commentaries, transcribed from recorded lectures, are available in the bookstalls of large monasteries on the mainland. His accomplishments as a practitioner and teacher are held in high regard, and the legacy of his flourishing activities in the West is a factor in his homeland reputation.

While Xuanhua's followers have disseminated his teachings across China by means of the techniques of modern publishing, some other teachers have made intensive use of the most contemporary technologies to re-enter the mainland. Professional quality productions of Xingyun's lectures can be seen on mainland television. The monk Jingkong (b. 1927), a controversial Pure Land teacher who situates himself in Yinguang's tradition, has produced numerous video compact discs of his lectures for free distribution and use for television broadcasts. In addition, his organization of lay disciples in Singapore transmits daily webcasts of live lectures.

I have raised the names of several influential "overseas" clerics. It is important to recognize that almost all of them (with the exception of

Taiwan-born Zhengyan) have mainland origins, and thus they have somewhat complicated insider/outsider relations to Buddhist circles in the PRC.

In addition to monastics, overseas lay devotees have played a fundamental role – economically and politically – in the effort to rebuild the material structures of Buddhist life in China. Their donations have gone not only to institutions for reconstruction projects, but also to congregations of monks and nuns at pilgrimage sites and large monasteries (sometimes in the form of sponsored vegetarian feasts, with "red envelope" monetary offerings distributed to each monastic participant), as well as significant gifts to elders. Also, some overseas devotees regularly come to the mainland to sponsor complex rituals such as the seven-day *shuilu* rites (for the liberation of all creatures of "sea and land"), thus enhancing monastic economies. This steadfast support, which continues to flow into Buddhist China, was crucial to the survival of Buddhist life after the Cultural Revolution.

"Buddhism" is posited by some as an international religion, and exists as such in the constructions of diplomatic and academic rhetoric, but in this present era it appears that Buddhists of most other cultural traditions seem to hold little real allure for Han Buddhists. Beyond the linguistic gap, which is significant, there are profound cultural gaps that seem insurmountable. Specifically in the Buddhist sphere, these include very different emphases or interpretations of Buddhist teachings and, most jarringly, different understandings of the codes of behaviour for monastic and lay practice. Thus Han Buddhists may feel that what others call "Buddhism" is not really the same thing, nor – very importantly – is it the "real" thing. There have been many friendly exchange visits between Han Buddhist dignitaries and various Buddhist groups from abroad, and generous economic support from Japanese Buddhist organizations has transformed some ancient Chinese sites important to Japanese lineage histories, but Buddhist teachers from outside Han circles do not seem to have made any substantial impact on the mainland. The significant exception lies in Tibetan worlds of teaching and practice.

The complex history of Tibetan-Han interchange in the 20th and 21st centuries is best told by specialists in those matters, as it is difficult and even treacherous for the uninitiated to penetrate the numerous layers of discourse produced by parties situated in a variety of positions. Still, I would like to attempt a brief sketch of the present state of this interchange in the specific realm of Han Buddhist practice and what is best understood as a Han Buddhist imaginary (*imaginaire*). This sketch portrays a set of contradictions – oppositions of views and oscillating attitudes.[8]

8. For a thoughtful and nuanced assessment of the current situation, see Matthew T. Kapstein, "A thorn in the dragon's side: Tibetan Buddhist culture in China," in Morris Rossabi (ed.), *Governing China's Multi-ethnic Frontiers* (Seattle: University of Washington Press, forthcoming 2003). For essential historical background, see Gray Warren Tuttle, "Faith and nation: Tibetan Buddhists in the making of modern China (1902–1958)," PhD dissertation, Harvard University, 2002. Among many significant points argued, Tuttle makes clear the importance of Taixu's work in fostering studies of Tibetan Buddhist traditions during the Republican period, and shows how this work was entangled with a range of political strategies and aspirations.

Over the past decade, there has been a small but steady flow of Han monks and nuns to the eastern Tibetan border regions of Amdo and Kham, such as beyond Kangding into the mountainous far western reaches of Sichuan. They travel there to study with Tibetan teachers, and often remain for a year or two to live under extremely harsh conditions. Groups of Han laypeople also have been travelling to well-known pilgrimage sites important to Tibetan Buddhists, sites in the Tibetan Autonomous Region as well as those in Tibetan culture areas within Sichuan and Qinghai provinces. Tibetan Buddhist books in Chinese translation, and books about Tibetan Buddhism, have been circulating on the mainland. Some are lurid, romantic accounts, others provide traditional biographies of saintly culture heros such as Milarepa, while others are demanding works that have become the focus of long-term lay study groups, such as the 14th-century Tibetan reformer Tsongkhapa's *Great Stages of the Path*. While a few Tibetans have become monastics in the Han tradition, for the most part the flow of learning has been in the opposite direction. What can be said about this phenomenon?

Principally, I think, there is the issue of difference, seen from several angles. Tibetan Buddhist forms and customs differ significantly from Han practices. Not only is the liturgy conducted in Tibetan language, but the daily rites are not at all the same as the thrice-daily communal rituals carried out in Han monasteries. The images in worship halls also are not the same: there are many figures in the Tibetan pantheon who are not encountered on Han altars. Practice methods also may differ, with a special emphasis on mantra and certain types of visualization methods as central elements of daily practice. In terms of daily sustenance, there are different customs for economic maintenance of monks and nuns, and importantly Tibetan monastics eat meat if it is available, in contrast to the strict vegetarian diet of Han Buddhists. And of course the altitude and harsh climate are challenging for outsiders to endure.

Thus, those who travel to these remote sites and are able to withstand the hardships to remain for a period of study are consciously looking for something strikingly different from the Han Buddhist teachings that are more easily available to them. In some cases they come to study with specific masters, whose charismatic reputations have filtered through to the heartland of Han Buddhism, mainly by word of mouth but also by photograph and descriptive flyer. Others make the long journey in hope of encountering one of these mysterious figures, who can initiate them into the powerful intricacies of a different Buddhism. There is something alluring about this difference, and something considered so valuable that one is willing to endure considerable physical hardship – something that these individuals are unable to find nearby.

Chinese media representations of Tibet and Tibetans have flip-flopped over the past few decades, depending on the political moment. These media representations have been absorbed by Buddhists in the Han population, as much as by any others who read newspapers and watch television. Some popular images of Tibetans focused on their undeveloped, wild, savage, child-like (or even sub-human) qualities, and emphasize the need to liberate, educate, civilize and discipline the population. While these images linger in popular consciousness, the opposite vision also has arisen, especially in recent years: the mysterious, supremely-accomplished, wonderfully pure, super-human Buddhist teachers of Tibet and the natural spirituality of the populace.[9]

Han Buddhist views about Tibetan Buddhist teachings, practices and teachers seem to mirror these extremes. They range from abhorrence of the difference and dismissal of its value, to absorbing attraction. Some monastics and lay Buddhists make the journey to Tibetan culture areas to fulfil fantasies or simply for the wild adventure of it. But in between these extremes, there are very serious individuals who endure the hardships in order to learn advanced meditative techniques and study practices aimed at overcoming and dissolving inner obstructions: traditional aims of Buddhist practitioners.

While Tibetans formerly were viewed as "other," attempts to integrate them within the Chinese nation-state have included media barrages that emphasize their place within the People's Republic, their kinship in the great Chinese family. And as this view permeates popular consciousness, study with Tibetan teachers has begun to seem increasingly reasonable to Han Buddhists. But still in the end the differences are so great that such study should be seen as a move out. For some, it is a distinctive mark of dissatisfaction or frustration with what commonly is available within the Han Buddhist environs.

Concluding Comments

In this article I have sought to identify several lines of coherence in the recent history and present activities of Buddhists in China. In order to accomplish a set of aims within a limited page space, I have made certain choices. Some modes of description, and some topics, have not been highlighted. There are no "tales of the field" here, at least not explicitly so, although this essay could not have been composed without field experience to reflect upon. I have not discussed at any length the world of nuns, whose numbers on the mainland are a good deal fewer than those of monks (in contrast to the situation in Taiwan). Given the strict gender separations maintained in this conservative aspect of Chinese society, many aspects of nuns' lives remain outside the experience of a male fieldworker. While interviews and observations suggest that the principal religious issues affecting nuns largely have been the same as the main issues confronting monks, my knowledge of the details of nuns' lives is not sufficient to venture substantive comments. Laypeople, like the clergy, come from all walks of society and have a wide range of motivations and understanding. Some are quite as dedicated to real engagement with Buddhist practice as the most serious monks and nuns, others find their place principally as generous donors who support monastic needs, others may only appear for rituals or advice in times of

9. A work by Michael Taussig, *Shamanism, Colonialism, and the Wild Man* (Chicago: University of Chicago Press, 1987), considers this type of cultural pathology in a different setting.

loss or trouble, others have reached their last years and prepare for death by chanting and other temple activities. A good deal of lay practice may be carried out privately before a family altar at home, and in this sense it is more difficult to observe and discuss – except on a case-by-case basis – than more public activities carried out in monastic halls.

This is not a comprehensive report but an inquiry into a world in process, set against the screen of its recent past. To conclude, I want to emphasize this matter of process. In 1968 or 1970, in the depths of the Cultural Revolution, it would have been difficult to foresee the astonishing Buddhist revival that has taken place over the past 15 years. Indeed, even ten years ago it might have been hard to imagine the liveliness of the current scene. While what the future now holds will only be seen as it occurs, for the Buddhist enterprise in China this future will continue to be shaped not only by individuals and groups within the Buddhist world, but also by powerful social, economic and political forces – as well as by powerful actors – within a China undergoing rapid change. At present the effect of the larger society on Buddhists often is visible, but the effect of Buddhists on the larger society is not at all clear. Whether that will change remains a question of no small importance in considering the vital future of Buddhists and their practices in a Chinese setting.

Islam in China: Accommodation or Separatism?

Dru C. Gladney

ABSTRACT Many of the challenges China's Muslims confront remain the same as they have for the last 1,400 years of continuous interaction with Chinese society, but some are new as a result of China's transformed and increasingly globalized society, and especially since the watershed events of the 11 September terrorist attacks and the subsequent "war on terrorism." Muslims in China live as minority communities, but many such communities have survived in rather inhospitable circumstances for over a millennium. This article examines Islam and Muslim minority identity in China, not only because it is where this author has conducted most of his research, but also because with the largest Muslim minority in East Asia, China's Muslims are clearly the most threatened in terms of self-preservation and Islamic identity. I argue that successful Muslim accommodation to minority status in China can be seen to be a measure of the extent to which Muslim groups allow the reconciliation of the dictates of Islamic culture to their host culture. This goes against the opposite view that can be found in the writings of some analysts, that Islam in the region is almost unavoidably rebellious and that Muslims as minorities are inherently problematic to a non-Muslim state. The history of Islam in China suggests that both within each Muslim community, as well as between Muslim nationalities, there are many alternatives to either complete accommodation or separatism.

China's Muslims are in the midst of the first decade of their second millennium under Chinese rule. Many of the challenges they confront remain the same as they have for the last 1,400 years of continuous interaction with Chinese society, but some are new as a result of China's transformed and increasingly globalized society, and especially the watershed events of the 11 September terrorist attacks and the subsequent "war on terrorism." Muslims in China live as minority communities amid a sea of people, in their view, who are largely pork-eating, polytheist, secularist and kafir ("heathen"). Nevertheless, many of their small and isolated communities have survived in rather inhospitable circumstances for over a millennium. Though small in population percentage (about 2 per cent in China), their numbers are nevertheless large in comparison with other Muslim states (just over 20 million). For example, there are more Muslims in China than Malaysia, and more than every Middle Eastern Muslim nation except Iran, Turkey and Egypt. China is also increasingly dependent on mainly Muslim nations for energy and as an export market (one recent estimate suggests that China will be as dependent on Middle-East oil as Japan by 2050 according to current growth rates).[1] As

---

1. Keith Bradsher, "China wrestles with dependence on foreign oil," *International Herald Tribune*, 4 September 2002, p. 1.

Jonathan Lipman[2] noted, these long-term Muslim communities have often been the "familiar strangers" found in small enclaves throughout Asia. And if Kosovo and Bosnia are to serve as lessons, failure to accommodate Muslim minorities can lead to national dismemberment and international intervention. Indeed, China's primary objection to NATO involvement in Kosovo centred on its fear that this might encourage the aiding and abetting of separatists, with independence groups in Xinjiang, Tibet and perhaps Taiwan clearly a major Chinese concern. The US and China's pressure on the United Nations to include the ETIM group as a terrorist organization reflects this ongoing fear over Muslim activism in China.[3]

This article seeks to examine Islam as it relates to Muslim minority identity in China, not only because it is where this author has conducted most of his research, but also because with the largest Muslim minority in East Asia, China's Muslims are clearly the most threatened in terms of self-preservation and Islamic identity. Because of the history of Chinese state integration and the recognition of Muslims along national minority lines, it is necessary to examine Islam from the perspective of Muslim identity in the Chinese nation-state. Indeed, as Islam makes no distinction between state and church, or politics and religion, to discuss it in the abstract in China without reference to minority identity would be to ignore the way it is experienced and practised in the daily lives of Muslims today. I suggest, however, that the wide variety of Islamic practice among Muslims in China indicates that there is no monolithic Islam in China, though there are many basic tenets of Islam upon which all Muslims everywhere, and not just China, agree. Most relevant is the thesis put forth that successful Muslim accommodation to minority status in China can be seen to be a measure of the extent to which Muslim groups allow the reconciliation of the dictates of Islamic culture to their host culture. This goes against the opposite view that can be found in the writings of some analysts of Islam in China, such as Raphael Israeli and Michael Dillon, that Islam in the region is almost unavoidably rebellious and that Muslims as minorities are inherently problematic to a non-Muslim state.[4]

Islam in China

Islam in China has primarily been propagated over the last 1,300 years among the people now known as "Hui," but many of the issues confronting them are relevant to the Turkic and Indo-European Muslims on

---

2. Jonathan Lipman, *Familiar Strangers: A History of Muslims in Northwest China* (Seattle: University of Washington Press, 1997), p. 2.

3. For the controversy over this unitary US–China policy, see Erik Eckholm, "US labeling of group in China as terrorist is criticized," *New York Times*, 13 September 2002, p. 1; Charles Hutzler, "US gesture to China raises crackdown fears," *The Wall Street Journal*, 10 September 2002, p. 3.

4. See Raphael Israeli, *Muslims in China* (London & Atlantic Highlands: Curzon & Humanities Press, 1978), p. 7; and Michael Dillon, *Hui Muslims in China* (London: Curzon Press, 1997), pp. 2–8.

China's Inner Asian frontier. "Hui teaching" (*Hui jiao*) was the term once used in Chinese to indicate "Islam" in general, and probably derives from an early Chinese rendering of the term for the modern Uyghur people. Although the official nationality figures from the 2000 census are not yet published, initial estimates suggest that they do not differ substantially from 1990. According to the reasonably accurate 1990 national census of China, the total Muslim population is 17.6 million, including Hui (8,602,978), Uyghur (7,214,431), Kazakh (1,111,718), Dongxiang (373,872), Kyrgyz (373,872), Salar (87,697), Tajik (33,538), Uzbek (14,502), Bonan (12,212) and Tatar (4,873). The Hui speak mainly Sino-Tibetan languages; Turkic-language speakers include the Uyghur, Kazakh, Kyrgyz, Uzbek and Tatar; combined Turkic-Mongolian speakers include the Dongxiang, Salar and Bonan, concentrated in Gansu's mountainous Hexi corridor; and the Tajik speak a variety of Indo-Persian dialects. It is important to note, however, that the Chinese census registered people by nationality, not religious affiliation, so the actual number of Muslims is still unknown, and all population figures are influenced by politics in their use and interpretation.

While the Hui have been labelled the "Chinese-speaking Muslims," "Chinese Muslims," and most recently, "Sino-Muslims,"[5] this is misleading, since by law all Muslims living in China are "Chinese" by citizenship, and there are large Hui communities who speak primarily the non-Chinese languages where they live, such as the Tibetan, Mongolian, Thai and Hainan Muslims, who are also classified by the State as Hui. These "Hui" Muslims speak Tibetan, Mongolian and Thai as their first languages, with Han Chinese the national language that they learn in school (having to learn Arabic and Persian, of course, in the mosque). Interestingly, since Tajik is not an official language in China, the Tajiks of Xinjiang (who speak a Daric branch language, distantly related to old Persian, and quite different from the Tajik languages spoken in Tajikistan), learn in either Turkic Uyghur or Han Chinese at school.

Nevertheless, it is true that compared to most other Muslim nationalities in China, most Hui are closer to the Han Chinese in terms of demographic proximity and cultural accommodation, adapting many of their Islamic practices to Han ways of life, which often became the source for many of the criticisms of the Muslim reformers. In the past, this was not as great a problem for the Turkish and Indo-European Muslim groups, as they were traditionally more isolated from the Han and their identities not as threatened, though this has begun to change in the last 40 years. As a result of state-sponsored nationality identification campaigns over the course of the last 30 years, these groups have begun to think of themselves more as ethnic nationalities, something more than just "Muslims." The Hui are unique among the 55 identified nationalities in China in that they are the only one for whom religion is the only unifying

---

5. For the debate over the definition of Hui and reference to them as "Sino-Muslims," see Lipman, *Familiar Strangers*, p. xxiv

category of identity, even though many members of the Hui nationality may not practise Islam.

Resulting from a succession of Islamic reform movements that swept across China over the last 600 years, one finds among the Muslims in China today a wide spectrum of Islamic belief. Archaeological discoveries of large collections of Islamic artefacts and epigraphy on the south-east coast suggest that the earliest Muslim communities in China were descended from Arab, Persian, Central Asian and Mongolian Muslim merchants, militia and officials who settled first along China's south-east coast from the seventh to the tenth centuries, and then in larger migrations to the north from Central Asia under the Mongol-Yuan dynasty in the 13th and 14th centuries, gradually intermarrying with the local Chinese populations and raising their children as Muslims. Practising Sunni, Hanafi Islam, residing in independent small communities clustered around a central mosque, these communities were characterized by relatively isolated, independent Islamic villages and urban enclaves, who related with each other via trading networks and recognition of belonging to the wider Islamic "Umma," headed by an *Ahong* (from the Persian, *akhun[d]*) who was invited to teach on a more or less temporary basis.

Sufism began to make a substantial impact in China proper in the late 17th century, arriving mainly along the Central Asian trade routes with saintly *shaykhs*, both Chinese and foreign, who brought new teachings from the pilgrimage cities. These charismatic teachers and tradesmen established widespread networks and brotherhood associations, including most prominently the Naqshbandiyya, Qadariyya and Kubrawiyya. The hierarchical organization of these Sufi networks helped in the mobilization of large numbers of Hui during economic and political crises in the 17th to 19th centuries, assisting widespread Muslim-led rebellions and resistance movements against late Ming and Qing imperial rule in Yunnan, Shaanxi, Gansu and Xinjiang. The 1912 nationalist revolution allowed further autonomy in Muslim concentrated regions of the north-west, and wide areas came under virtual Muslim warlord control, leading to frequent intra-Muslim and Muslim–Han conflicts until the eventual communist victory led to the reassertion of central control. In the late 19th and early 20th century, Wahhabi-inspired reform movements, known as the Yihewani (from *Ikhwan*), rose to popularity under Nationalist and warlord sponsorship, and were noted for their critical stance towards traditionalist Islam as too acculturated to Chinese practices, and Sufism as too attached to saint and tomb veneration.

These movements of Islam influenced all Muslim nationalities in China today; however, they found their most political expression among the Hui who were faced with the task of accommodating each new Islamic movement with Chinese culture. Among the north-western Muslim communities, especially the Uyghur, their more recent integration into Chinese society as a result of Mongolian and Manchu expansion into Central Asian has forced them to reach social and political accommodations that have challenged their identity. In terms of integration, the Uyghur as a people are perhaps the least integrated into Chinese society, while the Hui are at the other end of the spectrum, as a result of several historical and social factors that are discussed below.

Uyghur Indigeneity and the Challenge to Chinese Sovereignty

In 1997, bombs exploded in a city park in Beijing on 13 May (killing one) and on two buses on 7 March (killing two), as well as in the north-western border city of Urumqi, the capital of Xinjiang Uyghur Autonomous Region, on 25 February (killing nine), with over 30 other bombings, six in Tibet alone. Most of these are thought to have been related to demands by Muslim and Tibetan separatists. Eight members of the Uyghur Muslim minority were executed on 29 May 1997 for alleged bombings in north-west China, with hundreds arrested on suspicion of taking part in ethnic riots and engaging in separatist activities. Though sporadically reported since the early 1980s, such incidents have been increasingly common since 1997 and are documented in a recent scathing report on Chinese government policy in the region by Amnesty International.[6] A recent report in the *Wall Street Journal* of the arrest on 11 August 1999 of Rebiya Kadir, a well known Uyghur businesswoman, during a visit by the United States Congressional Research Service delegation to the region, indicates that China's random arrests have not diminished, nor is China concerned with Western criticism.[7]

To consider the interaction of Uyghur Muslims with Chinese society, three interrelated aspects of regional history, economy and politics must be examined. First, Chinese histories notwithstanding, every Uyghur firmly believes that their ancestors were the indigenous people of the Tarim basin, which did not become known in Chinese as "Xinjiang" ("new dominion") until the 18th century. Nevertheless, I have argued elsewhere the constructed "ethnogenesis" of the Uyghur, in which the current understanding of the indigeneity of the present people classified as Uyghur by the Chinese state is a quite recent phenomenon related to Great Game rivalries, Sino-Soviet geopolitical manoeuvrings, and Chinese nation-building.[8] While a collection of nomadic steppe peoples known as the "Uyghur" has existed since before the eighth century, this identity was lost from the 15th to the 20th centuries. It was not until the fall of the Turkish Khanate (552–744 CE) to a people reported by the Chinese historians as *Hui-he* or *Hui-hu* that we find the beginnings of the Uyghur Empire. At this time the Uyghur were but one collection of nine nomadic tribes, who initially, in confederation with other Basmil and Karlukh nomads, defeated the Second Turkish Khanate and then dominated the federation under the leadership of Koli Beile in 742.

Gradual sedentarization of the Uyghur, and their defeat of

6. Amnesty International, *Peoples Republic of China: Gross Violations of Human Rights in the Xinjiang Uighur Autonomous Region* (London, 21 April 1999).

7. Ian Johnson, "China arrests noted businesswoman in crackdown in Muslim region," *Wall Street Journal*, 18 August 1999.

8. Dru C. Gladney, "The ethnogenesis of the Uighur," *Central Asian Studies*, Vol. 9, No. 1 (1990), p. 3.

the Turkish Khanate, occurred precisely as trade with the unified Tang state became especially lucrative. This was accompanied by socio-religious change: the traditional shamanistic Turkic-speaking Uyghur came increasingly under the influence of Persian Manichaeanism, Buddhism and eventually Nestorian Christianity. Extensive trade and military alliances along the old Silk Road with the Chinese state developed to the extent that the Uyghur gradually adopted the cultural, dress and even agricultural practices of the Chinese. Conquest of the Uyghur capital of Karabalghasun in Mongolia by the nomadic Kyrgyz in 840, without rescue from the Tang, who may have become by then intimidated by the wealthy Uyghur empire, led to further sedentarization and crystallization of Uyghur identity. One branch that ended up in what is now Turpan took advantage of the unique socio-ecology of the glacier-fed oases surrounding the Taklamakan and were able to preserve their merchant and limited agrarian practices, gradually establishing Khocho or Gaochang, the great Uyghur city-state based in Turpan for four centuries (850–1250).

The Islamicization of the Uyghur from the tenth to as late as the 17th century, while displacing their Buddhist religion, did little to bridge these oases-based loyalties. From that time on, the people of "Uyghuristan" centred in Turpan who resisted Islamic conversion until the 17th century were the last to be known as Uyghur. The others were known only by their oasis or by the generic term of "Turki." With the arrival of Islam, the ethnonym "Uyghur" fades from the historical record. It was not until 1760 that the Manchu Qing dynasty exerted full and formal control over the region, establishing it as their "new dominions" (*Xinjiang*), an administration that lasted barely 100 years when it fell to the Yakub Beg rebellion (1864–1877) and expanding Russian influence.[9] The end of the Qing dynasty and the rise of Great Game rivalries between China, Russia and Britain saw the region torn by competing loyalties and marked by two short-lived and drastically different attempts at an independence: the proclamations of an "East Turkestan Republic" in Kashgar in 1933 and another in Yining (Ghulje) in 1944.[10] As Andrew Forbes has noted, these rebellions and attempts at self-rule did little to bridge competing political, religious and regional differences within the Turkic people who became known as the Uyghur in 1934 under successive Chinese KMT warlord administrations.[11] Justin Rudelson's recent work suggests there is persistent regional diversity along three, and perhaps four macro-regions: the north-western Zungharia plateau, the southern Tarim basin, the south-west Pamir region and the eastern Kumul–Turpan–Hami corridor.[12] The recognition of the Uyghur as an official Chinese "nationality" (*minzu*) in the

9. For the best treatment of the Yakub Beg rebellion, see Kim Ho-dong, "The Muslim rebellion of the Kashgar Emirate in Chinese Central Asia, 1864–1877," PhD dissertation, Harvard University, 1986

10. Linda Benson, *The Ili Rebellion: The Moslem Challenge to Chinese Authority in Xinjiang, 1944–1949* (New York: M.E. Sharpe, 1990).

11. Andrew D. W., Forbes, *Warlords and Muslims in Chinese Central Asia* (Cambridge: Cambridge University Press, 1986), p. 29.

12. Justin Jon Rudelson, *Oasis Identities: Uyghur Nationalism Along China's Silk Road* (New York: Columbia University Press, 1997), pp. 40–45.

1930s in Xinjiang under a Soviet-influenced policy of nationality recognition contributed to a widespread acceptance today of continuity with the ancient Uyghur kingdom and their eventual "ethnogenesis" as a *bona fide* nationality. The "nationality" policy under the KMT identified five peoples of China, with the Han in the majority. This policy was continued under the Communists, who eventually recognized 56 nationalities, with the Han occupying a 91 per cent majority in 1990.

The "peaceful liberation" by the Chinese Communists of Xinjiang in 1949, and its subsequent establishment as the Xinjiang Uyghur Autonomous Region on 1 October 1955, perpetuated the Nationalist policy of recognizing the Uyghur as a minority nationality under Chinese rule. This nationality designation not only masks tremendous regional and linguistic diversity, it also includes groups such as the Loplyk and Dolans who had very little to do with the oasis-based Turkic Muslims who became known as the Uyghur. At the same time, contemporary Uyghur separatists look back to the brief periods of independent self-rule under Yakub Beg and the Eastern Turkestan Republics, in addition to the earlier glories of the Uyghur kingdoms in Turpan and Karabalghasan, as evidence of their rightful claims to the region. Contemporary Uyghur separatist organizations based in Istanbul, Ankara, Almaty, Munich, Amsterdam, Melbourne and Washington, DC, may differ on their political goals and strategies for the region, but they all share a common vision of a unilineal Uyghur claim on the region, disrupted by Chinese and Soviet intervention. The independence of the former Soviet Central Asian Republics in 1991 has done much to encourage these Uyghur organizations in their hopes for an independent "Turkestan," despite the fact the new, mainly Muslim Central Asian governments all signed protocols with China in the spring of 1996 that they would not harbour or support separatist groups.

Within the region, though many portray the Uyghur as united around separatist or Islamist causes, they continue to be divided from within by religious conflicts, in this case competing Sufi and non-Sufi factions, territorial loyalties (whether they be oases or places of origin), linguistic discrepancies, commoner–elite alienation and competing political loyalties. These divided loyalties were evidenced by the attack in May 1996 on the Imam of the Idgah Mosque in Kashgar by other Uyghurs, as well as the assassination of at least six Uyghur officials in September 2001. It is also important to note that Islam was only one of several unifying markers for Uyghur identity, depending on those with whom they were in co-operation at the time. For example, to the Hui Muslim Chinese, the Uyghur distinguish themselves as the legitimate autochthonous minority, since both share a belief in Sunni Islam. In contrast to the nomadic Muslim peoples (Kazakh or Kyrgyz), Uyghur might stress their attachment to the land and oases of origin. In opposition to the Han Chinese, the Uyghur will generally emphasize their long history in the region. This suggests that Islamic fundamentalist groups such as the Taliban in Afghanistan (often glossed as "Wahhabiyya" in the region) will have only limited appeal among the Uyghur. It is this contested understanding of history that continues to influence much of the current debate over separatist and Chinese claims to the region.

Amnesty International has claimed that the round-ups of so-called terrorists and separatists have led to hurried public trials and immediate, summary executions of possibly thousands of locals. One Amnesty International estimate suggested that in a country known for its frequent executions, Xinjiang had the highest number, averaging 1.8 per week, most of them Uyghur. Troop movements to the area, related to the nation-wide campaign against crime known as "Strike Hard" launched in 1998 that includes the call to erect a "great wall of steel" against separatists in Xinjiang, have reportedly been the largest since the suppression of the large Akto insurrection in April 1990 (the first major uprising in Xinjiang that took place in the Southern Tarim region near Baren Township, which initiated a series of unrelated and sporadic protests). Alleged incursions of Taliban fighters through the Wakhan corridor into China where Xinjiang shares a narrow border with Afghanistan have led to the area being swamped with Chinese security forces and large military exercises, beginning at least one month prior to the 11 September attack, and suggesting growing government concern about these border areas. Under US and Chinese pressure, Pakistan returned one Uyghur activist to China, apprehended among hundreds of Taliban detainees, which follows a pattern of repatriations of suspected Uyghur separatists in Kazakhstan, Kyrgyzstan and Uzbekistan.

International campaigns for Uyghur rights and possible independence have become increasingly vocal and well organized, especially on the internet. Repeated public appeals have been made to Abdulahat Abdurixit, the Uyghur People's Government Chairman of Xinjiang in Urumqi. Notably, the elected chair of the Unrepresented Nations and People's Organization (UNPO) based in the Hague is a Uyghur, Erkin Alptekin, son of the separatist leader, Isa Yusuf Alptekin, who is buried in Istanbul where there is a park dedicated to his memory. Supporting primarily an audience of approximately 1 million expatriate Uyghurs (yet few Uyghurs in Central Asia and China have access to these internet sites) there are at least 25 international organizations and websites working for the independence of "Eastern Turkestan," and based in Amsterdam, Munich, Istanbul, Melbourne, Washington, DC and New York. Since 11 September, each of these organizations has disclaimed any support for violence or terrorism, pressing for a peaceful resolution of ongoing conflicts in the region. The growing influence of "cyberseparatism" and international popularization of the Uyghur cause concerns Chinese authorities, who hope to convince the world that the Uyghurs do pose a real domestic and international terrorist threat.

The second pressing issue is economic. Since 1991, China has been a net oil importer. It also has 20 million Muslims. Mishandling of its Muslim problems will alienate trading partners in the Middle East, who are primarily Muslims. Already, after an ethnic riot on 5 February 1997 in the north-western Xinjiang city of Yining that left at least nine Uyghur Muslims dead and several hundreds arrested, the Saudi Arabian official newspaper *al-Bilad* warned China about the "suffering of [its] Muslims whose human rights are violated." Turkey's Defence Minister, Turhan Tayan, officially condemned China's handling of the issue, and China responded by telling Turkey to not interfere in China's internal affairs. Muslim nations on China's borders, including the new Central Asian states, Pakistan and Afghanistan, though officially unsupportive of Uyghur separatists, may be increasingly critical of harsh treatment extended to fellow Turkic and/or Muslim co-religionists in China.

Unrest in the Xinjiang Uyghur Autonomous Region may lead to a decline in outside oil investment and revenues that are already operating at a loss. Recently, Exxon reported that its two wells came up dry in China's supposedly oil-rich Tarim basin of southern Xinjiang, with the entire region yielding only 3.15 million metric tons of crude oil, much less than China's overall output of 156 million tons. The World Bank lends over $3 billion a year to China, investing over $780.5 million in 15 projects in the Xinjiang Region alone, with some of that money allegedly going to the Xinjiang Production and Construction Corps (XPCC) that human rights activist Harry Wu has claimed employs prison *laogai* labour. International companies and organizations, from the World Bank to Exxon, may not wish to subject their employees and investors to social and political upheavals. As a result of these criticisms, many Bank and ADB projects have been curtailed in recent years.

China's trade with Central Asia is expanding at a rapid rate, with the opening of direct rail, air and six overland links since 1991. Energy economist James P. Dorian has noted that Xinjiang's trade with Central Asia increased from $463 million in 1992 to $775 million in 1996. The end of 1992 saw an increase of 130 per cent in cross-border trade, with Kazakhstan benefiting the most. China is now Kazakhstan's fifth largest trade partner. Xinjiang's top three trading partners are Kazakhstan, Xinjiang and Hong Kong, with China–Kazakhstan trade alone totalling more than Turkey's trade with all of Central Asia.[13] Additionally, China is hoping to increase revenues from tourism to the region, marketing it as an important link on the ancient Silk Road. It has been a tremendous draw to foreign Muslim tourists, as well as Japanese, Taiwanese, South-East Asian and domestic tourists, with touristic development assisting the establishment of five-star hotels throughout the region, including the Holiday Inn in Urumqi. Economic development in Urumqi alone has witnessed 80 new skyscrapers in the last ten years.

It is clear that Uyghur separatism or Muslim complaints regarding Chinese policy will have important consequences for Chinas economic development of the region. Tourists and foreign businessmen will certainly avoid areas with ethnic strife and terrorist activities. China will continue to use its economic leverage with its Central Asian neighbours and Russia to prevent such disruptions.

13. James P. Dorian, Brett Wigdortz and Dru Gladney, "Central Asia and Xinjiang, China: emerging energy, economic, and ethnic relations," *Central Asian Survey*, Vol. 16, No. 4 (1997), p. 466.

The third aspect is political. China's international relations with its bordering nations and internal regions such as Xinjiang and Tibet have become increasingly important not only for the economic reasons discussed above but also for China's desire to participate in international organizations such as the World Trade Organization and Asia-Pacific Economic Council. Though Tibet is no longer of any real strategic or substantial economic value to China, it is politically important to China's current leadership to indicate that they will not submit to foreign pressure and withdraw their iron hand from Tibet. Uyghurs have begun to work closely with Tibetans internationally to put political pressure on China in international fora. In an 7 April 1997 interview by this author in Istanbul with Ahmet Türköz, vice-director of the Eastern Turkestan Foundation that works for an independent Uyghur homeland, Mr Türköz noted that since 1981, meetings had been taking place between the Dalai Lama and Uyghur leaders, initiated by the deceased Uyghur nationalist Isa Yusup Alptekin. These international fora cannot force China to change its policy, any more than the annual debate in the US over the renewal of China's Most-Favoured Nation status. Nevertheless, they continue to influence China's ability to co-operate internationally. As a result, China has sought to respond rapidly, and often militarily, to domestic ethnic affairs that might have international implications.

As China goes through the process of reintegrating Hong Kong since 1997 with the hope of eventually reuniting with Taiwan, residents of Hong Kong will be watching how China deals with other problems of national integration. During the Dalai Lama's March 1998 visit to Taiwan, he again renounced independence, calling for China to consider Tibet under the same "two systems, one country" policy as Hong Kong, yet *Renmin ribao* (*People's Daily*) continued to call him a "separatist." Taiwan will certainly be watching how well Hong Kong is integrated into China as a Special Administrative Region with a true separate system of government, as opposed to Tibet and Xinjiang, which as so-called Autonomous Regions have very little actual autonomy from decision-makers in Beijing. China's handling of ethnic and integrationist issues in Xinjiang and Hong Kong will have a direct bearing on its possible reunification with Taiwan.

In addition, outside the official minorities, China possesses tremendous ethnic, linguistic and regional diversity. Intolerance towards difference in Xinjiang might be extended to limiting cultural pluralism in Guangdong, where at least 15 dialects of Cantonese are spoken and folk religious practice is rampant. Memories are strong of the repressions of the Cultural Revolution (1966–76), when all forms of diversity, political or cultural, were severely curtailed. If rising Chinese nationalism entails reducing ethnic and cultural difference, then anyone who is regarded as "other" in China will suffer, not just the Uyghurs.

Hui Muslims and Islamic Accommodation to Chinese Society

Islam in China has primarily been propagated over the last 1,300 years among the people now known as Hui. Yet many of the issues confronting them are relevant to the Turkic and Indo-European Muslims on China's Inner Asian frontier. Though Hui speak a number of non-Chinese languages, most Hui are closer to Han Chinese than other Muslim nationalities in terms of demographic proximity and cultural accommodation. The attempt to adapt many of their Muslim practices to the Han way of life has led to criticisms amongst Muslim reformers. The Hui are unique among the 55 identified nationalities in China in that they are the only one for whom religion (Islam) is the only unifying category of identity, even though many members of the Hui nationality may not practise Islam. As a result of Islamic reform movements that have swept across China, the Hui continue to subscribe to a wide spectrum of Islamic belief.

Many Muslims supported the earliest communist call for equality, autonomy, freedom of religion and recognized nationality status, and were active in the early establishment of the People's Republic of China. However, many became disenchanted by growing critiques of religious practice during several periods in the PRC beginning in 1957. During the Cultural Revolution (1966–76), Muslims became the focus for both anti-religious and anti-ethnic nationalism critiques, leading to widespread persecutions, mosque closings and at least one large massacre of 1,000 Hui following a 1975 uprising in Yunnan province. Since Deng Xiaoping's post-1978 reforms, Muslims have sought to take advantage of liberalized economic and religious policies, while keeping a watchful eye on the ever-swinging pendulum of Chinese radical politics. There are now more mosques open in China than there were prior to 1949, and Muslims travel freely on the Hajj to Mecca, as well as engaging in cross-border trade with co-religionists in Central Asia, the Middle East and increasingly South-East Asia.

Increasing Muslim political activism on a national scale and rapid state response indicates the growing importance Beijing attaches to Muslim-related issues. In 1986 Uygurs in Xinjiang marched through the streets of Urumqi protesting against a wide range of issues, including the environmental degradation of the Zungharian plain, nuclear testing in the Taklamakan, increased Han immigration to Xinjiang and ethnic insults at Xinjiang University. Muslims throughout China protested against the publication of a Chinese book *Sexual Customs* in May 1989, and a children's book in October 1993, that portrayed Muslims, particularly their restriction against pork, in a derogatory fashion. In each case, the government responded quickly, meeting most of the Muslims' demands, condemning the publications and arresting the authors, and closing down the printing houses.

Islamic factional struggles continue to divide China's Muslims internally, especially as increased travel to the Middle East prompts criticism of Muslim practices at home and exposes China's Muslims to new, often politically radical, Islamic ideals. In February 1994, four Naqshbandi Sufi leaders were sentenced to long-term imprisonment for their support of internal factional disputes in the southern Ningxia region that had led to at least 60 deaths on both sides and People's Liberation Army intervention. Throughout the summer and autumn of 1993 bombs exploded in several towns in Xinjiang, indicating the growing demands of organizations pressing for an "independent Turkestan." In February 1997, a major uprising in Ili led to the deaths of at least 13 Uyghur and the arrest of hundreds. Beijing has responded with increased military presence, particularly in Kashghar and Urumqi, as well as diplomatic efforts in the Central Asian states and Turkey to discourage foreign support for separatist movements. It is clear that Hui and Kazakh Muslims are critical of these separatist actions among the Uyghur, but it is not yet clear how much support even among the Uyghur there is for the violent acts, especially one recent attempt to assassinate a "collaborating" Imam in Kashgar. At the same time, cross-border trade between Xinjiang and Central Asia has grown tremendously, especially since the reopening in 1991 of the Eurasian Railroad linking Urumqi and Alma Ata with markets in China and Eastern Europe. Overland travel between Xinjiang and Pakistan, Tajikstan, Kyrgyzstan and Kazakhstan has also increased dramatically with the relaxation of travel restrictions based on Deng Xiaoping's giving priority to trade over security interests in the area. The government's policy of seeking to buy support through stimulating the local economy seems to be working at the present. Income levels in Xinjiang are often far higher than those across the border, yet increased Han migration to participate in the region's lucrative oil and mining industries continues to exacerbate ethnic tensions. Muslim areas in northern and central China, however, continue to be left behind as China's rapid economic growth expands unevenly, enriching the southern coastal areas far beyond that of the interior.

While further restricting Islamic freedoms in the border regions, at the same time China has become more keenly aware of the importance foreign Muslim governments place on its treatment of its Muslim minorities as a factor in its lucrative trade and military agreements. The establishment of full diplomatic ties with Saudi Arabia in 1991 and increasing military and technical trade with Middle Eastern Muslim states enhances the economic and political salience of China's treatment of its internal Muslim minority population. The official protocols signed with China's Central Asian border nations beginning in 1996 with the group known as the "Shanghai 5" (China, Russia, Kazakhstan, Kyrgyzstan, Tajikstan) and expanded in 2001 to include Uzbekistan (as the Shanghai Co-operative Organization), underlines China's growing role in the region and concerns over transnational trade and security. The increased transnationalism of China's Muslims will be an important factor in their ethnic expression as well as practised accommodation to Chinese culture and state authority.

Islam and Chinese Nationalism

Increased Muslim activism in China cannot but be nationalistic, yet a nationalism that may often transcend the boundaries of the contemporary nation-state, via mass communications, increased travel and the internet. Earlier Islamic movements in China were precipitated by China's opening to the outside world. No matter what conservative leaders in the government might wish, China's Muslims politics have reached a new stage of openness. If China wants to participate in an international political sphere of nation-states, this is unavoidable. With the opening to the West in recent years, travel to and from the Islamic heartlands has dramatically increased in China. In 1984, over 1,400 Muslims left China to go on the Hajj. This number increased to over 2,000 in 1987, representing a return to pre-1949 levels, and in the late 1990s, official Hajj numbers regularly surpassed 6,000, with many others travelling in private capacities through third countries. Several Hui students are presently enrolled in Islamic and Arabic studies at the Al-Azhar University in Egypt, with many others seeking Islamic training abroad.

Encouraged by the Chinese state, relations between Muslims in China and the Middle East are becoming stronger and more frequent, partly from a desire to establish trading partners for arms, commodities and currency exchanges, and partly by China's traditional view of itself as a leader of the Third World. Delegations of foreign Muslims regularly travel to prominent Islamic sites in China, in a kind of state-sponsored religious tourism, and donations are encouraged. While the state hopes that private Islamic investment will assist economic development, the vast majority of grants by visiting foreign Muslims have been donated to the rebuilding of Islamic mosques, schools and hospitals. As Hui in China are further exposed to Islamic internationalism, and they return from studies and pilgrimages abroad, traditional Hui identities will once again be reshaped and called into question, giving rise to new manifestations of Islam in China. Global Islam is thus localized into Hui Islam, finding its expression as a range of accommodations between Chineseness and Muslimness as defined in each local community.

While further restricting Islamic freedoms in the border regions, at the same time the state has become more keenly aware of the importance foreign Muslim governments place on China's treatment of its Muslim minorities as a factor in its lucrative trade and military agreements. The establishment of full diplomatic ties with Saudi Arabia in 1991 and increasing military and technical trade with Middle Eastern Muslim states enhances the economic and political salience of China's treatment of its internal Muslim minority population. The increased transnationalism of China's Muslims will be an important factor in their ethnic expression as well as in their accommodation to Chinese culture and state authority.

Internal Conversion

While Islamic associations are as confusing to the non-initiate as are the numerous schools of Buddhist thought in China, they differ in that membership in them is hotly disputed in China. Unlike Middle Eastern or Central Asian Islamic orders, where one might belong to two or even three brotherhoods at once, the Hui belong to only one. Among the Hui, one is generally born into one's Islamic order, or converts dramatically to another. In fact, this is the only instance of conversion I encountered among my sojourn among the Hui. I never met a Han who had converted to Islam in China without having been married to a Hui or adopted into a Hui family, though I heard of a few isolated instances. Fletcher records the conversion of 28 Tibetan tribes as well as their "Living Buddha" by Ma Laichi in Xunhua, Qinghai in the mid 18th century.[14] After the 1784 Ma Mingxin uprising, the Qing government forbade non-Muslims from converting to Islam, which may have had some influence on the few recorded Han conversions. This goes against the common assumption that Islam in China was spread through proselytization and conversion. Islamic preachers in China, including Ma Laichi, Ma Mingxin, Qi Jingyi and Ma Qixi, spent most of their time trying to convert other Muslims. Islam in China for the most part has grown biologically through birth and intermarriage.

Hui Islamic Orders and Chinese Culture

The tensions and conflicts that led to the rise and divisions of the Sufi *menhuan* in north-west China, and subsequent non-Sufi reforms, are impossible to enumerate in their complexity. They give evidence, however, of the ongoing struggles that continue to make Islam meaningful to Hui Muslims. These tensions between Islamic ideals and social realities are often left unresolved. Their very dynamism derives from the questions they raise and the doubts they engender among people struggling with traditional meanings in the midst of changing social contexts. Questions of purity and legitimacy become paramount when the Hui are faced with radical internal socio-economic and political change, and exposed to different interpretations of Islam from the outside Muslim world. These conflicts and reforms reflect an ongoing debate in China over Islamic orthodoxy, revealing an important disjunction between "scripturalist" and "mystical" interpretations.

In a similar fashion, the study of South-East Asian Islam has often centred on the contradiction and compromise between the native culture of the indigenous Muslims and the *shari'a* of orthodox Islam, the mystical and scriptural, the real and the ideal.[15] The supposed accommodation of orthodox Islamic tenets to local cultural practices has led scholars to dismiss or explain such compromise as syncretism, assimilation and "sinification," as has been described among the Hui. An alternative approach, and one perhaps more in tune with the interests of Hui themselves, sees this incongruence as the basis for ongoing dialectical tensions that have often led to reform movements and conflicts within

14. See Trippner, "Islamische Gruppe und Graberkult in Nordwest China" ("Muslim groups and grave-cults in north-west China"), *Die Welt des Islams*, No. 7 (1961), pp. 154–55.

15. This distinction was most fully articulated by William Roff, "Islam obscured? Some reflections on studies of Islam and society in Asia," *L'Islam en Indonesie* Vol. 1, No. 29 (1985), pp. 8–10.

Muslim communities.[16] Following Max Weber,[17] one can see the wide variety of Islamic expression as reflecting processes of local world construction and programmes for social conduct whereby a major religious tradition becomes meaningful to an indigenous society.

In the competition for scarce resources, these conflicts are also prompted by and expressed in economic concerns, such as the example of the non-Sufi *Xi Dao Tang* who were defeated by the Sufi Khufiyya – clearly a case of coveting his Muslim brother's wealth. Fletcher notes that one of the criticisms of the Khufiyya was that their recitation of the *Ming Sha Le* took less time than the normal Quranic suras by non-Sufi clergy, and therefore their Imams were cheaper to hire at ritual ceremonies. He suggests that this assisted their rise in popularity and criticism by the Gedimu religious leaders.[18] The Yihewani criticized both the Gedimus and Sufis for only performing rituals in believers' homes for profit, and advocated the practice, "If you recite, do not eat; if you eat, do not recite" (*nian jing bu chi, chi bu nian jing*). The Chinese state has generally found economic reasons for criticizing certain Islamic orders among the Hui. During the Land Reform campaigns of the 1950s, which appropriate mosque and *wagf* (Islamic endowment) holdings, they met great resistance from the Sufi *menhuan* which had accumulated a great deal due to their hierarchical centralized leadership. In a 1958 document criticizing Ma Zhenwu, the Jahriyya Sufi shaykh, the following accusations are quite revealing:

According to these representatives, Ma Chen-wu instituted many "A-mai-lis," or festival days to commemorate the dead ancestors to which the A-hungs must be invited to chant the scriptures and be treated with big feasts, thereby squeezing money out of the living for the dead. For example, he has kept a record of the days of birth and death of all the family members of his followers and has seen to it that religious services be held on such days. These include "Grandmother's Day," "Wife's Day," "Aunt's Day," and others, sixty-five of such "A-mai-lis" in a year. On the average, one such "A-mai-li" is held every six or seven days, among which are seven occasions of big festival ... All the A-hungs of the Islamic mosques have been appointed by Ma Chen-wu. Through the appointment of A-hungs he has squeezed a big sum of money ... Ma has regularly, in the name of repairing the "kung-peis" [tombs], squeezed the Hui people for money.[19]

The tensions arising from the conflict of Chinese cultural practices and Islamic ideals have led to the rise and powerful appeal of Islamic movements among Hui Muslims. One way of looking at this tension between cultural practice and Islamic ideals I explored in an earlier

16. See Dale F. Eickelman, *Moroccan Islam: Tradition And Society In A Pilgrimage Center* (Austin and London: University of Texas Press, 1976), pp. 10–13.

17. Max Weber, *Economy and Society*, 2 vols. (Berkeley: University of California Press, 1978).

18. Joseph Fletcher, *Studies on Chinese and Islamic Inner Asia* (London: Varorum Press, 1996), p. 21.

19. Quoted in Donald E. MacInnis, *Religious Policy and Practice in Communist China* (New York: MacMillan, 1972), pp. 171–72.

work.[20] In China there were many attempts to reconcile Chinese culture with Islam, leading to a range of alternatives. At one extreme there are those who reject any integration of Islam with Chinese culture, such as Ma Wanfu's return to an Arabicized "pure" Islam. Conversely, at the other extreme, there are those leaders of the Gedimu, such as Hu Dengzhou, who accepted more integration with traditional Chinese society. Likewise, Ma Qixi's *Xi Dao Tang* stressed the complete compatibility of Chinese and Islamic culture, the importance of Chinese Islamic Confucian texts, the harmony of the two systems, and the reading of the Quran in Chinese.

In between, one finds various attempts at changing Chinese society to "fit" a Muslim world, through transformationist or militant Islam, as illustrated by the largely Naqshbandiyya-led 19th-century Hui uprisings. The Jahriyya sought to implement an alternative vision of the world in their society, and this posed a threat to the Qing as well as to other Hui Muslims, earning them the label of "heterodox" (*xie jiao*) and persecution by the Chinese state. By contrast, other Hui reformers have attempted throughout history to make Islam "fit" Chinese society, such as Liu Zhi's monumental effort to demonstrate the Confucian morality of Islam. The Qadiriyya alternative represents resolution of this tension through ascetic withdrawal from the world. Qi Jingyi advocated an inner mystical journey where the dualism of Islam and the Chinese world is absolved through grasping the oneness of Allah found inside every believer. These various approaches represent socio-historical attempts to deal with the relationship of relating the world religion of Islam to the local Chinese realm.

Another way to examine this range of alternatives is to generalize about the Muslim nationalities themselves. In this scheme, the Uyghur can be seen to be much more resistant to accepting integration into Chinese society than other Muslim groups, in that they are the only Muslim minority in China expressing strong desires for a separate state (Uyghuristan) – although it is not at all clear that all Uyghur desire independence. At the other extreme, it could be argued that the Hui are the most integrated of all the Muslim minorities into Chinese society and culture. This is both an advantage and a disadvantage in that they often have greater access to power and resources within Chinese society, but at the same time risk either the loss of their identity or the rejection of other Muslim groups in China as being too assimilated into Chinese society, to the detriment of Islam. In between there is a range of Muslim nationalities who are closer to the Uyghur in resisting Chinese culture and maintaining a distinct language and identity (Uzbeks, Kazakh, Kyrgyz and Tajiks), and those who are much closer to the Hui in accommodation to Chinese culture (Dongxiang and Bonan). While much of this is due to historical interaction and locale, it can be a heuristic way of examining

20. Gladney, *Muslim Chinese: Ethnic Nationalism in the People's Republic* (Cambridge, MA: Harvard University Press, 1996), p. 75. This interpretive scheme is influenced by H. Richard Niebuhr's *Christ and Culture* (New York: Harper and Row, 1951).

the challenges faced by each Muslim minority in their daily expression of identity and Islam in Chinese society. Here, it must be clearly noted, however, that there are many exceptions to this overly generalized pattern, for example Uyghur (such as Party officials and secularists) who are quite integrated into Chinese society, and Hui (such as religious Imams and rebellious youths) who might live their lives in strident resistance to Chinese culture.

Ethnic Muslim Nationalism in an Age of Globalization

China is not immune to the new tide of ethnic nationalism and "primordial politics" sweeping Europe, Africa and Asia in the post-Cold War period. Much of it is clearly due to a response to globalization in terms of localization: increasing nationalism arising from the organization of the world into nation-states. No longer content to sit on the sidelines, the nations within these states are playing a greater role in the public sphere, which Jürgen Habermas suggests is the defining characteristic of civil society in the modern nation-state.[21] In most of these nationalist movements, religion, culture and racialization play a privileged role in defining the boundaries of the nation. In China, Islam will continue to play an important role in debates about the nation, especially in countries where nationality is defined by a mix of religion and ethnicity. These accommodations of China's Muslims are not unlike those made on a daily basis among other Muslim minorities in Asia and in the West. The only difference may be the increasingly post-modern contraction of time and space: accommodations that took over a millennia in China are now being required of Muslim diasporic communities in a matter of hours or days. For Muslims in China, Pakistani and Bangladeshi workers in Tokyo and Seoul, and the other wider diaspora, Muslims may be becoming increasingly "unfamiliar" strangers. If the "war on terrorism" widens to divide the West and China against Muslim communities in general, one can expect the Muslims in China will be increasingly regarded as a threat to state rule and social integration. This does not bode well for the future integration of Muslims into the Chinese leviathan.

---

21. Jürgen Habermas, tr. Thomas Burger and Frederick Lawrence, *The Structural Transformation of the Public Sphere* (Cambridge, MA: MIT Press, 1989 (1st ed. 1962).

Catholic Revival During the Reform Era

Richard Madsen

ABSTRACT This article focuses on three distinctive features of the revival of Catholicism in China: its relatively slow rate of increase, compared with other forms of Chinese religiosity; its relatively intense internal and external conflicts; and its peculiar mix of antagonism and co-operation with the government. These are explained in terms of three interpenetrating layers of the Chinese Catholic community: its priestly, sacramental religious vision, its social embodiment in rural society, and the legacy of political conflict between the Vatican and the PRC government. Though intimately interconnected, these layers of the Catholic Church have each developed at different paces and in somewhat different directions. The effects of this are seen most clearly in the problems faced by Chinese priests.

The Catholic Church in China is only a "little flock," comprising no more than one per cent of the population. Still, with 10–12 million members, the Church is not small in absolute numbers[1] – there are more Catholics than in Ireland! And probably more active Catholics. Compared with their European and North American counterparts, Chinese Catholics are very devout. Churches and chapels are packed for Sunday Mass, and overflowing on major feast days. Catholics are willing to make serious sacrifices to raise money to build new churches, and impressive numbers of them are willing to risk severe political harassment, even imprisonment, in order to practise their faith. The Catholic Church is a vital presence in China today.[2]

The revitalization of the Catholic Church in China is part of a general revival and growth of religion throughout China. True to its Marxist-Leninist ideology, the PRC did its best to eliminate religion during its first three decades of rule. Although the various constitutions promulgated by the PRC since 1949 have guaranteed freedom of religious belief, they have strictly restricted any public expression of religion. During the Maoist era, the PRC government subjected all citizens to militantly anti-religious propaganda, and, especially during the Cultural Revolution, destroyed places of worship, imprisoned religious leaders and "struggled against" religious believers. Most Western social scientists assumed that most forms of religious practice would have been destroyed by these

1. Jean Charbonnier, *Guide to the Catholic Church in China* (Singapore: China Catholic Communication, 2000), p. 14. Based on research done at the Holy Spirit Study Centre in Hong Kong, this handbook places the number of Catholics at 10 million. These figures, however, are based on research done in 1992. Cf. Anthony Lam, "How many Catholics are there in China?" *Tripod*, No. 71 (September–October, 1992), pp. 51–57. More recently, journalistic reports have been using the figure of 12 million Catholics. Suffice it to say that the number is imprecise.
2. Richard Madsen, *China's Catholics: Tragedy and Hope in an Emerging Civil Society* (Berkeley: University of California Press, 1998), pp. 1–20. In this book I list the sources, ethnographic, archival and bibliographical, upon which the above portrait is constructed.

assaults. Even influential Western religious leaders often assumed this. Catholic missionaries, for example, had often patronizingly thought that many of their Chinese Catholics were poorly educated and weak in the faith – "rice Christians" who could not be expected to survive the harsh persecutions of the Maoist era. But after new opportunities for religious practice opened up under Deng Xiaoping's policies of reform, there has been an astonishing efflorescence of all forms of religious practice.[3] By the government's own (probably underestimated) statistics, there are at least 100 million religious believers in China today, including an officially estimated four million Catholics (with the real figure, as noted above, perhaps being two or three times higher).[4]

Although still not fully explainable by conventional social scientific theories, this general revival can be attributed to factors like the collapse of Marxist ideology, increased social mobility, decreased government capacities for repression, and renewed communication with the outside world. But there are distinctive features of the Catholic revival that must be explained in more specific terms, and this article will concentrate on this level of analysis.

There are three specific features of the Catholic revival on which this article specifically focuses. First, compared with some other religious groups, the growth of the Catholic Church has been relatively static. The increase in the Catholic population – from about 3 million in 1949 to 10–12 million in 2001 – has roughly matched China's general population increase since the establishment of the PRC. Protestants, on the other hand, have expanded much more rapidly, from less than one million to a conservatively estimated 20 million today.[5] Certain "new religions," like the *falun gong*, based on some combination of folk Buddhism and *qigong*, have been born and grown extremely rapidly between the mid-1980s and the end of the 20th century. However, the slower rate of Catholic growth does not seem to be the result of a weakness in religious devotion. At least in terms of willingness to suffer for their faith, Catholics have shown levels of commitment every bit as high as Protestants or *falun gong* members.

A second distinctive characteristic of the Chinese Catholic Church is the relative intensity of its external and internal conflicts. Although there have been many conflicts between Protestants and the government, the conflicts with the Catholics seem to have been more systematic, linking grass-roots conflict with conflict at the national and international levels. As do some Protestant communities, Catholics get involved in confrontations with local authorities and with each other, and sometimes these lead

3. *Ibid.* pp. 25–45.

4. "Xinhua backgrounder views Catholicism in China," Xinhua, 20 August 2000. FBIS-CHI-2000–0820.

5. Alan Hunter and Kim-kwong Chan, *Protestantism in Contemporary China* (Cambridge: Cambridge University Press, 1993); for a higher estimate, see Tony Lambert, *The Resurrection of the Chinese Church* (London: Hodder and Stoughton, 1991); for a thorough discussion of the "numbers game," see Daniel H. Bays, "Chinese Protestant Christianity today" in this issue.

to violence. But unlike Protestants, these local confrontations extend to the national and international levels, in sometimes bitter wars of words between the Vatican and the PRC government. Something like this happens with the government's attacks on both the central leadership and local followers of the *falun gong*. However, unlike the *falun gong*, whose methods of resistance are more passive (being willing to suffer for their convictions and maybe – though this is controversial – even being willing to commit suicide), Catholics sometimes fight back actively. Although Catholic conflicts are not as violent as those of separatist Muslims in the western provinces, they have nevertheless involved more violence than most other religions. The most grisly case of violence thus far was the 1992 murder of a priest who was alleged to be a collaborator with the government, in which the priest was killed by poisoning the wine in his chalice at Mass.[6] A more recent case, also laced with religious symbolism, was the cutting off the ear of a collaborationist priest on Good Friday 2001, presumably in imitation of Saint Peter's cutting off the ear of the high priest's servant who came to arrest Jesus in the Garden of Gethsemene.[7]

But the relationship between the Catholic Church and Chinese society and government is by no means purely conflictual. A third special characteristic of the Chinese Catholic Church, at least as it has evolved in recent years, is the depth of its political ambivalence – its peculiar and paradoxical mix of antagonism and co-operation with the government.

After presenting a fuller description of these special characteristics in their historical context, this article attempts to explain them in terms of three interpenetrating layers of the Chinese Catholic community: its religious vision, social embodiment and political interests.

Chinese Catholicism in Historical Context

In 1949, there were about three million Catholics in China, the product of three-and-a-half centuries of missionary work, which began with the arrival of the Jesuit Matteo Ricci in Guangzhou in 1583, gained momentum in the 17th century, was interrupted in 1724 by the Yongzheng Emperor's declaration of Catholicism as a "heterodox faith," resumed in the mid-19th century with the support of European imperialists, suffered a setback in the Boxer Rebellion at the end of the century, and then underwent a period of vigorous growth in the first half of the 20th century, despite the obstacles posed by Chinese nationalist movements and by war. Although the early Jesuits were successful in converting Confucian elites in the 17th century and even gained official support from

---

6. UCAN News, 11 August 1992. As I wrote in *China's Catholics*, p. 156: "The murderer was tried and executed. He may have been deranged, and there is no evidence that his actions were deliberately planned or approved by any Catholic group. But the atmosphere of hostility in the Catholic Church was probably conducive to his crime."

7. UCAN News, 23 April 2001 and 30 May 2001. The priest whose ear was cut off was in Harbin and he was the head of the CPA in the Heilongjiang Diocese. One of the accused perpetrators was another priest, from Qiqihar.

the Kangxi Emperor, their efforts had been brought to a halt in the early 18th century when their ecclesiastical rivals convinced the Pope that the Jesuits had compromised the faith by adapting it to the rituals and philosophy practised by Chinese elites. Thereafter, the Church focused its efforts mainly on poor and uneducated rural people. Even in the early 20th century, Catholic missionaries thought that the cities were too devoted to "Venus and Mammon" to produce good Catholics.[8]

From the beginnings of the PRC, the clash between Chinese Catholics and the communist government was especially sharp. In 1949, the Vatican, led by the strongly anti-communist Pope Pius XII, forbade Chinese Catholics, under pain of excommunication, to co-operate in any way with the new Chinese regime. For its part, the new regime was determined to bring the Catholic Church, as all other religions, under tight state control. It expelled all missionaries and forbade any dependence on outside support. The regime established political structures to supervise and control the religious community, though of course such structures had existed before in republican and imperial China. The main state agency for this purpose was the Religious Affairs Bureau (RAB), which in turn was directed by the Communist Party's United Front Department. "Mass associations" were organized to be transmission belts between these agencies and the religious communities. The leaders of these were selected and supervised by the RAB.[9] Although they were not officially state employees, such religious leaders functioned as government cadres. They were paid by the government and their position was primarily dependent on their approval by political superiors rather than by most members of their communities. Although religious leaders could not openly be members of the Communist Party, because one of the requirements of Party membership was atheism, I have been told that some of the heads of these mass associations had secret Party membership. The mass organization to control the Catholic Church was the Catholic Patriotic Association (CPA).[10]

Because of the Vatican's strict stance against any co-operation with communism, however, it was particularly difficult to find any Catholic bishops or priests who would accept leadership positions within the CPA. Indeed, one requirement of accepting such a position was to sever one's allegiance to the Vatican, which for Catholics would have been seen as a major betrayal of their identity. (In the case of the Protestants, there were prominent figures like Wu Yaozong [Y.T. Wu], who had been long involved in leftist, nationalist movements and who had some genuine sympathy with the communist cause. There were no such figures among the Catholics.)[11] Catholic leaders, like Archbishop Ignatius Gong Pinmei

8. Madsen, *China's Catholics*, pp. 29–33.

9. In 2000, this bureau got a new name, the State Administration for Religious Affairs (SARA).

10. *Ibid.* pp. 34–39.

11. Gao Wangzhi, "Y. T. Wu: a Christian leader under communism," in Daniel H. Bays, *Christianity in China: From the Eighteenth Century to the Present* (Stanford: Stanford University Press, 1996), pp. 338–352.

of Shanghai, firmly resisted communist pressure. In the mid to late 1950s the most prominent of such Catholic leaders were sentenced to prison and labour camps. In 1957, the government found five bishops who were willing to assume leadership within the CPA, and, in violation of Church canon law, these bishops consecrated several other bishops without Vatican approval. Most Catholics, both clergy and laity, refused to participate in institutions controlled by these bishops. They carried on their faith in secret, sometimes under threat of severe punishment.[12]

During the Cultural Revolution even the CPA was shut down and priests associated with it imprisoned. All churches were closed and many demolished. All forms of religious practice were condemned as part of the "four olds." The same was true for other religions.

With reform and opening, the government replaced a policy of suppressing religion with one of co-opting and controlling it. For Catholics, that meant that many priests and bishops were released from prison in the late 1970s and early 1980s and allowed to resume their ministries. (But not the most prominent leaders like Gong Pinmei, who languished in prison until 1985, when he was paroled under house arrest on "humanitarian grounds" and then exiled to the United States for medical treatment in 1988.) It also meant the gradual reopening and rebuilding of churches, seminaries and convents. However, the official government policies (set forth in 1982 in Party Central Committee "Document 19") required that all Catholic religious activities be firmly under the supervision of the CPA.[13]

The new regulations made concessions to Catholic concerns about doctrinal and sacramental integrity. Most decisions on theological and liturgical matters were left to the Chinese Catholic Bishops conference, not to the CPA. Catholics were allowed to express their "spiritual allegiance" to the Pope, although they were not supposed to allow the Vatican to interfere in Chinese Church affairs. These conditions were acceptable enough that many Catholics, eager for the spiritual nourishment that they believed could only come through reception of the sacraments, flocked to the officially opened churches. About four million people are now associated with these churches.

But even more Catholics turned to other religious leaders who refused to work within the government's regulations. Perhaps six to eight million Catholics are associated with the so-called "underground church." Its development was facilitated by regulations that the Vatican had secretly directed towards the Chinese Church in 1978. Similar to other directives that the Vatican sent to churches under communist regimes in Eastern Europe, these regulations relaxed the requirements of canon law that bishops follow the Vatican's normal bureaucratic procedures in choosing

12. Madsen, *China's Catholics*, pp. 38–39.
13. *Ibid.* pp. 39–45. For the text of Document 19, see Mickey Spiegel and James Tong (eds.), *Chinese Law and Government*, Vol. 33, No. 2 (2000).

new bishops and training new priests.[14] The purpose was to allow bishops and priests operating clandestinely to run the affairs of the Church even though they could not maintain regular communication with Rome. Many Chinese bishops, operating without the approval of the CPA, went ahead and consecrated new episcopal successors and set up clandestine seminaries to train new priests. Since such clergy were not tainted by association with the CPA, they were seen as more acceptable to many Catholics. Moreover, since there were more Catholics than could be accommodated within the officially opened churches, many other believers who might not have had a principled antipathy toward priests associated with the CPA nevertheless turned to underground priests to fulfil their spiritual needs.[15]

There have thus developed two factions within the Chinese Catholic Church. Even though these are popularly called the "open" and "underground churches," many Chinese Catholics, on both sides, take pains to emphasize that as a matter of theology and even canon law, there is really only one Church, even though there are social and political divisions within it. Some underground Catholics, however, claim that the official church really is a separate church, in a state of schism from the true Church of Rome. They sometimes declare that leaders of the official church have been excommunicated and refuse to receive the sacraments from them.[16] But, for reasons explained below, this is increasingly a minority view, even among the underground, and it is not supported by statements from the Vatican.

The majority of Protestants belong to unregistered "house churches," which, like underground Catholic communities, are vulnerable to government repression. What differentiates the Catholic underground from most of them is its capacity for co-ordinated, nation-wide action. Although there are many unregistered Protestant communities, for example, they do not have a single, unified structure of authority. There is, however, an underground Catholic Bishops Conference, which operates in parallel with the officially sanctioned Bishops Conference. In the autumn of 1989, the inaugural meeting of the underground Bishops Conference, held in Shanxi province, was raided by the police and its leaders were sentenced to prison. This did not crush the underground movement, however, and its leaders manage to continue to issue joint statements, which receive wide circulation throughout China.[17]

In some places, the Catholic underground and open churches have been engaged in passionate, even violent struggle. The killing and mutilation

14. Latin text provided in Kim-kwong Chan, *Towards a Contextual Ecclesiology: The Catholic Church in the People's Republic of China (1979–1983): Its Life and Theological Implications* (Hong Kong: Photech Systems, 1987), pp. 250–53.

15. Madsen, *China's Catholics*, pp. 42–45.

16. *Ibid.* pp. 154–55. Also, Edmond Tang, "The Church into the 1990s," in Edmond Tang and Jean-Paul Wiest (eds.), *The Catholic Church in Modern China* (Maryknoll, NY: Orbis Books, 1993), pp. 32–35. Ma Ji, "My statement," Underground Bishop, "My vision of the Patriotic Association," and Joseph Yao Tianmin, "Who is not loyal to the Church?" all in *ibid.* pp. 120–141.

17. Madsen, *China's Catholics*, p. 43.

mentioned above were carried out by members of the underground church against priests in the open church. It must be stressed, however, that this violence is not common. Indeed, tensions between underground and official church factions have been diminishing rapidly in recent years. In some places, such as the area in Guangzhou studied by Eriberto Lozada,[18] there is no significant underground church, because believers seem completely satisfied with their officially approved priests. In other places, underground and official priests live together, share church buildings and even participate in religious services together. One important reason for this is that most official bishops – at least two-thirds of them – have quietly received "apostolic mandates," or official approval, from the Vatican.[19] There is no longer a stark division between one faction of the Church loyal to the Vatican and one faction loyal instead to the Chinese government. Still, as indicated by the recent ear-cutting incident, the evolution towards reconciliation is by no means completely smooth.

The remaining tensions are amplified and complicated by their connections to the international arena. Today, all the major Chinese religions are supported and influenced by transnational ties. Protestants, for example, receive large amounts of money and other aid from abroad, a good portion of it illegally smuggled in to nonregistered house churches by evangelical Protestants in North America. The *falun gong* receives instructions from its leader based in New York and financial support, where possible, from devotees around the world. Tibetan Buddhists receive help from the Dalai Lama's world-wide supporters, and Muslims from supporters in the Middle East.

Chinese Catholics also have a wealth of international contacts. Both the open and underground churches receive money not only from Taiwan and Hong Kong, but also from the United States and Europe. In addition, Hong Kong and Taiwan provide educational resources – books and video tapes, and teachers for seminaries and pastoral training workshops. Besides providing formal teachers, who in the nature of the case must go to institutions controlled by the open church, Hong Kong and Taiwan also send many visitors who informally communicate with the underground church about developments in the universal church. Finally, there are about 40 seminarians and priests, from both open and underground churches, receiving advanced training in Europe, and about 20 more in the United States.[20]

The international contacts of Chinese Catholics are brought into a very public focus in negotiations between the Vatican and the PRC government. The Vatican is the only state in Western Europe that maintains diplomatic relations with Taiwan. It has demonstrated willingness to shift

---

18. Eriberto P. Lozada, Jr. *God Aboveground: Catholic Church, Postsocialist State, and Transnational Processes in a Chinese Village* (Stanford: Stanford University Press, 2001).

19. Jeroom Heyndrickx, "Epiphany 2000: the Beijing–Rome confrontation," *The Tablet*, 13 January 2000.

20. Information from interviews in Hong Kong, November, 1999. As of October 2001, there have been 67 priests, seminarians, nuns and Catholic layworkers who have studied in the US since the late 1980s. There are currently 18 priests and three nuns studying in the US.

its ties to the PRC in exchange for getting more oversight over the religious life of Chinese Catholics. Negotiations have taken place on several occasions during the 1980s, in the early 1990s and most lately in 1999. They have usually taken place during periods of relative political openness in the PRC, and then broken down during periods of retrenchment. There seems to have been an evolution in the pattern of the negotiations, however. In the earlier years, according to one Vatican diplomat involved in the 1999 negotiations, "we were more eager for normalization than they were, but now they are more eager."[21]

The fundamental obstacle to reaching an agreement has been the selection of bishops. In the latest negotiations, the Vatican has been willing to accept the "Vietnam model," in which it agrees to chose bishops from a list nominated by the government.[22] However, the Vatican demands the final say in selection of bishops – a concession that the Chinese government is so far unwilling to make.

An Explanatory Framework

To understand these patterns of growth, organization, and conflict and co-operation with the government during the era of reform and opening, it is useful to refer to three interpenetrating layers of influence: the Catholic religious vision, its social matrix and its political legacies. Each of these layers has two dimensions, one rooted in Western traditions and the other in Chinese culture and society. Although each layer interacts with the other, they also each develop at their own pace and according to their own logics, creating a very complicated and ambivalent reaction to a modernizing and globalizing Chinese society.

The first and most basic layer is that of religious vision. Catholicism is a priestly, sacramental religion. It sees the Church as the embodiment of God's presence in the world. The Church is thus an institution greater than the sum of its individual members. One's relationship to God is mediated by the sacraments, the fundamental rituals of the Church. The sacraments, in turn, are administered by priests, whose most fundamental authority comes by the grace of God through ordination to priestly status, not through any personal charisma. In the doctrine of the Council of Trent, the sacraments impart grace *ex opere operato*, that is, just by the act of being performed properly, irrespective of the personal holiness of the minister of the sacrament. It is easy for such a doctrine to slip into a kind of magic, in which the rituals are simply instruments to obtain divine favour automatically without the need for any personal moral cultivation by the recipient. It was of course on these grounds that the Protestant

21. Author's interviews in Hong Kong. Unless otherwise noted, these were gathered at a meeting of Catholic Church China experts in November 1999.
22. For discussion of the "Vietnam model," see Eric O. Hanson, *The Catholic Church in World Politics* (Princeton: Princeton University Press, 1987), pp. 197–233; and Eric O. Hanson, *Catholic Politics in China and Korea* (Maryknoll, NY: Orbis Books, 1980), pp. 114–16.

reformers criticized the Catholic Church, and emphasized instead the prophetic dimensions of the Christian tradition.[23]

Since the late 20th century, especially after the Second Vatican Council of 1963–64, some of the contrasts between Catholicism and Protestantism have been blurred. It is emphasized that the sacraments are not mechanical instruments for obtaining grace but rather powerful symbols that both express and bring into being the faith of the Church. There is a renewed emphasis on how the Catholic Church, even though it incarnates the presence of God, must be continually reformed, because it is a frail human as well as divine institution. There is a new stress on the prophetic aspect of the Church – the divine command to stand apart from the world and to judge critically not just the Church but all human institutions.[24]

But the Catholicism that was brought to China, beginning with the Jesuit missionaries of the late 16th century, was a counter-Reformation version that emphasized the contrasts with Protestantism. Partially because the Chinese Catholic Church was cut off from developments in world Catholicism during the period of ferment aroused by the Second Vatican Council, the Chinese Church embodies the old counter-Reformation vision more fully than any other national Catholic community in the world. The clash between this counter-Reformation Catholicism and a post-Vatican II understanding can be seen in the following comment from a Church worker from Hong Kong who frequently goes to the mainland to give retreats to Chinese priests and nuns: "It is hard to get them to learn to pray, rather than just to say prayers."[25]

The classic priestly, sacramental vision of the Church resonates strongly with important elements within Chinese cultural traditions. The Confucian vision, as Tu Wei-ming describes it, was one of "transcendence in immanence," a vision that stresses the need to seek the *dao* through living within the primary institutions of this world, especially the family and the state.[26] The traditional emphasis on rituals of propriety seems very akin to the sacramental sense. The importance given to respect for hierarchical status corresponds with the Catholic stress on priesthood. Of course there are other strands in the Chinese tradition – indeed the early communist movement drew upon traditions of protest that have a closer affinity with Western Protestantism – but in spirit and practice the Catholic vision seems close to strands that remain influential

23. A succinct formulation of the difference between the Catholic and Protestant vision is in Paul Tillich, "The permanent significance of the Catholic Church for Protestants," *Protestant Digest*, Vol. 3, No. 10 (1941).

24. Compare the new *Catechism of the Catholic Church*, promulgated in 1992 (New York: Doubleday Image Books, 1994) with the *Catechism of the Council of Trent*, which was the basis for Catholic doctrinal education until the 1960s. The new Catechism has been published in Chinese translation. The version openly published in China, however, omits the sentence in Entry 2425 that reads: "The Church has rejected the totalitarianism and atheistic ideologies associated in modern times with 'communism' and 'socialism'." UCAN News, 14 October 1999.

25. Interview in Hong Kong, 1999.

26. Tu Wei-ming, "Confucianism," in Arvind Sharma, *Our Religions* (New York: HarperCollins, 1993), pp. 202–204.

among conservative Chinese, including much of today's communist political establishment. It also fits with the fascination for ritual that is often found in rural folk religion.[27] And it is the rural folk culture that disproportionately influences the ethos of the Chinese Church today.

Historically, the Catholic religious vision has become embedded in various forms of social life, which shape and constrain the way the vision can be understood. In Europe Catholicism attained its most elaborate flowering in the agrarian societies of the Middle Ages, and it gave meaning and moral regulation to the primary social relations of peasants and aristocrats. It has had a difficult (but not necessarily unsuccessful) time adapting to the social relations of urban middle classes in modern industrial societies. In China, even more than Europe, it became primarily embedded in the relations of village life, especially after it lost the credibility of scholar officials after the rites controversy. Catholic missionaries made an effort to convert whole villages, or at least whole lineages, in order to provide the social support for perseverance in the faith. Catholics embraced the extended family relationships that were central to village life.[28]

Indeed, in many Catholic villages, especially in those relatively closed to the outside world, a Catholic identity becomes almost identified with such familistic relationships. Some villagers may be "true believers" and others "lax," but even lax Catholics can never completely lose their identity. At the very least, they will have to be buried with Catholic rites, in order to maintain a connection with their ancestors.

Unlike the form which it took in the European Middle Ages, however, Catholicism in China could not easily provide moral links between peasant villagers and political and intellectual elites. After the Pope had rejected the Jesuit accommodation to the Confucian rites, the Church largely abandoned the effort to create an influential Catholic intellectual elite. Without the guidance that might have been provided by such an elite, rural Catholics, despite being warned against the dangers of "paganism," have gradually absorbed beliefs and devotional practices that seem analogous to heterodox folk-Buddhist sects: a strong devotion to the Virgin Mary not unlike the White Lotus Eternal Mother, an emphasis on miraculous salvation rather than ethical cultivation, a belief in miraculous healing and exorcism – and a rejection of the rationalistic scholarship that legitimated the status of imperial officials. Many of these features are still visible in many rural Catholic villages today, and they create a gulf between such villages and relatively well-educated Catholics in the cities.[29] Present-day Chinese Catholics are often reporting apparitions of

27. Richard Madsen, "Beyond orthodoxy: Catholicism as Chinese folk religion," in Stephan Uhalley, Jr. and Xiaoxin Wu, *China and Christianity: Burdened Past, Hopeful Future* (White Plains, NY: M.E. Sharpe, 2001).

28. Madsen, *China's Catholics*, pp. 50–53. For excellent ethnography of Catholic villages, see Wu Fei, "Maimangshangde shengyan: yige xiangcun tianzhujiaohui zhongde xinyang han shenghuo" ("Maimang's Holy Word: belief and life in a village Catholic church"), Beijing University MA thesis, 1999, and Lozada, *God Aboveground*.

29. Richard Madsen, "Beyond orthodoxy."

the Virgin Mary. Using rituals of dubious orthodoxy, rural priests cast out demons and perform miraculous healings.[30] Meanwhile, many urbanized Catholics drift away from the faith because it does not seem relevant to their modern experience. "I had no fear for our Catholics facing the challenge of persecution," says Bishop Jin Luxian, the bishop of Shanghai. "But, now, facing the challenge of modernization ... I have fears."[31]

A final layer of influence on the shape of Catholicism has been political: the relationship of the Church to political patrons and opponents. In the 19th century, Catholicism was often implicated with rightwing politics in Europe and with imperialism in China. These relationships continued until well into the 20th century. Even after the Catholic Church disavowed the imperialistic enterprise, it has often continued its association with the political right. Particularly in China (where the Church was cut off from currents of "liberation theology" that developed in Latin America and the Philippines after the 1960s), the Church has remained strongly associated with the anti-communist cause. Even though most Chinese Catholics wisely try to stay out of politics, there were some who hoped that the Church in China could help to accomplish what Church-inspired organizations like Solidarity in Poland accomplished, the destruction of communist regimes. This is undoubtedly part of the reason why right-wing Catholics in the United States, like Phyllis Schlafly and Robert Dornan, participate in organizations supporting the Chinese underground Church.[32]

Priesthood and the Growth of the Catholic Community

These religious, social and political influences affect many aspects of the Chinese Church. But their most crucial effects are upon the role of Chinese priests, and it is here that this analysis is focused.

Ritual status. Because of its sacramental vision, a properly ordained priesthood is essential to the Church. Catholics believe that they need the sacraments to receive God's grace, and the efficacy of the sacraments depends upon their being administered by a priest who has been validly ordained. Personal piety, no matter how deep and how sincere, cannot fully substitute for receipt of the sacraments. Unordained laypeople, no matter how holy, cannot substitute for a priest. Reverence for the priesthood gives Catholic communities a stable focal point and a sense of connection with a universal Church, which has helped sustain the Church in all its difficulties. However, dependence on priests makes it more

30. Fuller discussion of such apparitions and miracles can be found in Madsen, *China's Catholics*, pp. 91–95.

31. Bishop Aloysius Jin Luxian, "How the 'little flock' in China lives the gospel in the changing society of today," speech at a conference in Manila, 1994; xeroxed English text furnished by the Holy Spirit Study Centre, Hong Kong.

32. They are on the Board of Free the Fathers, which in turn in connected with organizations such as Freedom House, which urge the US government to take strong action in defence of religious freedom, especially for Christians, around the world.

difficult for Catholic communities to expand rapidly than for Protestants, who rely mostly on easily trained, often highly entrepreneurial lay preachers, female as well as male.

One of the agonies inflicted by the Maoist regime on Chinese Catholics was its denial of priests to them. While most of the clergy was jailed, Catholics carried on their faith through private devotions, but no matter how pious they were, they felt a pressing need for the sacraments and feared for the salvation of their souls if they were denied the services of priests to hear their confessions, give them Holy Communion, bless their marriages and administer the Last Rites. After the Maoist era, the government returned some of their priests to them – but not enough to meet the religious demand. Most of the priests were now old and frequently in poor health. Some of them had been compromised, in the eyes of many Catholics, because of their association with the Catholic Patriotic Association.

The supply of clergy has been improving, but there remain social and political obstacles to the recruitment of new priests and the appointment of new bishops. As of 1999, the average age of bishops in the open church was about 78. The demographic situation of priests is better. By the year 2000, about three-quarters of China's estimated 2,200 priests had been ordained during the past 12 years. In the 1980s, the government began to reopen seminaries, and there are presently about 1,000 seminarians in 19 approved major seminaries and five preparatory seminaries. In addition there are perhaps 700 in underground seminaries.[33]

Catholics must often rely on the underground church to fill gaps in the supply of priests. Disputes about the relative quality of underground and open church priests help create the strong factionalism that one finds in the Chinese Church. At the same time, common agreement on the importance of the priesthood helps bind the factions into a unity. While opposing Protestant communities can separate themselves from one another, opposing Catholic factions cannot. They are like rival factions within a traditional Chinese family, whose members stay together even when they are causing each other considerable pain.

Disputes among different Catholic factions over the priesthood centre not on the validity but on the licitness of one another's sacramental practices. In traditional Catholic theology, the administration of a sacrament may be "valid but illicit." That is, as long as it has been performed in the prescribed way by a priest who has been ordained in a properly performed ritual, it "works." But if it is performed in circumstances forbidden by canon law, for instance by a priest who does not have ecclesiastical permission to be functioning as a priest, the priest who performs it and the person who receives it commit a sin.

A priest is functioning licitly if he has been properly ordained by a bishop who is himself acting licitly and if the priest is working with the approval of the rightful bishop of his diocese. Church law says that to be licitly made a bishop, a priest must receive approval from the Vatican.

33. Charbonnier, *Guide*, pp. 14–15.

The official position of the CPA is that China's bishops do not need such permission. Nevertheless, about two-thirds of open church bishops have informally received Vatican approval. When they get consecrated as new bishops, they often go through elaborate manoeuvres to ensure that at least one and if possible all of the three bishops required for the ceremony have received Vatican approval. Priests too go through similar manoeuvres to ensure that their ordinations are licit. Even if they are planning to work within the open church, young men awaiting ordination often go to great lengths – even if this means postponing their ordination – to ensure that it will be done at the hands of a Vatican-approved bishop.[34] Meanwhile, the CPA tries to assert the principle that it should decide who gets consecrated a bishop or ordained a priest. The underground church has the advantage that all its priests and bishops are considered licitly ordained.

Claiming that priests in the open church are acting without permission from the Vatican, some underground priests warn Catholics that they are committing a mortal sin by receiving the sacraments in the open church. But even Church law says that it is permitted to receive the sacraments from any validly ordained priest under extraordinary circumstances, for instance if no other priest is available when one is in imminent danger of death.[35] The circumstances of the Church in China are extraordinary under any measure, but ambiguous enough that Catholics often feel that they have to make complicated decisions about how they receive the sacraments. Sometimes, they might attend Mass celebrated by a priest in an "open church," but they might not go to confession to such a priest, because they fear that he might come under pressure to report their sins to political authorities.[36] And when they were dying, if at all possible, they might want an underground priest to give them the Last Rites because they absolutely cannot afford to take chances that they might be illicitly receiving the sacrament.[37]

Social roles. The priest's role as a ritual leader is connected to his role as a community leader. Since the Chinese Church is so embedded in rural society, its priests take on many of the characteristics of local authorities. The intense concern over the ecclesiastical "lineage" of its bishops and priests, rather than, say, their preaching ability or their personalities, resonates with traditional emphases on particularistic, patron–client relationships. The effect of this is to encase Chinese bishops, priests and lay people within complicated informal, vertically organized networks. Because of factional divisions, sometimes within a locality there are at least two networks of loyalties running parallel to one another. One

34. Information based on author's interviews in Hong Kong.
35. Tang, "The Church into the 1990s."
36. *Ibid.*
37. During my ethnographic fieldwork near Tianjin in 1993, in a community where most members worshipped in an open church, there was a sudden flurry of whisperings that an underground priest had just slipped in and out of the village to give the Last Rites to someone who was dying. I never got to meet the priest personally, however.

extends towards the offices of the CPA, another, for most Catholics thicker and more morally compelling, extends towards the Vatican. But there are gaps in the networks. A network to the Vatican does not necessarily connect in an unbroken chain all the way to Rome. Contact with Vatican representatives is intermittent at best and accurate information about who stands where is hard to come by. Rivalries even between bishops and priests who are nominally approved by Rome can test the loyalty of Catholics lower down their networks.

Especially in the rural context, the overwhelming importance for Catholics of having a validly and licitly ordained priesthood creates a fluid but viscous pattern of Catholic community life. It is fluid because under current political circumstances Catholics must fulfil their need for priests by relying on informal networks rather than the regular bureaucratic procedures that both the Vatican and the PRC would for different reasons and incompatible purposes prefer. It is viscous because the need for a priesthood slows down processes of Church development.

But the embeddedness of the Church in rural life makes it difficult to get the kinds of priests it needs – effective local pastors who could link local piety with a theology fit for coping with the problems of modernization. Most recruits to the seminaries, both open and underground, in fact come from the countryside, often produced by large families in remote villages. Few modern urban youths seem attracted to the clerical life.[38] Part of the attraction of the priestly vocation to rural young men is the great status attributed to it by their families. But priests today – at least in the official Church – are trained in seminaries in the cities and receive enough of a modern education to alienate them from the customs of their home communities. They often develop aspirations for something other than a rural ministry. If they are sent to work in the countryside, they sometimes feel embarrassed at being put on a pedestal by Catholics in the villages and feel inadequate to live up to their expectations. Although they have enough education to alienate them from village customs, they do not have enough to deal with the social, political and cultural challenges of such an environment. The consequences of this are described in an article by a Beijing Catholic layman published in the Hong Kong Catholic journal *Tripod*:

The average young priest on the mainland is ordained after five or six years of post-secondary education. His educational environment in the seminary has been intense, enclosed and isolated from the outside.... After ordination, he finds himself in a different kind of world. He is thrust into an active ministry full of conflicts and difficulties, in which temptations are many and supports are few. Problems soon begin to surface: personal, social and ecclesiastical. He often finds himself over-worked, undervalued and lonely. For the strong, these are challenges to be met and overcome, merely steps along the way to progress.... But for those who come to their day of ordination still hampered by unresolved ambivalence, for those who choose to

---

38. For instance, at the seminary at Sheshan, close to Shanghai, one of the best seminaries in China that draws its students from across the nation, most seminarians in the 1980s came from Shanghai itself. Now, very few come from there. Almost all come from rural areas.

become priests more out of internal or external pressures than personal conviction, these problems are much more acute. Such young priests have the feeling that they are riding on the back of a tiger with no possibility of escape. As the years pass, their interest in pastoral work declines, and they turn to more material pleasures for solace. They cultivate a taste for "the good life." ... Soon they seek to fill a void in their lives with wining, dining, and the aimless pursuit of pleasures.[39]

Catholic theology itself does not give these young priests a clear model for how they should play out their role of a sacramental leader at the local level. In the absence of such a model, the role of the priest gets imagined in terms of the role of the village cadre. The pressures of modernization then help to produce tensions and even introduce kinds of corruption that one commonly finds among rural officials.

The processes of modernization also foster a generation gap among young priests:

Older priests have seniority and experience, but they appear to the younger priests as passive, sedate and conservative, anxious to avoid any disturbance or controversy. On their part, the older priests find it difficult to accept the new ideas of the young, and they tend to respond to them in a pedantic and patronizing way.... There are some bishops and leaders of the older clergy who have little respect for nor understanding of the younger priests. They stereotype them and demand total compliance with their own wishes. They are particularly distrustful of the brighter, more active ones, on whom they place enough restrictions to ensure that they do not act contrary to or independent of their own authority.[40]

Even in the tightly disciplined world of the seminaries, would-be priests get new ideas that they ought to have more autonomy, that faith must be more a matter of active, internal conviction than external obedience. The gap between their views and that of the older generation is intensified by the absence of a middle generation.

Political conflicts. Priests are also torn by political pressures coming from two directions: from the government and from the Vatican.

Catholics widely assume that government agents have infiltrated both the official and underground churches and, among other things, try to keep the Church off balance by fomenting discord. The aggressive attempts by the government to control the Church are not simply a result of standard government strategies to stifle all forms of independent association, no matter how innocuous. They are also the legacy of a long history of direct political conflict between the Catholic Church and the communist government. Especially after the Tiananmen demonstrations of 1989, the government has been utterly determined to stamp out any Catholic-inspired political activism – which, according to their standard operating procedures, means erring on the side of political security and repressing many forms of religious activity that would probably be considered a-political in a Western context.

39. Yu Min, "The Church in China: on-going concerns and challenges," trans. by Norman Walling, SJ, *Tripod*, Vol. 20, No. 117 (May-June 2000), pp. 27–28.
40. *Ibid.* pp. 31–32.

Standard forms of political repression do not seem to be working well, however. During the 1990s, the government subjected the underground church to waves of violence, including imprisonment, beatings and demolition of church buildings. This has not reduced the numbers of practising Catholics, and, by producing martyrs, may have increased the zeal of some Catholic activists and perhaps only increased their politicization. At the same time, the government has been powerless to prevent an evolution towards reconciliation among Catholics in the open and underground churches. The number of bishops in the open churches who have gained Vatican approval has been rapidly climbing, from perhaps 30 per cent in the early 1990s to over two-thirds today. There is now no clear distinction between an open church which the government controls politically and an underground church which it does not.

As I have argued elsewhere, it is perhaps best now to make a distinction between an official (*guanfang*) and unofficial (*wuguanfang*) church than between an official and underground church:

As used in modern Chinese parlance, "official" refers to the realm of activity that is publicly recognized and controlled by the state. "Unofficial" refers to a realm of private negotiations at least partly independent of state control. In ordinary Chinese speech, "unofficial" has a connotation of "unorthodox" or "deviant," reflecting a political system that denies the legitimacy of any forms of association not under state supervision. But "official" and "unofficial" are not neatly separated. They form a continuum. Most people have to live and work under the supervision of state-controlled organizations, but within those organizations (sometimes in complicity with the organization's leaders) they carry out a great deal of unofficial activity, which sometimes contradicts and subverts the stated purposes of the organization.

Thus, to regulate and supervise Roman Catholics, there are official government regulations for religious activity and officially recognized organizations, like the Catholic Patriotic Association and the Chinese Catholic Bishops Conference. But within this framework, Catholics are developing their own informal rules and unwritten procedures for establishing legitimate authority. As in much of the rest of China, this vigorously developing unofficial sector does not overtly defy government authorities but it subtly neutralizes them, and renders them increasingly irrelevant.

In the unofficial Church, people, ideas, and moral rules from the open and underground churches become blended together in new syntheses. And no matter what government officials or leaders of the Catholic Patriotic Association might desire, the religious life of unofficial Church is oriented toward communion with the universal Church, under the jurisdiction of the Pope.[41]

This leads to a certain convergence of interests between Beijing and the Vatican. Beijing has been trying to impose a rationalized system of bureaucratic control upon the Church, but is frustrated by the growth of an informal, unofficial organization of Church life. However the Vatican, too, would like to impose a more rationalized system of control upon this luxuriant informal undergrowth.

It was perhaps for this reason that the PRC government seemed

41. Richard Madsen, "Saints and the state: religious evolution and problems of governance in China," *Asian Perspective*, Vol. 25, No. 4 (2001), pp. 187–211.

increasingly willing in early 1999 to open negotiations with the Vatican on normalization of diplomatic relations. Normalization would enable the Vatican, through its papal nuncio, to impose a more effective bureaucratic discipline upon its bishops and priests. If the PRC could then convince the Vatican to ensure that its priests would not become politically active or socially disruptive, the PRC regime could get the kind of social stability that is in its interests.

The Vatican, on the other hand, had some reasons to be accommodating towards Beijing. The old battle between Catholicism and communism was mostly over. Chinese communism was ideologically dead. One of the Vatican's main concerns with the Chinese government was with its lawlessness and corruption. In spite of some continued repression, Catholics have been gaining a good deal of practical freedom to practise their religion, but this is not protected under the law. It is often gained through unofficial understandings with local officials, sometimes lubricated with bribes. Under these circumstances, Catholics are vulnerable to extortion. For example, when a diocese in Sichuan wanted to build a convent they had to pay inflated prices to a government-controlled construction company. Then officials from the CPA appropriated the buildings and rented them out for profit.[42]

The ambient corruption can seep into the Church. Along with other outsiders interested in providing financial aid to Chinese Catholics, Vatican officials have become concerned about a lack of accountability. Because there are no regular channels of communication with Catholics in China, especially with the non-official church, it is difficult for outsiders to evaluate requests for financial aid and determine if donations are properly spent.[43]

Regular channels of communication could also help the Vatican better evaluate the suitability of its bishops and priests, and to develop more systematic procedures for training and supervising them. In short, it could impose a bureaucratic rationalization on the priesthood. Such rationalization might not be entirely welcome among clergy and laity at the grass roots. In fact, as the negotiations for Sino-Vatican normalization were moving ahead in the autumn of 1999, underground bishops moved to consecrate a number of younger bishops (without having to go through the careful process of vetting that the Vatican would have been able to institute after normalization), thereby presenting both the CPA and the Vatican with fait accompli.[44]

A more rationalized hierarchy could be welcome to the government only if it had more say than the Vatican on the selection of bishops. The government insisted even more strongly on this point, especially by the autumn of 1999, as it used its campaign against the *falun gong* to tighten control over all forms of religious activity. The Vatican in the end could

---

42. Author's interviews in Hong Kong.
43. Author's interviews in Hong Kong.
44. Author's interviews in Hong Kong.

not yield the principle that it must have the final word on the selection of bishops. Thus, the 1999 round of Sino-Vatican negotiations collapsed.

The wary co-operation then turned into harsh conflict. On 6 January 2000, the Feast of the Epiphany, the CPA staged a consecration of five new bishops, none of them approved by the Vatican. Unlike other such rituals in recent years, the Cathedral of the Immaculate Conception in Beijing was almost empty. Police ringed the Cathedral, and those in attendance were mostly government cadres rather than practising Catholics. Even Catholics closely associated with the open church refused to attend. Buses sent to fetch 120 seminarians from the National Seminary in Beijing, an institution closely sponsored by the open church, returned empty. (The seminarians and their rector were later punished for this.)[45] The Vatican pointedly reminded Chinese Catholics that bishops who accepted consecration without an "apostolic mandate" were automatically excommunicated.[46]

In a document issued in the autumn of 1999, the Party centre had outlined a strategy for "winning over the majority" of Catholics and "isolating a minority."[47] It had now lost its hope of winning over the majority. By the spring of 2000, the government began to backtrack. In May, it allowed the consecration of a bishop who had very openly received approval from the Vatican. (A large, enthusiastic congregation attended the ceremony.) But then on 1 October the Vatican went ahead with plans to canonize 120 Chinese martyrs, most of whom had died in the 19th century, especially during the Boxer uprising. *Renmin ribao* denounced this for "hurting the feelings of the Chinese people," and it said that the so-called saints had "violated Chinese laws ..., playing accomplices to the imperialist and colonialist invasion of China, committing unpardonable crimes, and deserving the punishments they received."[48]

The leaders of the CPA dutifully echoed this, even repeating parts of the official government line verbatim, and organized meetings for clergy in the open church to add their voices of denunciation.[49] But many other clergy and laity were quietly joyful that the Church had for the first time proclaimed as saints Catholics nurtured on their own soil. At the officially organized meetings, some priests even stood up to defy the government line and to praise the newly canonized saints.[50]

In the political battle between Beijing and the Holy See the Vatican is clearly winning, because it commands the strong allegiance of the vast majority of China's Catholics. But why does there have to be a political

45. UCAN News, 4,6,7 January 2000; Fides News Service, 14 January.
46. UCAN News, 26 June 2000.
47. Document 26 "Regarding the strengthening of Catholic Church work in the new circumstances," supposedly issued by the Secretariat of Party Central on 17 August 1999. Translated in *Tripod*, Vol. 20, No. 116, pp. 32–36.
48. Editorial and article by Shi Yan, "The true colors of the 'saints'," *Renmin ribao* (*People's Daily*), 3 October 2000. Translated by FBIS, 2 October 2000.
49. "Foreign ministry statement against 'canonization' hailed," Xinhua, 2 September 2000. Translated in FBIS-CHI-2000–1002.
50. UCAN News, 17 September 2000.

battle? In present-day circumstances, it would seem to be in the interests of neither party to be in a political battle. The Vatican has no need – if it ever did – to combat a moribund communist ideology. The PRC cannot have any significant control over the behaviour of Catholics unless it has co-operative relations with the Vatican. For the reasons adduced above, however, the Church cannot fully escape its political legacy, even if Vatican diplomats wanted to. That legacy is embedded within the collective memory of many Catholics, especially older ones, and it deeply influences their religious and moral self-understandings. This is to no small degree the fault of a Chinese system which, especially during the Maoist era, forced people to politicize all spheres of their lives. Meanwhile, the PRC government is too insecure about its grip on the country to give the Catholic Church even a modest level of autonomy, even if doing so might work to the PRC's long-term best interests.

Conclusion

Though intimately interconnected, the various layers of the Catholic Church have each developed at different paces and in somewhat different directions. Influenced belatedly by the Second Vatican Council, the layer of sacramental, priestly vision has been moving away from an understanding of the sacraments as a means for gaining grace to an understanding of them as powerful symbols of faith. However, the process is slowed, not simply because of the difficulty of learning the lessons of Vatican II, but because of the resonance of the older vision with the lifestyles of the peasants who are the backbone of the Chinese Church.

The rural communities in which the church is embedded are changing at a different pace from changes in Catholic theology. The heartland of the faith is in small rural villages, which for several generations were largely cut off from urban life and even now are more cut off than most villages. The social practices of such villages remain extremely conservative, centred on loyalty to extended family and obedience to the authority of patriarchs and priests. Catholic rituals are seen as sanctifying and strengthening such practices. The closedness of such villages during the Maoist era only deepened the identification of village life with Catholic practice. Under the new socialist market economy, such villages are becoming more open now. As young people migrate outside of the villages and begin to get some distance on relations to family and kin, they begin to re-evaluate their faith – and often to lose it. Seminarians and young priests who get their training in the cities develop a more modern understanding of the faith, but sometimes this alienates them from the Catholic communities in which they grew up and to which they may eventually be sent to serve. Paradoxically, confusion over how to carry out the religious demands of the priesthood leaves young priests with the temptation to model themselves more after rural cadres than after modern religious pastors.

Although the political orientations of Chinese Catholicism are certainly shaped by its religious vision and its social matrix, they develop at their own pace, influenced both by historical inertia and by international forces that are outside the control of the Chinese Church. Historically, relations between the PRC and the Catholic Church have been more deeply politicized than relations between the government and any other world religion, except for Tibetan Buddhism. Because of the ways in which both the Vatican and the PRC government would like to impose more bureaucratic control over the Church, Rome and Beijing are engaged in a complex game of co-operation and conflict that is evolving in uncertain directions. This will affect the ability of the Chinese Catholic Church to renew its theology, recruit and train adequate clergy, and adapt its pastoral practices to an urbanizing, market-driven society.

Chinese Protestant Christianity Today

Daniel H. Bays

ABSTRACT   Protestant Christianity has been a prominent part of the general religious resurgence in China in the past two decades. In many ways it is the most striking example of that resurgence. Along with Roman Catholics, as of the 1950s Chinese Protestants carried the heavy historical liability of association with Western domination or imperialism in China, yet they have not only overcome that inheritance but have achieved remarkable growth. Popular media and human rights organizations in the West, as well as various Christian groups, publish a wide variety of information and commentary on Chinese Protestants. This article first traces the gradual extension of interest in Chinese Protestants from Christian circles to the scholarly world during the last two decades, and then discusses salient characteristics of the Protestant movement today. These include its size and rate of growth, the role of Church–state relations, the continuing foreign legacy in some parts of the Church, the strong flavour of popular religion which suffuses Protestantism today, the discourse of Chinese intellectuals on Christianity, and Protestantism in the context of the rapid economic changes occurring in China, concluding with a perspective from world Christianity.

Protestant Christianity has been a prominent part of the general religious resurgence in China in the past two decades. Today, on any given Sunday there are almost certainly more Protestants in church in China than in all of Europe.[1] One recent thoughtful scholarly assessment characterizes Protestantism as "flourishing" though also "fractured" (organizationally) and "fragile" (due to limits on the social and cultural role of the Church).[2] And popular media and human rights organizations in the West, as well as various Christian groups, publish a wide variety of information and commentary on Chinese Protestants. Here I intend first to trace the gradual extension of interest in Chinese Protestants from Christian circles to the scholarly world during the last two decades, and then to discuss salient characteristics of the Protestant movement today.

The phenomenon of rapid Protestant growth was first noted soon after 1980 by several church-related organizations and their publications in Hong Kong and the West. Some of these were reports issued by evangelical organizations which tended to speak for the "house church" (those not registered with the government) sector of Protestants.[3] Others were

---

1. Mark Noll, "The globalisation of Christianity: a report" (unpublished, 2001), p. 2. This is a summary of papers and discussions at a conference of the Currents in World Christianity Project (Westminster College, Cambridge, UK), held at the University of Pretoria, South Africa, 3–7 July 2001.

2. Ryan Dunch, "Protestant Christianity in China today: fragile, fragmented, flourishing," in Stephen Uhalley, Jr. and Xiaoxin Wu (eds.), *China and Christianity: Burdened Past, Hopeful Future* (Armonk, NY: M.E. Sharpe, 2001), pp. 195–216.

3. The Chinese Church Research Centre, formerly based in Hong Kong and now in Taiwan, and its affiliated organization China Ministries International, for over 20 years has

reports and analysis by China-related offices of ecumenical church bodies in the United States, Britain and Canada, which were more attuned to the officially sanctioned Protestant Churches linked to the Christian Three-Self Patriotic Movement (TSPM), the organization designed as a link between the Protestant community and the state which had first been set up in the early 1950s, was abolished in the 1960s, and re-established, together with the China Christian Council (CCC), at the end of the 1970s.[4] The reasons for the intense interest in the Chinese Protestant Church by many on the entire spectrum of Christian circles in the United States, Britain and Canada is itself a very interesting historical question, for the most part outside the scope of this article.[5] At any rate, a variety of Christian organizations based in the West continue to contribute to the discussion of Chinese Protestantism.

In the 1980s Western scholars based in universities and secular research bodies also began to take note of the revival of religions of all kinds in China, and by the end of the decade many were including Protestantism in the discussion.[6] In the early 1990s some excellent academic studies of Protestantism began to appear. One of the best of these, by Alan Hunter and Kim-Kwong Chan, set a benchmark as both an objective descriptive profile and an analysis of the dynamics of the social and political as well as religious dimensions of Protestantism.[7] Among research bodies dedicated to analysis of human rights issues in China, whereas religion and issues of religious persecution were not often

---

footnote continued

published a variety of reports and periodicals on Christianity in China, for example *China and the Church Today* and *Zhongguo yu fuyin* (*China and the Gospel*). Overseas Ministries Fellowship (now OMF International), organizational descendent of the China Inland Mission, also published reports throughout the 1980s on the revival of Protestantism, and continues to do so (e.g. in *China Insight*, written by Tony Lambert). Many other Christian groups publish newsletters in Chinese or English.

4. *China Notes* was published throughout the 1980s and until the early 1990s by the East Asia/Pacific Office of National Council of Churches (USA). In the UK, The China Study Project, now the China Department, Council of Churches for Britain and Ireland, from 1980 published *Religion in the People's Republic of China: Documentation*, which since 1986 has continued as *China Study Journal*. The latter has extensive translations of Chinese government policy documents as well as reports on the local religious scene for all religions in China. In Hong Kong, beginning in 1983 the ecumenical Christian Study Centre on Chinese Religion and Culture published bimonthly English and Chinese versions of *Bridge* (*Qiao*), with first-hand reports on visits to churches in China. *Bridge* ceased publication in the late 1990s. Drawing on many of these materials from Christian sources in China, Philip L. Wickeri wrote a generally favourable study of the TSPM and its place in Chinese society as a PhD dissertation at Princeton Theological Seminary, later published as *Seeking the Common Ground: Protestant Christianity, the Three-Self Movement, and China's United Front* (Maryknoll, NY: Orbis Books, 1988).

5. A thoughtful discussion of some aspects of this for the US, but which would partially apply to the UK and Canada as well, is Richard Madsen, *China and the American Dream: a Moral Inquiry* (Berkeley: University of California Press, 1995), esp. ch. 6.

6. For example, inclusion of Protestants in Julian F. Pas (ed.), *The Turning of the Tide: Religion in China Today* (Hong Kong: Royal Asiatic Society and Oxford University Press, 1989).

7. *Protestantism in Contemporary China* (Cambridge: Cambridge University Press, 1993). A study from an evangelical Christian perspective is Tony Lambert, *The Resurrection of the Chinese Church* (Wheaton, IL: OMF/Shaw Publishers, 1994). Wickeri, *Seeking the Common Ground*, is more sympathetic than either of these to the viewpoint of the TSPM.

covered in the 1980s, in the 1990s Amnesty International and especially Human Rights Watch/Asia have included extensive documentation on religion, including Protestants.[8]

In the meantime, in China during the 1980s both the TSPM/CCC[9] Church leadership in Shanghai and Nanjing, and secular scholars at universities and research institutes at various places in the country, began to study and publish materials concerning Protestantism. The Jinling Theological Seminary in Nanjing, the only graduate-level seminary among the more than 20 Protestant seminaries and Bible schools, began publishing the *Jinling shenxuezhi* (*Jinling Theological Review*), as well as *Zongjiao* (*Religion*).[10] Historians, social scientists and philosophers at major universities and in the Chinese Academy of Social Sciences and the Shanghai Academy of Social Sciences began including Chinese Protestantism in their expanding research on religion. A landmark volume in 1987 published the results of field research on religion which included several studies of Protestant believers.[11] In the 1990s, two bibliographical indexes of academic works on Christianity published since 1949 showed the rapid development of Chinese scholarly work on Protestantism, mainly by historians and philosophers, after 1980.[12] This academic interest has continued down to the present, now including, as described below, a certain number of Chinese intellectuals who have themselves in some fashion adopted Christian ideas or advocate Christian values as useful for Chinese society.

Thus there is no lack of material to consult in assessing Protestantism today. The problem is the widely varying points of view of the sources and their sometimes conflicting claims.

---

8. For example, Human Rights Watch/Asia, *Continuing Religious Repression in China* (June 1993), *China: Persecution of a Protestant Sect* (June 1994), and *China: State Control of Religion* (October 1997).

9. The TSPM is not a Church organization. It is a body set up specifically to act as an interface and conduit between the registered and therefore government-recognized local churches and the offices of the Religious Affairs Bureau (government) and the United Front Work Department (Communist Party). The China Christian Council, a parallel body which has considerable overlapping membership with the TSPM, is less political and more "pastoral" in function: it co-ordinates and assists the churches with training of lay leaders, published materials, etc.

10. The latter journal is jointly published by the seminary and Nanjing University. After 1985, an annual publication of translations of articles on theology and church issues from these journals and from other Chinese sources, *Chinese Theological Review*, has been published in the US. 14 issues have appeared. In addition, since 1991 the Amity News Service, based in Hong Kong and representing the TSPM/China Christian Council, has published a bimonthly English-language digest of articles from *Tianfeng* and other sources in China.

11. Luo Zhufeng (ed.), *Zhongguo shehuizhuyi shiqi de zongjiao wenti* (*Religious Questions During the Socialist Period in China*) (Shanghai: Shanghai shehui kexueyuan, 1987), published in English as *Religion under Socialism in China*, trans. Donald E. MacInnis and Zheng Xi'an (Armonk, NY: M.E. Sharpe, 1991).

12. An index of works published in China from 1949 to 1993 is in Zhu Weizheng (ed.), *Jidujiao yu jindai wenhua* (*Christianity and Modern Culture*) (Shanghai: Renmin chubanshe, 1994), pp. 429–489. An index of historical works only, published from 1949 to 1997, is in Zhuo Xinping and Xu Zhiwei (ed.), *Jiduzongjiao yanjiu* (*Study of Christianity*) (Beijing: Shehui kexue wenxian chubanshe, 1999), 1st collection, pp. 245–401.

How Many Chinese Protestants?

There is uncertainty even on the part of the best-informed analysts as to how many Protestants there are in China. Major reasons for this, and for the resulting widely varying claims of numbers, are: much Church growth in the last two decades has been in the countryside, where it is difficult to count any group with accuracy; and a certain number, perhaps more than half, of Protestant believers are in autonomous Christian communities ("house churches," as opposed to congregations registered with the TSPM). Some of these communities are quite large, numbering in the hundreds or thousands.

The "numbers game" is important because the social and political importance of a group of 15 million nation-wide is very different from that of a group numbering 75 million or more (these are the approximate parameters for the debate). By the late 1980s it was clear that there was a large gap between estimates of the size of the Protestant community made by the TSPM, which for the most part counted only those believers in registered churches and recognized smaller "meeting points," and those made by many groups outside China which attempted to include all believers. The careful 1993 study by Hunter and Chan concluded that the "official" figure of about five million Protestants was far too low, and that the actual figure was very likely to be 20 million or more.[13] In the most recent past, "official" TSPM estimates for 2000 claimed more than 13,000 churches, 35,000 meeting points and 15 million believers.[14] Almost certainly the real number of Protestants, including those not in groups recognized by the TSPM, is higher. But how much higher? It is nearly impossible to answer definitively. In recent years various Chinese government agencies have estimated the number of Protestants to be between 25 and 35 million.[15] An analyst in the evangelical Christian sector, Tony Lambert, estimates that the number "may be" 50 million, but he is reluctant to claim a specific figure.[16]

Two points should be made about the size and official/unofficial components of the Protestant community. First, there are clearly more Protestants than Catholics in China today. Estimates of the Catholic community centre on a figure of about ten million. This is a dramatic reversal of the proportions of a half-century ago, at the end of the missionary era, when there were about three million Catholics and somewhere between 700,000 and one million Protestants. Secondly, the Protestant bifurcation between TSPM-related churches and autonomous communities is not well-defined. In some areas there is contact, co-operation and individuals active in both. And the theological beliefs of TSPM and non-TSPM groups overlap a great deal. Why then the

---

13. Hunter and Chan, *Protestantism in Contemporary China*, esp. pp. 66–71.
14. *Chinese Theological Review*, No. 14 (2000), p. 155; *China Insight* (November/December 2000).
15. *China Insight* (November/December 2000). Tetsunao Yamamori and Kim-kwong Chan, *Witnesses to Power* (Carlisle: Paternoster Press, 2000), p. xiv.
16. Tony Lambert, *China's Christian Millions* (London: Monarch Books, 1999).

continuing importance of the distinction between registered and autonomous, TSPM and house churches? The answer lies partly in the role of
the state.

Church and State Issues among Protestants

Like all religious believers in China, Protestants have to live with state
control of and interference in their activities. For TSPM pastors and
congregations, that means monitoring by the state, required political
study for pastors, certain restrictions on acceptable topics for preaching
and intervention in church personnel matters. Autonomous groups are
vulnerable to much more coercive and punitive state action, including
physical harassment, detention, fines, and labour re-education or criminal
proceedings and prison sentences.[17]

There is nothing new about this pattern. Since imperial times, certainly
since the Tang dynasty (618–907 CE), state registration and monitoring
of religious activities, though irregularly exercised, was a constant reality
of organized religious life.[18] One reason this has been so is that the state
itself has had religious dimensions. The contemporary state structure and
Communist Party domination of public life have inherited this tradition
and have built upon it a pattern of ritual, vocabulary and public discourse
which is similar to that of theocratic organizations.[19] So legitimacy of the
state structure necessitates vigilance against dissenting or critical voices
arising from authentically religious sources. And for more than a decade,
since the fall of the communist regimes of Eastern Europe, the Party has
been aware of the contribution which Christian Churches, Catholic and
Protestant, made to the demise of several of those regimes. The bureaucratic control apparatus also evinces a purely administrative imperative in
its behaviour. According to a senior official interviewed in 1991, referring
to religious believers, intellectuals, and journalists:

In fact all policies concerning these people are the same. They are part of the overall
ideological control mechanism. The basic principle is simple: if they are obedient,
then we treat them well. If they are not, then we discipline them … Christians say
they must obey God, journalists say they are serving the public, intellectuals say they
are developing culture. But from our point of view these excuses are all irrelevant.
We treat these people as an administrative problem.[20]

Whether from religious principle, aversion to administrative interference or any number of other reasons, including personal animosities
towards TSPM leaders or the fact that in some rural areas no TSPM

17. Dunch, "Protestant Christianity," p. 209 has a concise description.
18. For a perceptive historical overview see Kim-kwong Chan, "A Chinese perspective on
the interpretation of the Chinese government's religious policy," in Alan Hunter and Don
Rimmington (eds.), *All Under Heaven: Chinese Tradition and Christian Life in the People's
Republic of China* (Kampen: J.H. Kok, 1992). For an example of the state's bureaucracy at
work in the Qing, see Vincent Goossaert, "Counting the monks: the 1736–1739 census of the
Chinese clergy," *Late Imperial China*, Vol. 21, No. 2 (2000), pp. 40–85.
19. See Alan Hunter and Don Rimmington, "Religion and social change in contemporary
China," in Hunter and Rimmington, *All Under Heaven*, pp. 11–37, esp. pp. 14–16.
20. Quoted in Hunter and Chan, *Protestantism in Contemporary China*, p. 28.

church exists nearby, many Protestants choose to function as autonomous entities. So it seems likely that sporadic tension between a substantial number of Protestants and the state will continue. But it is possible that the presence of both categories of Protestants actually helps both. In a recent survey of trends in relations between Protestants and the state in Asia, Africa and Latin America, Paul Freston speculates that in China, the house church option, and the likelihood that stricter state control might actually drive more believers out of the open churches into house churches, "means the TSPM has a greater margin of manoeuvre vis-à-vis the government than it would otherwise. And the TSPM's existence gains concessions for believers that house churches alone would not obtain."[21] This last observation points to the undoubted fact that were it not for the role played by the TSPM and its longtime leader K.H. Ting (Ding Guangxun), Chinese Protestants almost certainly would not enjoy even the limited protections and practical freedoms they now have.[22]

The Legacy of the Missionary Past

Foreign missionaries left China a full half-century ago, but in many urban churches the Western imprint is still visible in church architecture, liturgy, music and theology. Many Western visitors to TSPM churches today, seeing the robed choir, hearing familiar Western hymns sung in Chinese and an evangelical sermon they might have heard in the United States or Britain, may wonder how indigenous the Chinese Church really is.[23] This situation is not altogether surprising, because of the strength of the foreign model and the fact that the last generation of Church leaders to be trained before 1949, now well into their 70s and older, is still influential, though it is fast passing from the scene. Yet it is ironic that the TSPM, created explicitly to sever ties with the Western churches in the 1950s and create an indigenous post-denominational "self-supporting, self-propagating and self-governing" Church, has perpetuated much of the appearance and tone of the old missionary churches, at least in many urban congregations.

The urban house churches are also not free from the strong historical influence of the West. Many still use translations of old Western devotional classics such as *Streams in the Desert*, and in the words of one recent observer, much of their theology is "drenched in Dispensational-

21. Paul Freston, *Evangelicals and Politics in Asia, Africa, and Latin America* (Cambridge: Cambridge University Press, 2001), p. 105.

22. Bishop K.H. Ting, longtime Principal of Jinling Theological Seminary in Nanjing and chairman of both the TSPM and the CCC, is now officially retired, but is still influential. In both Chinese and foreign circles he has been praised by some for his astute leadership and success in reviving the public presence of Protestants, and reviled by others for alleged compromise and betrayal of the true Church. Recent publication of a large collection of his writings gives insight into this complex figure. Janice Wickeri (ed.), *Love Never Ends: Papers by K.H. Ting* (Nanjing: Yilin Press, 2000). This is an English translation by Wickeri of the Chinese volume published in 1998.

23. Alex Buchan, "Is the Chinese Church Chinese enough?" *ChinaSource*, Vol. 3, No.1 (2001), pp. 1–10.

ism and garnished with Creationism and Inerrancy – all theological exports from Europe and North America."[24]

In the top levels of the visible urban Protestant structures, including the TSPM/CCC and the seminaries, there seems to be increasing concern about what is perceived by some Chinese Church leaders as the persistence of obsolete or even "backward" theological currents of an evangelical or fundamentalist nature. This means doctrines stressing individual salvation and exclusiveness of the Christian community which were characteristic of the theology brought by Western missionaries in the first decades of the 20th century.[25] These are seen by some TSPM/CCC leaders as hindering relations between Protestants and the wider society of secular Chinese. It is undoubtedly true that adherence to this traditional theology makes it difficult to have dialogue between Protestants and Chinese intellectuals and scholars who, despite their interest in Christianity, find the level of intellectual discourse in the Church far too low, and have little interest in attending or interacting with the Church. It is precisely those traditional evangelical characteristics, however, which define the faith of the great majority of believers who attend the TSPM churches, as well as the house churches. It can also be argued that these characteristics helped enable Protestant communities to survive the decades of persecution before 1980. Thus it is an inherently complex and difficult task to try to change the theological orientation of the majority of Chinese Protestants, to which they seem strongly attached.

The Legacy of the Independent Churches

Traditional evangelical beliefs and doctrines are even more characteristic of autonomous Protestant communities than they are of TSPM congregations. Part of the house church sector of Protestants descends from Chinese independent churches founded early in the 20th century as a reaction against the missionary-run churches. These, some of which were individual churches and others of which were movements nationwide in scope (such as Watchman Nee's "Little Flock" or the True Jesus Church), were critical of the hierarchy and institutional complexity of Western denominations.[26] Most sought a return to primitivist Christianity, and put stress on direct spiritual experience of conversion or supernatural acts such as healing or prophecy, as well as practising considerable autonomy for local congregations.[27] Today, many in the autonomous Christian communities preserve the theological traditions and practices of

---

24. *Ibid.* p. 1.

25. *Chinese Theological Review*, No. 14 (2000) includes translations of presentations by top Chinese Church leaders from the nation-wide Protestant conference of late 1998 which were published in 1999 in the *Jinling shenxuezhi* from the Nanjing seminary, several of which stress this theme.

26. I use quotation marks for "Little Flock" (xiaoqun) because this is a name used only by outsiders.

27. Daniel H. Bays, "The growth of independent Christianity in China, 1900–1937," in Daniel H. Bays (ed.), *Christianity in China: From the Eighteenth Century to the Present* (Stanford: Stanford University Press, 1996), pp. 307–316.

these independent churches, especially Pentecostals, whose overt manifestations of being moved by the Holy Spirit (such as speaking in
tongues, praying loudly en masse, healing practices) are frowned on in
most TSPM churches because in their view they appear too much like
superstition rather than religion.[28]

At the same time, some Protestants in the tradition of the pre-1949
independent churches, for example the "Little Flock" and the True Jesus
Church among others, worship in TSPM congregations. Because the True
Jesus Church is Sabbath-observant – that is, they worship on Saturday –
TSPM churches where they are present usually have a Saturday service.
A Saturday service is also important for former Seventh Day Adventists,
descendants of members of the old American missionary denomination.
An important part of "Little Flock" practice is the breaking of bread (a
form of communion or the Lord's supper), usually on Sunday night. Thus
those TSPM churches with believers from this tradition sometimes have
a Sunday evening service which is mainly populated by these members.
At such a service, many of the women may cover their heads (another
"Little Flock" practice), and the congregation will break bread in the
manner of the tradition.[29]

Clearly, the Protestant scene today is thoroughly coloured by traditions
from both the old missionary-established denominational churches and
the several strands of the independent church movement dating back to
the early 20th century. Yet beyond either of these components, perhaps
the most striking feature of contemporary Protestantism is the large
number of new converts who come from none of these traditions, but are
products of Chinese popular culture.

The Rural Church, Chinese Popular Culture and Sectarianism

The great majority of Chinese Protestants live in rural areas, and many
have only minimal knowledge of the Christian doctrines and ritual
behaviour that would be familiar to most urban Christians. In their 1993
study, Hunter and Chan claimed that in understanding the appeal of
Christianity to many Chinese, especially in the countryside, we must
realize that in practical terms "many Christian activities ... are closely
related to traditional cultural patterns."[30] They went on to specify many
of those linkages to traditional popular culture, such as in the function of
prayer, requests for healing, charismatic phenomena like shamanism,
moral norms, ideas about sin and salvation, and the pragmatic aspects of
conversion.[31] In many ways, the tone of Chinese Protestantism on the

28. A brief description of some basic Pentecostal practices is in Hunter and Chan,
Protestantism in Contemporary China, pp. 145–155.
29. Many of the articles reporting local church practices in *Bridge* from the late 1980s to
the mid-1990s note this mixture of traditions in many TSPM churches. I have myself observed
it at churches in Shanghai, Fuzhou, Hangzhou and Jinan.
30. *Protestantism in Contemporary China*, p. 188.
31. *Ibid.* ch. 4.

local level of practice is very different from that of the West, despite having similar doctrinal tenets.

The growth spurt from the mid-1990s to the present has brought millions more into the churches or autonomous communities, and has stretched even further the scarce personnel resources of the TSPM churches and the body of trained clerical personnel available to provide pastoral leadership. The more than 20 seminaries and Bible schools cannot keep up with the demand. In 1999 there were only about 3,000 seminary graduates nation-wide, of whom 1,300 were ordained.[32] And even though annually there are over 2,000 provincial, county and munici-pal level short-term programmes of a few weeks or months sponsored by CCC bodies to train lay leaders for the burgeoning churches, these likewise result in only spotty provision of knowledgeable local leaders.

The result, insofar as can be inferred from scattered sources in the absence of formal field studies in the rural areas, has been the flourishing of an entire spectrum of sectarian groups, ranging from identifiably Protestant to quasi-Christian. Two of the apparently better organized of the more or less orthodox Protestant groups are the Chongsheng pai (Born again sect) and the Quanfanwei jiaohui (Full scope church), which stresses a dramatic conversion experience including copious weeping.[33] The religious culture of these groups, in the words of a recent study, typically stresses "direct personal experience of God, centered on literal reading of the Bible, spread by itinerant preachers with little in the way of formal education (theological or otherwise), but a great deal of dedication and enthusiasm. Suspicion of the state, and of the TSPM/CCC for its ties to the state, are characteristic, as is an otherworldly and often eschatological orientation."[34]

A recent study by Leung Ka-lun of Hong Kong documents thoroughly the phenomenon of Protestant sectarian groups in the countryside taking up practices of traditional popular culture. Their millenarianism (stressing the imminent second coming of Jesus, but reminiscent as well of the anticipated advent of Buddhist saviour figures), utilitarian agendas in conversion, and emphasis on magic and the supernatural, all facilitated by minimally trained leaders, make some of them a reflection of traditional cultural patterns as much as of Christianity.[35]

These tendencies in the countryside have resulted in some extreme groups evolving into sects which most Christians would unhesitatingly label heretical. Groups such as the Beili wang (Established king), Men-tuhui (Disciples sect), and many others often have a charismatic leader who proclaims himself to be Christ or otherwise divine, and who creates

32. *Chinese Theological Review*, No. 14 (2000), p. 155.

33. Summary description, with several sources noted, in Dunch, "Protestant Christianity," p. 201.

34. *Ibid.* p. 201.

35. Leung Ka-lun (Liang Jialin), *Gaige kaifang yilai de Zhongguo nongcun jiaohui (China's Rural Churches Since the Perform Period)* (Hong Kong: Jiandao shenxueyuan, 1999). Excerpts translated in *China Study Journal*, Vol. 14, No. 2 (1999), pp. 22–34. Also see Claudia Wahrisch-Oblau, "Healing prayers and healing testimonies in mainland Chinese churches," *ibid.* pp. 5–21.

new sacred instructions or scriptures. They typically denounce orthodox Christian congregations, perform alleged spectacular miracles, promise deliverance from an imminent apocalypse, and demand obedience and resources from their followers. In some respects they are similar to various popular religious sects in late imperial China, or even the Taipings of the 19th century. For the past two decades such groups have troubled the Protestant movement in China and have siphoned off many rural Christians from the mainstream of the faith. The sects have also recruited in urban areas. In the late 1990s both the national TSPM/CCC offices and leading house church groups published booklets denouncing many of these sects.[36] National Church leaders routinely point out the dangers of heretical sects in their discussions of Protestant affairs.[37]

These recent tendencies towards rural sectarianism may indicate that whereas most observers of Protestantism in China have in the past drawn the major fault line between registered, state-recognized TSPM churches and unregistered house churches whether urban or rural, perhaps that line should be drawn between urban and rural Protestant expressions whether registered or not. This is similar to the suggestion by Richard Madsen that for Chinese Catholicism we should look below the elite level of national organizations and relations with the Vatican and view rural, lay-led Catholic communities as a variant of Chinese folk religion.[38] A major question for the present and future is the urban impact of those sectarian Christians who are part of the massive migration from the rural areas to the cities in search of work. Will they be reconverted to orthodox Protestantism (or Catholicism), or will they perpetuate their sometimes heterodox sectarianism in the urban setting?

Protestantism Among Ethnic Minorities

The Chinese mainland officially has 55 national minorities. They number over 100 million, and inhabit areas constituting about 60 per cent of China's territory, mainly in strategic border areas. Some of these ethnic groups responded very favourably to Christianity before the communist period, such as the Hua Miao.[39] In Protestant conversion it seems that some minorities found social and psychological resources to resist domination and oppression by both the Han majority and by other

36. Four articles in *China Study Journal*, Vol. 13, No. 3 (1998), pp. 6–32. Tony Lambert, "Modern sects and cults in China," pp. 6–9; Lu Yunfeng, "Report on an investigation into the illegal organisation, the 'Disciples sect'," pp. 9–16; Luo Weihong, "The facts about the activities of the heterodox sect 'The established king'," pp. 17–21; and Zhong Guofa, "A survey of newly emerged religious sects in the republican era," pp. 22–32.

37. One example is Ma Jianhua, "The development of rural Christianity in China and its challenges," *Chinese Theological Review*, No. 13 (1999), pp. 65–71.

38. See Richard P. Madsen, "Beyond orthodoxy: Catholicism as Chinese folk religion," in Uhalley and Wu, *China and Christianity*, pp. 233–249, and also Madsen's article in the present volume.

39. For an overview of the pre-1949 pattern, Ralph R. Covell, *The Liberating Gospel in China: The Christian Faith among China's Minority Peoples* (Grand Rapids: Baker Books, 1995). Also Norma Diamond, "Christianity and the Hua Miao: writing and power," in Bays, *Christianity in China*, pp. 138–157.

minorities, and others found reinforcement for traditional cultural or religious identities. Some minorities that had substantial numbers of Protestants were strikingly loyal to their faith despite persecution after 1949.[40]

There has always been a widely varying pattern in the willingness of some minority groups and the unwillingness of others to convert to Christianity.[41] In the recent and present situation in China, the minorities who inhabit inaccessible interior areas in the south-west are being bypassed by the national movement towards modernization, and more-over are often victims of extreme poverty, drug addiction and social breakdown. Some of these groups have been very receptive to Protes-tantism. Moreover, some county governments in these areas, in an ironic reversal of the past stance of government vis-à-vis religion, but desperate to combat the drug problem and its dangers to public health and law and order, have actively promoted the conversion to Christianity of the afflicted peoples, and have facilitated their evangelization by Chinese Protestants.[42]

Chinese Intellectuals and Protestantism: the Phenomenon of "Cultural Christians" and the Missing Public Role of the Church

The first part of the article referred to the fact that since the 1980s there has been an increasing number of Chinese intellectuals who do research on Protestant Christianity, especially historians and philosophers. Some believe that Protestantism was centrally involved in the overall process of modernization that fuelled the economic development, political democra-tization and world-wide expansion of the West in the past few centuries. Others have found Protestant ethics and patterns of community formation interesting or attractive. Some intellectuals have actively advocated China's adoption of some aspects of Christianity as part of its own modernization efforts, and a certain number of these intellectuals have themselves become Christians.[43]

One of the first, most prolific and well-known of "cultural Christians" was Liu Xiaofeng, who began writing in the 1980s and now lives in Hong Kong. Several other intellectuals, both overseas and at universities and research units within China, are serious and knowledgeable scholars of Christianity, especially of Protestantism, and in recent years these schol-ars have published an impressive array of books and articles analysing

---

40. Diamond, "Christianity and the Hua Miao," and T'ien Ju-k'ang, *Peaks of Faith* (Leiden: Brill, 1993).

41. See the concluding chapter of Covell, *The Liberating Gospel*.

42. Case studies in Yamamori and Chan, *Witnesses to Power*, pp. 18–35.

43. For recent views, see the following. Zhuo Xinping, "Discussion on 'cultural Christians' in China," in Uhalley and Wu, *China and Christianity*, pp. 283–300. Chen Cunfu, "Historical and cultural background to the emergence of scholars in mainland China studying Christianity (SMSCs)," in Samuel Ling and Stacey Bieler (eds.), *Chinese Intellectuals and the Gospel* (San Gabriel, CA: China Horizon, 1999), pp. 83–108. Edwin Hui, "The 'cultural Christian' phenomenon in immediate context, with theological reflections," in *ibid.* pp. 109–136.

Christianity.[44] Some of these scholars may be Christian believers as well, but it is very difficult to know with certainty.[45] Whereas sometimes Chinese Christian intellectuals outside China are willing to participate in conferences and publications revealing their identity as Christian believers, intellectuals in China who study Christianity, including those who may be believers, have very little or no connection with the organized Church, whether TSPM or autonomous Christian communities, and normally do not reveal their personal beliefs.[46] Public knowledge that one is a religious believer can be of no help, and would almost certainly be a detriment, to one's career. Moreover, the paths of secular and religious studies of Christianity only infrequently cross. Academic conferences and publications on Christianity seldom include participation by Protestant representatives such as Church leaders or seminary professors, and with few exceptions meetings of Protestant leaders and seminary academics do not include secular academics.[47] One basic explanation for this, in addition to the personal career consideration just mentioned, is the perceived low level of academic discourse in the Protestant seminaries and publications, and the traditional, somewhat anti-intellectual, theology of the Church. Hence the desire of some TSPM leaders to "modernize" Protestant theology and establish more discourse with secular intellectuals.

The separation of Protestant intellectuals in the churches from those intellectuals interested in Christianity but who function in the secular realm of research institute or university is representative of the gulf between Protestantism and public issues in China today. Although some individuals who have run foul of the state for labour organizing or for attempting to organize political movements independent of the Communist Party apparently have partly been motivated by their beliefs as Protestant Christians, formal Church authorities, whether in the TSPM or the autonomous communities, refrain from comment on public issues. The Protestant magazine *Tianfeng* often has articles or answers to letters from readers which attempt to help believers cope with the stresses of economic and social change, family problems, or intra-church conflict.

44. A few of many possible items include: Gao Shining and He Guanghu (eds.), *Jidujiao wenhua yu xiandaihua* (*Christianity and Modernization*) (Beijing: Zhongguo shehui kexue chubanshe, 1996); Liu Xiaofeng and He Guanghu (eds.), *Jidujiao wenhua pinglun* (*Christian Culture Review*), No. 6 (Guiyang: Guizhou renmin chubanshe, 1997); He Guanghu and Xu Zhiwei (eds.), *Duihua: Rushidao yu jidujiao* (*Dialogues Between Confucianism, Buddhism, Daoism and Christianity*) (Beijing: Shehui kexue wenxian chubanshe, 1998); He Guanghu, *He Guanghu zixuanji* (*Selected Works of He Guanghu*) (Guilin: Guangxi shifan daxue chubanshe, 1999).

45. A leading scholar of Christian studies in China has warned observers to distinguish carefully between those Chinese intellectuals interested in the study of Christianity ("scholars in mainland China studying Christianity") and the much smaller number among them who have actually become believing Christians themselves. Zhuo Xinping, "Discussion on 'cultural Christians' in China."

46. An example of Chinese intellectuals overseas speaking frankly of their faith is Yuan Zhiming *et al.*, *Soul Searching: Chinese Intellectuals on Faith and Society* (Wheaton, IL: China Horizon, 1997), with ten essays by seven different scholars.

47. For a partial exception see Philip Wickeri and Lois Cole (eds.), *Christianity and Modernization: A Chinese Debate* (Hong Kong: DAGA Press, 1995).

There is a small but potentially important Protestant presence which has been established in the area of social services, provided mainly through the Amity Foundation, to groups neglected by the government and the larger society, such as the physically disabled.[48] And in recent years churches have willingly participated in relief efforts and contributed to relief funds at times of floods or other calamities. Beyond this, however, Protestantism has practically no public presence: no radio or television, no Christian bookshops (except the book table or book room in TSPM churches), no social or political commentary, or personal connections to those in high office.[49] Protestant seminary students did join the democracy marchers in a few cities in May 1989, but nothing like that has occurred since. Of course no non-state organizations have been able to establish an audible public voice; against that background there is no reason to expect that Protestants could have done so.

Despite this extremely modest public presence, there is some debate as to whether the very existence of a substantial number of believers organized into supportive local communities constitutes a form of "civil society." A recent thoughtful discussion of this question concludes that although it does not and probably will not oppose the Communist Party or play any formal political role, Protestantism in China does indeed "constitute part of an emerging 'civil society' in China in the sense that the ongoing struggle to claim an autonomous space for religious activity is at the core of the Protestant experience, both in the open and in the autonomous churches."[50] This quest for space could have political consequences in the future, although it does not seem to now.

Protestantism and Socio-economic Change

If it ever was true in the 19th century that Chinese Protestant converts to Christianity were poor and marginalized, that picture began to change at the turn of the century. Largely through the social mobility provided by the Protestant school system established by foreign missions, prosperous middle-class urban congregations began to develop early in the 20th century, especially in the coastal cities of Shandong, Zhejiang and

48. The Amity Foundation was created in the 1980s to give the Protestant church an entrée into society. It is closely linked to the TSPM/CCC, but its board of directors includes non-Church people, even non-Christians. The foundation maintains an overseas co-ordination office in Hong Kong, and publishes a bimonthly bulletin there in English, *Amity News Service*.

49. In the early part of the 20th century, in some areas Chinese Protestants were extremely influential in local and national politics, effectively making their views known on a whole range of national issues. See Ryan Dunch, *Fuzhou Protestants and the Making of a Modern China 1857–1927* (New Haven: Yale University Press, 2001). In the 1930s and 1940s the fact that Chiang Kai-shek and members of his family and entourage were Christians gave Chinese Church leaders occasional special access to the ear of government.

50. Dunch, "Protestant Christianity," p. 214. *Ibid.* pp. 209–214 discusses many aspects of this issue. Also see Richard Madsen, *China's Catholics: Tragedy and Hope in an Emerging Civil Society* (Berkeley: University of California Press, 1998), and Kenneth Dean, "Ritual and space: civil society or popular religion?" in Timothy Brook and B. Michael Frolic (eds.), *Civil Society in China* (Armonk, NY: M.E. Sharpe, 1997), pp. 172–192.

Fujian.[51] In some of these same cities, by the 1990s the resurgence of Protestantism seemed linked to the market economy. *The Wall Street Journal* reported in 1995 that in Wenzhou, Zhejiang province, where some think that as many as 10 per cent of the population are Christians: "Just as they drink Coke and carry Motorola pagers, entrepreneurs show off their cosmopolitan savvy by erecting the finest houses of worship. Taxi drivers sermonize passengers. Factory foremen lure their workers to Sunday services. So the Chinese people are discovering what Max Weber theorized long ago: capitalism and Christianity can be self-reinforcing."[52]

This portrait of urban Protestants, whether or not it is representative of more than a small portion of those believers who live in relatively prosperous coastal enclaves like Wenzhou, is certainly not true of rural believers. Many of them are extremely poor, and for them their adherence to Protestantism is less a manifestation of status than a strategy for survival. Those believers who have joined the throngs of workers migrating from rural to urban China, and who live day-to-day by temporary labour opportunities, constitute a very different social and cultural element in the urban Protestant community from the established middle-class congregations. Are these workers supported socially and psychologically by the rural communities whence they came, associating with fellow believers from the same locales, like them sojourners in the urban day-labour market? Do they attend established churches, whether TSPM or autonomous? Do those churches welcome them? What of those rural migrants who are already members of a heterodox sect? Do they find fellow sectarians in the cities? Do they convert to more orthodox Christianity? And what of those migrant workers who were not believers before their move to the city; are they attracted to the community and mutual support of Protestant congregations? The size of the recent and present population shift from countryside to city makes this a very interesting set of questions, not just for Protestantism but for other religions as well.[53]

China has finally joined the World Trade Organization. That may mean even more rapid economic and social change as, under the pressure of international competition, state-owned industries and the entire public sector shrink even more rapidly and private enterprises and economic networks grow. This might constitute an opportunity for further expansion of Protestantism in China. As a Chinese business and technocratic class in urban China becomes more like its counterparts in Singapore, Penang, Vancouver and Silicon Valley, the growth of Protestantism in all

51. Daniel H. Bays, "A Chinese Christian 'public sphere'? Socioeconomic mobility and the formation of urban middle class Protestant communities in the early twentieth century," in Kenneth G. Lieberthal, Shuen-fu Lin and Ernest P. Young (eds.), *Constructing China: The Interaction of Culture and Economics* (Ann Arbor: University of Michigan Center for Chinese Studies, 1997), pp. 101–117. This is also an important theme of Dunch, *Fuzhou Protestants*.

52. 16 June 1995, article by Joseph Kahn, "China's Christians mix business and God: Wenzhou church thrives on new capitalists' wealth," cited in Bays, "Chinese Christian 'public sphere'," p. 101.

53. For the different rural and urban worlds of Chinese Catholicism, see Madsen, *China's Catholics*, especially ch. 4.

of those places outside China may constitute a model for its future religious trajectory within China as well, at least in urban areas.

Conclusions

In their 1993 study, Hunter and Chan had one large definitive conclusion, that "Chinese Protestantism is now a sustainable force." They also had a more speculative conclusion, that "China may become an increasingly important part of the world Protestant community."[54] The correctness of their first conclusion is confirmed by the picture drawn here of the state of Chinese Protestantism in 2001. The size, resources and virtually nation-wide presence of the Protestant movement makes it one of the most important of non-governmental entities in China today. This is true despite the divisions and tensions which exist within Protestantism, and despite the failure so far of its leaders and institutions to make more than a faint contribution to public discourse on national issues.

Protestantism seems thoroughly rooted in Chinese society, with some aspects of it strongly reflecting affinity to traditional cultural patterns and others appealing to modernity. It offers varied appeals to its followers: its beliefs provide an explanation of suffering, an ethical code and a promise of salvation, all at a much cheaper cost than traditional rituals in local communities, because of less expense for ritual offerings, operas and feasts. Socially, it provides fellowship in a wide variety of organizational forms, from small home groups to large congregations. Yet it also offers personal affirmation and, especially for women and young people, an outlet for their energies and development of musical, organizational or preaching skills. For example, numbers of rural teenagers have found in networks of Protestant groups a vocation of travelling evangelism. Psychologically, different forms of Protestantism can offer for intellectuals or the urban middle class an identification with the West and modernization, or an eschatological prospect which may appeal to poor peasants left behind by the economic reforms.[55]

In their attitudes towards and relationships with Protestants outside China, Chinese Protestants take a variety of positions. Although the Chinese Church has long since ended its formerly close ties to the Western missionary movement and (for the most part) its aura of being a foreign religion, TSPM leaders and publications sometimes speak as though Western Christians and outside evangelization of China were still a threat to the independence of the Chinese Church. They speak of the importance of the three-self ideal, and denounce outside organizations which attempt to "infiltrate" China by establishing links with autonomous groups. At the same time the TSPM and CCC, supported by the govern-

54. Quotations from Hunter and Chan, *Protestantism in Contemporary China*, pp. 278, 280.
55. Yamamori and Chan, *Witnesses to Power*, pp. xiv–xvi, have an extensive list of factors which help explain the growth of Protestantism.

ment, try to maintain good relations with churches around the world, and warmly welcome foreign church leaders who wish to visit China. The CCC was admitted to the World Council of Churches in 1991, Chinese seminarians study in the West, and outside assistance enabled the building of a modern press in Nanjing to print large quantities of Bibles and other Protestant literature. The Amity Foundation assists in the placement of foreign teachers at Chinese schools that otherwise could not afford them. For their part, some autonomous Protestant communities also have an often lively intercourse with evangelical organizations based outside China. These organizations bring in ("smuggle," as the TSPM sees it) Bibles and other literature, provide money or other resources, conduct short-term classes or training, and altogether carry on a range of contacts that are considered by Chinese Church and Party authorities to be both illicit and an infringement of Chinese sovereignty.[56]

In my view, all these various foreign contacts do not constitute diminishment of the extent to which Protestantism has been domesticated in Chinese society in the past few decades. The majority of Chinese Christians were converted by other Chinese, not by foreign missionaries, even before 1949, and that is overwhelmingly true today. Christian groups outside China can participate in the further development of the Protestant movement within China in various ways – by sending teachers or other "foreign experts" to fill educational or training needs, by assisting activities of either TSPM or autonomous Protestant groups in China, or by evangelizing Chinese students and scholars who come to the West for training.[57] But none of these outside elements is essential to the continued viability and growth of Chinese Protestantism, which has established its own momentum of development on the basis of its own resources.

To view Chinese Protestantism on the broadest scale, as part of a world-wide phenomenon, it is apparent that it has certain features in common with the Protestant movement in other parts of the world in recent decades. In its piety, its concern for both salvation and tangible this-worldly benefits, its relentless sectarian diversity within a context of disintegration of old denominational affiliations, and its association with an expanding market economy, Chinese Protestantism has much in common with world-wide trends. Even the predilection towards Pentecostalism, on the surface "unmodern," insofar as it facilitates individual self-development, can be associated with adaptation to modernizing economic change, as it has been in Latin America.[58] Within the past few decades Christianity in its Protestant and Catholic expressions alike has become a primarily non-Western religion in terms of both numbers of adherents and local practice. For the near future it may be more useful to view Chinese Protestants as part of that new centre of gravity outside

56. Yamamori and Chan, *Witnesses to Power*, pp. xxi–xxii.
57. There is a wide range of Protestant individuals and organizations outside China who engage in various forms of such activities.
58. This point is made in Dunch, "Protestant Christianity," p. 215.

Europe and North America, rather than to discuss it in terms and categories more familiar in the West but now increasingly distant from Chinese reality.[59]

---

59. For example, even terms like Pentecostalism, while used to describe more or less similar phenomena world-wide, when used in some places outside the West (including China, in my opinion) are "imported concepts." Noll, "The globalization of Christianity," p. 4.

Healing Sects and Anti-Cult Campaigns*

Nancy N. Chen

ABSTRACT Charismatic forms of healing can be found both in Chinese medicine and spiritual practices. This article examines how *qigong* healing sects in contemporary China became subject to state regulation and medicalization. Such a move was intended to eradicate masters who were viewed as promoting superstition (*mixin*) or heterodox spiritual practices. Yet, the rise of masters who intertwined healing with spirituality was facilitated by market reforms that enabled entrepreneurial forms of medicine. When other popular forms of healing emerged in the late 1990s, the previous state response to *qigong* facilitated containment practices which continue into the 21st century. Recent state policy towards sectarian organizations based on the promotion of science are compared with the regulation of *qigong* a decade earlier.

At the onset of the 21st century, the Chinese state bureaucracy faces the recurrent issue of how to retain social order with ongoing market reform. Despite robust exports and access to new goods and job opportunities, the domestic economy has produced not only *nouveaux-riches* but also vastly poorer individuals without a familiar net of state welfare or services available. In the midst of market expansion, alternative healing practices gave meaning to those who were being displaced in the new economic order and who came to embody social disorder. Followers were drawn to the messages of inclusion where anyone could participate, especially those who had lost jobs or health care benefits. Such a context created a broad-based interest in healing, setting the stage for entrepreneurial masters and the formation of new healing practices.

This article examines how sectarian groups based on communal forms of healing have shaped recent state discourse about religion and science. Such communities and their leaders do not claim to be religious organizations, nor does the Chinese state recognize them as official religion. Yet, the networks and experiences of charismatic healing in such groups facilitate social movements similar to sectarian faith organizations. Perhaps what is shared more commonly between healing sects and faith groups is the scrutiny of state officials and tightening of regulatory policies. Determining membership and classification of these recent forms has been a serious endeavour of officials concerned with maintaining state authority. As scholars of science such as Bowker and Star have

* I am grateful to Professor Daniel Overmyer for inviting me to contribute to this special volume and for his useful editorial feedback. Diana Lary, Raoul Birnbaum and conference participants offered incisive suggestions for revisions. Special thanks to the Fundação Oriente and Dr Richard Edmonds for the Arrabida conference which enabled invaluable discussions. The earlier research on which this article is based was made possible with funding from the Committee for Scholarly Communication with the PRC (CSCPRC). My discussion of science, *qigong*, and *falun gong* is based on more extensive analysis in *Breathing Spaces: Qigong, Psychiatry, and Healing in China* (Columbia University Press 2003).

indicated, classification is a form of political shorthand to define boundaries of legitimacy.[1] Such demarcations were especially important in the light of public concerns about corruption and a deepening crisis of faith in the government to provide basic services. Individuals who were drawn to the healing and spiritual practices, ordinary people in their 40s to 70s, were the very people who had sacrificed themselves in the forgoing of the nation. In what follows, I examine the local conditions which led to widespread interest in *qigong* and other forms of popular healing.

The Social Context of Healing

In the post-Mao period, fervent discussions about the power of *qigong* (deep breathing exercises, meditation and healing practices) took place throughout China. The immense popularity of masters and highly visible practices taking place in parks or in large stadiums opened conversations and debates about the miracles of *qigong* among strangers, acquaintances and family members. Experiences of healing for chronic illnesses or somatized disorders were profoundly moving, leading many participants to spread the word. In a sense, *qigong* reframed the very boundaries of public and private spheres, opening up different possibilities for the organization of daily life in time and space. Rather than co-ordination with state-imposed spatial and political order, *qigong* practitioners sought personal balance and self-cultivation through attention to healing practices. The variety of participants from all walks of life including intellectuals, industrial workers and cadres indicates how far reaching the practice could be. Moreover, *qigong* offered opportunities for belonging that did not rely on existing state categories such as work units, communes or the Party.

The broad-based appeal of *qigong* in the post-Mao era, accompanied by the explosion of mystical movements, emerged for several reasons. The most common reason, according to both practitioners and masters, was people's desire to heal themselves rather than relying upon continually ingesting numerous medications, either biomedical prescriptions or traditional Chinese herbs, each day. Many of the afflicted sought *qigong* for initial relief and eventual transformation of their health status from incurable to healed. Especially for somatized complaints or congenital defects, *qigong* provided a cheaper alternative to the systems of Western and traditional Chinese medicine accompanied by immediate changes. Many retirees took up the practice for chronic illnesses. Younger practitioners in their 30s and 40s also used it to feel energetic and ready for long days at work. It is important not to overlook the affective qualities or emotional release of *qigong* practice. Most of the practitioners that I observed in the mid-1980s and interviewed in the early 1990s described

---

1. Geoffry Bowker and Susan Leigh Star, *Sorting Things Out: Classification and its Consequences* (Boston: MIT, 1999).

how *qigong* helped to reframe their lives in positive ways and overcome illnesses as a result of decades of political trauma.

For example, Mrs Guo, a retired chemistry teacher in her 60s, started *qigong* practice after several colleagues told her of their experiences of miraculous healing. She had suffered from debilitating migraine headaches and lethargy for nearly a decade. After attending a mass lecture and demonstration among thousands in a packed gymnasium led by a famous master, she felt inspired to try it herself. When I met Mrs Guo during the winter of 1990, she had already been practising for several years. She described how her daily practice helped end her suffering while bringing a new sense of vitality. She looked forward to morning visits to her local park to meet other regular practitioners who also focused on self-cultivation. Mrs Guo did not subscribe to any religion or spiritual practice, especially with her training in science. However, her experience of well-being led her to have faith in the deeply meditative form of her *qigong* master.

The momentous changes in the health care system were a key catalyst for the pursuit of these more accessible forms of medicine. They provoked a deep crisis in faith in the government's ability to provide for its citizens, especially the elderly who were loyal supporters. Concern about falling through the cracks of the existing medical system was thus a critical backdrop to the increased popularity of *qigong* as an alternative form of healing. Many people relied on self-medication with herbal remedies, special foods or tonics, often prepared by family members, before seeking medical advice. *Qigong* was thus part of the shift to market medicine. Promoted both by the state and by medical practitioners and masters, *qigong* fitted well with people's desires for better health and less costly prescriptions. As the state health care system became entrepreneurial so too did Chinese medicine and other healing practices. Compared to costly and time-consuming visits to clinics, practitioners found that *qigong* was more convenient, inexpensive and enjoyable. Practitioners claimed that it decreased stress and anxiety, and gave energy immediately.

The combination of the withdrawal of state funds, emergence of charismatic masters and a long tradition of self-cultivation all fuelled the explosive growth of healing sects. Informal social networks helped to support the power of masters with little or no formal medical training recognized by the government, so that these individuals accumulated ephemeral powers of health and wealth in a socialist market economy. Like popular entertainers, they had much charisma and gained great attention and respect wherever they went. Their emergence depended upon the renewal of the social sphere referred to as *minjian* (folk) that was non-governmental and increasingly influential. Healing sects were initially tolerated by the state because many officials were clients themselves, actively seeking masters and other healers for a wide range of ailments. As long as such activities remained in the realm of medicine, practitioners could work without any official notice. Moreover, the patronage of well-known and well-positioned officials was crucial for the formation of a master's social networks. However, once healers amassed large followings, accumulated vast material resources or participated in visibly questionable activities, it was likely that they would be viewed carefully.

From the perspective of the state bureaucracy it became necessary to call for regulation in a practice where *luan* (chaos) had taken over. Accusations of corruption and superstition (*mixin*) were directed at specific masters who had amassed tremendous capital during mass healing sessions or in private. In what follows, the use of science to contain the widespread interest in *qigong* and healers is examined.

The Mandate of Science

In the 21st century, late socialist anti-cult campaigns rely heavily upon discourses of scientific rationality and civilization. The notion of science as critical to nation-building is a particular ethos that pervaded most of the previous century. As with reformers in the early 20th century, science continued to be embraced by Chinese state leaders as a national platform essential for modernization at the end of the century. The use of scientific discourse to create new categories of "real, scientific" and "false, unscientific" *qigong* evolved after specific interest groups came together. Such classifications reflected a particular desire to define order with science rather than adopt already existing categories within *qigong* practice.

The patronage of Qian Xueshen, China's premier scientist, and the invocation of science by *qigong* masters as well as by bureaucrats led to the privileging of science to measure the authenticity or power of *qigong*. Below are explored some of the concerns and debates that led to science as a form of "national consciousness" about modern life.[2] Especially during the 20th century, science represented a potent field of meanings in both the production of knowledge and subject citizens. *Qigong* presented a critical tension between "superstition" and science on the authority of expert, official knowledge. In order to combat superstition or pseudoscience, scientists vehemently opposed popular claims about the practice. If *qigong* was supposed to promote a better life, then modern science was necessary to prove its reality and efficacy. However, many masters already invoked science, claiming that their forms were sound. How would it be possible to combat pseudoscience when scientific discourse had already been appropriated in the popular context? The mobilization of allegiances between bureaucrats, scientists, physicians and *qigong* masters was crucial to the formation of "scientific" *qigong*. Scientific and medical *qigong*, for instance, emphasized the material elements of *qi* as a source of energy rather than the spiritual qualities of healing, which can be far too subjective. Chinese scientists were very outspoken about the need to define clear boundaries between authentic *qigong* and the more contaminated category of pseudoscientific *qigong* promoted by masters.

2. Tang Xiaobing, *Global Space and the Nationalist Discourse of Modernity: The Historical Thinking of Liang Qichao* (Stanford: Stanford University Press 1996), p. 23.

Policing the newly constructed categories would eventually co-evolve with a state campaign for social order.

In the 1990s a loosely organized web of government representatives became galvanized in a campaign for the regulation of *qigong*. Official state discourses began to engage with popular *qigong* debates. While testimonial accounts of healing continued to abound informally and in the popular press, there were calls by state bureaucrats to differentiate between "real" (*zhen*) and "false" (*jia*) *qigong* masters and forms. This was an attempt to separate those individuals who claimed to be masters and healed for lucrative purposes from those with "true" abilities. The state-appointed bureau to regulate *qigong* invoked the new category of scientific *qigong* (*kexue de qigong*) as a means to cleanse and discipline the ranks of "false" masters. Such categories were quite porous and difficult to maintain as the criteria for "true" abilities differed greatly among laypersons and officials. For ordinary Chinese the subjective experience of being healed was enough evidence of a master's abilities. However, for scientists and bureaucrats, double-blind tests, laboratory studies and board examinations were deemed crucial to determining "true" abilities. The state and its representatives thus became crucial gatekeepers to counter runaway popular imaginations of *qigong* masters. Science and visions of the modern life were an integral part of this construction. It became clear that the oppositional boundaries created between true science and false practices were defined by bureaucrats rather than practitioners in order to regulate *qigong* as a state enterprise. While charismatic masters and mystics were threatening to state order and not to be tolerated, *qigong* overall was tolerated because the healing practice worked. Both ordinary citizens and high-level cadres still sought masters for chronic ailments and still practised themselves in spite of the new regulations.

The move to demystify and secularize *qigong* was taken up by scientists. Scientists, especially physicists, were involved in empirical research to test the phenomena of *qi*. Publications in Chinese journals such as *Ziran* (*Nature*) tried to establish *qi* as a physical element similar to wave particles. Another project based at Qinghua University involved experiments with masters on measuring *qi* quantitatively. The overlap between traditional Chinese medicine and *qigong* healing was further institutionalized as several traditional Chinese medicine clinics offered *qigong* as a new addition to their services. Yet its classification as a part of traditional Chinese medicine was not entirely satisfactory to the medical scientists. The number of masters with no formal training who claimed to be able to cure anything was still legion. Such healers were viewed as contrary to a medical system that was founded on scientific principles. Popular practices, such as mass healing lectures or practices in public parks, began to be cast as *mixin* (superstition). Secular and medicalized versions of *qigong*, referred to as medical *qigong*, which reduced more hallucinatory effects and removed the need for charismatic masters, were introduced.

The state regulation of *qigong* became even more aggressive in 1991.

Private entrepreneurial book carts were raided by public security officers for any titles that promoted "unscientific" (*wu kexue*) or "false" (*jia*) *qigong*. As one state official told me, it was necessary to reduce the feverish interest in *qigong* (*jiangwen*). Masters who wished to practise officially were required to register with the state *qigong* association. They could become licensed in several ways: by already having a medical degree and taking additional courses at a traditional medical school; by training with an officially recognized master; or by performing before a select board of officials and bringing in former patients to certify their healing powers. State authority was also inserted into parks in two ways. Practitioners must also be formally registered members of an official school. For those individuals who practised without such markers, regular raids by public security were conducted. Practitioners of banned forms were taken in by local police to be questioned. A close examination of anti-superstition regulation of *qigong* is very revealing for subsequent anti-cult legislation a decade later. In many respects, the containment of *qigong* masters and illegalized forms was a precursor to later attempts at suppression.

The state logic of scientism continued in the second half of the 1990s. Discourses about pseudoscience were used to distinguish between practices that undermined the credibility of scientific knowledge and national progress, and state sanctioned forms of enterprises which embraced the scientific spirit that cultivated the nation state. Many masters relocated their quasi-empires away from Beijing, the centre of the *qigong* regulation campaign, to more favourable climes elsewhere, in the provinces and, more notably, abroad. Extensive networks of overseas Chinese and foreigners greeted charismatic leaders with much enthusiasm for what would be promoted as traditional healing as an alternative to biomedicine.

Transnational Healing Sects

The potential for *qigong* masters and leaders of new healing forms to expand their followings into transnational networks was irresistible. The entrepreneurial logic of healing sects during the 1990s in mainland China resonates with Robert Weller's finding of millenarian sects as "good business" in Taiwan.[3] This section traces the development of one healing sect, *falun gong* (*FLG*), which the Chinese government declared in 1999 to be an evil cult (*xie jiao*). Though *xie jiao* has been translated as heterodox teachings in other periods of Chinese history, in the 21st century the notion of evil cult has been increasing used as the official translation. *Falun gong* is significantly different from *qigong*. Though initially it was promoted as a form of *qigong* within China, abroad *FLG* has evolved into a new social movement based on healing and spiritual meditation practices that are more new age than Buddhist or Daoist. The term *falun* refers to the wheel of Dharma while the term *gong* is the same

3. Rob Weller, "Living at the edge: religion, capitalism, and the end of the nation state in Taiwan," *Public Culture*, Vol. 12, No. 2 (1999), pp. 477–498.

as in *qigong*. Many of its practitioners also refer to *falun dafa* in which *dafa* is translated as great teaching, release or law. During the 1990s its founder, Li Hongzhi, began to lecture and set up teaching stations in north-east China. Similar to other *qigong* practitioners, *FLG* enthusiasts expressed their initial interest in healing as the main reason to start practising. The amalgam of *qigong*-like exercises with esoteric notions of cultivation and iconography seemed familiar and provided quick relief. Some practitioners even renounced taking medication, which has been a problematic issue.

FLG organizers utilized certain strategies to enable rapid growth through recruitment of members. First, in contrast to most *qigong* classes in China which charged fees, all classes were free to interested parties. Though lay practitioners still purchased books or tapes, this was less expensive than regular weekly or monthly payments. Once practitioners became regulars, they were encouraged to spread the news about self-cultivation and to bring in new members. This was perhaps the main reason for rapid dissemination. Eventually an elaborate web of practice sites, instruction centres, teaching centres, branches, and city or provincial headquarters became established.[4] The group was possibly one of the largest organizations to have emerged in the 1990s, though estimates by the government (2 million) and by the group (100 million) widely differed. When I returned to China in 1996, many of my colleagues mentioned this new form of healing. Established bookstores and small book carts throughout Beijing sold Li's text, the *Zhuan falun* (*Turning the Dharma Wheel*). Such a publication followed the 1990s boom in *qigong* texts which are reminiscent of early sectarian traditions of *baojuan* (precious volumes).[5]

FLG became rapidly established outside China as well. In 1996, its leader moved to Flushing, NY where he continued to promote his form of self-cultivation and healing, initially to the Chinese immigrant community.[6] Lessons were promoted not only by word of mouth but also via the internet. Rather than maintaining a internally closed unit, information about representatives and practice sites was available to any interested parties. Despite the claims by *FLG* followers that it was not an organization, the numerous websites with names and telephone numbers of local practitioners in cities across the United States, Canada, Australia and Europe reflected its impressive networks and organizational forms.

FLG initially competed for membership with other *qigong* groups

4. John Wong and William T. Liu, citing *Mingbao*, 31 July 1999 in *The Mystery of China's Falun Gong: Its Rise and its Sociological Implications* (Singapore: World Scientific Publishing, 1999), p. 25.

5. Daniel Overmyer discusses early forms of *baojuan* in *Precious Volumes: An Introduction to Chinese Sectarian Scriptures from the 16th and 17th Centuries* (Cambridge, MA: Harvard University Asia Center, 1999). He notes that "Pao chuan teaching is proclaimed to be a new revelation, long concealed but now available to all who believe, particularly those with the proper karmic affinity or destiny" (p. 4).

6. Zhibin Guo discusses the different generations, linguistic communities and classes in the Chinese American and immigrant community in Flushing, NY. See *Ginseng and Aspirin: Elderly Chinese in New York* (Ithaca, NY: Cornell University Press, 2000).

when it emerged both in China and the United States. Its practices spurred debate among *qigong* practitioners. On the one hand, *FLG* emphasized meditation and movements similar to standard *qigong* forms. Some *qigong* practitioners even managed to practise several forms including *FLG*, at different times of the day. However the primary focus on spiritual cultivation through the spinning wheel was quite different from concentrating just on *qi* energy. Followers were told that the wheel spun in the air or within one's belly to promote healing.

On an organizational level, each cell or practice site had a volunteer spokesperson and organizer. These individuals were ordinary practitioners who had been recruited to gain more practitioners. Sharing stories of healing experiences and group practice sessions were important means of recruitment. Regular "experience sharing" conferences, in which new and experienced followers described how they were healed and how their lives were saved, took place across the United States. Rather than emphasizing the power of the master through the performances of his or her ability followed by public healing for supplicants, the power of healing narratives took centre stage. A whole day would be based on testimonials of followers who claimed to be healed by thinking of the master and the wheel of law. Member after member would get up to share their healing story read aloud from scripted pages. Organizers also devoted much effort to petitioning municipal offices across the United States to recognize their leader with mayoral proclamations.

Beyond these activities, *FLG* stood out for one primary reason. In China whenever any negative criticism was publicly raised about the sect in the form of news editorials, published articles or television programmes, immediate response in the form of protests by followers often followed. Though hundreds of *qigong* masters and forms were active in post-Mao China, few overtly criticized the state. The *FLG* organization was the only group which resorted to surrounding media offices with dozens, sometimes hundreds of protesters as early as 1994. The *Washington Post* noted in July 1998 that several dozen supporters had protested in front of the Beijing Television Station building after a programme that warned about the dangers of *qigong* had been broadcast.[7] The continued mobilization of followers to contest institutions and bureaucrats that offered negative views about *FLG* began to resemble responses by past followers of sectarian organizations. Scholars of Chinese sects indicate that official opposition and non-recognition can sometimes backfire, generating more fervent support. David Ownby's study of Qing brotherhoods and secret societies, such as the *Tiandihui* (Heaven and Earth Society), traces how some mutual aid groups became criminalized and then considered rebellious when they asserted their own legitimacy.[8] Studies of White Lotus adherents also indicate similar dynamics of

7. Michael Laris, "Chinese TV twits a popular pastime and gets an earful on its merits," *Washington Post*, 13 July 1998, p. A13.

8. David Ownby, *Brotherhoods and Secret Societies in Early and Mid-Qing China: The Formation of a Tradition* (Stanford: Stanford University Press, 1996).

contestations over official repression. Barend ter Haar has argued that the term White Lotus was used perjoratively in Qing legal records as a way to indicate an institutional stance towards rebels.[9] Even so, such imperial disdain did not prevent potential members from joining and further facilitated the entrenchment of established followers. As Blaine Gaustad has indicated, White Lotus groups were quite localized, fragmented at times, but in many occasions functioned as support groups for travelling believers across long distances.[10] These networks of solidarity and support were tolerated when sect or secret society projects forged close alliances with bureaucrats or included officials in their membership. However, during periods of official repression or adversity, followers were mobilized into greater levels of commitment. Such actions would transform *FLG* followers who initially sought healing and self-cultivation into a political organization that has come to plague the Chinese leadership. A core group of organizers and followers based on martyrdom became distinguished from ordinary practitioners who simply practised for healing purposes.[11]

On 26 April 1999 *FLG* became front-page news in the international press when an estimated 10,000 or more members staged a silent protest outside Zhongnanhai, the official state compound where leaders reside. The timing of the event, on a Sunday in the spring when several key historic moments of the 20th century are remembered, such as the May Fourth movement, the tenth anniversary of the Tiananmen protests and especially the 50th anniversary of the People's Republic of China, reached an already primed foreign press waiting to hear of any demonstrations or acts of protest. The spatial dimensions of the gathering also made clear the intentions of the group and the significance of its public act. Had the protest been in a park where *qigong* is regularly practised and accepted as a daily event, few people outside the city would have ever heard about it. Instead its location took many, including military guards, by surprise. Eyewitnesses from the scene indicated that the thousands of protesters, mostly in their 40s to 60s, lined up silently in orderly rows with designated appointees to speak to onlookers or reporters. Without the usual signs, banners and slogans shouting their demands, even public security officers were hesitant to start moving the crowd, who easily outnumbered them. Residing in the United States, its leader claimed to have nothing to do with the protest in Beijing. However his organization and the protesters that day demanded a meeting with Premier Zhu Rongji and a retraction of an article published in the Tianjin youth science and technology journal that warned about the dangers of cults. The protest directly confronted socialist leaders, which transformed

9. Barend J. ter Haar, *The White Lotus Teaching in Chinese Religious History* (Leiden: E.J. Brill, 1992).

10. Blaine Gaustad, "Prophets and pretenders: inter-sect competition in Qianlong China," *Late Imperial China*, Vol. 21, No. 1 (June 2000), pp. 1–40.

11. The effect of official opposition to shape sectarian group formation is noted by fellow contributors to this volume. See also the articles by Madsen, Gladney and Bays.

this healing sect into a political organization that challenged state legitimacy.[12]

The Anti-Cult Campaign of 1999

At the end of the 20th century, Chinese officials were involved in a concerted anti-cult campaign against *FLG* and other unofficial sects. State leaders reportedly left Zhongnanhai to assess the situation outside its gates personally. The organized rows of middle-aged and elderly dissenters presented a sight that was disturbing not merely for its large numbers. These were not impulsive youths as was the case a decade earlier. Instead the protestors came from the backbone of Chinese society. Many of the older participants were contemporaries of the leadership who underwent the same formative experiences of nation-building and sacrifice. Their presence before the state compound indicated deeper rifts beyond claims of misrepresentation in the media. Moreover, their ability to amass such a large group without detection was especially disconcerting. The power of assembly through combined low tech (word of mouth) and high tech (internet) means of dissemination (*chuan*) was unexpected.

The protest on 22 April was declared illegal. When more practitioners arrived to protest, swift action was taken to round up any demonstrators immediately. On 30 April, an official warning was issued ordering citizens, especially officials, not to participate in forthcoming demonstrations. Whenever protestors tried to show up in large numbers, they were either turned away or detained and sent back home. There was a delay of several weeks before further official action was undertaken. Then on 22 July 1999 a concerted anti-*FLG* campaign unfolded. This highly visible and orchestrated crackdown began with the arrests of over 70 key figures and a ban on all practice. All *FLG* books, posters, audiotapes and videotapes were ordered to be destroyed; neighbourhood committees, work units and other social units were brought in to collect these materials. The *Liberation Daily* claimed that over 1.55 million copies were confiscated and destroyed.[13] Large-scale book burnings were organized in major cities and provinces. To counter the wide circulation of such materials, the government presses quickly published their own texts. In December 1999 the People's Press Bookstore, a dazzling six-storey building with massive columns newly located on West Changan Avenue, contained to the left of the entrance a large shelf filled with texts about China's bid to join the World Trade Organization (WTO), while directly to the right was an equally large bookcase filled with anti-*FLG* texts and histories of cults. Nearby a poster with graphic images of victims, whose deaths were attributed to *FLG* psychosis or *FLG*-induced mania, was prominently displayed. The concurrent framing indicated how intricately

12. Vivienne Shue, "State legitimization in China: the challenge of popular religion," paper presented at American Political Science Association annual meeting, San Francisco, CA 2001.
13. Agence France Press "Falungong founder's arrest sought as China keeps up anti-sect blitz," 29 July 1999.

linked the eradication of this group was to economic progress and modernity.

In the ensuing two years (1999–2001) a predictable logic of demonstration and containment evolved into rituals of popular protest which Elizabeth J. Perry has described as a "magnetic, mimetic connection between the Chinese state and its would be challengers."[14] Both spatial and temporal dimensions of official meaning would be contested by protestors. Whenever there was a notable Chinese date, especially on major holidays such as 1 May (International Worker's Day), 1 October (National Day) or the lunar new year, a handful of *FLG* protestors would try to evade police blockades at Tiananmen Square. There the demonstrators would briefly shout slogans and unfurl banners before being briskly surrounded by waiting guards and plain-clothes police. Security forces became accustomed to preparing for symbolic protests by a lone or small group of protestors during such periods and would step up their watch. By the winter of 1999 even local Beijing citizens could sketch a profile of the typical protestor. A taxi driver explained it in this way: "They look like they are from out of town (*waidilaide*). But instead of going to the square to take photos like ordinary tourists, they carry plastic bags or small satchels with their toothbrush and washcloth because they know they'll be in the slammer for a while." Between 30 April 1999 and June 2001, several thousand protestors, including supporters with foreign passports, participated in such demonstrations.

The purge of sect members extended far beyond the visible arrests of protestors. All major institutions, beginning with Party members, then the military, media and work units underwent a thorough cleansing of the ranks. During the summer and autumn of 1999 each of these entities made public announcements of support for the anti-*FLG* campaign with self-criticisms of former members. Alliances between scientists and medical doctors that were forged during the early 1990s concerning the regulation of *qigong* came back into play. According to state media, 753 deaths related to *FLG* were reported. News stories and television broadcasts told how followers died after stopping their medication or suffered a form of psychotic reaction which led to violent death. Leading scientists spoke out vehemently against the group, denouncing it as a cult that promoted superstition and disorder, the antithesis of science.

The war against *FLG* and *mixin* was waged on several media fronts. Like faxes and international radio broadcasts during the unrest of 1989, in 1999 the internet proved to be a complicated entity to control. When the PRC government announced its own ban, several websites quickly posted "eyewitness" accounts of the crackdown from practitioners. The battle to present the "truth" to Chinese and international audiences was being waged on the internet.[15] Within a few days all *FLG*-related websites

14. Elizabeth J. Perry, "Challenging the mandate of heaven: popular protest in modern China" *Critical Asian Studies*, Vol. 33, No. 2 (2001), pp. 163–180.
15. Timothy Barrett, in his discussion at Arrabida, noted that Benjamin Penny has pointed out how the internet is an unstable textual environment as web information constantly mutates.

operating within the mainland were shut down, while various official government news sources went online with new accounts about the false and superstitious practices that *FLG* represented. Access to the internet for users in China became restricted as many servers were shut down. Even though followers began to rely on alternative forms of communication, the widespread presence of *FLG* on the internet drew officials' attention to this medium. Subsequently, some owners of cyber cafes and the operators of dissident web sites were also arrested.

Television was a key medium to illustrate why the state viewed the sect as an evil cult. On 21–25 July 1999 a government documentary on *FLG* was repeatedly shown on national television. Regular programming was cancelled while this special presentation aired even as far away as Tibet. Family tragedies such as members who committed suicide, participated in violent acts or died from ceasing medication took centre stage. Sobbing relatives told wrenching stories while accompanying graphic images were televised. Such narratives served to illustrate how the sect had "disrupted social order" (*pohuai shehui wending*). The video contrasted claims by its founder with testimonials of former disciples to proclaim that *FLG* was not a higher form of knowledge. Towards the end of the documentary, ordinary practitioners who simply sought healing were excused for being duped. However they were urged to undergo serious revamping of their thoughts (*sixiang*). In sum, the five-week anti-*FLG* campaign followed a familiar path of attacking heterodox rebellion and establishing legitimacy with strict countermeasures. Despite retractions by its leader, such as claiming not to be a deity or reincarnation of Buddha but an "ordinary man," and stating that he was not responsible for organizing the protests, the line had already been crossed. When over 10,000 followers placed themselves in front of Zhongnanhai with additional provocation from an internet campaign, the Chinese leadership was impelled to save face through strict countermeasures.

Many observers have remarked on the similarities of *FLG* to secret societies and millenarian sects in China's past. The dramatic confrontation before state compounds and apocalyptic pronouncements by its leader certainly supported this view. The anti-*FLG* campaign was similar to historic responses of various Chinese rulers to rebellions. A comparative view of the Qing government response to White Lotus rebels in the 19th century is instructive. After an unsuccessful attempt by the sect in 1813 to take over the imperial palace in the Forbidden City, officials took the following steps, according to Susan Naquin: "In order to quell the Eight Trigrams rebellion, the Ch'ing government undertook both organizational and propaganda measures to counteract rebel claims to legitimacy. In the first place it was necessary for the government to secure the loyalty and assistance of the non-rebel population, particularly the local

---

footnote continued

See Benjamin Penny, "Qigong, Daoism, and science: some contexts for the qigong boom," in Mabel Lee and A.D. Syrokomla-Stefanowska (eds.), *Modernization of the Chinese Past* (Canberra, Australia: Wild Peony, 1993), pp. 166–179.

elites. In the second place, it was important to induce the majority of rebel followers to 'return their allegiance' to the Ch'ing."[16] Then, as now, the bureaucracy sought to distinguish between varying levels of involvement and to reinstate disengaged citizens back into the folds of official policy. Followers who merely practised for health reasons would be viewed as misguided. Organizers who engaged in actions to disrupt social order would be placed in the category of rebels.

When sectarian movements develop into political entities and amass great resources, often in the forms of human labour, monetary and social capital, it is not surprising that such challenges to existing rule eventually lead to struggles for representation and survival. Sect leaders denounce the corruptness of regimes while espousing their own hierarchical utopia as an alternative. The Chinese government in the imperial period inevitably responded with full crackdowns to maintain the sacred principle of social order – usually with death for sect leaders and re-education for followers. The long history of shared struggles between millenarian organizations and the Chinese body politic formed a deep pattern of institutional memory which continues to inform contemporary bureaucrats in their responses to recent challengers. The contemporary anti-cult campaign to eradicate the influence of the *FLG* within China resonates powerfully with this history. State classification practices which defined certain masters, healing forms and spiritual practices as either authentic or false, superstitious and evil were critical means by which boundaries were created.

Even though *FLG* presented many continuities with past millenarian movements, there were also significant differences in its membership. Most of the pre- and early 20th century rebellions were rural-based with peasants as the primary participants. The Boxers and White Lotus rebels, among others, were overwhelmingly described as young and male, with few women. In contrast, the majority of *qigong* practitioners, including *FLG*, tended to be urban-based with more-or-less equal distribution among male and female practitioners at the initiate level. Most *qigong* devotees were notably older retired workers, intellectuals and cadres – people who were solidly based in the socialist system. As the modes of transmission in the contemporary world have shifted from the vernacular and visual to include more textual sources such as autobiographical novels, "how-to" manuals and the internet, potential members have shifted to include more literate, educated and elite audiences that also include cadres and scientists. Finally, the more cosmopolitan travel of masters via circuits of "greater" China and diaspora communities has meant that the political arena of containment at home has been entirely transformed. Using foreign press coverage as an intervention in the Chinese mainland has meant that the state also needed to respond at a broader and more unified level at home and abroad. Questions about membership (such as numbers, mobility and networks) were constantly

16. Susan Naquin, *Millenarian Rebellion in China* (New Haven: Yale University Press, 1976), p. 232.

raised by local and foreign media, state officials and even *FLG* organizers. Such obsession with counting is a reminder of the inherent power of numbers in late socialist China. Another way to rethink membership might be to delineate between different forms of membership or levels of engagement with *FLG*, such as initiates, core followers and leaders. While the majority of practitioners took up the practice for healing purposes, an inner core of organizers and martyrs began to evolve as state containment policies began in earnest. A key contradiction also emerged: how to sustain the core followers who incurred much suffering when *FLG* promoted itself as a healing practice?

Regulations imposed by state authorities on all forms of healing and spiritual practices increased as a result of the anti-cult campaign. During the 1990s, *qigong* practice in parks continued openly despite the medicalization of *qigong* deviation and licensure of masters. In the winter of 1998 it was still possible to find many eclectic *qigong* groups practising in Beijing parks. However in the round-up of *FLG* followers, which included sweeps in urban parks across the country, many practitioners of other forms found themselves subject to scrutiny and questioning as well. This has had a great impact on the practice of *qigong*, and many groups have gone underground. Practitioners quietly practise by themselves at home or retreat to the mountains away from official surveillance. The return of psychotic incidents attributed to *FLG* practice also provided a key opportunity for the state to call for the hard-strike campaign. The state media claimed that over 1,200 deaths occurred as a result of delusions and psychotic reactions to practice. Gruesome details of some of the most sensational cases of FLG-induced mental instability leading to violent acts were aired in a state-produced television documentary.

On the eve of the Chinese New Year in 2001, five presumed *FLG* members, protestors including a 12 year-old child, doused themselves with petrol and set themselves on fire. Though guards and police on watch at Tiananmen Square rushed to the scene, all the demonstrators suffered severe second and third degree burns. Graphic images were televised to audiences who were previously inured to daily stories about *FLG* as an evil cult. Such footage and subsequent stories about the child's death polarized viewers.

Since the immolations, *FLG* supporters have relied on several strategies to continue its campaign in different contexts. First, regular practice sessions as political demonstrations are held in front of Chinese embassies or consulates world-wide as well as at international meetings where Chinese officials will attend. In other spaces such as major airports and hotel lobbies, supporters frequently staff information booths or fill tables with brochures. Secondly, with the detention of local organizers and supporters, foreign members became more visible representatives in protests on Tiananmen Square. Finally, the *FLG* organization has become more litigious, serving visiting officials to the US with papers for lawsuits. On the second anniversary of the anti-*FLG* crackdown, the organization staged a march to Washington DC to urge American policy makers to exert more pressure on this issue. By 2002, most organizers and followers within China had either renounced their beliefs or were in reform camps. Since the first strike in 1999, the state has sent hundreds of *FLG* followers to detention camps for re-education and training. However, the accumulation of support and influence outside China continue to provoke the leadership at home.

What's in a Name: Sect or Cult?

Classification, membership and experience are critical frameworks for understanding the strategies of both sectarian healing movements and the Chinese bureaucracy. Classification practices offer a useful means to map the boundaries of officially recognized projects. The recruitment and membership of followers in spiritual healing groups are organized along shared feelings of cohesion and experiences of healing in a social context. This has been reclassified by the state as deluded or pathological. Official categories work to situate sect membership in terms of legitimacy rather than in terms of powerful experiences of charismatic healing and belonging. Especially as *FLG* does not fall into the recognized category of organized religion, the state has gone to extreme measures to classify the group as a cult.

The official term for cult, *xie jiao*, incorporates pathological notions of "twisted," "perverse" or "malignant" associated with evil.[17] Such a linkage goes beyond an earlier notion of cult as religious worship (*zongjiao chongbai*) of figures or deities specific to local regions (see Fan Lizhu's discussion in this issue).[18] Renewed emphasis on defining sects (*zong pai*), even those which solely focus on healing and do not claim to be religious, as superstitious or pseudoscientific further blurs the already thin line between sects and cults. Sects and sectarian activity are considered to be social formations with high potential to evolve into cults, especially if their leaders have extensive networks both within and outside China. Just as sects and cults point to China's extensive social history of sectarian activity while promising the future, the state has recycled anti-sectarian policies which promise a different future – one that promotes order based on science and modernity. Healing of any sort, whether medical or spiritual, requires licensed practitioners who promote secular forms of healing over popularized sectarian forms.

The expansion of the anti-*FLG* campaign into a broader anti-cult campaign indicates how seriously Chinese officials view any obstacles to economic and social progress. Other sectarian groups, mostly Christian evangelical, have also come under state scrutiny and share the common experience of being redefined as evil cults. Many of these groups are viewed as a cancerous growth with tentacular extensions into rural regions. The closures and demolition of "unofficial" churches and

17. Michel Strickmann translates *xie* in this way with regard to evil agents of disease in Daoist epidemiology. See Bernard Faure (ed.), *Chinese Magical Medicine* (Stanford: Stanford University Press, 2002), p.72.

18. *Concise English–Chinese, Chinese–English Dictionary* (Oxford: Oxford University Press and the Commercial Press, 1986).

temples in China reveal intense concerns for maintaining social stability. Yet, in the context of massive closures of state factories and the privatization of state health care, many participants in heterodox sects "come to faith through illness," according to a seminary teacher in Nanjing.[19] At first glance, the desires for healing seem to fit well with long-standing state premiums on social stability. Healthy bodies are, after all, crucial to a healthy economy. However, notions of healing and cultivation promoted by heterodox sects are deeply unsettling to the very existence of the bureaucracy precisely by contesting the meanings of order and the legitimacy of progress. The membership of a broad spectrum of individuals who resembled the membership of the Party – intellectuals, military and even mid-level cadres – posed an immense threat of destabilization. The potential for popular sects with leaders wielding flexible and even transnational followings to challenge legitimacy remains unacceptable to state leaders.

19. Matthew Forney DengFeng citing Faye Pearson in "Jesus is back and she's Chinese," *Time*, 4 November 2001.

Glossary of Chinese Terms

The following is a glossary of Chinese terms used in the main text of all articles and research reports. All characters have been supplied authors.

Romanization	English equivalent	Chinese characters
Ahong, Aheng	Ahong (Imam)	阿訇，阿洪，阿衡
A-maili (ermaili)	festival day	尔麦力
baishen	to worship deities	拜神
Baiyun guan		白云观
Balizhuang		八里庄
Bao'an	Bonan	保安
Bao'an		宝安
Baoding		保定
baoju shi	"master who guarantees"	保举师
baojuan	precious volumes	宝卷
Baren		巴仁
Baxian gong		八仙宫
Beidi	God of the North	北帝
Beili wang	Established king	被立王
Beiqi		北齐
Benhuan		本焕
bian'e	placard	匾额
biguan	"sealed retreat"	闭关
buzhao	ministry's licence	部照
Cangu nainai	Silkworm Mother	蚕姑奶奶
Chai Wan		柴灣
Chan		禅
Chang Hsun		張珣
Changchun guan		长春观
Changdao guan		常道观
Chaozhou		潮州
Chegong	General Che	車公
Chen Liansheng		陈莲笙
Chen Shui-bian		陳水扁
Cheung Chau		長洲
Chiang Ts'an-t'eng		江燦騰
Chin-men		金門
Chiu Hei-yuan		瞿海源
Chongsheng pai	Born again sect	重生派

chuan	disseminate	传
chuandu shi	"master who initiates and transmits"	传度师
chuanjie	ordination	传戒
chuanjie lüshi	ordination master	传戒律师
Chuzhen jie	Initial Precepts of Perfection	初真戒
Ciji		慈济
Ciji gongde hui	Compassionate Relief Merit Society	慈濟功德會
cun	village	村
Dade	Great Virtuous Ones	大德
Dajia le	Everybody's Happy	大家樂
Dajia Zhenlangong		大甲鎮瀾宮
Dajue si	Dajue Monastery	大觉寺
Dan		蛋
dang lingdao renmin zhiding falü, ye lingdao renmin zunshou falü	the Party leads the people in enacting the law and leads the people in observing the law	党领到人民制定法律，也领到人民遵守法律
Dangtian	Heaven God	當天
daofeng	"spiritual atmosphere"	道凤
Daohui si	Bureau for Daoist Assemblies	道会司
Daoji si	Bureau for Daoist Institutions	道集司
Daojiao	Daoism	道教
Daojiao xintu	Daoist follower	道教信徒
Daojiao zhengyipai shoulu chuandu jingjiaoji	Collected essays on the scriptures and instructions for the ordination of Zhengyi sect of Daoism	道教正一派授箓传度经教集
Daojiao zhishi zhuanxiuban	Higher educational classes for Daoists	道教知识专修班
Daolu si	Bureau for Daoist Registry	道录司
daoshi	Daoist priest	道士
daotan	Daoist altar	道坛
Dawangdian		大王殿
Dayi		大邑
Dazhong ye	"Lord of the Hordes"	大眾爺
Delin		德林
diandeng	lantern lighting (a festival)	點燈
difangzhi	local chronicles	地方志
Ding Guangen		丁关根
Ding Guangxun	K.H. Ting	丁光训
Ding xian (Ting Hsien)	Ding county	定县
Dingguang Fo	Dingguang Buddha	顶光佛

Dixian		谛闲
Dizang An	Dizang Abbey	地藏庵
Dizang wang pusa	Bodhisattva Dizang	地藏王菩薩
dizhu	landlord, Master of the Site	地主
Dongxiang		东乡
Duanwu	Duanwu (a festival)	端午
fahao	religious names	法号
falun	wheel of Dharma	法轮
falun gong		法轮功
faming	"Dharma name"	法名
fang yankou	"releasing the burning mouths"	放焰口
fangzhang	abbot	方丈
fengshui	geomancy	风水
Foguang shan		佛光山
foxue yuan	Buddhist study academies	佛学院
Foyuan		佛源
Fu Yuantian		傅圆天
Fuzhou		福州
gaishan minjian jidian jieyue banfa	improving frugality in folk sacrifices	改善民間祭典節約辦法
Gaochang	Khocho	高昌
Gaomin si	Gaomin Monastery	高旻寺
Gedimu		格底木（苏非派）
Gong Pinmei		龚品梅
gongbei (kung pie)	domed tomb/tomb of the saint	拱北
gongde	virtue and merits	功德
Guandi	God of War	关(關)帝
guanfang	official	官方
Guanghua		广化
Guangsheng tang		广生堂
Guangze zunwang		广泽尊王
Guanyin	Goddess of Mercy	观(觀)音
Guanyu daojiao gongguan guanli banfa	Methods for administering Daoist temples	关于道教宫观管理办法
Guanyu daojiao sanju zhengyipai daoshi guanli shixing banfa	Tentative methods related to the administration of the Zhengyi priests who live at home	关于道教散居正一派道士管理试行办法
Guanyu quanzhenpai chuanjie de guiding	Rules about the transmission of precepts for the Quanzhen order	关于全真派传戒的规定
Guanyu zhengyipai daoshi shoulu de yiyi	The significance of the conferral of registers to Zhengyi Daoists	关于正一派道士授箓的意义

Guanyu zhengyipai daoshi shoulu guiding	Rules related to conferring registers of ordination for the Zhengyi priests	关于正一派道士授箓规定
guiyi zheng	certificate	皈依证
guomin liyi fanli	models for citizens' rites and ceremonies	國民禮儀範例
guomin shenghuo xuzhi	what citizens should know about daily life	國民生活須知
Hami		哈密
Han		韩
Handan		邯郸
Hangzhou		杭州
Hanshan Deqing		憨山德清
He Canran		何灿然
Heming shan		鹤鸣山
Hongsheng	God of the South Sea	洪聖
Hongwu	(Emperor) Hongwu	洪武
Hongyi		弘一
Hsin hsin-wen	*The Journalist*	新新聞
Hsin-chuang		新莊
Hsu Hsin-liang		許信良
Hu Dengzhou		胡登洲
Hua Miao		花苗
huapao	flower cannons	花炮
huapaohui	flower cannon associations	花炮會
Huayan jing		华严经
Hui		回
Hui-he		回纥
Hui-hu		回呼
Hui jiao	Hui teaching (Islam)	回教
Huiming		慧明
Huizhou		惠州
huoju daoshi	Daoists living at home	火居道士
Idgah	Idgah Mosque	艾提尔尔大寺
Ili		伊犁
jia	false	假
jiandu shi	"master who examines"	监度师
Jiang Zhilin		江至霖
jiangwen	reduce temperature, contain fever	降温
Jianyue Duti		见月读体
Jiao	Jiao (festival), offering rituals	醮
jiaoluo	village neighbourhood	角落

jieba	ordination scars	戒疤
jiedie	ordination certificate	戒牒
Jigong	a 12th-century monk deity	濟公
Jin Luxian		金鲁贤
Jing'an (Bazhi Toutuo)		敬安 (八指 头陀)
Jingkong		净空
jinglu	register	经箓
jingshe	small residential temples	精舍
Jinling shenxuezhi	*Jinling Theological Review*	金陵神学志
jushi	layperson	居士
jushi lin	lay association halls	居士林
kaiguang	consecration	开光
kaijizu	"foundation-building ancestor"	開基祖
kang	clay bed	炕
Kangding		康定
Kangxi		康熙
Kashi	Kashgar	喀什
Keelung		基隆
Kejia	Hakka	客家
kexue de qigong	scientific *qigong*	科学的气功
Kōminka	Kōminka Movement	皇民化
Koxinga		鄭成功
Kwun Tong		觀塘
Laiguo		来果
Lam Tsuen		林村
Langfang		廊坊
Lao zushen	Ancestor God	老祖神
laogai	labour through reform	劳改
laorenhui	old folks associations	老人会
Laotian	Old Heaven	老天
Laoye	Laoye (temple)	老爷
Laozi		老子
Lengyan jing	*Suramgama sutra*	楞严经
li	Ming-dynasty ritually differentiated sub-canton	里
Li Hongzhi		李洪志
Li Ruihuan		李瑞环
Li Yangzheng		李养正
Liang Jialin	Leung Kalun	梁家麟
Lien Chan		連戰
Lin Mei-rong		林美容

ling	spiritual efficacy	灵
Lingyan shan		灵岩山
Lingyin si	Lingyin Monastery	灵隐寺
Liu Xiaofeng		刘小枫
Liu Zhi		刘智
Lok Fu		樂富
Longhu shan		龙虎山
longmai	"dragon vein"	龍脈
Longzang	*Dragon Treasury*	龙藏
Louguan tai		楼观台
luan	chaos	乱
Luerhmen		鹿耳門
Lung Yeuk Tau		龍躍頭
Luo Gan		罗干
luodanzu	"carrying-pole-releasing ancestor"	落擔祖
Luofu shan		罗浮山
Lüshan		閭山
lusheng	"students of register"	篆生
Lüzu	Immortal Lü	呂祖
Ma Laichi		马来尺
Ma Mingxin		马明心
Ma Qixi		马启西
Ma Wanfu		马万福
Ma Zhenwu		马震武
mahoujing	horse-monkey demon	马猴精
Maoshan		茅山
Mawei		馬尾
Mazu (Matsu)	A popular deity, originally goddess of the sea	妈(媽)祖
Meizhou		湄州
Menguan	Door God	門官
menhuan	saintly descent group	门宦
Mentuhui	Disciples sect	门徒会
Miao	Hmong	苗
miao	temple	庙
miaobei	temple inscriptions	廟碑
Miaojing		妙境
Min		闽
Minbei		闽北
Mindong		闽东
minjian	folk	民间

minjian xinyang	folk beliefs	民間信仰
Minnan		闽南
Minnan foxue yuan	Minnan Buddhist Study Academy	闽南佛学院
minzu	nationality, ethnicity	民族
mixin	superstition	迷信
Mulian		目连
Nanhua		南华
Nanputuo si	Nanputuo Monastery	南普陀寺
nanwu (nam mo)	professional Daoist priest	嗬嘸
Ngau Tau Kok		牛頭角
nian Fo shi shei?	"who is it who is mindful of the Buddha?"	念佛是谁?
nianjing bu chi, chi bu nianjing	If you read the Quran, you do not dine, if you dine, you do not read the Quran	念经不吃，吃不念经
Ningbo		宁波
Ningxia		宁夏
Nuoxi	masked exorcistic theatre	傩戏
Ouyi Zhixu		藕益智旭
Pai Hsiao-yen		白曉燕
Pai Ping-ping		白冰冰
Pat Heung		八鄉
Peng Zhen		彭真
Ping Shan		屏山
Pinghai		平海
po'an	solving the case	破案
pohuai shehui wending	disrupt social order	破坏社会稳定
Pu'an jiao		普庵教
Pudu		普度
Putian		莆田
Puxian		莆仙
qi	air, vital energy	气(氣)
Qi Jingyi		祁静一
qianghuapao	"flower-cannon catching"	搶花炮
qianshi	auspicious poem	籤詩
qigong	breathing, meditation and healing practices which move the *qi*	气功
qijing	village ritual alliances	七境
Qingcheng shan		青城山
Quanfanwei jiaohui	Full scope church	全范围教会

quan shen	all the gods	全神
quan shen luozuo	"all the gods are here"	全神落座
Quanzhang		泉漳
Quanzhen	Total Perfection	全真
Quanzhou		泉州
Renmin ribao	*People's Daily*	人民日报
Rongcheng		容城
san ju hua	"three sentences"	三句话
San min zhuyi	"Three Principles of the People"	三民主義
San-hsia		三峽
sanju daoshi	Daoists who live at home	散居道士
Sanping zushi		三坪祖师
Santan dajie	Great Precepts of the Threefold Altar	三坛大戒
Sanyijiao	Three in One	三一教
Sanyue	Sanyue (temple)	三岳
Sau Mau Ping		秀茂坪
Shanghai daojiao	*Shanghai Daoism*	上海道教
shanshu	morality books	善書
Shap Pat Heung		十八鄉
shaqi	"killing air"	煞氣
Shatin		沙田
She		舍
shejidao qian baiwan qunzhong	affects the masses of a billion people	涉及到千百万群众
Shen Hsueh-yung		申學庸
sheng	hierarchical, ordering, central power	圣
Shengyan		圣严
shenshen guigui	superstitious	神神鬼鬼
shentan	household shrine	神壇
shenting	deity hall	神廳
shi gui, shi zuxian, xianjia nongde	from ghosts, ancestors or supernatural beings	是鬼，是祖先，仙家弄的
Shiba wang gong	18 Lords cult	十八王公
shifang conglin	"public monasteries" of Quanzhen Daoism	十方丛林
Shijiazhuang		石家庄
shizheng linian yu mubiao	guiding principle and objectives	施政理念與目標
shoulu	conferring of register	授籙
shuilu	"sea and land" (rites)	水陆
simiao	temple	寺庙

sixiang	thoughts	思想
Sung Ch-u-yu	James Soong	宋楚瑜
Ta-chia		大甲
Tai O		大澳
Taichung		台中
Taiqing gong		太清宮
Taishan	Mount Tai	泰山
Taiwan zongjiao xuehui	Taiwan Association of Religious Studies	臺灣宗教學會
Taixu		太虛
Takelamagan	Taklamakan	塔克拉玛干
Talim	Tarim	塔里木
Tanxu		倓虛
Tianhou	Empress of Heaven	天后
Tiandihui	Heaven and Earth Society	天地会
Tianfeng		天风
Tianshi	Heavenly Masters	天师
Tianshidong		天师洞
Tiantai		天台
Tiantong si	Tiantong Monastery	天童寺
Tianxian dajie	Great Precepts of the Celestial Immortals	天仙大戒
tongsheng	almanac	通勝
Tsuen Wan		荃灣
Tudi	Earth God	土地
Tuen Mun		屯門
Tulufan	Turpan	吐鲁番
Tung-kang		東港
waidilaide	outsider	外地来的
Wang Ch'iu-kuei		王秋桂
Wang Zhaoguo		王兆国
Wangye	Royal Lords	王爺
Weiwuer	Uyghur	维吾尔
wen'an	investigate a case history	问案
Wenfu hui	Committee for the Revival of Chinese Culture	文復會
Wenhua jianshe weiyuanhui	Council on Cultural Affairs	文化建設委員會
Wenhua ju	Bureau of Culture	文化局
wenhua zhongxin	cultural centre	文化中心
Wenjian hui	Council on Cultural Affairs	文建會
wenmipo	shaman ("rice-asking women")	問米婆
wenshi ziliao	literary and historical materials	文史资料

Wenzhou		温州
Wolong si	Wolong Monastery	卧龙寺
Wong Tai Sin	Immortal Huang	黄大仙
Wu		吴
wu kexue	unscientific	无科学
wu sheng lao mu	sectarian Eternal Mother	无生老母
Wu Yaozong		吴耀宗
Wudang shan		武当山
wuguanfang	unofficial	无官方
Wulumuqi	Urumqi	乌鲁木齐
Xi Dao Tang	"western school or mosque"	西道堂
Xiamen		厦门
Xianghua		香花
xiao san tong	"three small links"	小三通
Xiaoxicun		小西村
xiejiao	sects, "evil cult;" heterodox teachings	邪教
Xin shenghuo yundong	New Life Movement	新生活運動
Xinghua		兴化
Xingtai		邢台
xingxiang	"walking the sub-district"	行鄉
Xingyun		星云
Xinjin		新津
xinxing zongjiao	"new religions"	新興宗教
Xishan	West Mountain	西山
xiuxing ren	practitioners	修行人
Xu Zhenjun		徐真君
Xuanhua		宣化
xunding	patrol/security force	巡丁
Xunhua		循化
Xushui		徐水
Xuyun		虚云
yamen	government office	衙門
Yang		杨
Yanghouwang	General Wang	楊侯王
Yangzhou		扬州
Yao		猺
Yaochi jinmu	Golden Mother of the Jasper Pool	瑶池金母
Ye Xiaowen		叶小文
Yekai		冶开
Yen Ch-ing-piao		顏清標

Yiguan dao	Unity Sect	一貫道
Yihewani	Yihewani (Ikwan)	依黑瓦泥
Yinguang		印光
Yining		伊宁
Yisilan jiao	Islam	伊斯兰教
yixin nian Fo	"single-minded concentration on the Buddha"	一心念佛
Yongzheng		雍正
Yu Guang-hong		余光弘
Yuanfu wanninggong		元符万宁宫
Yuanying		圆英
Yue		越
yue (Cantonese, yuek)	alliance/agreement	約
Yulan	Hungry Ghost	盂蘭
Yunju shan		云居山
Yunmen shan		云门山
Yunqi Zhuhong		云栖袾宏
Zaojun	Kitchen God	灶君
zhai	funeral rites	斋
Zhang Enpu		张恩溥
Zhao Puchu		赵朴初
zhen	township	镇
zhen	real, authentic	真
Zhengyan		证严
Zhengyi	Celestial Master Daoism	正一
zhengyipai daoshizheng	Daoist certificate belonging to the Zhengyi sect	正一派道士证
Zhenlan Gong	Zhenlan Gong (temple)	鎮瀾宮
Zhenren fu	Heavenly Masters' office	真人府
zhidie	registration certificate	职牒
Zhiwuying		智武营
zhizhao	licences	执照
Zhongguo Daojiao		中国道教
Zhongguo Fojiao xiehui	China Buddhist Association	中国佛教协会
Zhonghua wenhua	Chinese culture	中華文化
Zhonghua wenhua fuxing weiyuan hui	Committee for the Revival of Chinese Culture	中華文化復興委員會
Zhonghua wenhua fuxing yundong zonghui	General Committee of the Movement to Revive Chinese Culture	中華文化復興運動總會
Zhongji jie	Intermediate Precepts	中极戒
Zhongnan shan	Zhongnan mountains	终南山
Zhongnanhai		中南海

Zhongyuan wenhua	KMT vision of Chinese culture	中原文化
Zhou Niankao		周念考
Zhu daxian	Immortal Zhu	朱大仙
Zhu Xi		朱熹
Zhuan falun	*Turning the Dharma Wheel*	转法轮
Zibo Zhenke		紫柏侦可
Ziran	*Nature*	自然
zisun miao	"hereditary monasteries"	子孙庙
zong pai	sect	宗派
Zongjiao	*Religion*	宗教
zongjiao chongbai	cult, religious worship	宗教崇拜
zongjiao shiwuju	religious affairs bureau	宗教事务局
zongtan	highest doctrinal altar	宗坛

Index

Abdurixit, Abdulahat 152
Ahern, E.M. 96
alliance temples in local religions 78–9
Alptekin, Erkin 152
Alptekin, Isa Yusuf 152, 154
Amita Buddha 128
Amity Foundation 194
Amnesty International 149, 152, 183
Amorim, J. 1
ancestors worship in local religions 74, 77, 83
ancestral halls in local religions 76–8
Arkush, R.D. 54
autonomous Protestant churches 186–7
  legacy of 188–9

Barrett, T. 1
Bays, D.H. 7, 182–98
Beg, Yakub 151
Beile, Koli 149
Beili wang (Established king) group 190
Benhuan 138
Birnbaum, R. 5, 122–44
birth rituals 77
Born again sect 190
Bowler, G. 199–200
Boxer Rebellion 164, 211
Brim, J. 78
Buddhism 5–6, 122–44
  academies 130, 134–6
  clergy
    generation gap in 133–4
    post-Mao development of 133
    training for 134–5
  ethnic traditions 124
  in Hong Kong 139–40
  as international religion 141
  in late Qing/Republican period 124–32
  laypeople 123, 126
    overseas 141
  leadership of 137–8
  and local religions 36
  long-term retreat 131–2
  monasteries
    destruction of 124–5
    economic changes to 136
    economic support for 125–6, 136–8
    types of 125
  monastic life 132–9
    post-Mao revival 132–4
    purpose 126–7
    social position in 135–6

recognized 14
reform and renewal 126–7
  conservative approach 127–8
  modernizing approach 128–39
  texts for 128
  training for 130, 134–5
rituals, performing 137
suppression of
  in Cultural Revolution 132
  in Tibet 27–8
  in Taiwan 4, 89, 92, 139–40
  in Tibet 141–3
    differences from Han Buddhism 142–3
    regulation of 22
    suppression of 27–8
Bureau of Culture (Taiwan) 97

Catholic Bishops Conference 167
Catholic Patriotic Association 23–4, 165, 167, 173–4, 179
Catholism 6–7
  consecration of bishops 179
  factions 167
    tensions between 167–8
  historical context of 164–9
  hospitals in Taiwan 90
  intellectual elite within 171
  international contacts 168–9
  numbers 162, 163
  open (official) church of 167, 174, 177
  political relationships 172
  recognized 14
  regulation of 23–4
  religious vision of 169–71
  resistance by 28
  revival in post-Mao China 162–81
    clergy 172–80
    framework of 169–72
    growth 163
    political conflicts 176–80
    ritual status 172–4
    social roles 174–6
  social life of 171–2
  underground church of 166, 167, 173–4, 177
  and village life 171
Central Art Institute 43
Chan Kim-Kwong 183, 185, 189, 196
Chang Hsün 103
Chegong, worshipped 73
Chen, Nancy N. 2, 8, 199–214

CPSIA information can be obtained at www.ICGtesting.com
Printed in the USA
BVOW010334040113

309796BV00002B/13/A

9 780521 538237